Learning iCloud
Data Management

Addison-Wesley Learning Series

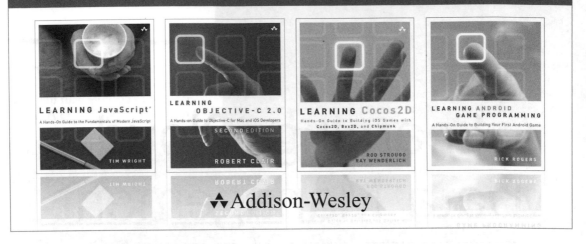

Visit informit.com/learningseries for a complete list of available publications.

The Addison-Wesley Learning Series is a collection of hands-on programming guides that help you quickly learn a new technology or language so you can apply what you've learned right away.

Each title comes with sample code for the application or applications built in the text. This code is fully annotated and can be reused in your own projects with no strings attached. Many chapters end with a series of exercises to encourage you to reexamine what you have just learned, and to tweak or adjust the code as a way of learning.

Titles in this series take a simple approach: they get you going right away and leave you with the ability to walk off and build your own application and apply the language or technology to whatever you are working on.

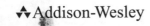

Learning iCloud Data Management

A Hands-On Guide to Structuring Data for iOS and OS X

Jesse Feiler

✦▾Addison-Wesley

Upper Saddle River, NJ • Boston • Indianapolis • San Francisco
New York • Toronto • Montreal • London • Munich • Paris • Madrid
Capetown • Sydney • Tokyo • Singapore • Mexico City

For information about buying this title in bulk quantities, or for special sales opportunities (which may include electronic versions; custom cover designs; and content particular to your business, training goals, marketing focus, or branding interests), please contact our corporate sales department at corpsales@pearsoned.com or (800) 382-3419.

For government sales inquiries, please contact governmentsales@pearsoned.com.

For questions about sales outside the U.S., please contact international@pearsoned.com.

Visit us on the Web: informit.com/aw

Library of Congress Cataloging-in-Publication Data

Feiler, Jesse.
  Learning iCloud data management : a hands-on guide to structuring data for iOS and OS X / Jesse Feiler.
    pages   cm
  Includes bibliographical references and index.
  ISBN 978-0-321-88911-9 (paperback : alkaline paper)
  1. iCloud—Handbooks, manuals, etc. 2. Cloud computing—Handbooks, manuals, etc. 3. Database management—Handbooks, manuals, etc. 4. iOS (Electronic resource)—Handbooks, manuals, etc. 5. Mac OS—Handbooks, manuals, etc. I. Title.
    QA76.585.F45 2014
    004.67'82—dc23
                                                              2013043333

ISBN-13: 978-0-321-88911-9
ISBN-10: 0-321-88911-8
Text printed in the United States on recycled paper at RR Donnelley in Crawfordsville, Indiana.
First printing, February 2014

Editor-in-Chief
Mark L. Taub

Senior Acquisitions Editor
Trina MacDonald

Development Editor
Michael Thurston

Managing Editor
John Fuller

Full-Service Production Manager
Julie B. Nahil

Project Editor
Anna Popick

Copy Editor
Carol Lallier

Indexer
Jack Lewis

Proofreader
Anna Popick

Technical Reviewers
Jon Bell
Erik Buck
Rod Strougo

Editorial Assistant
Olivia Basegio

Cover Designer
Chuti Prasertsith

Compositor
Shepherd, Inc.

Contents at a Glance

Contents

Preface

When Apple announces new products or new versions of its operating systems, there is usually a big press event, and frequently there are lines of people waiting at Apple stores. There's generally a pattern to these announcements. In the case of the operating systems, the major announcements are made at the Apple Worldwide Developers Conference in June. In some years, developer previews of one or both operating systems are made available earlier in the spring. Over the course of the summer, developer releases are made available. Rumors of the availability of the new iPhone begin circulating, and, sometime in the fall, Apple sends invitations to a media event to be held in a week. At that event, a new version of iOS is shown to the public along with a new iPhone. The public release of iOS comes a week later, followed by the availability of the new iPhone. Later (often the following month) the process is repeated for the iPad, Macs, and OS X.

This has been the schedule over the past few years, but there is no guarantee it will be repeated. What is important to note is that there are specific dates for the announcement and release of the products and operating systems. iCloud is a very different matter. Over a number of years, Apple has built a significant hardware and telecommunications support structure to power iCloud and its other network operations. As is the case with many such infrastructures, the details of it are kept confidential. We know the location of some of Apple's data centers because they often require building permits and other public documents and permissions, but they are usually kept out of the public view. There has been no ribbon cutting or turning of a key to launch iCloud—it has been a years-long process (and it will continue for years to come).

In addition to the hardware infrastructure, iCloud has a software component. However, that, too, has been a years-long development process. As you will see in this book, parts of iCloud are implemented in the user interface of the operating systems, and other parts of it are implemented with relatively small changes to existing frameworks and APIs. For developers as well as consumers, public announcements about iCloud have been part of the announcements of new versions of the operating systems as well as of hardware.

In short, iCloud is not a product: it's a pervasive technology and a companywide strategy for Apple. Unlike Apple's hardware and software products, iCloud has no part number and no version. It is part of products across the company.

For that reason, it is not easy to write about iCloud or to learn to develop for it. This book was first envisioned in early 2012, but as it took shape, it became clear that some of the most powerful pieces of iCloud were not yet in place. Rather than rushing out a partial book and relying on the possibility of a revised edition sometime in the future, Trina MacDonald and Addison-Wesley agreed to push back the publication date so as to include the information from WWDC in June 2013, and I'm very grateful to them for doing that.

As you will see, the book culminates in what I call the iCloud Round Trip. In the final chapter, you'll see how to build an iOS app and an OS X app that let you share data via iCloud on both OS X and iOS. Having the tools to be able to implement the Round Trip seems to me to be a good time to publish the book. That's as close to a product launch event as you can get in the world of iCloud.

Who Should Read This Book

This book is written for developers who want to explore iCloud. Because iCloud is implemented in so many areas of the operating systems, you need a bit of familiarity with many parts of Cocoa and Cocoa Touch. As the book presents iCloud, an attempt has been made to at least summarize the various components that it touches. This means that the discussion of a topic such as notifications is at a fairly high level: some people will think "everyone knows that" and other people may think that more details are needed.

The attempt has been to provide a medium road for both experts and novices in the various Cocoa technologies that interact with iCloud. Apple's documentation on developer.apple.com provides the primary resource for more details if you feel you need them. If you hit an area where you feel that you already know the topic, feel free to skip to the details of iCloud. Even among engineers at Apple, there are many areas of Cocoa that they know inside out (and may have written) and other areas with which they're not familiar.

In terms of skills and knowledge, you should have a basic knowledge of Cocoa and/or Cocoa Touch as well as of Xcode. Objective-C is a must for understanding the code. The author's *Sams Teach Yourself Objective-C in 24 Hours* provides an introduction to that topic.

In addition, you should have experience in using iCloud. It is always amazing how many people attempt to develop for a technology that they have not used. There's nothing like hands-on user experience.

Downloading the Example Files

The example files for each chapter that has them can be downloaded from the author's site at http://northcountryconsulting.com and from http://informit.com/title/9780321889119. In addition to the examples, you will find any updates and corrections on both sites. Some of the downloadable examples contain additional code, such as an iPad interface in addition to the iPhone interface for Chapter 14, "Working with File Wrappers in iCloud."

The files are arranged by chapter, and they represent the code as of the end of the chapter. Thus, in the cases where one chapter builds on the previous chapter's code, download the previous chapter and work through it to add the new chapter's code.

iCloud requires code signing, so you'll see in this book how to set up your projects to accomplish that. Note that the code in this book and in the downloadable code contains code signing that will not work on your computer. You must use your own developer credentials. Rather than leaving the code signing information blank, I have used my own credentials (the password is not provided, and even the developer account name has been changed). This means that the code will not run unless you customize it for your own developer account. This is deliberate and necessary.

The code has been written against Xcode 5.0 and OS X Mavericks (10.9).

How This Book Is Organized

There are four parts to this book.

Part I: Introducing iCloud

The first part provides perspectives on iCloud from the user's point of view and from that of the developer.

- Chapter 1, "Exploring iCloud and Its User Experience": As iCloud has evolved, it has been incorporated into apps such as the iWork suite. You'll see the user interface aspects of iCloud for apps and the operating systems.

- Chapter 2, "Setting Up iCloud for Development": This chapter provides an overview of the API structure of iCloud. It's a roadmap to the rest of the book.

Part II: Using the APIs

This part explores how you use iCloud data that the user enters and maintains. For many users, iCloud plays some role with the storage of their music and with the synchronization of their calendars and contacts. There are APIs that allow developers to tap into this synchronized user data, and they are described in this part of the book. This use of iCloud can reap big payoffs for the developer: the engineers at Apple and the users have done all the work—all you have to do is empower the users to employ their own data in new and imaginative ways.

- Chapter 3, "Introducing the APIs and the First Apps": The simplest part of iCloud consists of the APIs that manage user data. This chapter provides the roadmap to this part of the book.

- Chapter 4, "Working with the AddressBook API for Contacts": The AddressBook API lets developers access and update address book data. This chapter shows you the basics of doing so.

- Chapter 5, "Managing Calendars and Reminders with the Event Kit API": You'll see how to leverage calendars and reminders in this chapter.

- Chapter 6, "Protecting the Privacy of User Data": iCloud brings up many privacy issues that you need to address in your apps. This is user data, and you have to play by the rules described in this chapter.

Part III: Using the Technologies

Various data management technologies and design patterns are integrated with iCloud. Using these technologies can mean that your apps can take the most advantage of iCloud synchronization. These technologies are integrated with iCloud, but they existed long before iCloud came to be. It's the integration that's new.

- Chapter 7, "Introducing Blocks, Threads, and Notifications": This chapter provides a roadmap to the technologies in the context of iCloud. Even if you know the technologies, it's important to review them in the iCloud world.

- Chapter 8, "Using Key-Value Coding (KVC)": Key-value coding has been used in Cocoa for years. It's a very efficient way of storing relatively small amounts of data. And it works very easily for you and your users with iCloud.

- Chapter 9, "Using Preferences, Settings, and Keychains with iCloud": Preferences (OS X) and Settings (iOS) are a special case of key-value coding. This chapter shows how you can add them to your apps so that they apply to all of a user's devices. You'll also see how to exclude certain preferences and settings from iCloud if they don't make sense for a specific device.

- Chapter 10, "Managing Persistent Storage with Core Data": Core Data is the major data persistence tool in Cocoa and Cocoa Touch. This chapter provides a high-level overview. It is followed on by Chapter 17, "Working with Core Data and iCloud."

- Chapter 11, "Using Xcode Project Workspaces for Shared Development": Introduced in Xcode 4, Xcode workspaces make it easy to set up multiple targets within a project and to share certain files among the targets. For example, this will enable you to share a Core Data data model (schema) and its specific managed object classes with an OS X/iOS Round Trip.

- Chapter 12, "Adding Data to Apps with Bundles and Resources": This is one of the most general ways of managing data in apps. It doesn't use iCloud directly, but it may be an appropriate addition to an iCloud app to complement iCloud-synchronized data.

Part IV: Using iCloud Documents and Data

The final part of the book brings together the APIs and technologies in documents and file wrappers. You'll see how to implement them on OS X as well as on iOS. In addition, you'll see how to complete a Round Trip as the documents synchronize across iOS and OS X.

- Chapter 13, "Adding the iCloud Infrastructure": This chapter shows you the basic infrastructure to use with iCloud—the code to establish contact with iCloud, manage changes in iCloud availability, and make iCloud account changes. Note that this is code that will need to be implemented in any of the following chapters. In order to focus on the specific issues of the following chapters in this part of the book, it is not repeated in them.

- Chapter 14, "Working with File Wrappers in iCloud": File wrappers implement a structure akin to packages in the finder: a collection of files that appear to be a single file to the user. They are a very efficient structure to take advantage of iCloud synchronization.

- Chapter 15, "Working with iOS Documents": This chapter provides the iOS document model based on UIDocument. You'll see how to monitor changes in your iCloud documents in real time.

- Chapter 16, "Working with OS X Documents": On OS X, Cocoa takes care of the changes in iCloud documents for you, so you have less work to do than in Chapter 15. However, there is still work to be done, and this chapter shows you how to use NSDocument to accomplish what is necessary.

- Chapter 17, "Working with Core Data and iCloud": This chapter provides you with the code you'll need to manage Core Data-based apps with iCloud. It builds on Chapter 10.

- Chapter 18, "Completing the Round Trip": Finally, you'll see how to put together a Round Trip. Remember to add the code from Chapter 13 to both of your targets (OS X and iOS).

Acknowledgments

As always, Carole Jelen at Waterside Productions provided help and guidance in bringing this book to fruition. At Addison-Wesley, Trina MacDonald helped move this book along from idea to publication. Michael Thurston provided excellent editorial advice. The production manager, Julie Nahil, kept things moving along in the very complicated process of creating a technical book. Anna Popick, the freelance project manager, and Carol Lallier, freelance copy editor, contributed mightily to the book's development. The elegant cover design is by Chuti Prasertsith.

Notwithstanding the help of these and many other people, any errors are the author's.

About the Author

Jesse Feiler is a developer and author. He has been an Apple developer since before it became fashionable. His books include *Sams Teach Yourself Core Data for Mac and iOS in 24 Hours* (Sams Publishing, 2011), *Sams Teach Yourself Objective-C in 24 Hours* (Sams Publishing, 2012), *FileMaker 12 in Depth* (Que Publishing, 2012), and *iWork for Dummies* (Wiley, 2012).

Jesse has written about Objective-C and the Apple frameworks beginning with *Rhapsody Developer's Guide* (Academic Press, 1997) and *Mac OS X Developer's Guide* (Morgan Kaufmann, 2001). His books on Apple technologies such as Cyberdog, OpenDoc, ODF, Bento (in both incarnations), and Apple Guide occupy a special place on the shelf of developer books.

He is the author of Minutes Machine, the meeting management app for iPad, as well as the Saranac River Trail app for iPhone and iPad. They are available on the App Store; more details are available at champlainarts.com.

A native of Washington, DC, Jesse has lived in New York City and currently lives in Plattsburgh, New York, where he serves on the board of the Plattsburgh Public Library and as chair of the Saranac River Trail Advisory Committee.

He can be reached at http://northcountryconsulting.com.

We Want to Hear from You!

As the reader of this book, you are our most important critic and commentator. We value your opinion and want to know what we're doing right, what we could do better, what areas you'd like to see us publish in, and any other words of wisdom you're willing to pass our way.

You can email or write me directly to let us know what you did or didn't like about this book—as well as what we can do to make our books stronger.

Please note that we cannot help you with technical problems related to the topic of this book and that due to the high volume of mail we receive, we might not be able to reply to every message.

When you write, please be sure to include this book's title and author as well as your name and phone or email address.

Email: trina.macdonald@pearson.com
Mail: Reader Feedback
Addison-Wesley Learning Series
800 East 96th Street
Indianapolis, IN 46240 USA

Reader Services

Visit our website and register this book at **informit.com/register** for convenient access to any updates, downloads, or errata that might be available for this book.

Introduction

Cocoa and Cocoa Touch consist of frameworks that contain classes as well as protocols, defined constants, and some other supporting items including dynamic sharable libraries. The most basic frameworks are Foundation, UIKit (Cocoa Touch—iOS) and AppKit (Cocoa—OS X). More specialized frameworks, such as the Core Audio Kit Framework, are used as needed by developers.

iCloud is different. Don't search for an iCloud framework: there is none. Don't even search for an iCloud API. There are a couple iCloud-specific methods, but they are few and far between. In fact, they're very far between in the sense that they are scattered across various classes and frameworks. `URLForPublishingUbiquitousItemAtURL: expirationDate:error:` is part of the `NSFileManager` class (there are seven iCloud-related methods among the 52 methods in this class), while `NSPersistent-StoreDidImportUbiquitousContentChangesNotification` is part of the `NSPersistentStoreCoordinator` class (it is one of two iCloud-related notifications in this class).

The implementation of iCloud in this way means that existing apps that don't use iCloud aren't affected. In addition, because iCloud spans multiple devices as well as both operating systems (OS X and iOS), it is hard to imagine how it could have been implemented in a single framework or API.

Along with these few additions to the Cocoa and Cocoa Touch APIs, the implementation of iCloud relies on long-time best practices, which now have been converted to essential practices. Design patterns such as key-value coding that date back to the very early versions of NeXTSTEP have been used for a quarter of a century now, and they are used in new ways in iCloud, although in most cases you don't have to do anything to take advantage of the iCloud functionality.

Core Data, which has long been the most powerful solution to managing an app's persistent data, is deeply integrated with iCloud. However, that integration is largely (but not totally) done behind the scenes. If you don't use iCloud, your existing Core Data code is just fine. Perhaps the most significant impact of iCloud on Core Data is that, in the past, there were two ways of creating a data store that could be distributed with an app. You could place a seed database in the app's bundle, or you could add seed data programmatically to an empty data store that you create the first time the app launches (or whenever the seed data needs to be recreated). Both techniques have been used for years. The biggest impact that iCloud has on Core Data is that with iCloud, the second technique needs to be used; the first one will not work properly. This is scarcely a major change.

Perhaps the most visible impact of iCloud on developers is the enhancement of entitlements that control what an app can do in its runtime environment. Entitlements implement the new sandboxing rules that come into play with shared documents on iCloud. Explicit entitlements and sandboxing define the functions and capabilities of the operating system that an app will use along with the specific parts of disk storage where the app can write data. They increase the stability and security of both operating systems. They are required on iOS and are optional on OS X. On both operating systems, they are more aggressively implemented. Furthermore, from a developer's point of view, you'll probably be happy to hear that the developer-facing interface for entitlements in Xcode 5 is now vastly changed and dramatically simplified. (Sandboxing is related to iCloud, but they are two separate functionalities.)

The implementation of iCloud has proceeded over several years; in mid-2012, the release of OS X Mountain Lion (10.8) and iOS 6 brought together some of the pieces that had been released over the previous year. In the fall of 2013, OS X Mavericks (10.9) and iOS 7 refined iCloud and expanded its behind-the-scenes tools for developers. If you have not used any of the iWork apps (Numbers, Pages, and Keynote), try one of them on multiple iCloud-enabled devices. They provide the best demonstration of iCloud from the user's point of view.

Actually, that statement is wrong. They provide the best demonstration of iCloud from the user's point of view—until you write *your* iCloud-enabled app.

Introducing iCloud

Exploring iCloud and Its User Experience

As is the case with many of Apple's technologies, iCloud just works: users don't have to do much of anything to take advantage of its features. As a user, the main thing that you have to do is leave some of your old habits and preconceptions at the door because iCloud can make your life easier and much more productive.

As a developer, things are a bit different. There's a saying that "all the tedious work can make for one inspired moment" (it's attributed to various people). Behind the scenes, you do have some work to do so that users can use iCloud easily—it just works after you've done your work. This book helps you understand iCloud from the developer's point of view; it shows you what you can do with iCloud and how to do it. In fact, you'll see several different ways of using iCloud, and you'll learn how to pick and choose among them for your various projects.

This chapter is different from the others in the book because it introduces you to iCloud from the user's point of view. You may be using iCloud now in "it just works" mode, but in this chapter you start to explore details of iCloud that most users never think about. It is these details that you'll be working with as a developer.

Looking at Cloud Computing

The exact origin and first use of the term *cloud computing* is unclear (you can find some history in Wikipedia). Basically, the term seems to have arisen as people sketched diagrams of systems that incorporated various computers and storage facilities. It was simple to identify a specific computer by name or a given disk drive by its code. Some diagrams dating back to the 1980s were quite fanciful, as designers used metaphors for the components of systems. (I worked on one rather complex system that incorporated computers in various locations as well as several data transfer processes that were identified as bridges and tunnels.) Sometimes, data storage as well as processing was identified as happening in a cloud—a remote and opaque location about which the designers did not have to worry because it was under the control of other people who worried about issues such as backups, redundancy, and even the licensing of shared software.

The availability of reliable high-speed Internet connections made cloud computing available to vast numbers of people in the early years of the 21st century. Without these speedy connections, storing data or using processing resources in the cloud carried significant performance degradation costs, and cloud computing was used primarily by organizations that had their own high-speed networks. With these high-speed connections widely available, the benefits of cloud computing became widely available. The economies of scale that are available with such shared resources dramatically brought down the costs of processing and storage so that users could use remote storage in the same way that they used an external disk drive that sat next to their computer.

Figure 1.1 shows a desktop environment in the Finder on a Mac. In the Devices section, you see various devices (they happen to be disks in Figure 1.1, but they also could include other computers). Whether these connections are over a wireless network or across the Internet, the same basic structure applies: these devices that are connected over the network (rather than with a local cable) can function very much as if they were wired into the Mac, and you can access their files directly. Below that, in the Shared section of the sidebar, you see a disk that is shared over the network rather than being directly connected to the Mac. (In fact, it's directly connected to an AirPort Express and is shared over the Internet using an Apple ID.)

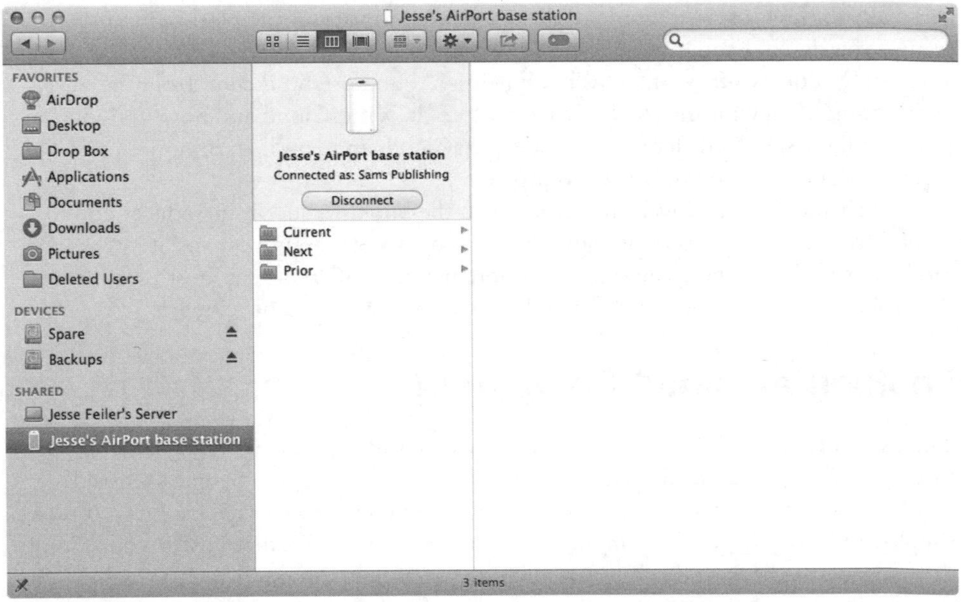

Figure 1.1   Using local and remote devices for storage

As you can see in Figure 1.1, the Finder provides a way to manage files across various devices. You can rename them, move them, and generally do anything you want with those files. If the files are located on a shared server, you may not have to worry about backing them up. If you have set up Time Machine backup, you don't have to worry about backing them up provided that, periodically, you check to make certain that your backups are running properly.

If you are even a moderately sophisticated computer user, you know all this. It may have taken you a while to get used to the various adventures involved in using files on internal disk drives, external disk drives, shared servers, and in the cloud, but you have learned it.

Congratulations: you're a power user who can manage your files no matter where they happen to be.

And now, it's time to forget all that. As generally used, the term *cloud computing* means putting some of your resources (both data and processing resources) in a network-accessible location. The way in which you work with those resources is basically unchanged. In fact, that's a big part of cloud computing: you don't care where those resources are because everything works as if it were local. (You can turn this around and suggest that you don't care where the resources are because everything behaves as if it were in the cloud.)

iCloud uses cloud technology to implement a new paradigm of resource management. It is important to realize that iCloud is not a synonym for cloud computing: it uses cloud computing to implement this new paradigm.

Understanding the iCloud Paradigm

The iCloud paradigm doesn't focus on *where* documents are located—either the disk or the folder within the disk. Instead, iCloud focuses on *what app* manages the document. As you will see in this section, this has a number of advantages, not the least of which is the capability of implementing sandboxing, which increases overall operating system and stability.

In addition, sandboxing can be handled automatically by the operating system: it organizes files by the apps that manage them. As you will see, iCloud is able to manage documents that are shared by several apps; however, on the way to taking full advantage of iCloud, you may have to change a few organizational tasks you have learned over the years with the Finder. The change basically consists of not bothering with your own organization of documents, folders, and disks.

Organizing Files by App

The Finder, shown in Figure 1.1, lets you manage files, folders, and devices in one place. Now take a look at Figure 1.2, which shows you iCloud and its new paradigm.

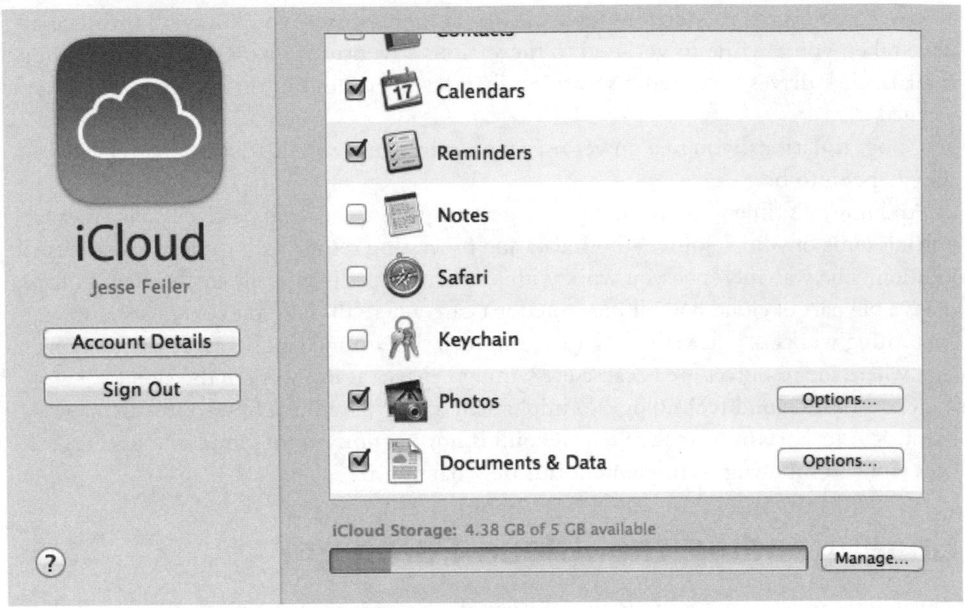

Figure 1.2   Storing documents by app in iCloud

No longer are you concerned with *where* documents are: instead, you are concerned with *what* they are and what app can manage them.

What makes this so powerful and important is that when you have iCloud enabled on your various devices, the documents in iCloud are automatically available on each device. Figure 1.3 shows Pages documents as shown in Pages running on a Mac.

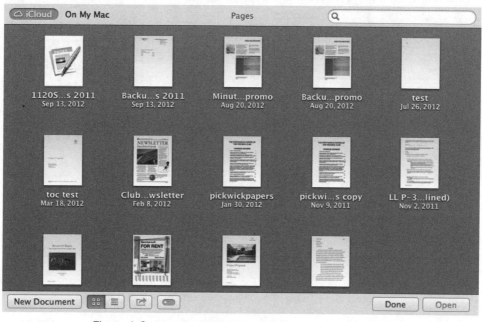

Figure 1.3   Viewing iCloud Pages documents on your Mac

Figure 1.4 shows the same documents in Pages on an iPad.

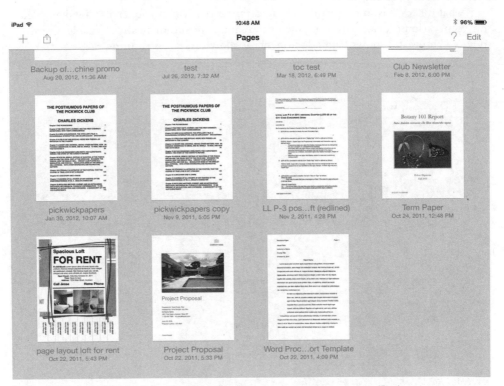

Figure 1.4   Viewing iCloud Pages documents on your iPad

Figures 1.3 and 1.4 are very similar, but there's an important difference in the top left corner. In Figure 1.3, you can choose between storing documents in iCloud or on your Mac. If you choose to store documents on your Mac, you use the same interface you're used to: the interface shown in Figure 1.1.

You can also manage the documents for each iCloud-enabled app from iCloud in System Preferences on your Mac, as shown in Figure 1.5. Click Manage in the bottom right of the screen to open this view of your apps and documents in iCloud.

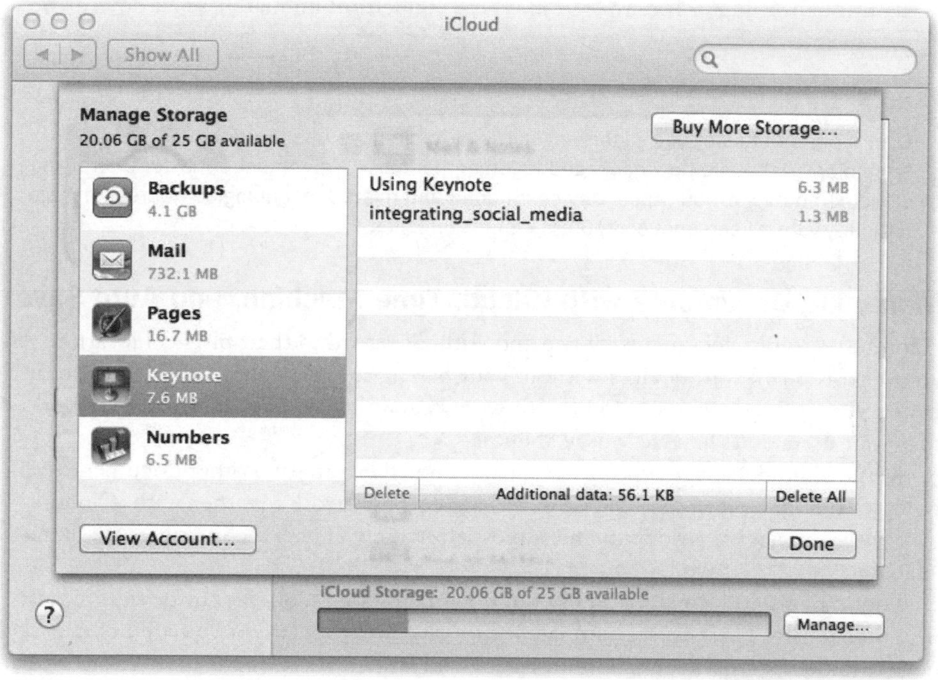

Figure 1.5   Viewing iCloud Keynote documents on your Mac using iCloud in System Preferences

The advantage of using iCloud is that you don't have to do anything other than click that iCloud button in the upper left of the Mac version of Pages: iCloud does the synchronization work (with a bit of help from Pages). You don't have to remember where you put the document: what you have to remember is what you want to do with it. (Many iCloud-enabled apps remember where you were in a document so that you can continue reading or listening from where you left off no matter what device you were using.)

> **Note**
>
> Over a period of many years, the engineers at Apple have been working on the technologies that are now packaged together in iCloud. It's not just a matter of bringing cloud computing to your Apple devices: iCloud and related technologies address a major difficulty with all personal computers—managing files.

Managing Documents with iCloud, Time Machine, and Auto Save

iCloud stores your documents by app and without regard to their physical location. All your data is on all your devices without your having to worry about it. Although, in your role as a developer, you do have to worry about it: you have to do a bit of work so that your users don't have to worry about it.

While iCloud manages your users' documents, there are two other document technologies that have been introduced in recent years that work together with iCloud to let users manage their documents almost effortlessly. These technologies are Time Machine and Auto Save.

iCloud by itself is timeless: all of your documents are on all of your devices almost instantaneously. There is a certain latency involved, particularly if you are not connected to the Internet at some point, but by and large, everything is on every device at all times. That is the behavior that most people want and expect most of the time for most of their data.

However, sometimes time matters. Time Machine automatically backs up documents on your Mac at periodic intervals: every hour for a day, every day for a month, and every week thereafter as long as there is space on the backup disk. As part of its operations, Time Machine periodically culls the backup files to get rid of hourly backups after a day, daily backups after a month, and so forth. This enables you to go back to files that have been modified or deleted and recover them. The scope of Time Machine's backups is your Mac's hard disk. iCloud files or files on external disk drives are not backed up unless you have copied them to your hard disk (sometimes people do this specifically to get documents into Time Machine).

Auto Save is a feature that appeared first on iPhone and iPad. Data is simply stored as necessary by the operating system and its apps. You don't have to worry about explicitly saving your data. For decades, computer users have been taught to save their files periodically and to even store backup copies of their files in a safe place. Because Time Machine automates the process of backing up copies of files, you don't have to worry about backups in the way that you did in the past. Now, with Auto Save, you don't have to worry about unsaved changes being lost: it's all done for you.

Part of Auto Save is the ability to create *versions* of documents. You may have gotten in the habit of doing this yourself by making copies of documents with titles such as Before Conference, After Conference Revisions, and the like. Now, you can use versions to store these versions and then browse them in a Time Machine–like display.

Put together, iCloud, Time Machine, and Auto Save document versions means that you can forget a lot of the document management tasks that you have learned and developed over the years.

Syncing Data Across Devices

There's another aspect to iCloud that makes it valuable to users beyond the fact that all of your data can be almost instantaneously available to your apps on all your devices. Time Machine and Auto Save provide convenient mechanisms for making copies of entire documents for backup and archival purposes. That's not something that iCloud does, which is why these products work so well together. What iCloud adds to the mix is the ability to sync data across devices.

Data often lives in documents, but it can be stored in other types of containers, such as key-value coding data stores, preferences, and Core Data persistent stores. iCloud doesn't just share your data among your devices; it can merge changes together so that the data that winds up being available on all of your devices may actually contain updates that were made separately on two or more devices.

Syncing changes across devices is something that has been supported in the operating systems and apps from Apple for a number of years. By now, you probably don't give a second thought to the fact that a phone number you enter into Contacts on your Mac shows up on your iPhone very quickly. Other apps from Apple also provide such automatic syncing—these include Calendar and Reminders as well as iPhoto, iTunes, and iBooks.

These syncing apps work quickly and efficiently to keep your data consistent. This process is made possible precisely because the apps do not worry about making complete copies of your contacts, iTunes library, or your iPhoto library as Auto Save and Time Machine do. Instead, your data is divided up into individual photos, contacts, reminders, and songs, and only the ones that have changed are synced.

This is the key to the process, and it bears repeating: you can keep your address book containing 10,000 contacts synchronized across devices because most of the time, what needs to be synced is a single contact that has changed. (In fact, it may be only a single contact's telephone number.) This divide-and-conquer strategy is the key to fast and efficient synchronization.

This means that your data has to be structured and organized. For most data and most users, that's not particularly difficult because the data in an address book, calendar, or library of music or photos is logically viewed as collections of specific items. This book helps you navigate through and choose from the wide variety of data management tools you'll find on iOS and OS X.

Making the Round Trip

This book helps you, the developer, learn how to implement what I call the Round Trip: synchronization of data between iOS and OS X apps. Although iCloud presents users with an app-centric view of their data (rather than a location-centric view), the heart of that app-centric data is a shared data container that iCloud can access directly. You configure your apps to access that shared data, and iCloud does most of the rest. There are many consequences to this that include benefits to the user and a bit more work for the developer. It's not a great deal of work for you, but the benefits for the user can be great.

In order to make the Round Trip, you need two apps: one to run on OS X and the other to run on iOS. Before you panic, consider what Apple has done in the last few years to make this work easier. First, on the iOS side, storyboards have been implemented to help you build your user interface. Used properly (and that means with Xcode 4.4 or later as well as iOS), this means that you can use separate storyboards for iPhone and iPad, but the differences in code outside the storyboards are minimal. That saves a great deal of time.

In addition, the new Auto Layout system on Cocoa and Cocoa Touch makes it easier to describe dynamic sizing and placing of views to accommodate varying screen sizes and orientations. Its basic concept is defining relationships between views as a series of prioritized constraints. This means that at runtime, the operating system can size and align views using a variety of constraints you have described. This makes UI design much easier than before.

Furthermore, the new (in Xcode 4.4) workspace feature lets you build multiproject workspaces. Projects are structured as they have always been, but you can combine two or more in a single workspace. This means that you can factor your code among an iOS project, an OS X project, and shared classes. Workspaces make developing Round Trip apps much, much easier than would be the case otherwise.

Chapter Summary

In this chapter, you've seen the basics of how iCloud looks to the user. The most important feature is that documents are app-centric and can be synchronized across devices and across pairs of apps (OS X and iOS). Apps can choose to use either (or both) ways of storing documents.

In addition, iCloud plays a role in managing data that may not be stored in documents. This data can range from preferences and settings to data that is stored out of sight in Core Data shoebox (or library) apps. (You'll find out more about Core Data in Chapter 10, "Managing Persistent Storage with Core Data.")

Exercises

1. If you haven't done so already, register at developer.apple.com. There are various registration categories that are designed for different types of developers. The paid levels of developer registration include technical support assistance (two incidents for the basic programs). There are also free registrations that provide no support but do allow you to download Xcode or obtain it for free at the Mac App Store.

2. Even though you may be chomping at the bit to start writing your own Objective-C code, take the time to explore several Xcode templates. At the least, on iOS, explore the Master-Detail Application template, and on OS X, explore the Cocoa Application template. Get used to the workspace window, and make certain to build templates with the downloaded settings before you modify them. In the case of the basic Mac OS X Cocoa application (the basis for most of your Mac OS X work), the basic template puts up an empty window. It is supposed to do that, so do not think you have done something wrong. Your job will be to fill that window.

3. Among the earliest iCloud apps are the iWork suite: Pages, Keynote, and Numbers. If you do not have them, buy them from the App Store or the Mac App Store. At the very least, get Mac and iOS versions of one of the apps so that you can see how iCloud synchronizes them across devices.

4. TextEdit supports iCloud documents; it is installed as part of the OS X installation. Experiment with it and particularly note how iCloud has been integrated into the File Save dialog. You can access this dialog from your own code when you instantiate NSDocument objects.

2

Setting Up iCloud
for Development

In Chapter 1, "Exploring iCloud and Its User Interface," you saw how iCloud looks to users. For many users, it's just a logical way of working, and iCloud really isn't an issue that they think about. For other users who have become used to managing their own files and folders on their various devices and desktops, there can be a significant effort at familiarization—an *unlearning* process. As technology advances, these unlearning events happen from time to time, but in the long run, the old way of doing things is forgotten. You may have had to configure a dial-up modem with bit rates and parity settings, for example. Now, even dial-up modems are automated and managed with handshakes to adjust their own settings. Dial-up modems are (fortunately) becoming artifacts of the past. And reports are surfacing of mystified children who don't know what a computer mouse is in the world of touchscreens that they inhabit.

This chapter looks at iCloud from the developer's perspective. As noted in the Introduction, iCloud isn't a monolithic API or framework that you just plug into your code. It's a collection of additions and modifications to many parts of Cocoa and Cocoa Touch. In this chapter, you'll find a high-level view of those additions and modifications with particular emphasis on setting up iCloud in your app.

iCloud involves synchronizing data across a user's devices, and as soon as you start thinking about sharing data among various devices, you have to consider the security issues involved. Fortunately, the engineers at Apple have done this: iCloud takes advantage of the security mechanisms that are built into the App Store and the Mac App Store. App security has not changed dramatically over time; however, configuring security has been difficult for many developers. In part, this is because it is a relatively complex process that, for most developers, is done relatively infrequently. That combination is a classic recipe for difficulty.

With the introduction of Xcode 5 in 2013, the implementation and setup of app security has changed insofar as the developer interface is involved (the underlying security mechanism is not changed). The changes make it easier for you to set up your app's security, but for many developers, it is a new process. Once again, there is an unlearning process involved when you use the new and simpler tools. Because iCloud requires security to be in place and because the way in which you implement it is changed, this chapter begins with an introduction to the new, improved, 2013 version of app security.

Managing App Security on iOS and OS X

The heart of the app security system is digitally signing your code with two digital signatures. Both of these signatures are generated by Apple, and each one references the other. (This is a common security mechanism that you can read about on Wikipedia in articles such as "Code Signing," which explains the process.) These signatures will not match if either the one identifying Apple or the one identifying the developer has been altered; in addition, part of the digital signature contains a checksum mechanism that causes the security system to fail if the code has been altered since it was signed.

Part of the complexity arises from the use of these digital signatures. The security for apps is built on a combination of developer.apple.com tools, Xcode tools, and Keychain Access tools. It is important to note that Apple IDs are used to identify people, and there are two categories of people (thus Apple IDs) that come into play: During development, you as a developer have an Apple ID. At runtime, the user's Apple ID comes into play with iCloud.

Identifying Yourself and Your App on developer.apple.com

Along with changes in Xcode 5, during 2013 developer.apple.com was revisited to consolidate the process of managing certificates, identifiers, devices, and provisioning profiles. These are the components of the security system for apps on iOS and OS X. Although the terminology hasn't changed, the layout of developer.apple.com has changed. Furthermore, with Xcode 5, it is easier to manage these security features, but the process is slightly changed.

Here is an overview of the process. It is required for you to set up your app to use iCloud as well as to ultimately distribute it.

After you register on developer.apple.com, go to Certificates, Identifiers & Profiles (currently at the right of developer.apple.com). It handles security for both your iOS and OS X apps. However, you can now do this through Xcode 5 and later: it's much easier there.

- You must identify yourself as a registered developer with a signing identity.
- You must identify your app with an App ID.
- You must identify the devices that you want to use for testing your app during development.
- You must create a provisioning profile that brings together your developer ID, your app ID, and the IDs for your test devices.

Managing Your Developer Signing Identity

A key part of the security mechanism is the certificate that you can download for each signing identity that you create. That is the link between developer.apple.com and Keychain Access on your Mac. The certificate is a portable and secure representation of your signing identity. In developer documentation, you may find the terms used interchangeably.

You can manage your signing identities in Xcode or on developer.apple.com. Xcode 5 introduced the ability to manage one or more Apple IDs for developer accounts, as you can see in Figure 2.1. A given Apple ID does not uniquely identify a specific developer account because a developer can be invited to join one or more development teams. You normally continue to use your developer Apple ID even though you may be working on several teams. Figure 2.1 shows the simplest scenario: a single developer Apple ID working on a single team. For iOS and Mac, one developer can have different roles.

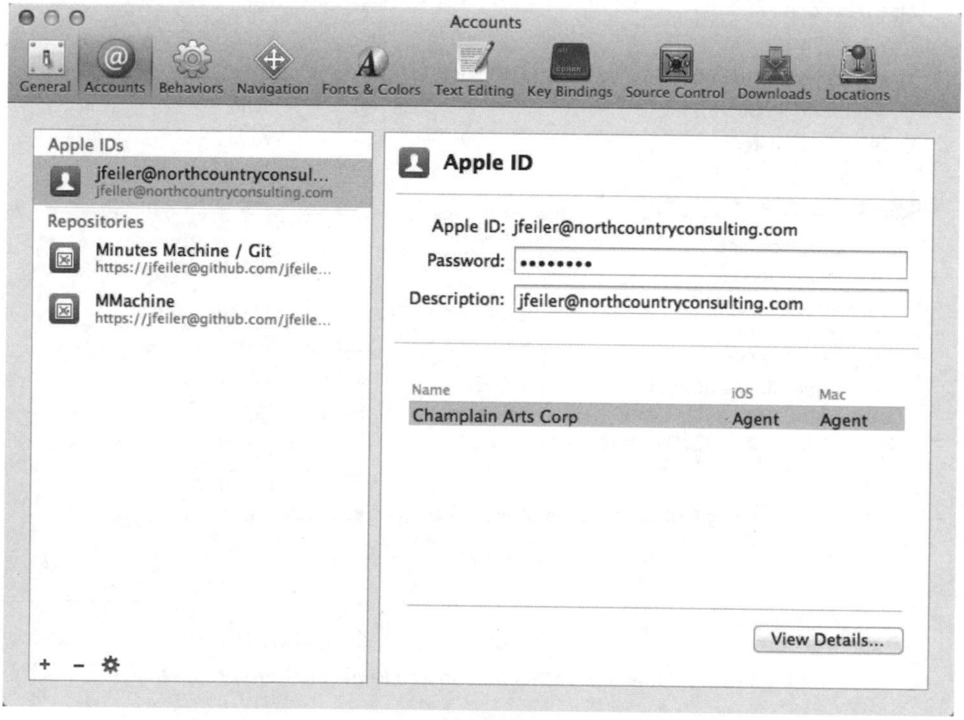

Figure 2.1   Manage your accounts on Xcode

Perhaps the most important point to take away is that you must use your own Apple ID to avoid compromising the security system for apps. Use the tools described on developer.apple.com to manage development teams so that developers can be assigned to the appropriate team without destroying the security structure.

Select the team you want to work with, and click View Details (shown at the lower right of Figure 2.1) to see its signing identities and provisioning profiles, as you see in Figure 2.2.

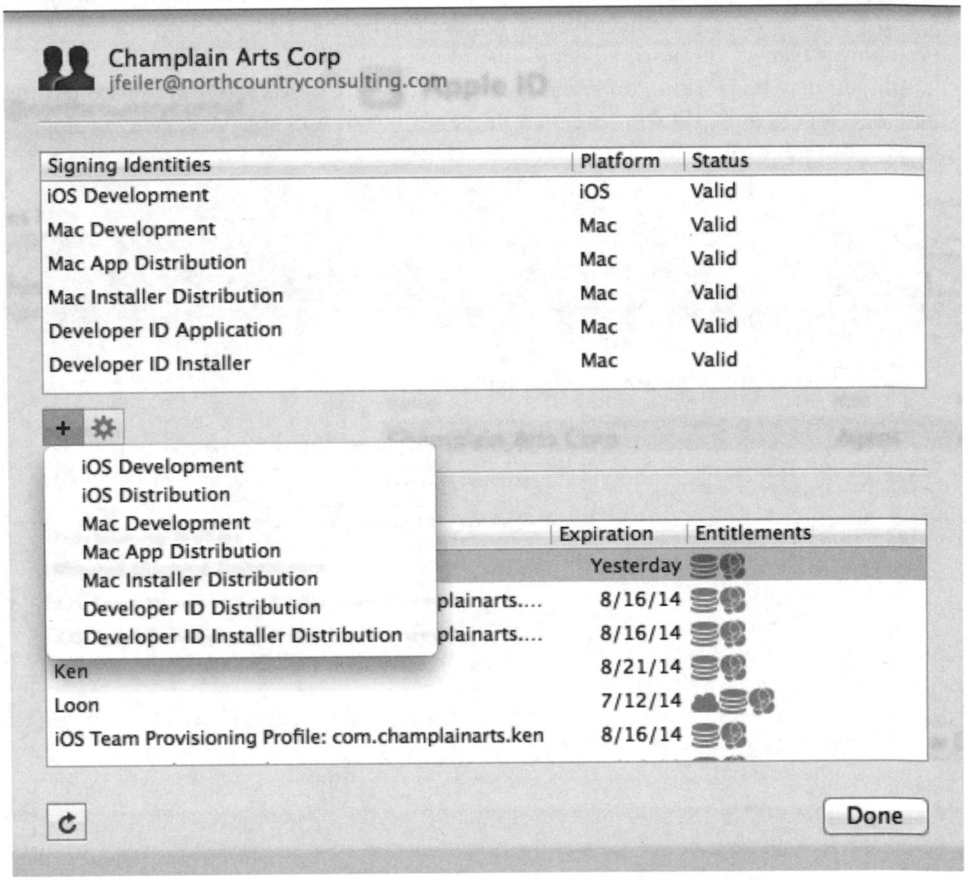

Champlain Arts Corp
jfeiler@northcountryconsulting.com

Signing Identities	Platform	Status
iOS Development	iOS	Valid
Mac Development	Mac	Valid
Mac App Distribution	Mac	Valid
Mac Installer Distribution	Mac	Valid
Developer ID Application	Mac	Valid
Developer ID Installer	Mac	Valid

iOS Development
iOS Distribution
Mac Development
Mac App Distribution
Mac Installer Distribution
Developer ID Distribution
Developer ID Installer Distribution

	Expiration	Entitlements
	Yesterday	
plainarts....	8/16/14	
plainarts....	8/16/14	
Ken	8/21/14	
Loon	7/12/14	
iOS Team Provisioning Profile: com.champlainarts.ken	8/16/14	

Done

Figure 2.2   Manage certificates in Xcode account preferences

Figure 2.3 shows the list of Mac certificates for a developer on developer.apple.com. Note that each one has a name that you provide, a type that you choose, and an expiration date that is set and enforced by Apple.

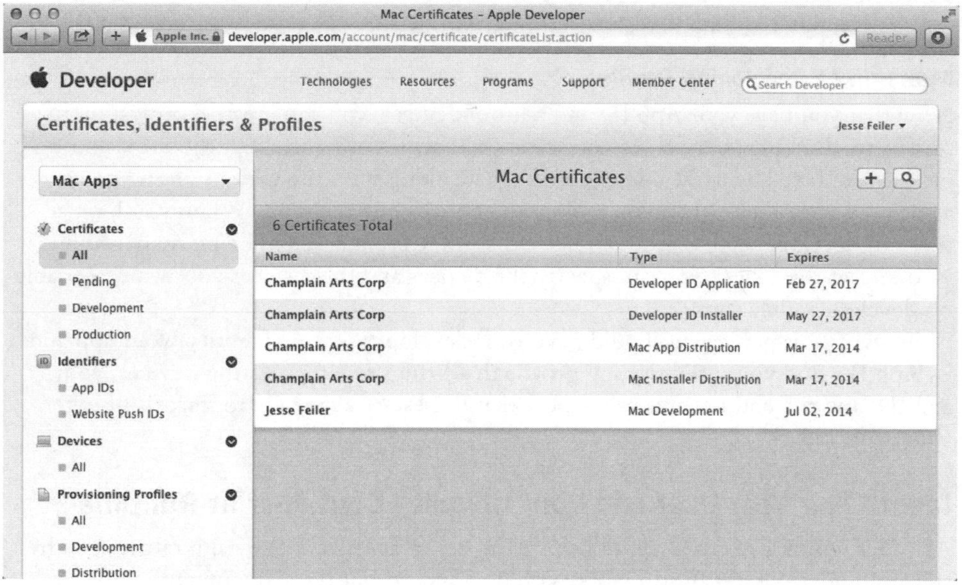

Figure 2.3   Manage certificates on developer.apple.com

Managing Your App ID

Unlike your developer signing identity, which can be edited on developer.apple.com through Xcode accounts, your App ID must be managed for the most part on developer.apple.com. You give the app a name, which can be changed later on if you want. (This is not the name the user sees.) What is important to note is that when you register your App ID, you can enable services that you want to use, such as Game Center, In-App Purchase, Maps, Push Notifications, and most important for this book, iCloud.

Although you cannot create an App ID through Xcode, when you turn on a capability such as iCloud, Xcode offers to update your App ID to add the iCloud capability automatically. (You'll see this demonstrated in Figure 2.9 later in this chapter.)

Managing Your Devices

You can register a number of devices that can be used for testing your apps. (As of this writing, the number is 100.) When you recruit people to test your app, ask them for the UDID (iOS) or UUID (OS X) of the device they want to test with. These people do not need to be registered developers, and sometimes it's a good idea to recruit one or two testers who are "real people" as opposed to developers. The rules for managing devices are detailed on developer.apple.com. There are limits to how many times you can change the list: this limit prevents you from allowing your app to be installed on a large number of devices without going through the App Store. (Ad hoc distribution is a specific option you may want to explore in this case.) You have one list of devices for your developer account. The provisioning profiles associate them with App IDs.

Managing Provisioning Profiles

Now that you have your App ID and a list of devices, you can create a provisioning profile to combine the two. As you see at the bottom of Figure 2.2, the provisioning profiles are listed by name and expiration date along with the various entitlements associated with them when you look at them in Xcode accounts. When you look at them in developer.apple.com, you'll see that some are marked as being managed by Xcode. For the others, you can specify the devices and the services you want to enable on developer.apple.com.

Thus, at this point, you should have your developer signing identity; your app and its App ID; and your provisioning profile that brings together testing devices, your app ID, and the entitlements or services that it uses. You're ready to start thinking about runtime.

Identifying Your User and Your Ubiquity Container at Runtime

As you saw in Chapter 1, iCloud helps users organize their data by app rather than by file and folder. Users can still work with documents, but those documents aren't on a visible file system in most cases: they're in iCloud. But where is iCloud?

As with all cloud computing, the cloud is an artifact of the Internet and large server farms. If you follow the trail of bits, you see that these server farms synchronize and store data so that it is accessible on an as-needed basis by users. The physical location of the data doesn't matter, and in fact, the actual storage is so often duplicated across servers that there is frequently no single primary data store among the many stores that come into play.

A user's data is available (subject to security constraints) whenever a user accesses the cloud with the appropriate account information and password. That's not the model with iCloud. With iCloud, data is available with the presentation of two identifiers:

- **Apple ID:** This identifies the user.
- **A ubiquity container identifier:** A ubiquity container is the object that holds the iCloud data for the app. It typically is a bundle identifier such as com.champlainarts.colby. It is prefixed automatically by your developer Team ID.

When the user connects to iCloud (usually this happens through the iCloud System Preference panel whenever the user logs in), the Apple ID is made available to all apps that are entitled to use iCloud. The ubiquity container identifier is usually set in the

Capabilities tab of the target in Xcode. As you will see in Chapter 18, "Completing the Round Trip," a shared ubiquity container may have an identifier that does not correspond to an app bundle identifier. In the case of the Round Trip, the two apps are com.champlainarts.ColbyOSX and com.champlainarts.ColbyiOS. They share a ubiquity container called com.champlainarts.Colby. It is the last component of the ubiquity container identifier that shows up in the System Preferences iCloud pane shown previously at the left in Figure 1.5.

With these two pieces of information, you can connect to the appropriate iCloud ubiquity container. That is your first task when your app starts to run.

Looking Inside the iCloud Basics

Bundle identifiers and Apple IDs have been around for a long time, but now they have key roles to play in iCloud. Both of them are needed to gain access to a section of iCloud. This is the implementation of the app-based file structure described in Chapter 1.

You might expect to find standard log-in methods in the iCloud API that enable your app to present an Apple ID and a bundle ID to iCloud in order to gain access to the data. That's not how it happens. Remember that there is no explicit iCloud API; beyond that, the notion of logging in to iCloud for an app isn't what happens. (Users do log in to iCloud—often automatically with their settings in the iCloud pane of System Preferences.)

Your app interacts directly with a local copy of the iCloud data for the user and the app. This copy of the iCloud data for the user and app is stored locally in a ubiquity container. The ubiquity containers are stored on the local device, and their contents are synchronized by the local OS and its interaction with iCloud. Just as is the case with any other local data access, you can read and write as necessary, and you can expect (and even check on) the results of those read and write statements.

Because you are not reading and writing to the iCloud data directly in most cases, you can't expect the changes that you have made to the local ubiquity data to be propagated to iCloud immediately. If you want to get into naming things, iCloud is an asynchronous and declarative implementation of cloud technology.

The key components of iCloud are

- Apple ID
- Bundle identifier
- Entitlements and capabilities
- Ubiquity container

The following sections cover the basics of what you need to know about them.

Declarative Programming

As is the case with more and more software today, iCloud relies heavily on *declarative* programming techniques. Declarative programming is distinguished from other styles that specify what happens and, frequently, in what order. (Common names for that style are *imperative*, *functional*, and *procedural* programming.) Declarative programming simply describes what should be done without specifying a control flow.

You find examples of declarative programming throughout OS X and iOS with more examples showing up with each new iteration of the Cocoa frameworks. Blocks, for example, allow you to specify code that is executed for each element of an enumerator or on completion of some task, but you do not hang around waiting for that trigger to occur. You define the block and then send it off (often as a parameter of a method), and it is executed at the appropriate time. You are out of the traffic-cop business, and, not coincidentally, multithreading at the system level is much easier for the OS to manage in your absence.

If you're not familiar with declarative programming or are still not comfortable with it, explore the topic online (Wikipedia is a great place to start for this type of research).

Apple ID

We're now looking at iCloud runtime behavior. The Apple ID discussed here is the user's Apple ID.

An Apple ID uniquely identifies . . . something. It started in 2000 as an account name on Apple's early Internet service, iTools, which provided free email accounts as <accountname>@mac.com. Over time, <accountname>@mac.com became <accountname>@me.com (MobileMe) and then <accountname>@icloud.com. With the advent of the iTunes store, customers used an Apple ID for their purchases. The email account name served as the first Apple IDs, but, particularly after Apple began charging for email accounts, Apple IDs no longer consisted of me.com or mac.com addresses. Every Apple ID did have to have an email address associated with it (for verification if for no other reason) and, for purchases in iTunes Store, a credit card number.

The idea that an Apple ID uniquely identifies an individual person has long gone away. An Apple ID has a name, a password, an email address, an optional rescue email address (in case the primary address is unreachable), and, if used for purchases, it may have a credit card associated with it. Apple suggests that people not share Apple IDs, but we know that sometimes a family or even a small business will share one.

Apple suggests that people may like to have one Apple ID to identify themselves to iTunes and another to identify themselves for other purposes such as iCloud, FaceTime, and the like. Developers often have one or more Apple IDs for their personal life and another for their developer account. iBook authors need their own Apple ID, so a developer who is also an iBook author needs two right there.

There is a unique identifier underneath all the attributes, so email address, name, password, and credit card can all be changed without creating a new Apple ID. Every iOS device requires that the user has an Apple ID in order to gain access to downloads of the operating system as well as any purchased apps or music.

On OS X, although the installation process encourages it, you do not need an Apple ID. If you want to use iCloud, you do need an Apple ID. Apple has recognized the proliferation of multi-Apple ID individuals in OS X Mountain Lion (10.8) and later versions of OS X. Figure 2.4 shows part of the Users & Groups pane in System Preferences.

Figure 2.4   You can have multiple Apple IDs on OS X.

If you click Change, you see a list of the Apple IDs you have associated with this account. You can add or delete some and create a new one, as shown in Figure 2.5.

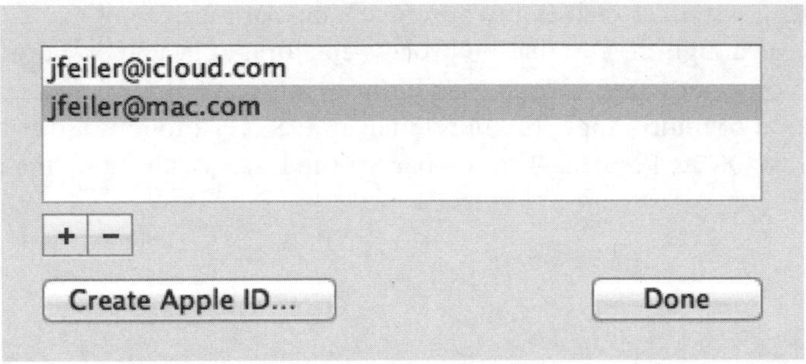

jfeiler@icloud.com
jfeiler@mac.com

`+` `−`

Create Apple ID...   Done

Figure 2.5   Switching Apple IDs on OS X

Most of the time, people don't pay attention to their Apple ID when they set up a device beyond checking that their email works (if it uses the Apple ID). However, for ongoing support of your iCloud app, remember (and let your tech support people remember) that the Apple ID is a critical part of iCloud access. If someone in an office uses an OS X account for business and another for personal matters, the iCloud documents created under those two OS X accounts may be using different Apple IDs. A Pages document under one account will not be shared with the other, although you can do so with sharing commands implemented in Pages and other apps.

The Apple ID that a user has used to sign into iCloud is available to the operating system at runtime, and that is how the Apple ID part of the iCloud authentication takes place: you don't do anything.

Bundle Identifier

The bundle identifier is set in your app's target settings in Xcode (in the General tab of the target). As you step through the process of creating a new project, you are asked for information, including the product name and the company identifier. You provide the product name, and the company identifier is editable (it actually is sticky—you start with the last company identifier you used).

> **Note**
>
> The management of bundle identifiers, product names, and targets, as described in this section, has been a matter of concern for a number of developers over the years. You can find many references on the Internet to what is going on. Unfortunately, some of them (particularly those from several years ago) are misleading. The information in this section is current as of Xcode 5, which is the version released with iOS 7 and OS X Mavericks (10.9).

The bundle identifier that Xcode starts with is the combination of the company identifier (which is usually your reverse domain name) and the product name, as in `com.yourcompany.yourproductname`.

If you look at the Info tab of your project, as shown in Figure 2.6, you'll see that the bundle identifier is set to your product name. The product name is also used as the target name, so you begin with identical values for your target and the last component of your bundle identifier. You can change your target name in the left side of the project editor: just double-click and type in a new name. You'll see that the last component of the bundle name also changes, because, as you see in Figure 2.6, it is picking up the product name.

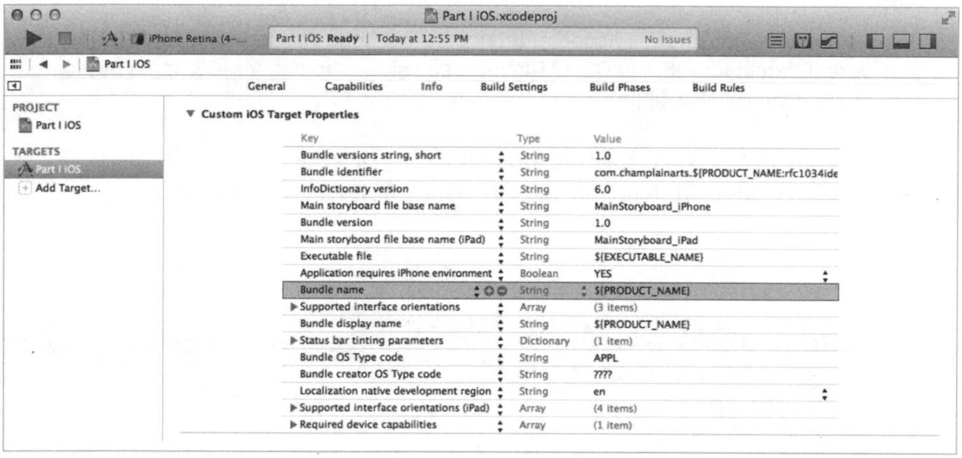

Figure 2.6   Editing the bundle identifier in Info

However, you can edit the bundle identifier itself in the General tab. As initially set up, it is set to `com.yourcompany.${PRODUCT_NAME:rfc1034identifier`. If you trace through the various settings, you'll see that product name (in the Packaging section of Build Settings) is set to `$(TARGET_NAME)`. This means that if you change the target name, the product name will change, and because it's used as the last component in the bundle identifier, that, too, will change. Anywhere along the line, you can double-click to edit the setting. If you change Product Name to be MyProject instead of `$(TARGET_NAME)`, you will change the product name, and indirectly, the last component of the bundle identifier. Generally, the best place to edit a bundle identifier is in the General tab of the project itself rather than in the Info tab. That is because the Info tab sets up the naming structure with placeholders such as `$(TARGET_NAME)` and the General tab lets you type in the actual name that you want to use, which overrides the placeholders.

Most of the time, the default settings are fine, and you don't have to worry about them. However, they come into play with iCloud when you need a ubiquity container that is shared among several apps. (Perhaps most commonly, one is a Mac app and the other is an iOS app.)

Entitlements and Capabilities

Entitlements specify what your app can do. The Capabilities tab shown in Figure 2.7 lets you configure the capabilities and the related entitlements and other settings. As you can see, there's a simple switch for each capability—iCloud, Game Center, Passbook, In-App Purchase, and more (still more are likely to come in the future).

> **Note**
>
> The Capabilities tab is new in Xcode 5. It replaces previous entitlements configurations that were different for iOS and OS X. The interface shown here is for iOS apps, but it is almost identical for OS X apps.

If a given capability is off, turning it on will also open the disclosure triangle to show you what additional steps you and/or Xcode must take, as you see in Figure 2.7.

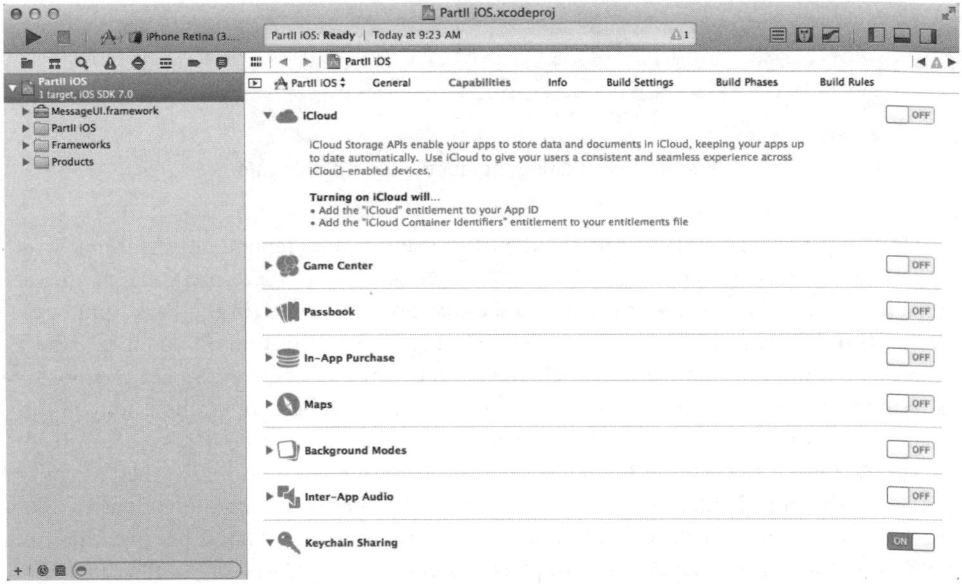

Figure 2.7   Turn capabilities on and off.

When you turn a capability on, you'll be asked to choose a development team to use in provisioning, as you see in Figure 2.8.

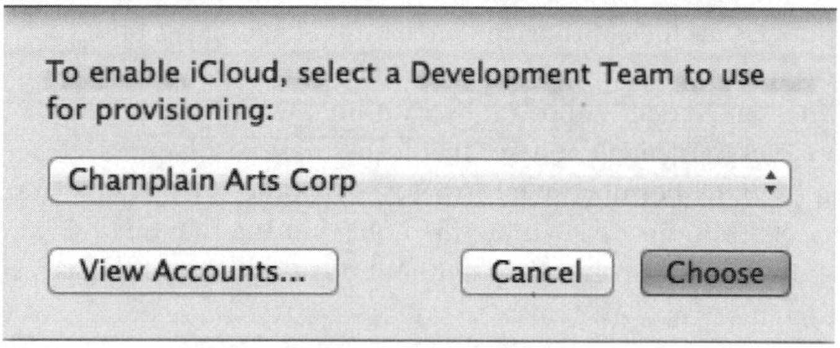

To enable iCloud, select a Development Team to use for provisioning:

Champlain Arts Corp ⇕

View Accounts...   Cancel   Choose

Figure 2.8   Choose a development team.

The steps that need to be taken, as shown in Figure 2.7, are checked off or, if a problem occurred, you are usually given an opportunity to have Xcode fix it, as you see in Figure 2.9.

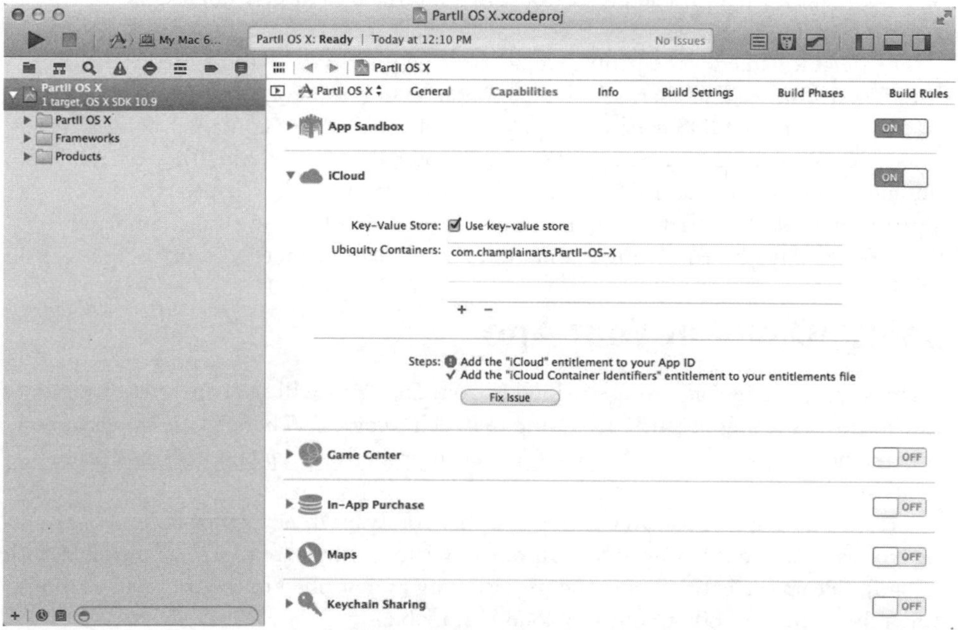

Figure 2.9   Managing Capabilities

Beginning in Xcode 5, this process replaces the manual configuration that you had to do in the past on developer.apple.com. You can still do that, and that is still the best place to actually see the details of your identities, provisioning profiles, and app IDs, but for many if not most of your transactions, Xcode will take care of those tasks. Also note that Xcode sets up the appropriate entries in your project's plist.

As you can see in Figure 2.9, when you enable iCloud, you'll be able to choose the entitlements file, but Xcode will begin by naming one for you. If you want to use a key-value store, you can enable it here: that is the topic of Chapter 8, "Using Key-Value Coding (KVC)." For documents (that is, data other than KVC data), you use a ubiquity container. You may have more than one, but the first one is always assumed to be the main one. If you are using KVC without documents, you don't need a ubiquity container.

Ubiquity Container

As you can see in Figure 2.9, you can specify ubiquity containers for your app. The first one you create has a default name set by Xcode, and it has a special role to play. (You can change the default name if you want, and in some cases, you must, as you'll see in the next paragraph.) The first ubiquity container is the *primary* ubiquity container. On OS X, its contents are displayed in the open and save dialogs available in NSDocument. (On iOS, you create your own interface to display documents in iCloud if you use them.)

The default name for the primary ubiquity container is the bundle identifier. In cases where you want to share a ubiquity container among several apps (such as an OS X version and an iOS version), change one of the ubiquity container names to the other one so it is shared. As you will see in Chapter 18, "Completing the Round Trip," the shared ubiquity container may have any name you want. In Chapter 18, the two apps have bundle identifiers of com.champlainarts.ColbyiOS and com.champlainarts .ColbyOSX. The shared ubiquity container is com.champlainarts.colby.

Using iCloud in Your App

At this point, you're ready to use iCloud in your app. You will see concrete examples of how to do so starting in Part III, "Using the Technologies." There is one step that you can take now to confirm that your app has been properly set up and that the entitlements and provisioning are correct.

Create a new app or use an existing app that you want to enable for iCloud (starting from a new app is a simpler way in the long run until you're more comfortable with iCloud). Set up the entitlements and provisioning as described in the previous sections. Add a single line of code to test if iCloud is available:

```
id currentiCloudToken = [[NSFileManager defaultManager]
                         ubiquityIdentityToken];
```

On OS X, it should go in `applicationDidFinishLaunching:`, and on iOS, it should go in `application:didFinishLaunchingWithOptions:`. In both cases, it normally goes after your other initializations. (Note that this method was added in iOS 6 and OS X Mountain Lion (10.8). You can find older and more complex ways of performing this task on the web.)

The iCloud token that is returned is an opaque object identifying the iCloud account (that means that you can't see inside it). There are two possibilities when you ask for the token:

- If it is nil, the user is not signed into an iCloud account.
- Although you can't see the account details, you can check if a token is the same as another token using `isEqual:`. This lets you check to see if the user has changed iCloud accounts.

Note that if a user has been signed into an iCloud account and turns on Airplane mode or turns off networking on a Mac, the token is still returned. You can access the local copy of your ubiquity container's data. When Airplane mode is turned on again, iCloud will take care of syncing the two stores and will let you know if there is anything for you to do. Because the operating systems manage these disruptions in connectivity, resist the temptation to store extra copies of data locally in the app's sandbox.

Apple recommends as a best practice that you use either iCloud storage or sandbox storage. Mixing the two provides a suboptimal user experience. Along those lines, ask users if they want to use iCloud the first time they run your app. Unless they reinstall the app, don't ask them again.

The iWork apps are a good example of how to manage documents in iCloud. Over the last few years, they have moved to an explicit Export command, which, among other things, can let you export the contents of an iCloud document to another format and to a non-iCloud location.

Chapter Summary

In this chapter, you've seen the basics of how iCloud works. iCloud for document data relies on a ubiquity container, which is identified by a user's Apple ID and your app's bundle ID and is enabled by entitlements. You can share ubiquity containers across several apps by using a single app's bundle ID for all of them.

A high-level overview of the provisioning process has shown you where you enable iCloud for your app. Provisioning is done by registered developers on developer .apple.com and in Xcode accounts. Provisioning profiles as well as identity certificates are then downloaded. You install provisioning profiles in Xcode accounts, while certificates are installed automatically in Key Chain.

Exercises

1. If you have any doubts about the wisdom of Apple's advice to either use iCloud for all storage or local (sandbox) storage for all storage, try to come up with a user interface of your own to manage them.

2. Set up entitlements for an iCloud-enabled app as described in this chapter. Start by following the steps exactly—either those in this chapter or those on developer .apple.com. Don't take any shortcuts until your first provisioning profile is running properly. Then you can experiment.

3. TextEdit supports iCloud documents; it is installed as part of the OS X installation. Experiment with it and particularly note how iCloud has been integrated into the File Save dialog. You can access this dialog from your own code when you instantiate NSDocument objects.

Using the APIs

II

3

Introducing the APIs and the First Apps

This part of the book shows you how to take advantage of the data your users have placed in iCloud either directly or indirectly by using apps that synchronize their data with iCloud. These apps include Contacts, Reminders, and Calendar as well as iPhoto on OS X or Camera on iOS. iCloud makes this data available to users on all their devices. The opportunity for you as a developer is to build apps that let users take this data and work with it. Their contribution is their data; your contribution is an understanding of what they may want to do with their data. The apps from Apple provide powerful support for the most common tasks that people want to perform with their data, but there are literally thousands (make that hundreds of thousands) of apps that let people combine their data with your ways of working with it.

This chapter introduces the project you'll be working on in this part of the book. You'll see what it can do, and you'll set it up with Xcode.

Getting Started as an Apple Developer

You'll find documentation and tools on Apple's Developer website at developer.apple .com. You need to register with an Apple ID for access to many parts of this content. You can use an existing Apple ID (such as one you've used in the App Store or iTunes) or you can create a new Apple ID that you will use with your developer's hat on. There is no charge for an Apple ID.

Each Apple ID has an email address associated with it along with your identity. Apple confirms your identity automatically by sending an email to the email address you provide. When you reply, Apple knows that—at least at that moment—you are the person associated with that email address. You can change any part of this supporting information at any time by logging in to appleid.apple.com, as shown in Figure 3.1. You repeat the verification process if you change your email address.

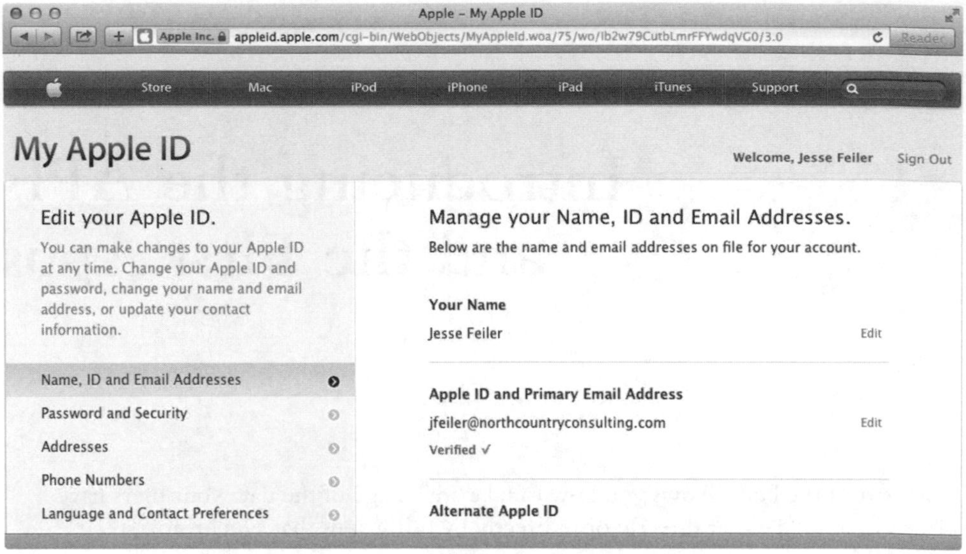

Figure 3.1   Configuring your Apple ID

To gain full access to developer resources on developer.apple.com, you need not only an Apple ID but also to register as a developer. You can find the details on developer .apple.com: they vary from country to country and they also change from time to time. There are separate programs for iOS and Mac developers; each costs $99 per year in the United States at the time of this writing. That fee covers access to the full site as well as two technical support incidents in which Apple engineers can help you with your code. There is an additional program for Safari developers, which is free.

In addition, there are specialized programs for in-house developers (the Enterprise Program) and for university-level teachers (the University Program). Rounding out the developer programs is the MFi Program, which is designed for manufacturers of accessories for the iOS devices. There are full details on developer.apple.com.

You can continue with this book with just an Apple ID (no charge), but you will need a developer registration in order to proceed to steps such as deploying your apps on iOS devices as well as creating entitlements to use iCloud. You may already have access to a developer account through the University Program or the Enterprise Program, so make inquiries before getting out your credit card.

As noted, many aspects of the developer programs are available without registration; however, from now on this book assumes that you have access to a developer account. Furthermore, this book assumes that you have downloaded and installed a current version of Xcode, the development tool—version Xcode 5 or later. If you have not used Xcode before, take a few moments to experiment with it. It comes complete with templates for projects that you can build and run either on the iOS simulator, your iOS devices, or on your Mac.

Looking at the APIs

As developers, we look at software very differently than users do. Of course, we're users as well as developers, and we use Mail and Safari along with other users. We also have our own apps to work with, foremost among them Xcode, which is the integrated development environment (IDE) that we use to build apps. When it comes to user data (appointments, notes, contacts, and the like) we work with the application program interfaces (APIs) that are implemented in the frameworks that we use to build our apps.

Most of the APIs that relate to user data have a common architecture. They let you (that is, you as a developer, not you as a user) locate objects such as photos, add new ones, delete old ones, and modify the data. In this part of the book, we focus on AddressBook and Calendar: once you have built a project using both of those APIs, moving on to other APIs should be relatively easy (and you'll do so throughout the book).

The APIs that are involved with the management of user data are found in the documentation section of developer.apple.com under the Data Management section, as you see in Figure 3.2. This section has a large selection of APIs in it. Note that the names of the APIs generally reflect the names they had when they were developed. Sometimes (as is the case with AddressBook) the consumer tools for using the data has a different name—Contacts. To avoid breaking existing code, the names of the API and its classes generally do not change.

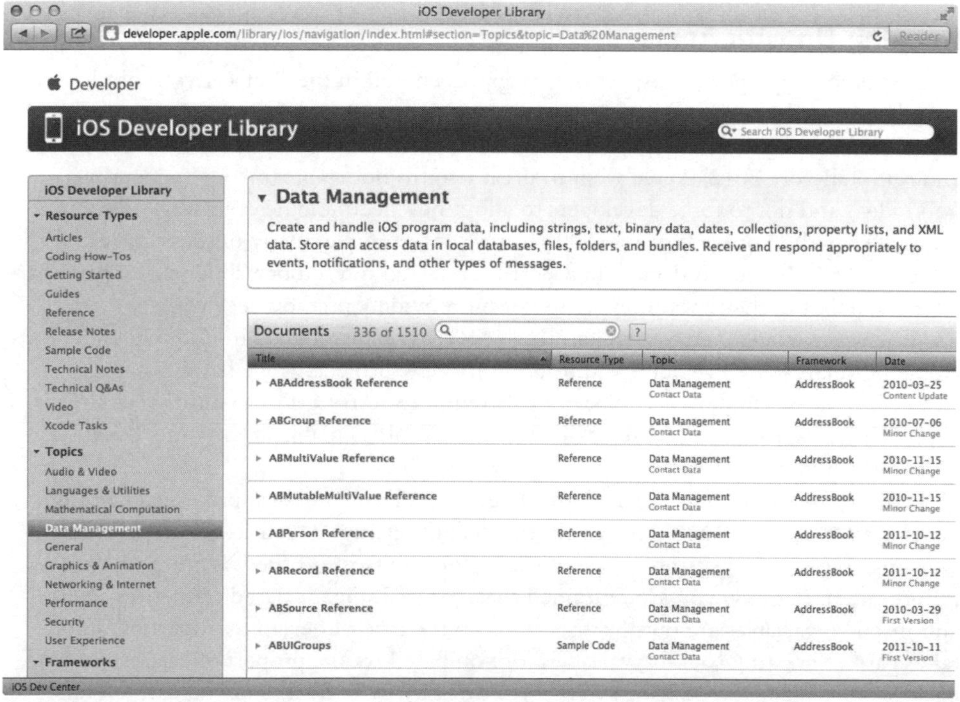

Figure 3.2   Browsing the Data Management APIs

The APIs that relate to user data are

- AddressBook
- ALAsset (for photos and videos on iOS)
- Calendar and Reminders

As Lao-Tzu said, the journey starts with a small step, so at the beginning the focus will be on AddressBook as well as Calendar and Reminders.

Introducing the Built-In Data Apps

In this part, we build an app that lets you type in a brief message and send it to someone in your address book. You'll be able to add reminders along with the message.

This app may seem like a reimplementation of a very small part of Mail, but it is an example of how you can combine the user's data with functionality that you create. From this basic step that does, indeed, duplicate a small part of Mail, your app can grow so that in addition to your message, you can add a reminder to the message. That reminder will automatically be synced to all of the user's devices (assuming that iCloud is enabled—that point won't be repeated from this point on). The evolution of the app as described in this part demonstrates how adding specific functionality can make the app much more useful to users.

Keeping Up with Apple

There is another important aspect of this app. As noted in the Preface, you should already be familiar with Objective-C and the Cocoa and Cocoa Touch frameworks as well as how to use Xcode. This book is based on Xcode 5, OS X Mavericks (10.9), and iOS 7. Before 2012, Apple went to great lengths not to break code (generally a good idea) and not to force developers to adopt new technologies and ways of coding that they did not want to use. That is why, for example, many of the features of Objective-C 2.0, such as declared properties, released in October 2007 (just 4 months after the debut of the first iPhone), are not more widely used by developers.

When Automatic Reference Counting (ARC) was introduced in iOS 5 (2011), Apple's guidance to developers was to use it for new projects as well as for major extensions to existing projects, but not to attempt to retrofit it onto old projects. This approach was necessary because of the developer tools available at the time, but it slowed the adoption of ARC.

In Xcode 4.4 (Summer 2012), Apple began to roll out a new approach to helping developers keep up to date. First of all, the default settings began to generate Xcode warnings when new features were not used. You can turn off the warnings or even ignore them, but now you are reminded that, for example, declared properties are in and instance variables are out. Furthermore, in the case of declared properties, Xcode takes care of creating backing variables for you based on the property declaration. The backing variable for `myProperty` is `_myProperty` by default, and you can reference it in your implementation file. You no longer need to write @synthesize statements because Xcode can generate them for you behind the scenes. All in all, to use a declared property, all you need is the property declaration: Xcode does the rest.

To further encourage the use of these new features, Xcode 4.4 adds two new commands to the Refactor submenu in the Edit menu. Both are self-explanatory: Convert to Objective-C ARC and Convert to Modern Objective-C Syntax. Both scan your project and suggest changes in the Version editor. You can go through comparing the before and after code and then decide if you want to save it.

With these new tools and the new approach to framework and tool changes, there is no reason to be concerned: if you knew Objective-C, you still know it, and the same goes for Xcode and the frameworks. Because this chapter introduces the book's first app, as part of that introduction, a few points of the new styles are pointed out, and they are used without further comment throughout this book.

With Xcode 5, more simplifications have been made: specifically, the complete redesign of project settings and the addition of the Capabilities tab has made the process of configuring your app's entitlements much easier. (You saw these features in Chapter 2, "Setting Up iCloud for Development.") All of these initiatives have a common goal of pushing changes to the language and frameworks into developers' apps sooner rather than later.

A good example of these changes is available in "View Controller Catalog for iOS" on developer.apple.com. This document shows the way in which the basics of Objective-C, Cocoa and Cocoa Touch, and Xcode evolve over time. It formerly was part of "View Controller Programming Guide for iOS" but was rewritten and published on its own in January 2012.

As people began to work with iPhone and iPad (people both within and outside Apple), they discovered new ways of working and new interface possibilities. Today, you can search the web for advanced techniques involving iOS views, including such complicated issues as placing a split view controller within a tab bar. You can find code examples that you can use.

Apple addressed these issues of advanced view techniques, and what had been an advanced topic became much simpler. Although the catalog is 70 pages long, you really only need to know two points:

- Apple now distinguishes between *content view controllers* and *container view controllers* such as split view controllers, tab bar controllers, and navigation bar controllers.

- If you use container view controllers, the order of containment is now specified clearly by Apple. If you use them, they must be used with the split view controller (if used) as the topmost view; then (if used) a tab bar controller and, within it, a navigation controller if you use it; and finally, content view controllers and page view controllers. The examples of placing split view controllers within tab bar controllers that you can find on the web may work, but they are now clear violations not just of the human interface guidelines but also of the order of containment, and they may not work in the future.

Thus, something that was an advanced topic in view management as well as an unclearly defined topic has become a basic principle that can be expressed in two thoughts. Sometimes, working with the excitement of new technologies means observing (and participating in) the evolution of those technologies. Many of us find the most exciting part of this evolution to be the synthesis of different ideas that makes things easier. Unfortunately, this does mean that from time to time we need to revisit the basics because they have changed.

These changes can ripple through the APIs and development tools, but it is important to stress the point that you're not back at the beginning. Many things are easier (and clearer), and occasionally you have a new way of working. Continuing with the issue of container views, you'll note that in Xcode, some of the library objects that you drag into storyboards come complete with attached and connected container views. Together with the clear containment order from the catalog, this complex process is now simpler and very clearly documented. Your existing knowledge and skills are leveraged.

Fortunately, long-time Apple developers have observed that these changes are reasonably predictable. They revolve around Apple's Worldwide Developers Conference (WWDC) that is held in June. WWDC typically includes details of new versions of iOS and OS X as well as Xcode. If there are cleanups to existing technologies (such as the view catalog), these typically happen with revised documentation in the first half of the year. New technologies are often announced at WWDC, and documentation pertaining to them is released at that time. As a result, if you want to keep up with Apple's developer technologies once a year, log in to developer.apple.com a few weeks after WWDC to see the announcements, documentation, and videos. (Beginning in 2013, Apple released videos of the sessions on the same or next day to all registered developers.)

Finally, over time, the pace of the major changes slows down as Apple generalizes concepts and rewrites the basics with the goal of making OS X and iOS development simpler and easier to learn. (Of course, at the same time, the pace of other changes steps up. Read the unofficial Apple blogs to see what Apple may or may not be working on in the next few years.)

App Overview

Think of how this app can be used. It is based on the Broken Swings app built for Steve Peters, superintendent of recreation for the City of Plattsburgh, New York. A parks supervisor can use it on periodic inspections to note broken swings, trees that need pruning, or any other issue. The supervisor can use the app to send that information to a staff member. The reminder can be used to ensure the worker or the supervisor follows up on the issue. In the domain of a park, you can start to build an app that goes far beyond the generality of Mail. For example, instead of asking the supervisor to type in the problem, you can provide a checkbox set with these choices:

- Broken equipment
- Pruning (tree)
- Pruning (bush)
- Water fountain

If the app is running on a device with a camera, the user can add a photo of the offending item. And if the device also has location capabilities, that, too, can be added to the email message.

This type of app is ideally suited to one of the iOS devices because it can be used in the field even by a large number of people. The email messages can go to a central address where someone can forward them or place them in a database.

This app lets you take advantage of iCloud without writing a single line of code: address book and calendar data is automatically synced across devices so that the possible recipients of the email message are on whatever device your user is using. Likewise, the reminder can be automatically added to all of the user's devices using iCloud.

Thus, the simplest way of building a sophisticated iCloud app can be to build an app that uses iCloud-enabled built-in apps and their APIs.

Creating Separate Xcode Projects for iOS and OS X

The first step is to create a project and run it. For projects that will run on both iOS and OS X, it is common (but not required) to create a single Xcode project with two targets. For a project such as this first project, though, you will be letting iCloud do its work behind the scenes, so you do not need common code that will run on both operating systems. The code will be comparable, but you do not need to create a single project with two targets. Because this structure is a little simpler than the multitarget structure, these first apps will have two separate Xcode projects: one for iOS and one for OS X. (You'll see how to build a single project with both an iOS and OS X app in Chapter 11, "Using Xcode Workspaces for Shared Development.")

Note that this is one of the places where recent features of Xcode are demonstrated. Previously, Xcode templates that used two targets used scenarios such as one target for OS X and another for Spotlight support. Now, the two targets, at least for iCloud projects, can be iOS and OS X. That is a long-awaited goal that is now achieved.

In both the iOS and OS X Xcode projects, you will produce a (minimally) working version of the app using the graphical user interface of Xcode. The only typing involved in the creation of each project is typing in the name of the app (and, if you haven't done so before, the name of your company). There is no code to type in for these projects, but rest assured there will be plenty to type in throughout the rest of the book.

Creating the iOS Xcode Project

As a general rule, the templates built into Xcode are the most up-to-date code you can find. If you are working from a previously downloaded sample, check to see if a new version has been created on developer.apple.com and also check the date of the most recent version. With the addition of the refactor commands in the Edit menu, it seems that the sample code can be updated more easily than before. If you're working from your own older code, seriously consider at least refactoring it to use modern Objective-C syntax and ARC.

Bearing this in mind, the best way to start your new iOS app is to create a new iOS project using the Single View Application, as shown in Figure 3.3.

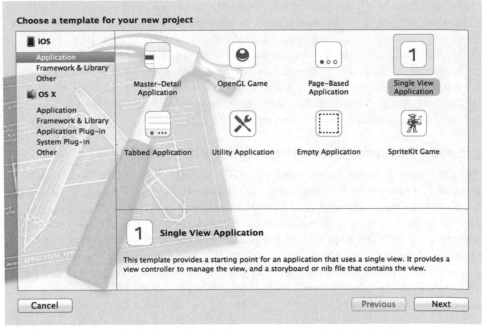

Figure 3.3 Using the Single View Application template

Select the options, as shown in Figure 3.4.

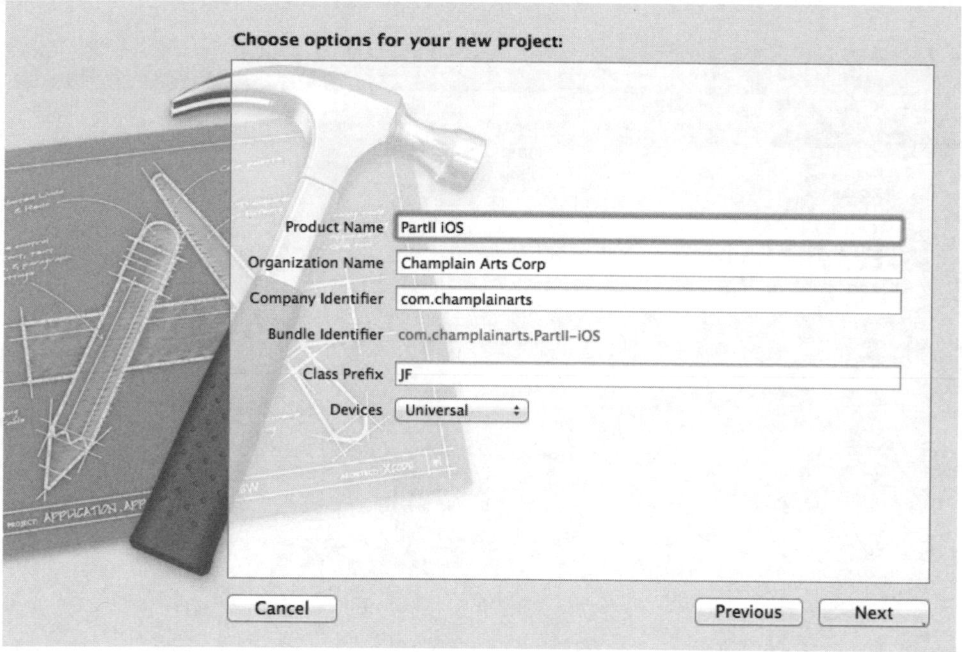

Figure 3.4   Selecting options

When requested, save the project. When the workspace window opens, as shown in Figure 3.5, choose Universal for Devices. The other settings are fine to leave as-is.

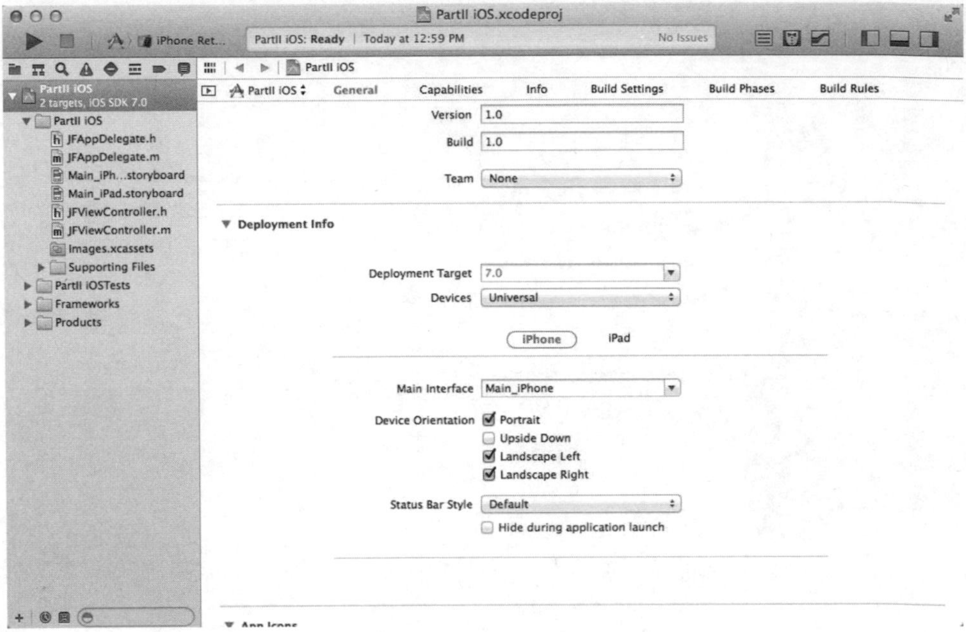

Figure 3.5   Choosing Universal for the Devices setting

Choose the iPhone simulator for your scheme (you can use any iPhone or iPad), and then click the Run button at the upper left of the workspace window to run your new project on the simulator. You should see no error messages, and, in fact, nothing except the blank simulator. Any other result indicates that there's something wrong either with your Xcode installation or with some configuration within it. The Apple Developer Forums can be helpful here if you run into problems.

Now that you've verified that the template runs for you, the first steps you add to this project will let you enter some text into a text view. To make that happen, open the iPhone storyboard, and then drag a text view from the objects library into the storyboard, as shown in Figure 3.6.

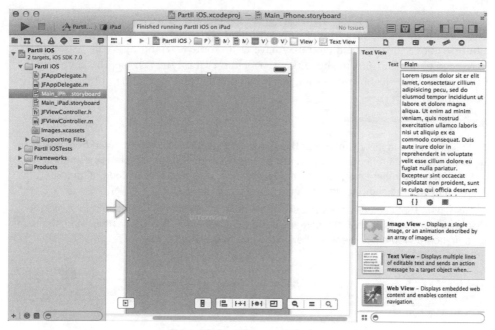

Figure 3.6   Adding a text view

Run the app now, and you'll see your text view with placeholder text. As you see in Figure 3.7, you'll be able to edit the text in the simulator. (Also note that Retina displays use pixel doubling; on the simulator, this may result in a double-size image.)

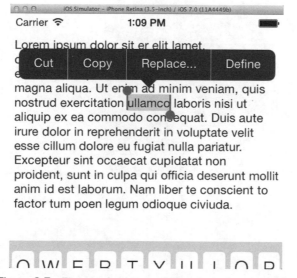

Figure 3.7   The text field is ready for use in the simulator.

Now you have an app that you can run; it contains a text field into which you can type text. You'll want to do something with that text, so, as shown in Figure 3.8, add a button above the text field (you may have to do some rearranging). The reason you may need to add the button above the text field is that on the iPhone, the keyboard may pop up over the button as soon as you tap in the text view if the button is at the bottom of the screen.

> **Note**
>
> You will notice in this chapter that the Xcode workspace window is changed from one figure to the next. That reflects the way many people work: the navigation area is sometimes critical, but at other times you can hide it and use the space for the code editor. Similarly, you may want to show or hide the utility area as you work.
>
> Also, note that in many cases you see the iPhone storyboard in figures in this book. The reason for that is simple: the screen size is the smallest of the iOS devices, and so those storyboards reproduce best on the limited size of a printed page.

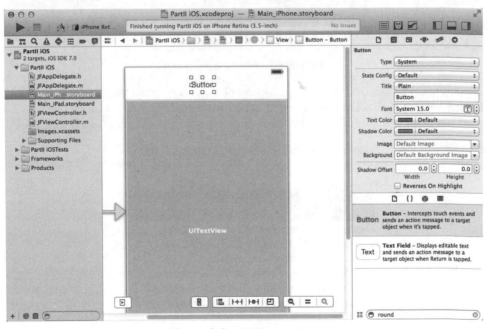

Figure 3.8   Adding a button

Creating the OS X Xcode Project

Now, you can turn your attention to creating a comparable OS X app. As is the case with the iOS app, you won't be typing any code at this stage for an OS X app, but, as you'll see, when you get into the functionality of the app, there are major similarities.

Begin by creating an OS X project in Xcode. In the OS X section of the New Product sheet, choose Application and Cocoa Application. (You do not have the variety of templates that you have with iOS.) Name the project PartII OS X, as shown in Figure 3.9. Do not choose any of the other options.

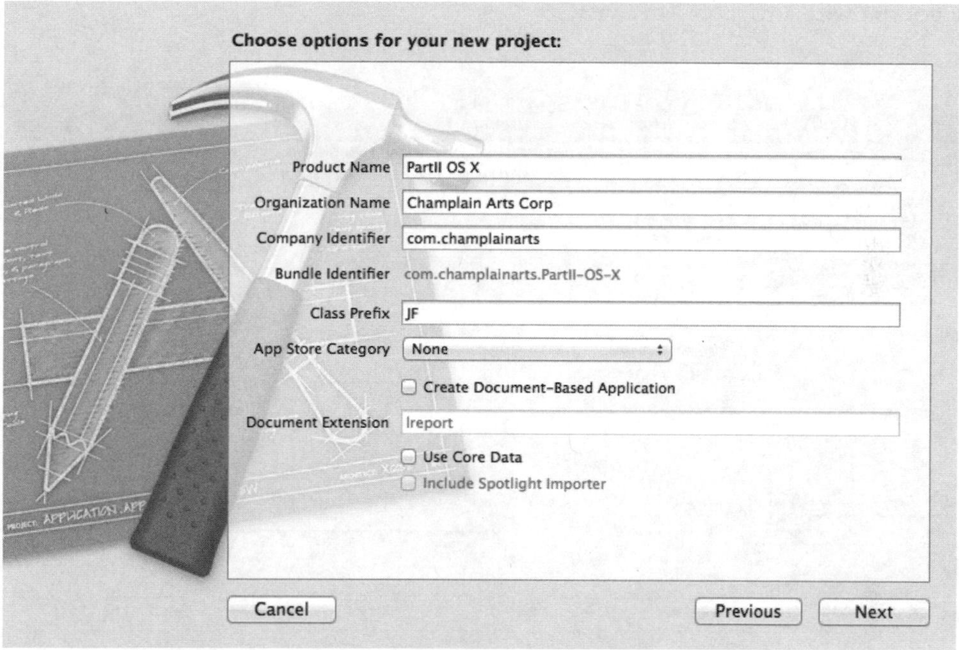

Figure 3.9   Using the Cocoa application template

As you did with the iOS project, start by attempting to run it. Again, you should see no errors or warnings, and not much of anything except the app's empty window.

Because there are no storyboards in OS X projects, you use nib and xib files to build your interface graphically.

> **Note**
>
> nib files got their name when OS X was first developed at NeXT. nib is an acronym for NeXT Interface Builder. In a major restructuring of Interface Builder, nib files were implemented in a different format that relies on XML, and the file extension became .xib. Many people pronounce xib as "nib" for reasons of history as well as the difficulty of figuring out what the correct pronunciation would be.

On both operating systems, you can also create the interfaces programmatically, although the classes you use in your code are not identical. Open the MainMenu.xib file to begin editing the interface, as shown in Figure 3.10. The project template provides you with a window and a view.

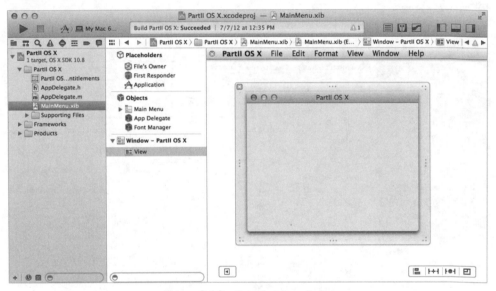

Figure 3.10   Opening the nib file

Explore the nib file. Just as you did for iOS, add a text view to the window's view. (The objects in the OS X library are not always identical to those in the iOS library, but they are mostly similar.) Figure 3.11 shows the field added to the view.

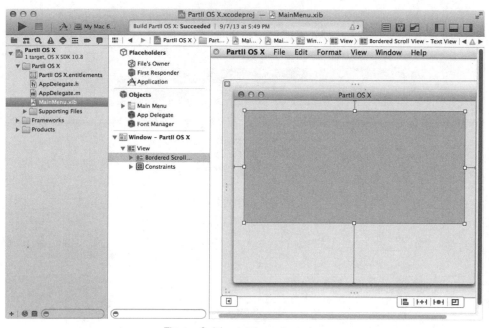

Figure 3.11 Adding a text view

Resize the text view and add a button, as you did for iOS. You should see the results shown in Figure 3.12.

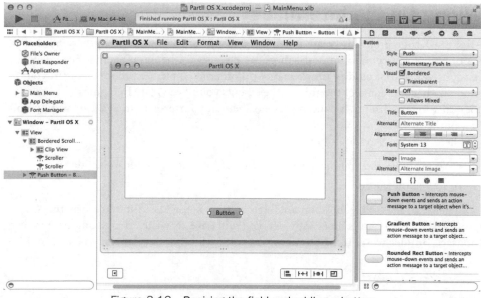

Figure 3.12 Resizing the field and adding a button

Now run the app. Figure 3.13 should match your results. (The app's menu bar is not shown in Figure 3.12, but it's there at the top of the screen.)

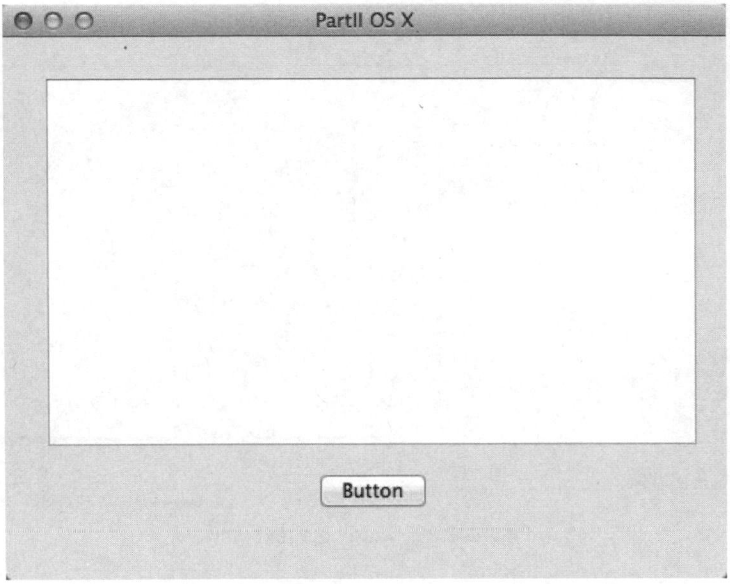

Figure 3.13   Running the app

Wiring Up the Interfaces

After the Xcode project is created, you can make whatever modifications are needed. Among the most common modifications are changes to the interface that become necessary as you add or modify functionality. In order to implement those changes, you generally have to connect the interface elements you have created graphically to the code that manipulates them and represents them in your project (that's the "wiring up" part of the process).

There are two ways of doing this:

- You can use the graphical user interface of Interface Builder in Xcode.
- You can write code.

In general, the two techniques are interchangeable for basic interface structures. However, there are some cases in which you will have to write code to augment your Interface Builder work. In addition, as you talk with other developers, you will find that some prefer one technique over the other. The only absolutely clear guidance is to use whichever technique is most comfortable for you at any given moment. Furthermore, if you are having difficulties building an interface, if it's possible to switch that particular part of the code from the graphical user interface of Interface Builder to code in your project, switching techniques may help you hone in on the problem. Both techniques are illustrated throughout this book in part because, regardless of your preferences, you're going to have to use both techniques from time to time. (View Controller Catalog for iOS sample code referenced previously generally shows the storyboard and programmatic techniques together.)

This section shows how you can make the connection between interface elements and code in Interface Builder. This basic technique is almost identical on iOS and OS X. The graphical user interface lets you see the relationships between interface elements and code objects. In later chapters, you will sometimes see code-based connections. The underlying structure of connections is exactly what you see in the figures of this chapter, but sometimes, instead of drawing lines with the mouse, you achieve the same goal with code.

There is an additional technology for managing these connections—*binding*—that can be used on OS X. It is deliberately omitted in favor of using a technique that works on both iOS and OS X.

Wiring Up the iOS Interface

In iOS, the links between interface elements and your code are *connections*, and you can manage them with the Connections inspector in the utility area of Xcode if you are using Interface Builder. Perhaps the most common connection that you need is the link between the `view` property of a view controller's code to a view in a storyboard. Without that link, those two pieces of functionality can't come together. You may not notice this because, in much of the downloadable sample code from developer.apple.com and in the Xcode project templates, the connection is often made for you. Also, when you drag a view controller from the library onto the canvas, it comes with a view already created and connected to the controller. You can subsequently delete the view (perhaps to replace it with another), but the connection is made for you.

For the interface elements that you add, you'll need to connect them. In Figure 3.8, you added a text view and a button. You'll need a connection in order to extract the text the user has typed in from the text view. Notice in the document outline view at the left of Interface Builder that, by default, all of the views are named generically. In order to keep your sanity, make it a practice to rename any view you'll be working with. Figure 3.14 shows the text view selected and renamed using the Label field in the Identity inspector. As soon as you leave the field, the name is changed in the document outline as you see in Figure 3.14.

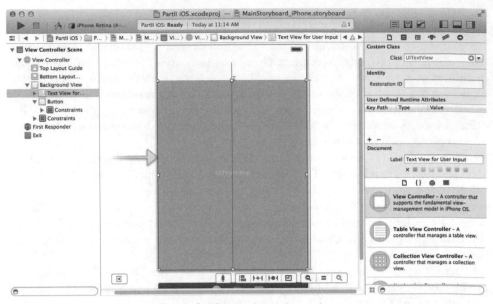

Figure 3.14   Naming the text view

Using the Assistant, open ViewController.h next to your storyboard. Select the text view either in the document outline or on the canvas. Holding down the Control key, draw a line from the text view to the interface in ViewController.h. When you release the mouse button, you'll be able to specify that this is a new outlet, and you can provide a name for it, such as userTextView. The storage type is typically weak: use strong for the top-level view in a view controller. Your actions result in a new property declaration for your view controller:

```
@property (weak, nonatomic) IBOutlet UITextView *userTextView;
```

Back in Interface Builder, you will see that you have made the connection to the new userTextView property in the referencing outlets section of the Connections inspector, as shown in Figure 3.15.

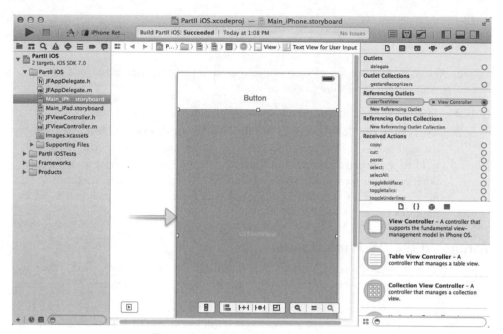

Figure 3.15   The connection is made.

Now that you have created the connection, you can use a similar technique to create an action that will access the text when the button is tapped. Control-drag from the button to the interface of ViewController.h. This time, instead of choosing an outlet from the pop-up menu, choose an action. Name it `tapButton`. By default, the action for a button is Touch Up Inside and the argument is Sender: both of these can remain, as can the `id` type. This means that all you need to do is make sure the pop-up menu is set to Action and that you have provided a meaningful name. (As you can tell from the name of the action, the action that actually starts things moving is the release of the button.)

This has created the following line of code in View Controller.h:

```
- (IBAction)tapButton:(id)sender;
```

Xcode has also created a shell of the action for you in ViewController.m. It will be called when the button is tapped. You can now proceed to add the code to that action that will retrieve the user's text:

```
- (IBAction)tapButton:(id)sender {                           //1
   NSLog (@" %@", _userTextView.text);                       //2
}                                                            //3
```

This code is a combination of your implementation and the code generated by Xcode as you created the action graphically.

1, 3 These are the lines that Xcode created for you.

2 This line is the only line you need to write for this example. You extract the text from the text view and display it in the log. By connecting the field to the declared property in Interface Builder, you can now access it whenever you want. In practice, although some of your action methods may consist of a single line of code, in many cases they involve much more complex code.

Wiring Up the OS X Interfaces

Although the process of wiring up the OS X interfaces is quite similar to iOS, there are three minor differences between the connections on OS X and those on iOS:

- Instead of a text view, you may want to use a text field (NSTextField). This is because text views on OS X are very powerful, but if you're used to dealing with text fields on iOS, the added power and complexity of a text view isn't necessary for the example app that you're building here. By default, the text view in the library for OS X is embedded in a scroll view. It is generally easiest to open the scroll view in the document outline to reveal the embedded text view and then connect it to the AppDelegate.

- NSTextView on OS X is a descendant of NSText. UITextView on iOS is not. To get the content of an NSTextView, you use the string property; to get the content of a UITextView on iOS, you use the text method.

These are the lines of code Xcode will create for you in AppDelegate.h as you attach a button and a text field:

```
#import <Cocoa/Cocoa.h>

@interface JFAppDelegate : NSObject <NSApplicationDelegate>

@property (assign) IBOutlet NSWindow *window;
@property (weak) IBOutlet NSTextField *userTextField;

- (IBAction)tapButton:(id)sender;

@end
```

And these are the lines of code created in AppDelegate.m. You must enter the body of `tapButton`:

```
]);
#import "JFAppDelegate.h"

@implementation JFAppDelegate  .

- (void)applicationDidFinishLaunching:(NSNotification *)aNotification
{
  // Insert code here to initialize your application
}

- (IBAction)tapButton:(id)sender {
  NSLog (@" %@", [_userTextField stringValue]);
}

@end
```

Chapter Summary

When a user turns on iCloud (and the corresponding options), contact, reminder, and calendar data automatically populates all of the user's devices through iCloud. Along with the data, photos, music, and videos may also be shared.

As a developer, you can add value to a user's data by massaging it and combining it in new ways. The basic APIs let you access the user's data in your app. Other shared data, such as music, iBooks, and videos, are generally not available through public APIs but instead are managed by iTunes and iBooks.

In this chapter, you've seen an overview of the user data that is automatically synced through iCloud. In order to start building apps for this part of the book, you have seen how to build an iOS and an OS X app that let a user enter data and then retrieve it. That's the building block for a sample app. In the next chapter, you'll see how to take the data the user has entered and email it to someone in the user's address book.

Exercises

1. If you are relatively new to Xcode and Cocoa or Cocoa Touch, experiment with the interfaces of the sample app to make them look better and behave differently.

2. Add a date picker to the app by dragging it out of the library and putting it in the app's interface. Create a property for it and extract the date in the `tapButton` method, just as you did for the text view. There are date pickers in both Cocoa and Cocoa Touch, but they look different.

3. Add a second button. One button will extract the text view data and post it to the log, as it does now. The other will do the same for the date picker. This multibutton/ multifield interface will be built on throughout this book.

4. If you have followed through the examples in this chapter, you have been working with the iPhone storyboard. If you change the schema to the iPad simulator, you won't see anything because the iPad storyboard is blank. Build the storyboard in the same way you did for the iPhone storyboard, but consider the fact that the iPad screen is much larger. Think about how you will let users take advantage of that screen.

5. Do you have an app in mind that you can build based on this chapter's apps? If so, think it through so that you can work on it in this part of the book. Remember, the app will let users enter some data, email to someone in their address book, and post a reminder through iCloud to all their devices. How could you use that basic functionality?

4

Working with the AddressBook API for Contacts

Now that you have a barebones app in place, it's time to add various iCloud features to it. The chapters in this part of the book focus on the user data that can be synchronized across the user's devices (subject to settings on the various devices, of course) using iCloud. Some of that data is entered explicitly either with the keyboard, with Siri or dictation, or with options in Mail and other automated hooks. The data discussed in this chapter—AddressBook data—can be entered explicitly, but it also frequently is added as a result of your normal actions, such as addressing an email message. This chapter shows you how to access that data as well as how to update AddressBook data.

Considering the AddressBook API on iOS and OS X

OS X and iOS both implement the AddressBook API, and you can synchronize your data through iCloud very easily. However, as you will see, the programmatic API for generating email messages is different on the two operating systems. Just as with bindings (implemented on OS X but not on iOS), the generation of email messages uses different tools—AppleScript on OS X and the MessageUI framework on iOS (AppleScript does not exist on iOS).

Also, as has been pointed out previously, don't worry about the distinction between AddressBook and Contacts. AddressBook is the API and was originally the name of the app that provided a user interface on OS X. The apps have been renamed now (Contacts on both operating systems), but the API retains is original title.

The ability to quickly send an email message to someone in your address book (be it in AddressBook or Contacts) is a very basic part of any computer that supports email. For that reason, it's available on both iOS and OS X, albeit in different implementations. It's another aspect of the operating system that "just works." On iOS, the "just working" part is courtesy of `MFMailComposeViewController` and its framework. As you'll see, you can type in a message, tap a button, and send it on its way. What you don't see in this chapter is that when you're addressing that email message, as you type names, type-ahead logic shows you possible addresses. To accomplish this, you as a developer do nothing more than use the standard compose sheet for email messages (it's described in this chapter).

On OS X, you build the functionality of `MFMailComposeViewController` into your code. There are several reasons for this. Perhaps the most important one is that on OS X, there never was a framework such as `MFMailComposeViewController`. Over the years (decades, in fact), developers have built and shared interfaces to interact with AddressBook. You can find them in sample code on developer.apple.com as well as in various places on the web if you search for them. There was no such resource on iOS at the beginning, so Apple created one very early on.

Another issue to think about with regard to the interface is that, in real-world deployments, the entry and editing of AddressBook data is often done on mobile devices on an as-needed basis (or, rather, on a meeting-someone-and-getting-their-contact-info basis). Much more commonly, contact data is synchronized from WebDAV or Exchange servers where an organization and its IT department manage the data. To be sure, there are many, many environments where contact information is managed from a desktop or laptop computer, but the mobile and shared server configurations are very strong players in the field of contact management.

Sending Mail from the iOS App

The MessageComposer sample app (downloadable from developer.apple.com) gives you a firm basis for implementing in-app email. It relies on the `MFMailComposeView-Controller` class that was introduced in iOS 3.0. It provides a view controller interface to Mail along with the necessary methods (very few, as you will find out). In fact, your basic do-nothing shell of an app is ready to send email with just a few additions. Figure 4.1 shows the interface as it appears on iPhone 5.

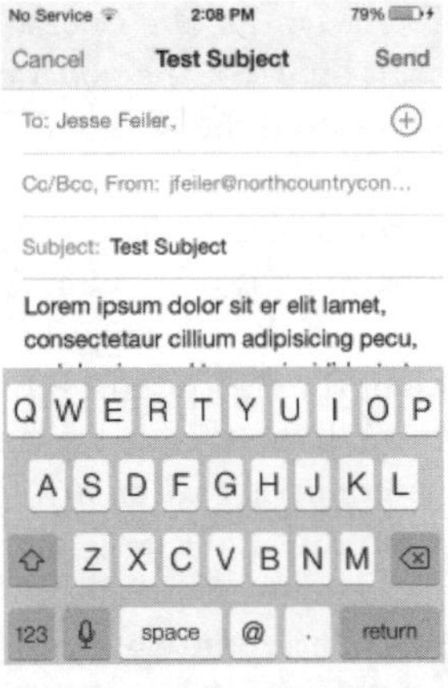

Figure 4.1   Sending email from your app

As is often the case with Cocoa and Cocoa Touch, your implementation of functionality consists of a number of adjustments to settings and wiring up of components old and new.

Note that `MFMailComposeViewController` takes care of sending the email once the user taps Send. If you are testing your code on the simulator, you can't send email. Thus, for testing, you will have to provision your app for distribution (actually ad hoc distribution), as described in developer.app.com. If you are using a development provisioning profile, you can't send email. You can pose the sheet on the simulator, but all you can do is tap Cancel. Furthermore, you may notice that the message field doesn't contain all of the text you expect it to (this is particularly true if your message is lengthy). Before you panic, use a distribution profile and test it on an actual device.

Making Sure You Can Send Mail

The code in this chapter builds on the code from the end of Chapter 3, "Introducing the APIs and the First Apps." You need to perform two tests:

- Make certain that Mail is configured on the iOS device.
- Make certain that you have an Internet connection.

The sequence of these tests is important. If Mail is not configured, you can forget about sending email. All is not lost, though, because you can advise the user to configure Mail and then continue with your app. If Mail is configured but there is no Internet connection, you can warn the user, but there is no reason to stop. The message can be configured, and Mail can put it in its queue to be sent. When there is an Internet connection, the message will automatically be sent.

Most people use a variation on code from the Reachability sample code on developer.apple.com to perform these tests. Here are the steps to take to modify the code from Chapter 3:

1. Download Reachability. As is always the case with downloading sample code, it makes sense to quickly run it to make certain that all the pieces are present. Look at the date of last modification and read the comments about the version you have downloaded.

2. Open the project and locate Reachability.h and Reachability.m. Add them to your app's target. You can do this either by dragging them into the navigator or by selecting your project in the navigator and using File, Add Files. (The right mouse button also brings up this command as one of the commands in the shortcut menu.)

3. Select your project in the navigator, and then click the General tab. In Linked Frameworks and Libraries, use + to add SystemConfiguration.framework. This is needed by Reachability.

4. Still in Linked Frameworks and Libraries, add MessageUI.framework.

Sending the Message

With this preparation, you're ready to move the text from the text view into a new email message. This section shows you the code for that process: the checks for Internet and email will come in the next sections.

Expanding the `tapButton` Method

You'll expand on the `tapButton` method that you have created in `ViewController`. Add the declaration of a new method to `ViewController.h`, as shown in Listing 4.1. This message will use `MFMailComposeViewController` to send the message. As you will see, you need to provide a delegate that conforms to `MFMailComposeView-ControllerDelegate` to handle the send result.

Listing 4.1   **Adding a New Method to View Controller**

```
#import <UIKit/UIKit.h>

@interface ViewController : UIViewController
@property (weak, nonatomic)
  IBOutlet UITextView *userTextView;

- (IBAction)tapButton:(id)sender;

- (void)displayComposerSheet;                              //1

@end
```

1   This is the declaration of the new method.

Importing the Frameworks to ViewController.h

You'll need to add new files to ViewController.m. Listing 4.2 shows what the top of that file will look like now.

Listing 4.2   **Importing a New File to ViewController.m**

```
#import "ViewController.h"                                 //1
#import "Reachability.h"                                   //2
```

```
#import <MessageUI/MessageUI.h>                                    //3
#import <MessageUI/MFMailComposeViewController.h>                  //4

@interface ViewController ()                                       //5

@end                                                               //6

@implementation ViewController                                     //7
```

1   This is the only line in the original file.

2, 3, 4   These are the added lines at the top of the file.

5, 6   This is the empty class extension that is automatically added to .m files beginning in Xcode 4.4. Use it to declare properties and methods.

7   This is the beginning of the implementation: there are many more lines following this one in the code that you have, but they don't need to be changed at this point. In Listing 4.4, you'll add another method at the bottom of the file.

Adopting the `MFMailComposeViewControllerDelegate` Protocol

You'll be setting `ViewController` to be the `MFMailComposeViewController-Delegate` delegate. So the interface in ViewController.h should look like Listing 4.3 at this point.

Listing 4.3   Adding `MFMailComposeViewControllerDelegate` Protocol

```
#import <UIKit/UIKit.h>                                            //1
#import <MessageUI/MessageUI.h>                                    //2
#import <MessageUI/MFMailComposeViewController.h>                  //3

@interface ViewController : UIViewController
  <MFMailComposeViewControllerDelegate>                           //4
@property (weak, nonatomic) IBOutlet UITextView
  *userTextView;

- (IBAction)tapButton:(id)sender;

- (void)displayComposerSheet;                                     //5

@end
```

1, 2, 3   This imports the framework.

    4   This adds the delegate protocol to your view controller.

    5   This is the method you will add later in this chapter.

Implementing the Protocol for `MFMailComposeViewControllerDelegate`

For readability, it's often a good idea to bracket delegate protocol code with a pragma, as shown in Listing 4.4. Despite the spacing, this consists of a single line for the method declaration and a single line of implementation.

Listing 4.4   **Using Pragmas to Bracket Protocol Code**

```
#pragma mark MFMailComposeViewControllerDelegate

-(void)mailComposeController:
  (MFMailComposeViewController*)controller
    didFinishWithResult:
      (MFMailComposeResult)result
      error:(NSError*)error
{
  [self dismissViewControllerAnimated:YES completion:nil];
}
```

Calling the New Method from `tapButton`

Now, call the new method from `tapButton`, which you created in Chapter 3, and provide the definition of the new method, as shown in Listing 4.5. Note that this is just the shell of the new method: for it to function properly, you'll have to add the code shown in the following sections. However, this preliminary code is provided to give you an idea of where you are going.

Listing 4.5   **Defining `tapButton`**

```
- (IBAction)tapButton:(id)sender {
  NSLog (@" %@", _userTextView.text);

  [self displayComposerSheet];                              //1


}

-(void)displayComposerSheet {
  MFMailComposeViewController *composer =                   //2
    [[MFMailComposeViewController alloc] init];             //3

  composer.mailComposeDelegate = self;                      //4
  [composer setSubject: @"Test Subject"];                   //5
```

```
[composer setMessageBody: userTextView.text
  isHTML: NO];                                              //6

[self presentViewController: composer                      //7
  animated: YES completion:NULL];
}
```

1   This is the call to the new method. After the text from the text view is written to the log, it will display a sheet to let you create the email message.

2, 3   This creates an instance of `MFMailViewController`.

4   This sets the delegate to this view controller.

5   This sets the message subject.

6   This sets the message body to the same text you wrote to the log.

7   This presents the new view controller. This is a method of `UIViewController`. It needs no completion handler.

Checking That Mail Is Configured and the Internet Is Available

Listing 4.6 shows the code that performs both checks. You can replace the direct call to `displayComposerSheet` in `tapButton` with this code, which incorporates the necessary checks before it either calls `displayComposerSheet` or posts an alert. This code is based on the MessageComposer sample app.

Listing 4.6   Checking That Mail Is Configured and Available

```
- (IBAction)tapButton:(id)sender {                         //1
  NSLog (@" %@", _userTextView.text);

  Class mailClass = (NSClassFromString(@"MFMailComposeViewController"));
  if (mailClass != nil)                                    //2
  {
    // We must always check whether the current device is configured for
    // sending emails
    if ([mailClass canSendMail])
    {
      NetworkStatus networkStatus = [[Reachability
        reachabilityForInternetConnection] currentReachabilityStatus];
      if (networkStatus == NotReachable) {
        [self showCantSendMailAlert];                      //3
      } else {
        [self displayComposerSheet];                       //4
      }
    }
```

```
  else
  {
    [self showCantSendMailAlert];                                    //5
  }
}
else
{
  [self showCantSendMailAlert];                                      //6
}


}
```

1   `tapButton` was created in Chapter 3 and should already be in ViewController.m.

2   This checks that you have a `mailClass` class.

3, 5, 6   These display alerts for the absence of the `mailClass` class, no email configuration, or no network connection.

4   This composes and sends the message.

In Listing 4.7, you see the code to show the error alert as well as the code to actually display and send the email.

Listing 4.7   **Sending the Message or Showing the Alert**

```
-(void)displayComposerSheet {
  MFMailComposeViewController *composer =
  [[MFMailComposeViewController alloc] init];                        //7

  composer.mailComposeDelegate = self;

  [composer setSubject: @"Test Subject"];                           //8

  [composer setMessageBody: userTextView.text isHTML: NO];          //9

  [self presentViewController: composer
     animated: YES completion:NULL];                                //10
}

-(void)showCantSendMailAlert                                        //11
{

        UIAlertView *alert = [[UIAlertView alloc]
                    initWithTitle: @"Email Not Configured"
                    message: @"You can continue with the message
                    but you will not be able to email it."
```

```
                    delegate:nil
                    cancelButtonTitle:@"OK"
                    otherButtonTitles:nil];
        [alert show];
}
```

7   This allocates the compose for the message.

8   This sets the subject.

9   This sets the message body to the text the user has typed in.

10   This presents the composer to the user.

11   This is the alert to display when an error occurs. You could parameterize it with alternate wording for the different errors. Alternatively, you might log specifics to the console from this method.

Sending Mail from the OS X App

OS X does not have a class that's comparable to `MFMailComposeViewController` that combines the sending of mail with the interface of AddressBook. In part, that's because AddressBook is integrated so tightly into iOS. On OS X, the integration of AddressBook with sending email is something that you implement at the app level.

The SBSendEmail sample app on developer.apple.com lets you send email to an address that your user types in, whereas on iOS devices, the address field (like the copy fields) has that AddressBook integration with type-ahead. On a Mac, the interface and the functionality are different, and, once again, much of that difference is attributable to the presence of multiple windows on the Mac.

Sending Mail from the OS X app is implemented based on SBSendEmail; because it's not directly an iCloud function, you should explore SBSendEmail on your own. Its integration with AddressBook is explored in the following section.

Using Property Lists for Storing and Syncing

You rarely need to look inside the AddressBook API: you usually use accessors and even higher-level methods. However, it is a good idea to know the basic outline of what's going on—if only because it's the same basic design pattern you'll find with events and reminders as well as a number of other classes throughout Cocoa (and other systems). It's a design pattern (architecture, if you prefer) that you may have already used yourself. If you haven't already used it, you may want to consider using it. From the perspective of iCloud, this design pattern helps to build a robust and easily synchronized data structure.

If you've used AddressBook, you have seen that you can manage people and groups. As is common in the digital world, groups (like albums and playlists) are not places.

This means that a person (or photo or song) can be in several groups at the same time. The AddressBook API implements this with two classes: `ABPerson` and `ABGroup`. Both are subclasses of the `ABRecord` abstract class. Because it's an abstract class, you never directly instantiate an `ABRecord` object. However, because it's the superclass of `ABPerson` and `ABGroup`, every time you instantiate an object of one of those classes, it inherits from `ABRecord`.

When AddressBook (or any other API) needs to access group or person information, it uses the appropriate class—`ABPerson` or `ABGroup`. However, when anything needs to access both types of instantiated classes, it can use the abstract superclass. "Syncing your address book/contacts" means syncing both of the instantiated subclasses, so it's not hard to guess that the actual sync process syncs `ABRecord` objects. As noted, this design pattern reappears over and over in Cocoa, and it's key to efficient syncing for iCloud.

If you look inside the ABRecord Class Reference on developer.apple.com, you'll see that it's very simple. Each instance is associated with a specific address book (by default, the shared address book), and each instance has a unique identifier (`uniqueID`). In addition, each instance can be marked as read-only (or not).

Then, you'll notice a set of four methods that manipulate properties within an instance of `ABRecord`:

```
- (id)valueForProperty:(NSString *)property
- (BOOL)setValue:(id)value forProperty:(NSString *)property
- (BOOL)setValue:(id)value forProperty:(NSString *)property error:(NSError **) error
- (BOOL)removeValueForProperty:(NSString *)property
```

Deep down, the data for properties is stored in a property list, and these four methods let you manipulate it. Property lists are well suited to storing the properties for an object because you get and set those properties using the key strings in the property list. If the property list has keys that you do not care about (or for which you do not know the key string), you never see them. And if you add a property to a property list, no one else sees it. This is how apps can add properties to the address book without breaking things. The lists of key strings are in "Address Book Programming Guide for Mac" on developer.apple.com.

Both the use of the abstract class and the use of flexible property lists to store data for the abstract class instances are important designs to remember as you build your own classes to easily sync with iCloud.

Chapter Summary

This chapter took your first app and added iCloud data to it in the form of address book contacts. This is user data—data that the user has entered (or obtains through synchronization with WebDAV or Exchange). On iOS, users can manipulate the data with apps that use the `MFMailComposeViewController` framework, which you've seen how to use. Both OS X and iOS use the same AddressBook API, but on OS X, you need to build your own updating interface to the data.

You've also seen the overall structure of the AddressBook API. It involves an abstract superclass that supports `ABPerson` and `ABGroup` classes, which you instantiate. It is this abstract superclass that iCloud syncs, and you'll see this design pattern in use through iCloud synchronizations. (In addition, you'll probably use the structure yourself.)

Exercises

1. To properly test your AddressBook code, create a new Apple ID for which you can create your own data at https://appleid.apple.com/cgi-bin/WebObjects/MyAppleId.woa/ (there is no charge), then assign it to a separate user account in Users & Groups on OS X. This will create a new address book for this new Apple ID. In order to test iCloud syncing, assign this Apple ID to an iOS device. (Most developers don't assign this ID to their own iPhone. Instead, find an iPhone that is not important to you. Do be careful, because if you use an older iPhone that can't run iOS 7 or later, you may not have a current version of iCloud.)

2. In order to understand how property lists can work for flexible data, add some new properties to your address book contacts. Use the test account you created in the first exercise.

3. In this chapter, you've seen how to modify the iPhone version of your app to use the AddressBook API. Modify the app for iPad. The changes should be in the storyboard: your code should not need changing.

5

Managing Calendars and Reminders with the Event Kit API

iCloud manages calendars and events, synchronizing them across devices just as it does with contact information. This is data that your users have entered, even if that entry is indirect, such as with data detectors in an email message or via an invitation. It is data that your users have already seen, although they may have forgotten specific details (that's the reason for calendars and reminders).

Both calendars and reminders are managed by the Event Kit framework, which provides access to the Calendar database that is built into OS X and iOS. If iCloud is enabled, the Calendar database is what is synchronized. It is the responsibility of apps on the various devices and different operating systems to manipulate the database data.

Just as is the case with AddressBook, there is a framework, `EventKitUI`, that provides view controllers for the iOS devices. `EventKitUI` provides a standard interface for users regardless of what app they're using. In this chapter, however, you'll see how to use your own interface. The code you'll use works on both iOS and OS X.

Structuring Events and To-Do Item Data

The synchronization of the Calendar database can extend to Exchange and CalDAV because it is based on calendar standards. There are extensions to the standards that provide additional functionality, and you can provide your own extensions. Finding the right way to organize calendar data has been a long task for the software industry. Standard calendar formats have been around for many, many years (and there is a multitude of such standards).

If you go back to the datebooks that people used in precomputer days (and that many people still use), you can see that people often entered events or appointments (the terms are basically interchangeable) as well as to-do items. There is a benefit to entering to-do items in a separate format because even if they are tied to a specific date, they are often done before or after that date, whereas events are tied to a definite date and time as well as, often, to other people. Keeping a separate list of to-do items means that you don't have to carry unfinished to-do items forward from date to date, but it also means that to find out the appointments and to-do items for a specific date requires you to look in two places.

This has been addressed in the Event Kit framework with two classes. The main class is `EKCalendarItem`. It has a subclass: `EKReminder`. This means that reminders and events sometimes behave the same way (for example, both can be assigned to calendars), and sometimes they observe slightly different behavior. The distinction between the two classes is clear at the user interface level even though there is some shared code underneath.

The distinction between to-do items and appointments is clear and logical, but when you come right down to it, the answer to the question "What do I have to do today?" shouldn't require consulting two lists (appointments and to-do items). Perhaps by designing for the most complex needs of large organizations, we have wound up with tools that make it awkward to note that tomorrow you have to buy cat food and have lunch with Earnest at noon. As it stands now, on OS X and iOS, you use the Calendar database to manage both types of data, but the interface and functionality are provided separately by Calendar and Reminder apps.

Exploring the Event Class Hierarchy

The interaction between events and reminders is reflected in the relative complexity of the class hierarchy. This background information shows you what happens behind the scenes.

There is a new subclass of `NSObject`: `EKObject`. It is an abstract superclass of all Event Kit classes. As you can see, most of the methods of this class have to do with synchronization: the heart of iCloud. There are five methods and no properties. All Event Kit classes inherit these methods:

- `hasChanges`: Returns a `BOOL` value if this object or any objects it contains has changes.
- `isNew`: Returns a `BOOL` letting you know if it has ever been saved.
- `refresh`: This method also returns a `BOOL` value. It accesses the copy of this event in the store and refreshes the object's data with the current store values except for the values that have been changed locally. Thus, your object will contain the latest values from the data store along with your changes. The result value is `YES` if all goes well. If the object has been deleted from the store, it returns `NO`.

- `reset`: Gets rid of local changes to the object and restores it to the value in the store. With regard to your changes, refresh is nondestructive and reset is destructive.

- `rollback`: Gets rid of any local changes and sets the object to the values it had when it was first fetched. If the object in the store has changed since the first fetch, `reset` will incorporate them into your local object, and rollback will not.

Setting OS X Permissions

When you set up an OS X project that will use calendars, you need to set it up using the new Capabilities tab in Xcode 5. After you create the project, go to Capabilities and turn on Contacts, Location, and Calendar, as shown in Figure 5.1. (Strictly speaking, Location isn't essential at this point, but it often is used.) Note that you don't have to turn iCloud on to get the benefits of synchronization. Once you have access to Calendar and Contacts, your choices in Settings (iOS) or System Preferences (OS X) control iCloud's access to Calendar and Contacts. You don't need to adjust capabilities on iOS for this project.

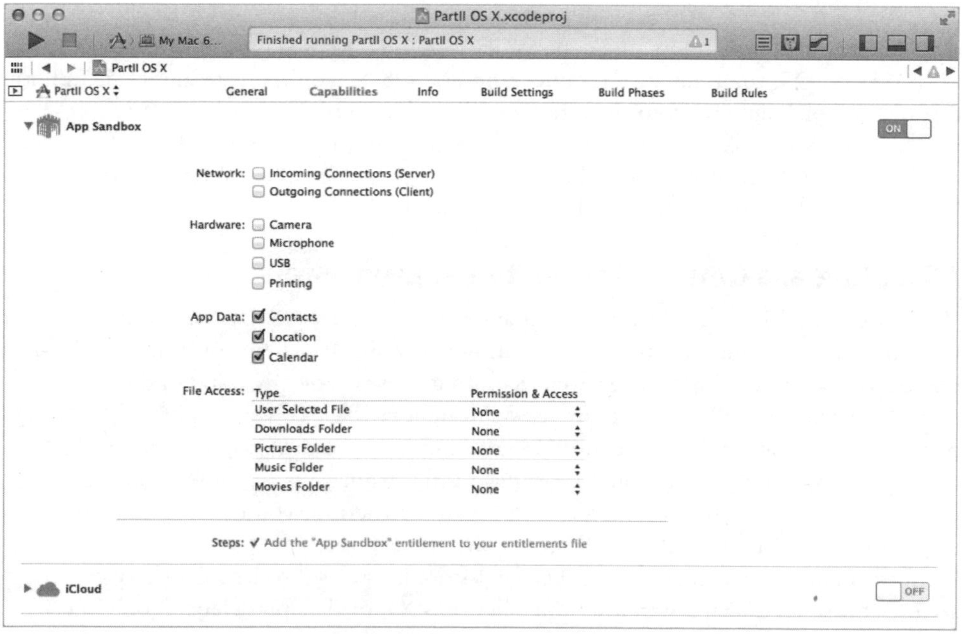

Figure 5.1   Setting up capabilities for your OS X project

Working with the Calendar Database

The Calendar database stores both events (appointments) and reminders (to-dos). Although the syntax is different (and despite that there are differences between OS X and iOS), the overall architecture or design pattern is the same:

- Events and reminders are stored in the Calendar database. From your code, you access it as a data store: EKEventStore. The overhead in creating this object is significant, so you generally keep it around while your app is running. Get rid of it after you are finished with all your Event Kit processing.
- Once you have the data store, you request access to specific types of entities within the Calendar database using EKEntityTypeEvent and EKEntityTypeReminder.
- At this point, you can create a new event or reminder.
- You can also search for an existing event or reminder.
- Having created or found an event or reminder, you can set or modify its properties.
- When you are finished working with the store and its calendar data, you must commit all unsaved data in the store. (If you use Core Data, this process will be familiar to you.)

In the sections that follow, the code for each of these steps is provided for OS X and for iOS. On iOS, you'll create a reminder, and on OS X, you'll create an event. In both cases, you'll pick up text from the interface just as you did in Chapter 4, "Working with the AddressBook API for Contacts." As you'll see, the iOS/reminder code is very similar to the OS X/event code. The few differences are pointed out in the chapter. You will start from the code as of the end of Chapter 4.

Allocating and Getting Access to the Event Store

You allocate and init a variable in your app for the event store. By convention, it is called store, but you can call it anything you want. If a view controller on iOS is associated with all your event handling, this is typically done in the viewDidLoad method. If events are used throughout the app, you might want to call it from application:didFinishLaunchingWithOptions: in the app delegate. On OS X, you may want to call it from your window controller's windowDidLoad method or, for a more pervasive structure, you might call it from applicationDidFinishLaunching: in the app delegate.

In the code snippets that follow, the event store is assumed to be a property of a view controller (iOS), a window controller (OS X), or the app delegate (on either). It is named eventStore.

Listing 5.1 shows how the event store can be declared in a class declaration. On OS X, this code could be placed at the top of AppDelegate.h. On iOS, it might be at the top of your view controller interface file. Note the import statements at the top of the file. You also need to add the `EventKit` framework to your project from the General tab. The code in Listing 5.1 also declares a new reminder button that will create a reminder from the text in `userTextView`.

Listing 5.1 **Declaring the Event Store on iOS**

```
#import <UIKit/UIKit.h>                                              //1
#import <EventKit/EventKit.h>                                        //2

@interface ViewController : UIViewController
@property (weak, nonatomic) IBOutlet UITextView *userTextView;
@property (nonatomic, strong) EKEventStore *eventStore;             //3

@end
```

1   This is the Cocoa Touch framework that you almost always start with.

2   Add the `EventKit` headers. Remember to add the `EventKit` framework in the General tab of your project.

3   This is the event store object for your class.

On OS X, the corresponding code may be placed at the top of AppDelegate.h, as you see in Listing 5.2.

Listing 5.2 **Declaring the Event Store on OS X**

```
#import <Cocoa/Cocoa.h>                                             //1
#import <EventKit/EventKit.h>                                        //2

@interface AppDelegate : NSObject <NSApplicationDelegate>

@property (assign) IBOutlet NSWindow *window;
@property (nonatomic, strong) EKEventStore *eventStore;            //3
@property (nonatomic, strong) EKCalendar *defaultCalendar;          //4

@end
```

1   This brings the Cocoa headers into the class.

2   This is the import of `EventKit` headers. Remember to add the `EventKit` framework in the General tab of your project.

3   This is your class's event store object.

4   This is the default calendar for reminders. You will need it to create new events or reminders, but you can always get it from the event store. In this version, it's stored in a public property. In the iOS version, it is obtained as needed from the event store.

This is the code to access the event store object for iOS:

```
EKEventStore *self.eventStore = [[EKEventStore alloc]init];
```

Once you have your local store, you can then request further access to it. (Before iOS 6, you did not need to request this access.)

Listing 5.3 shows the code for iOS 6 or later and OS X Mavericks (10.9) or later.

Listing 5.3   Requesting Access to Events on iOS 6 or Later and OS X Mavericks (10.9) or Later

```
self.eventStore = [[EKEventStore alloc] init];                       //1

[self.eventStore requestAccessToEntityType: EKEntityTypeEvent
    completion:^(BOOL granted, NSError *error)                       //2
{
    if (!granted) {                                                  //3
    // handle error
    }
}];
```

1   Allocate and `init` a new event store.

2   This is the request for access to events.

3   This is the block for the completion handler.

Note that the code shown in Listing 5.3 is slightly different in OS X Mavericks (10.9) than in previous versions. It has been tweaked to make it identical to the iOS version in Mavericks.

Similarly, Listing 5.4 shows the allocation and access requests for reminders on iOS 6 or later and OS X Mavericks (10.9) or later.

Listing 5.4   Requesting Access to Reminders on iOS 6 or Later and OS X Mavericks (10.9) or Later

```
[self.eventStore requestAccessToEntityType: EKEntityTypeReminder
    completion:^(BOOL granted, NSError *error)                       //2
{
    if (!granted) {
        //handle error}
}];
```

2   This is the only difference between Listing 5.3 and Listing 5.4—the constant specifying events (`EKEntityTypeEvent` in Listing 5.3) or the constant specifying reminders (`EKEntityTypeReminder` in Listing 5.4).

Creating a New Event or Reminder

The syntax for creating a new event or reminder is parallel in OS X and iOS. You use a class method to create the new object; you pass in your event store. You get the new event or reminder back, and you can then set its values. The values are not saved until you commit the changes.

As noted previously, the code in this chapter builds on the code from the end of Chapter 4.

Listing 5.5 shows the code to implement the button that will create a new event. This code can be used on iOS or OS X provided that you choose *either* line three (for OS X) or line four (for iOS).

Listing 5.5   **Create a New Event in an Event Store**

```
- (IBAction)tapEventButton:(id)sender {
  EKEvent *newEvent = [EKEvent eventWithEventStore: _eventStore];        //1
  newEvent.title = @"Test Event";                                        //2
  newEvent.notes = [[_userTextView textStorage] string];                 //3
  newEvent.notes = userTextView.text;                                    //4
  newEvent.calendar = [_eventStore defaultCalendarForNewEvents];         //5
  newEvent.startDate = [NSDate date];                                    //6
  newEvent.endDate = [NSDate date];                                      //7
  NSError *error = nil;                                                   //8
  [_eventStore saveEvent: newEvent span:EKSpanThisEvent                  //9
    commit:YES error:&error];
}
```

1   This is where you create a new event.

2   This sets the title.

3   This sets the notes from an iOS UITextView. Use only line 3 or line 4.

4   This sets the notes from an OS X NSTextView. Use only line 3 or line 4.

5   This sets the calendar for the new event. As you will see in Listing 5.6, you can also get it from the event store rather than storing it in a property.

6, 7   Events must have a start and end date (date and time in an NSDate). Without a start and end date (called an NSSpan), you will get an error.

8   Create a variable for the error message

9   Save the event.

Listing 5.6 shows the code to implement the button that will create a new reminder. This code can be used on iOS or OS X provided that you choose *either* line three (OS X) or line four (iOS).

Listing 5.6   **Creating a New Reminder in an Event Store**

```
#pragma mark - Create Reminder Button
- (IBAction)tapReminderButton:(id)sender {
  EKReminder *newReminder =
    [EKReminder reminderWithEventStore: _eventStore];

  newReminder.title = @"Test";
  newReminder.notes = [[_userTextView textStorage] string];
  newReminder.notes = userTextView.text;
  newReminder.calendar = [_eventStore defaultCalendarForNewReminders];
  NSError *error = nil;
  [_eventStore saveReminder: newReminder commit:YES error: &error];
}
```

Every instance of EKEvent or EKReminder has a unique identifier. That unique identifier is assigned when the object is created. If you want to be able to retrieve this specific item in the future, you can store it (see the following section for searching). Remember that reminders are subclasses of calendar items, so the calendarItem-Identifier property is available for both reminders and calendar items. This is a legacy of the class structure described in the sidebar at the beginning of the chapter. If you want to break all existing reminders and calendars, you can come up with a more streamlined class structure, but that's not an option in most cases.

Here is the unique identifier property for both EKEvent and EKReminder instances:

```
@property(nonatomic, readonly)
  NSString *calendarItemIdentifier;
```

As soon as you receive the new event or reminder back from the class method that creates it, you can access this unique identifier. However, until you commit the store, the object won't be saved and the unique identifier will do you no good in the future. Note that this is not an argument for immediately committing the store: that may unnecessarily slow down your app. It is, however, an argument for making certain that you do commit the object (particularly before your app is suspended on iOS), and it's a reminder of something to check if, during testing, you discover that your app is some-times losing new events and reminders.

Searching for an Event or Reminder

There are two ways to search for events or reminders (and, because reminders are a subclass of events, in this chapter both will be referred to as events—which they are).

If you have an event identifier, you can use it to retrieve the event. Although identi-fiers are unique, in the case of recurring events, there can be multiple objects returned from this method. Only the first occurrence is returned. Here is the method of the store to call:

```
- (EKEvent *)eventWithIdentifier:(NSString *)identifier
```

You can also search based on dates in a *predicate*. Predicates are widely used in databases to select the records for inclusion (or exclusion) in a query. In SQL-speak, predicates are very roughly the WHERE clause. You use them with events just as you use them elsewhere in Cocoa and Cocoa Touch (they are particularly important in Core Data).

You create a predicate using a method of an event store as follows:

```
- (NSPredicate *)predicateForEventsWithStartDate:(NSDate *)startDate
                                         endDate:(NSDate *)endDate
                                       calendars:(NSArray *)calendars
```

You use the predicate to get an array of matching objects as in this code:

```
- (NSArray *)eventsMatchingPredicate:(NSPredicate *)predicate
```

You can also use the predicate to drive an enumerator, which executes a block for each object returned, as shown in Listing 5.7.

Listing 5.7   **Enumerating Events with a Predicate and Block**

```
- (void)enumerateEventsMatchingPredicate:(NSPredicate *)predicate
                               usingBlock:(EKEventSearchCallback)block
```

Thus, you have three ways of getting events:

- You can retrieve them using the unique identifier. You get the first of any recurring events in this case. The unique identifier is found either when you first create an event or if you take it from one of the events returned with a predicate.
- You can get all of the matching events in an array. It is common to immediately sort that array.
- You can enumerate through the matching events running a block on each one.

These are all standard Cocoa operations, so they are not described further here.

Setting or Modifying Properties

The properties for calendar items and reminders fall into two groups:

- Simple items
- Groups of items

Table 5.1 shows the simple items and their types. With very few exceptions (the properties with types beginning EK), these are standard Cocoa types, so they are not described in detail here.

Table 5.1   **Simple Properties of Calendar Items**

Property	Type
calendarItemIdentifier	NSString
calendarItemExternalIdentifier (read-only value from calendar server)	NSString
calendar	EKCalendar
title	NSString
location	NSString
creationDate	NSDate
lastModifedDate	NSDate
timeZone	NSTimeZone
URL	NSURL

The groups of items are shown in Table 5.2. Unless otherwise noted, they return an array and a BOOL indicating if there are any of the items.

Table 5.2   **Group Properties of Calendar Items**

Property	BOOL Method	Type
alarms	hasAlarms	NSArray of EKAlarm objects
attendees	hasAttendees	NSArray of EKParticipant objects
notes	hasNotes	NSString
recurrenceRules	hasRecurrenceRules	NSArray of EKRecurrenceRule objects

In addition, there are methods to add and remove recurrence rules and alarms.

Finally, the properties for EKReminder objects beyond those for calendar items are shown in Table 5.3.

Table 5.3   **Simple Properties of Reminders**

Property Name	Type
completionDate	NSDate
completed	BOOL
dueDateComponents	NSDateComponents
startDateComponents	NSDateComponents

completed and completionDate work together. Setting completed to YES sets completionDate to today, and setting it to NO sets completionDate to nil. Likewise, setting completionDate to a value (or nil) sets completed accordingly.

The NSDateComponents class represents a remarkably flexible and powerful way of specifying dates along with calendars that refine them. All fields of the object are optional. If you are not familiar with this class, it's worth looking at the class reference. They were one of the most admired features of NeXTSTEP (and then OPENSTEP and now OS X and iOS).

Committing Changes

As noted previously, your changes to reminders and events are not saved until you commit the changes to the store. When you commit a save or remove action, the changes are propagated to the event's calendar, which may be on another computer or environment (CalDAV or Exchange, for example). These changes do not wait for a sync process via iCloud.

You must always ask the user's permission before you modify the Calendar database. You have the option of committing changes as you make them or batching the updates for a single commit. The remainder of this section shows the methods you will use. The reminder methods are shown first because they are simpler than the event methods.

The commit parameter is a BOOL indicating whether the commit should be performed now or should wait for a batch commit later on.

To save a reminder, use the code in Listing 5.8.

Listing 5.8   **Saving a Reminder**

```
- (BOOL)saveReminder:(EKReminder *)reminder
             commit:(BOOL)commit
              error:(NSError **)error
```

To remove a reminder, use the code in Listing 5.9.

Listing 5.9   **Removing a Reminder**

```
- (BOOL)removeReminder:(EKReminder *)reminder
               commit:(BOOL)commit
                error:(NSError **)error
```

Events are a bit more complicated because they can recur. Thus, there is an added span parameter, which takes one of two constants: EKSpanThisEvent or EKSpanFutureEvents. The companion methods are discussed next.

To save an event, use the code in Listing 5.10.

Listing 5.10 **Saving an Event**

```
- (BOOL)saveEvent:(EKEvent *)event
              span:(EKSpan)span
           commit:(BOOL)commit
            error:(NSError **)error
```

To remove an event, use the code in Listing 5.11.

Listing 5.11 **Removing an Event**

```
- (BOOL)removeEvent:(EKEvent *)event
                span:(EKSpan)span
             commit:(BOOL)commit
              error:(NSError **)error
```

Finally, if you have uncommitted changes, make certain to commit them all to the store before you are finished with it:

```
- (BOOL)commit:(NSError **)error
```

Adding a Reminder to the App on iOS

This is the full code for you to use to add a reminder by tapping a button on iOS. In Chapter 4, you moved the contents of the text view into a new email message. Now, you can add a Reminder button to that app to move the text from the text view into a new reminder. The next section shows you the code to implement an Event button on OS X. Remember that you can mix and match the code—take the relevant parts of this code to implement adding a reminder on iOS or the relevant parts of the following code to implement adding an event on OS X. The listings earlier in the chapter focus on the key lines for each operating system as well as for events and appointments.

To prepare, add the EventKit framework to your project in the Linked Frameworks and Library section of the General tab. At the top of ViewController.h, add the following line:

```
#import <EventKit/EventKit.h>
```

You'll also need the Reachability.h from the sample code on developer.apple.com, as described in Chapter 4.

You'll also need an event store, so add this code to your view controller's interface:

```
@property (nonatomic, strong) EKEventStore *eventStore;
```

Begin by declaring the store as shown in Listing 5.12. This code can go conveniently into ViewDidLoad of your view controller.

Listing 5.12   **Declaring the Store on iOS**

```objc
#import "ViewController.h"
#import "Reachability.h"

#import <MessageUI/MessageUI.h>
#import <MessageUI/MFMailComposeViewController.h>

@interface ViewController ()

@end

@implementation ViewController

- (void)viewDidLoad
{
  [super viewDidLoad];
  // Do any additional setup after loading the view, typically from a nib.
  self.eventStore = [[EKEventStore alloc] init];

  [self.eventStore requestAccessToEntityType: EKEntityTypeReminder
    completion:^(BOOL granted, NSError *error)
  {
    if (!granted) {
      UIAlertView *alert = [[UIAlertView alloc]
            initWithTitle: @"Error"
                  message: @"Can't access reminders"
                 delegate: nil
        cancelButtonTitle: @"OK"
        otherButtonTitles: nil];
      [alert show];
    }
  }];
}
```

Now that the store is declared, you need to create it and gain access to it, as shown in Listing 5.13.

Listing 5.13   **Creating the Store on iOS**

```objc
#import "ViewController.h"
#import "Reachability.h"

#import <MessageUI/MessageUI.h>
#import <MessageUI/MFMailComposeViewController.h>

@interface ViewController ()
```

```
@end

@implementation ViewController

- (void)viewDidLoad
{
  [super viewDidLoad];
  // Do any additional setup after loading the view, typically from a nib.
  _eventStore = [[EKEventStore alloc] init];                              //1

  [_eventStore requestAccessToEntityType: EKEntityTypeReminder
                  completion:^(BOOL granted, NSError *error)             //2
  {
    if (!granted) {                                                       //3
      UIAlertView *alert = [[UIAlertView alloc] initWithTitle: @"Error"
                                  message: @"Can't access reminders"
                                  delegate: nil
                        cancelButtonTitle: @"OK"
                        otherButtonTitles: nil];
      [alert show];
    }
  }];

}
```

1 Create the event store.

2 Request access.

3 If access is not granted, warn the user. Note that this is a placeholder type of message.

Create a reminder button and wire it up to a new method in the same way that you wired up the Email button in Chapter 4. Listing 5.14 shows what you need to do. The only choice that you have to make is whether to move the contents of the text view to notes or the reminder title. This is the same issue you confront with email. Because a text field is more limited than a text view, a text field is more appropriate for an email subject or a reminder title than a text view, which is more appropriate for the body of an email or a note.

Listing 5.14 **Creating the Add Reminder Button on iOS**

```
# #pragma mark - Create Reminder Button
- (IBAction)tapReminderButton:(id)sender {
  EKReminder *newReminder =
      [EKReminder reminderWithEventStore: _eventStore];               //1
```

```
newReminder.title = @"Test";                                        //2
newReminder.notes = _userTextView.text;                             //3
newReminder.calendar = [_eventStore defaultCalendarForNewReminders]; //4
NSError *error = nil;
[_eventStore saveReminder: newReminder commit:YES error: &error];   //5
}
```

1 This creates the new reminder in your store.

2 This sets the title.

3 This sets the notes.

4 This sets the calendar from the event store.

5 This saves and commits the reminder.

Adding an Event to the App on OS X

This code builds on the code from the end of Chapter 4 or the code you have just created to implement a button that adds an event to the app. Listing 5.15 shows the declaration of the store. It can go into AppDelegate.h or a window controller. It just needs to be available before any access to the store is needed.

Listing 5.15   **Declaring the Store on OS X**

```
#import <Cocoa/Cocoa.h>                                             //1
#import <EventKit/EventKit.h>                                       //2

@interface AppDelegate : NSObject <NSApplicationDelegate>

@property (assign) IBOutlet NSWindow *window;
@property (unsafe_unretained) IBOutlet NSTextView *userTextView;
@property (nonatomic, strong) EKEventStore *eventStore;            //3
@property (nonatomic, strong) EKCalendar *defaultCalendar;        //4

- (IBAction)tapButton:(id)sender;
- (IBAction)tapEventButton:(id)sender;                             //5
@end
```

1 This line imports the basic Cocoa headers.

2 This imports the EventKit headers. Make sure to add it to your frameworks in the General tab.

3 This line adds the event store property.

4 This is the default calendar property. You can also get it at runtime from the event store.

5 This is the new action for the new button.

In Listing 5.16, you see the code to create the store.

Listing 5.16   **Creating the Store on OS X**

```
- (void)applicationDidFinishLaunching:(NSNotification *)aNotification
{
  // Insert code here to initialize your application
  self.eventStore = [[EKEventStore alloc] init];
  [self.eventStore requestAccessToEntityType: EKEntityTypeEvent
    completion:^(BOOL granted, NSError *error) {
    if (!granted) {
      // Handle error
    }
  }];
}
@end
```

Finally, you provide the code for a button to actually do the work of adding the event, as shown in Listing 5.17.

Listing 5.17   **Supporting the Button**

```
- (IBAction)tapEventButton:(id)sender {
  EKEvent *newEvent = [EKEvent eventWithEventStore: self.eventStore];   //1
  newEvent.title = @"Test Event";                                       //2
  newEvent.notes = [[_userTextView textStorage] string];
  newEvent.calendar = [_eventStore defaultCalendarForNewEvents];        //3
  newEvent.startDate = [NSDate date];                                   //4
  newEvent.endDate = [NSDate date];
  NSError *error = nil;                                                  //5
  [_eventStore saveEvent: newEvent span:EKSpanThisEvent
    commit:YES error:&error];                                           //6
}
@end
```

1   This line creates the event store.

2   This line and the following line set the title and notes.

3   This gets the default calendar for new events from the event store.

4   This line and the following line set the span of the event.

5   This line creates an error instance and sets it to nil.

6   This line creates the event. If an error occurs, it is returned in a new error object.

Chapter Summary

Your interaction with events and reminders is quite similar to your interaction with email. In both cases, you're facilitating access to the user's data that is synchronized through iCloud with various devices and, possibly, external servers such as Exchange. In Chapter 4, you saw how to use the `MFMailComposeViewController` class on iOS to provide your user interface. There is a similar interface for events available to you on iOS: `EventKitUI.framework`. In this chapter, you saw how to work directly with the Event Kit, so this code will work on both iOS and OS X.

Exercises

1. Move the code to iOS (and a real device). Add the EventKitUI framework to provide a graphical user interface for managing events. Use it to look at and edit your event. You might want to look at SimpleEKDemo from the sample code on developer.apple.com.

2. Instead of using separate buttons for mail and reminders in your interface, explore other interface possibilities. For example, on iPad, you might use an action sheet.

3. Get used to testing iCloud. That means working with multiple devices (and a single Apple ID). Create, view, edit, and delete data across the devices. After your first experiments, you might want to prepare a standard protocol so that you can run through it as needed. Vary it by reversing or randomizing the steps where it's possible so that you catch errors.

4. On iOS devices, turn Airplane mode on and off as part of your testing. On your Mac(s), turn WiFi on and off and unplug Ethernet. You want to make certain that your code works properly, and you want to give iCloud a chance to catch conflicts.

6

Protecting the Privacy of User Data

This chapter is unlike any other in this book, and in some ways, it's the most important chapter of all. iCloud lets people share data across all their devices. The data can also be synchronized with CalDAV and Exchange servers. This is all remarkably convenient for users because their data is wherever they want it to be.

It also brings up a host of privacy and security issues. This chapter provides an overview of the issues and the steps that you can take to implement the privacy that users expect for their data—privacy that in some cases is even required by law.

The Need for Privacy

With the newest operating systems from Apple (as well as from other vendors), the wide-open access that developers had in the past to resources, such as the local file system on a computer, is being constrained. *Sandboxes* for apps are such constraints, as are the limits on apps that can be installed on devices. Thus, what previously was often relegated to a footnote in a reference to developers now needs to be part of your planning from the very beginning.

As more and more people are becoming increasingly dependent on technology and more used to dealing with it on a daily basis, privacy has become a major concern. Every week brings headlines about privacy issues from somewhere in the world, and there also are headlines about proposed new legislation somewhere in the world. Yes, privacy can make it more difficult for legitimate users to use your app, but locks on doors make it more difficult for you to get into your home, yet you probably wouldn't leave your door unlocked.

People, governments, and organizations are aware that privacy can be a key to physical safety as well as security for objects, information, and money. Wishing that it were not so and that everyone in the world respected everyone else equally is wonderful, but that is not the world we live in.

Looking at Apple's Rules and Guidelines

Both the App Store and the Mac App Store have guidelines regarding privacy (they are described here as well as on developer.apple.com if you search for "store guidelines"). Violating these guidelines gets you a speedy rejection from the store.

The privacy sections of the App Store Review Guidelines and Mac App Store Review Guidelines (on developer.apple.com) are identical at the time of this writing. They are simple and far from unusual. Here is how Apple expresses the three key points:

- Apps cannot transmit data about a user without obtaining the user's prior permission and providing the user with access to information about how and where the data will be used.

- Apps that require users to share personal information, such as email address and date of birth, in order to function will be rejected.

- Apps that target minors for data collection will be rejected.

The App Store Review Guidelines mention privacy in another place: all included URLs in an app must be functional when the store reviews it, and that includes a privacy policy if there is one.

If you are distributing your app through ad hoc distribution or another method that does not involve one of the stores, the rules and guidelines may not apply to you. However, that doesn't mean that you don't have to be concerned about privacy: laws may govern your app's use of data, either directly or as they affect the organization for which you're building your app.

Best Practices in App Privacy

The best practices in app privacy are not complicated. If they are not part of your standard procedures, you should start to implement them. Many of the best practices listed here are scarcely unique to Apple, but others deal specifically with issues regarding the App Store and Mac App Store.

An important point to keep in mind is that these best practices, along with specific privacy policies, change from time to time. Apple notifies developers of changes as they happen, but it is easy to miss them. The most important policy changes in all areas of the developer programs are usually highlighted at the right side of the landing page at developer.apple.com. These updates typically appear there for several months, so periodically look at them for updates.

Know What Should Be Private

As Apple uses the term *privacy*, they are generally referring to personal information that the user provides. However, privacy comes into play in other areas of the guidelines.

The devices can collect data automatically (location data is one good example). The use of location data is governed not by the privacy section of the guidelines but by a section specifically devoted to location. However, the policy is the same: you must notify the user and obtain consent before "collecting, transmitting, or using" location data.

Device identifiers, IP addresses, and anything that can identify the user or the data has to be treated with care. And to be a responsible citizen in today's cyber world, you need to bend over backwards. For example, we know that most people reuse passwords. Knowing that, if you ask people to choose a password, recognize that, even if you provide a warning, you may wind up with the password to their online bank account, so treat it accordingly and, if you store it, make certain that it is encrypted.

If you watch or read thrillers, you often see that it is a combination of events and data that provides the clue to the murderer or some other solution to a puzzle. That is why any data that the user enters could wind up being part of a puzzle that reveals something that should not be revealed.

Use Good Programming Style to Enforce Privacy

Objective-C 2.0 introduced properties to the language. Xcode has added sophisticated support for properties (particularly in Xcode 4.3 and 4.4) so that it is no longer necessary for you to declare instance or backing variables. Xcode can create them automatically from the property (the backing variable is the property name preceded by an underscore, which previously was merely a recommendation of style).

Properties provide strict encapsulation because you never touch the backing variable directly from outside the implementation file for a class. The accessors that are created for the property handle the variable. You can create your own accessors that do directly interact with the variable, and there are examples where a nil value of the variable is replaced by the accessor with a specific default value or even a newly created object. It is this level of indirection that helps keep your code clean, and this design carries over to many of the accessors to data in frameworks. The accessor can manage security, and that's where privacy can be enforced.

If you are used to handling instance variables directly, make sure you adopt the modern style so that you will be able to insert your privacy-respecting code in accessors as necessary. As the various Cocoa frameworks are revised, this design pattern is consistently implemented.

Be Careful When Debugging

One common cause of privacy violations is the inclusion of debugging code in a shipping product. If you do not already do so, bracket debugging code with defines so that you can turn it on or off automatically. Xcode projects define DEBUG. Some developers add a separate define (perhaps with your initials—JFDEBUG) so that you can turn your debugging code on or off independently of the general debugging code.

Ask Permission and Explain What You'll Do with the Data

The first part of this guideline is the simplest: ask the user for permission whenever you want to access personal data or pass it along. As you saw in Chapters 4 and 5, this is built into the syntax for connecting to AddressBook or EventKit, so you don't have to do anything special: your app's attempt to use those frameworks handles the permission. If it isn't granted, you're blocked from accessing the data.

Every app and site that asks users to enter personal data has a comparable standard. Often, an app or website posts a privacy policy that spells out how data will be used, and a request to the user will reference that policy. What particularly infuriates many people is when data is obtained from them under false pretenses (or even under no pretenses at all). There are many people who will not use Facebook or other social media sites because they do not believe their data will remain under their control. There are many people who will not use online banking for the same reason. Whenever a data breach makes headlines, people start to revisit their data and how much control they have over it.

A particular issue of concern to many people is scrubbed or anonymized data. To improve its search services, Google has stored queries without the identification of who posted the query. Researchers were able to prove that with the right analysis (and some luck with regard to the queries in question), they could discover the identity of the person who posed the query.

The iCloud data you have accessed in this part of the book (AddressBook and Events) is among the most critical data that people enter. Users trust that their data on their Mac or iOS device belongs to them and is safe. It may fly back and forth across the Internet as it is synchronized, and it may be transferred to and from servers such as Exchange, but people trust that it is safe.

Look at privacy policies on the web and read media reports on this subject. Ideally, you should explain why your app wants certain data, but you should then go one step further to say what will happen if it is stored. If you want the email address of someone to whom to send a message from your app (as shown in Chapter 4), that's a simple request, and it makes sense. However, if you ask for that email address in order to send the message *and if you then proceed to store that address,* you're in trouble. Ideally, you should ask for the address to send the message and, in most cases, ask the user if the address should be stored for future use. You can even go further in asking if the address should be stored in the address book or in local app storage because some people like to have multiple address books.

Many experts in the privacy field suggest that the burden should be on the app that is storing data: don't store data unless it is absolutely necessary. Many people and apps collect data because it "might be useful in the future," but that's not going to get too many people agreeing to give you their data.

The cautions about data collection apply to apps that you build for the public. Apps that are used in the course of work play by different rules—particularly if the apps (and even the devices in some cases) are owned by a business or other organization.

Somewhere along the line the users should know quite clearly what is their data and what is the organization's data. An argument can be made (if supported by documentation) that the addresses of websites an employee visits at work from company-owned devices is corporate data and not personal information.

Do Not Require Personal Data to Unlock Your App

The App Store and the Mac App Store both work with Apple IDs, and through them, the stores can identify the individual. Your app should not duplicate that process by forcing users to give you their email or other personal information before running. This has been a matter of much discussion, particularly with subscriptions to magazines. The ownership of the subscriber data is (at the moment) given to the relevant app store. Apple has approved some subscriptions that ask the user to provide that information to the app developer, but in the cases where this has been done, it is not required: the user can say no and still use the app.

Add Extra Measures to Protect Minors

Read the App Store Review Guidelines. This sentence from the introduction brings up a point that applies far beyond the App Store:

> We have lots of kids downloading lots of Apps, and parental controls don't work unless the parents set them up (many don't). So know that we're keeping an eye out for the kids.

It's not just about kids: we know that many (perhaps most) people leave the security settings on the routers and computers set to their defaults (sometimes even including "Password" as a password). Some adults actively bypass the security of minors by purchasing alcohol and cigarettes for them, but more often, they passively bypass their security by not adjusting privacy and security settings.

Relying solely on privacy and security settings may be within the letter of the law, but it is not always a responsible policy. If your app is targeted to kids or is particularly attractive to kids, many people would advise that you take extra steps to manage security.

A particularly valuable resource is onguardonline.gov. It consolidates the US government's online resources from a number of federal agencies; it is managed by the Federal Trade Commission. It is primarily geared to consumers, but the information is also relevant to developers. Geared directly to businesses and developers, "Children's Online Privacy Protection Rule: A Six-Step Compliance Plan for Your Business" at http://www.business.ftc.gov/documents/bus84-childrens-online-privacy-protection-rule-six-step-compliance-plan-your-business has more information.

Provide Privacy for Support Materials

In common with everything from refrigerators to vitamins and TV shows, apps are frequently part of a communications network. If you have a question about any of those items, you may well turn to the web, expecting to find a web page. Sometimes, the web page you find is an official page, and sometimes it isn't. If you are supporting your app with a web page, make certain that it adheres to privacy standards just as much as your app does. Separate standards and best practices exist for websites and apps, but they often overlap.

One area that has been problematic with apps, support materials, and privacy is the use and sharing of personal information. If you collect personal data on your website and then allow your app to access it (possibly with an account name or number), make certain that the sharing is revealed and explained on both ends of the transaction. This is particularly important when you allow users to fine-tune their settings.

Users often leave their privacy settings set to the defaults. The defaults often are a middle-range setting that balances risks and benefits. Many privacy advocates recommend that the default setting be total privacy; other people advise total openness. Obviously, the content in question helps determine the appropriate setting. If you do allow more than just on/off settings, make certain that the mid-range settings are consistent on your app and on your support materials, such as a website.

Consider User Issues

Finally, remember that users will be using your app and adjusting privacy settings. One of the easiest ways to destroy any semblance of privacy is to force users to adhere to security settings that are impossible to manage. Many users use password managers (on OS X, Keychain Access provides this feature, and it's implemented on iOS behind the scenes). However, not everyone uses a password manager. As soon as you make security and password settings too difficult, most reasonable users resort to writing down their passwords and even posting them on an easy-to-find location. (If you want to discover someone's passwords, look at the bottom of his laptop: you may find passwords taped there.)

For security to be effective, it needs to be unobtrusive and automatic if at all possible. The engineers at Apple now provide two such tools. Beginning with the iPhone 5S in fall of 2013, Touch ID uses your finger's touch on the Home button to match your fingerprint to a stored fingerprint you have set up. (It's a touch for the fingerprint scan rather than a tap—a button press—to use the Home button, as you have always done.) You can set up multiple fingerprints to allow multiple users. The encoded fingerprints are compared inside the processor so that all the processor reveals is that a given fingerprint does or doesn't match whatever is stored. Touch ID promises to make security almost effortless to implement and that, in turn, may encourage more people to lock their phones.

Furthermore, beginning in iOS 7 and Mavericks, iCloud Keychain can store passwords and credit card information and synchronize it through iCloud to all your devices. (It also can generate and fill in passwords for websites.) Between Touch ID and iCloud Keychain, security is moving to an increasingly automatic and behind-the-scenes feature. As a developer, you should use these features whenever you have a choice.

Chapter Summary

This chapter addressed issues of privacy and security about which you need to be aware. From the start, iOS has enforced a degree of app-level security that was not enforced on OS X (and, to be fair, many other operating systems). As time goes on, app-level security is being more tightly controlled on more environments. In addition, legislation, best practice, and media reports are addressing privacy issues more aggressively.

The basic rules are quite simple:

- Make certain users know what your app is doing with regard to their privacy and personal data.
- Ask permission to do it, and if permission is declined, don't do it.
- Publish and abide by your policies.

In many ways, privacy and security don't pose new issues for developers. They are just further examples of how we must design and implement software in which the user is in control.

Exercises

1. Make an aggressive effort to follow issues of security and privacy. Follow proposed legislation and court cases in your country. Media outlets typically respond to current events, and after some well-publicized data breach or cyber attack, there may be a lot of information published. As is the case with all news, sometimes details are missing. Make a point to read about security and privacy issues in the lulls between the headlines.

2. If you haven't already, read the App Store guidelines and other documents on the app stores you work with. Check for updates regularly. (Apple typically updates them and their developer guidelines and contracts with the release of a new OS version.)

3. Listen to or read nontechnical articles about privacy and security. Try to understand the issues that people care about.

4. Follow organizations like the Electronic Frontier Foundation (www.eff.org) that are active in the privacy and security arenas.

III

Using the Technologies

7

Introducing Blocks, Threads, and Notifications

In Part II, "Using the APIs," you saw how to use APIs to get at the iCloud data that users enter and manage. Contacts, Reminders, and Calendar work with iCloud if the user has registered and turned it on, but the APIs work just as well if the user doesn't use iCloud or does use it but has no network connection at the time. In this part of the book, "Using the Technologies," you start to deal explicitly with iCloud itself.

As you saw in Chapter 2, "Setting Up iCloud for Development," iCloud is not a single framework or API. You won't be sitting down to write line after line of code. Instead, you'll be setting up the iCloud structure for your app with Apple IDs, a bundle ID, entitlements, and in many cases, a ubiquity container. The tools you use for these tasks are developer.apple.com and Xcode. As you'll see in this chapter, you'll be using notifications along with other pieces of code that you insert into various parts of your app.

Also in this chapter, you'll find a basic overview of blocks (relatively new in Objective-C) and threading. As with much of iCloud, existing technologies are being adopted and pressed into service. Threads, for example, have been around for a long time to help you optimize your app's performance, but in the context of iCloud, they're not just an optimization tool. Certain iCloud operations, such as obtaining the URL of the ubiquity container for the user's account, must not be performed on the app's main thread because the latency in getting a result returned can be unacceptable to the user. Using blocks, notifications, and multithreading means that you can perform a multistep process as independent steps that are performed as necessary.

Syncing blobs of data across devices can be a lengthy process. (In this case, "blob" is used both in its technical sense of *binary large object* and its common sense of a shapeless mass). Anything that you can do to structure the data is likely to make it easier to sync. The most commonly cited example is that many people may have an address book with hundreds or even thousands of contacts, but at any given time, most of those entries probably don't need to be synced. From time to time, one or two may require syncing. Part II of this book helps you use technologies to structure data to make it easier to manage and to sync.

iCloud May Change User Behavior

iCloud is the start of a new era in computing. It builds on the general concept of cloud computing, but in its focus on app-centered content rather than a file system with files and folders, it breaks new ground. How the technology and its use evolve remains to be seen. In addition to studying technical documentation, spend some time keeping up to date with the behavioral changes people adopt with mobile devices.

One particularly useful resource is the Pew Research Center's Project for Excellence in Journalism. In its paper, "The Future of Mobile News: The Explosion in Mobile Audiences and a Close Look at What it Means for News," published in October 2012 and available online at www.journalism.org/files/legacy/Futureofmobilenews%20_final1.pdf, Pew's research shows that mobile readers of news are reading more and longer news stories on their mobile devices.

This flies in the face of some early theories that mobile devices were suited to shorter articles (these theories were particularly popular with regard to smartphones with small screens, but the mobility and ease of access may be counterbalancing the small screens). It is quite possible that iCloud is also going to change the way people use apps and devices. The ability to continue reading, listening to, or working with data over time and across devices as well as while moving around may well change behavior.

Catching Up with Blocks and Threads

Many experienced OS X and iOS developers haven't used blocks and threads. They are relatively new to both operating systems, having been introduced in iOS 4 and in OS X Snow Leopard (10.6). Grand Central Dispatch (GCD) provides support for concurrent code execution on multicore systems. Blocks (sometimes called *closures* in other programming languages) often are used together with threads.

Queues and Threads

Before GCD, it was possible to use multiple threads on a multicore system, but it was a somewhat complex process. The complexity arose from the fact that software engineers basically had to construct their own threading mechanism, sometimes even modifying it depending on the number of cores in the processor running the app. This complexity didn't cause too many problems because multicore processors were not in widespread use. However, the trend was clear, so Apple developed GCD to allow people to use threads for multicore processing.

There are two abstractions at the heart of GCD:

- A *thread* is a sequence of instructions that is executed on a single processor or core.
- A *queue* is a collection of tasks that are managed on available threads by the operating system.

Most often, the tasks are actually *blocks*. There are three types of queues in GCD:

- *Main* is the main thread. It is where most tasks are performed. The tasks (blocks) queued on the main thread are executed serially.

- *Concurrent* queues have their tasks dequeued serially in first-in/first-out (FIFO) order. When multiple threads are available, the operating system assigns them to threads as they become available. Although the dequeuing sequence is FIFO serial, the completion sequence is undetermined.

- *Serial* queues execute their tasks in FIFO order and one at a time. Thus, the sequence of completion is the same as the sequence of enqueuing.

You can further manage your app's multiprocessing by requesting concurrent queues that run at varying priorities. This structure provides abstractions that work across various multicore configurations without your having to change your code.

Blocks

The blocks that you enqueue in a queue are a relatively new (iOS 4 and OS X Snow Leopard (10.6)) feature. Whether or not their appearance a year before the launch of the iPad may be part of the story, they certainly are important on all the devices today. A block is a section of code that is much like a function. Like a function, it can be named. It can also be pointed to just as a pointer can point to a function's inline code.

Unlike a function, a block can contain bindings to variables from the scope of the block's declaration. Functions only manage data passed in through argument or global to the function (which is a poor programming practice). A block locks onto variables and can use them whenever it executes. Thus, if you enqueue a block that is bound to variable X outside the block, control may pass out of the code that created the block and X is no longer present—except that the block is still locked to it. Whenever the block is executed by the queue, it has access to that variable. This makes it an excellent tool for asynchronous or concurrent processing. (The access is actually to a copy unless the variable is declared with __block preceding the type in the declaration.)

Block declarations and definitions use the ^ character to introduce the declaration or definition. Thus, a block declaration of myBlock can be written as

```
int (^myBlock)(int)
```

This describes myBlock, which takes an int argument and returns an (int) value.

A block definition can be written as

```
^(int amount) {return amount + runningTotal;}:
```

In the definition, the int argument is given a name: amount. The body of the block definition contains the return value.

You can combine them in

```
int RunningTotal = 0;
int (^myBlock)(int) = ^(int amount) {return amount + runningTotal;}:
```

Because blocks often are relatively short, and also because they commonly are used only in one place, it is common not to bother with a declaration.

Getting Up to Speed with Notifications

Blocks and GCD (not to mention iCloud) are new technologies. There's another technology that is very important in using iCloud: notifications. Notifications aren't new. In fact, they are one of the basic building blocks of the operating systems. There are three ways in which objects can communicate with one another:

- An object can communicate with another if it has a reference to the second object (and vice versa). Most often, this reference is made by setting a field in the first object to the second object.

- A looser link occurs when the first object communicates with a delegate, which, in turn, finishes the communication. The first object isn't aware of the object that will be receiving the message: it just knows about the delegate (the intermediary).

- Notifications are the loosest coupling. There is no linkage between the two objects. It uses a broadcast model: the first object broadcasts a notification to any object that happens to be listening. The second object receives the notification. The first object *posts* a notification; other objects *register* for notifications. The intermediary is an NSNotificationCenter, which each process has access to at runtime.

Notifications are one of the features of Cocoa that are used constantly by some developers and never by others. This section provides a high-level overview to get you up to speed for using notifications with iCloud.

The reason that notifications are so important for iCloud is that, due to their very loose coupling, they work very well in asynchronous processing. When you tightly couple two objects together, the communication between them is as fast as possible. Even delegation is normally quite speedy. But when you are dealing with processes that may be running on different computers and across the network, you need a communication mechanism that doesn't assume instantaneous and always-available communication. Notifications fit the bill. In fact, it is hard to think of a way to implement an iCloud-enabled app without using notifications.

The basics of notifications are quite simple:

- You obtain a reference to the process's notification center.

- If you want to register to receive specific notifications, you register as an *observer* of the specific notification.

- If you want to send notifications, you *post* them to the notification center.

- Notifications themselves are lightweight objects of the NSNotification class. Among their properties are a name: that's how the linkage between registration and posting is made.

Notification Properties

A notification is a lightweight object that contains three properties:

- name—An NSString containing the name of the notification object. Both observer and poster need to know this name. Usually it is defined as a constant in a project so that there's no possibility of confusing the name between observer and poster. This property is required.
- object—The id of the object posting the notification or, occasionally, another object related to the notification. When you observe a notification, you supply the name of the notification to observe; by passing a non-nil value for object, you can refine the observation so that only notifications from object are observed.
- userInfo—An NSDictionary containing any information you want to pass along with the notification. Like object, it is optional.

If you want to create a notification, you can use either of the following NSNotification class methods:

```
+ (id)notificationWithName:(NSString *)aName object:(id)anObject
+ (id)notificationWithName:(NSString *)aName object:(id)anObject
    userInfo:(NSDictionary *)userInfoGetting the Notification Center
```

As is the case with blocks (and for many of the same reasons), it is common not to bother with explicitly creating notifications. Instead, they are created as part of the methods that post them to the notification center, as you will see in the following sections.

Note
This section discusses local notifications within a single process. Distributed notifications are also available.

Registering for Notifications

To register for a notification, get the process's notification center and register as an observer. The code to get the notification center for a process is

```
[NSNotificationCenter defaultCenter]
```

Whether you store the notification center or obtain it as you need it is up to you.

To register for a notification, you become an observer of it. The method is

```
- (void)addObserver:(id)notificationObserver
  selector:(SEL)notificationSelector
  name:(NSString *)notificationName
  object:(id)notificationSender
```

The parameters are

- `notificationObserver`: This is often `self`; it cannot be nil.
- `notificationSelector`: This is a message that will be sent when the notification is received. It must have one parameter: an `NSNotification`, which is the incoming notification.
- `notificationName`: This identifies the notification you want to observe by name.
- `notificationSender`: This identifies the notification by `object` (usually the sender).

Note that the last two parameters are optional. By setting only one of them, you can receive all notifications from a specific object, or you can receive all of a given notification no matter who sent it.

Posting Notifications

You usually create and post a notification with one message:

```
- (void)postNotificationName:(NSString *)notificationName
  object:(id)notificationSender
  userInfo:(NSDictionary *)userInfo
```

Although you often observe as well as post, with iCloud apps you are more frequently an observer than a poster.

Receiving Notification of iCloud Availability Changes

The most basic notification you need to register for is `NSUbiquityIdentityDid-ChangeNotification`. You receive this notification when the user logs out and logs in again; you also receive this notification for a log out from iCloud without a new log in. After receiving this notification, use `ubiquityIdentityToken` to find the new identity, if any, as described in Chapter 2. If the token is nil, the user has signed out of iCloud or turned off Data & Documents for the iCloud account. Note that turning on Airplane mode does not generate this notification. iCloud just stores changes until Airplane mode is turned off.

This code shows how you can combine obtaining a reference to the notification center with registration for `NSUbiquityIdentityDidChangeNotification`. It is assumed that you have a method called `handleiCloudAvailabilityChange` that will be triggered by the notification. You typically register for this notification (indeed, for many notifications that are not specific to a given window) in your application's launch process. On iOS, that is `didFinishLaunchingWithOptions:` for the App

Delegate. On OS X, that is `applicationDidFinishLaunching:`, also for the App Delegate.

```
[[NSNotificationCenter defaultCenter]
  addObserver: self
     selector: @selector (handleiCLoudAvailabilityChange:)
         name: NSUbiquityIdentityDidChangeNotification
       object: nil];
```

Introducing the Second Project

This part of the book focuses on the techniques for managing data on iOS and OS X as well as on iCloud's interaction with these data technologies. Accordingly, the second project in this book provides hands-on examples of the various types of data management. It builds on the first project by letting the user enter text data and categorize it. Because the app is iCloud-enabled, the data can be synchronized across a user's devices.

This project brings together the generalized snippets you have seen about connecting to iCloud and maintaining that connection even when iCloud is not available. The project also lets you adjust settings and preferences and save them. In general, settings are managed on iOS by the Settings app (it manages them for all apps). Preferences are normally used to describe items that are managed by the app itself. In the case of iCloud-enabled apps, settings often are device specific, and preferences are often data-specific. Until iCloud, it wasn't necessary to make this distinction.

Getting Ready to Move On

In order to test your work from this point onward, you need to be a registered developer and have a test device. To test synchronization across iOS devices, you'll actually need at least two test devices, and preferably three; likewise, you'll need two OS X devices. You won't have to break the bank for this: you only need OS X and iOS devices with Internet connectivity. On OS X, that can be wired or WiFi, and on iOS it generally is WiFi (at least for testing). At this point, you don't need to test Internet connectivity over the mobile network, so you don't need a data plan.

You also don't need the latest devices, although ideally you should have iOS 7 or later and OS X Mavericks (10.9) or later. Fortunately, these run on several recent generations of hardware. Before you go shopping on eBay, ask around because you are likely to find people who have older devices sitting in drawers or closets.

With Xcode 5, the simulator is now able to simulate iCloud access. However, iCloud synchronization is a menu command you use on the simulator. Only with actual devices will you see the synchronization process in action on its own. The menu command is a great way to test your synchronization code, but once you have done that, you must use actual devices to ensure that the synchronization happens when you're not around to start it from the simulator menu command.

One strategy for setting up test devices to test iCloud development is to create a new Apple ID (there's no cost for this). Your Apple ID lets you register for iCloud with 5 GB of storage (at the time of this writing). Keeping your testing Apple ID separate from your own Apple ID (or IDs) is a good idea. In fact, it's a very good idea.

For your testing environment, you may not want to link to iTunes. If you start synchronizing your books and music with your test environment, first of all, you will start to mingle test and actual data. Second, you may find that you're using up your basic iCloud storage unnecessarily. If you want to listen to music, check your email, or look up contacts, keep your personal iPhone handy while you work on other devices for testing.

Chapter Summary

This chapter has shown you some of the basic techniques that you'll use in actually managing iCloud data. In particular, you've seen how block and multithreading with Grand Central Dispatch along with notifications let you take advantage of multiple core processors as well as how to manage the latency that frequently accompanies networked operations such as iCloud.

Exercises

1. Within your testing Apple ID, experiment with the basics of iCloud—contacts, reminders, and events. Do some informal testing with your three (ideally) devices. First, enter a new contact on one of the devices, and then watch it propagate to the other devices. Now, start experimenting with Airplane mode on the iOS devices and turning off WiFi on the OS X devices. Try to create collisions so that you get the hang of it. With all devices on, enter a new contact. Now, turn on Airplane mode and disable WiFi. Make a controlled change to the data you entered (like just changing a telephone number). Make a different change on each device. Then, reenable WiFi on two devices. Practice until you can consistently create conflicts. The reason for doing this is so that when you test this situation on your own code, you're confident that you're properly exercising the code. Not having conflicts when you should have them may encourage you to think that your code is working, but the absence of errors or warnings may, in and of itself, be an error.

2. Pay attention to the latency involved in iCloud. As you start testing your own code, you may fall into the trap of assuming that updates propagate instantaneously. You may discover certain patterns of iCloud performance. They may actually be patterns of iCloud performance, or they may turn out to be patterns of Internet access performance. Particularly on shared connections such as cable TV, look for certain times of day or days of the week where connectivity is better or worse.

8

Using Key-Value Coding (KVC)

With this chapter, you write your first iCloud apps. You've used iCloud data in apps from Part II of this book, but iCloud stayed in the background there. Now, it's time to work directly with iCloud. Not only do you work directly with iCloud, but you do it twice: once on iOS and once on Mac OS X. This is your first pair of Round Trip apps.

There are two types of storage in iCloud: document storage and key-value (KVC) storage. KVC is the simpler of the two, and it is used in many, if not all, apps. (Apple recommends that it be enabled in all apps submitted to the App Store.)

KVC uses simple data types such as numbers, strings, dates, and so forth. It is limited to 1 MB per app on a user's device. It is best suited for data such as preferences and configuration. In part because of its lightweight storage, it requires less attention than documents and other more complex data stores.

In this part of the book, you'll move from the simplicity of KVC on to property lists, Core Data (the most powerful data store), and specialized types of data stores such as resources in app bundles. By the end of Part III, you should be familiar with all of the iOS and OS X data storage mechanisms. Furthermore, in Part III and into Part IV, you'll see how to use them with iCloud either directly (as is the case with KVC), in documents (the case with Core Data), and in file wrappers that combine several store types.

> **Note**
>
> The code shown in this chapter (and downloadable as described in the Preface) is based on the Utility Application (iOS) and Cocoa Application (OS X). It uses key-value coding to store a text string in iCloud. It also stores the current value in local settings on each device. Normally, the most recent value is the best value for synchronization, but there are cases in which older values are better to use. Sometimes, you can write code to automatically choose among conflicting values, and sometimes you will need to ask the user. That code depends on your app, so its location is pointed out here, and you can implement whatever conflict resolution you choose.

Setting Up a Controlled Testing Environment

As you work with KVC, you'll see how to synchronize data across a user's devices. Because KVC is designed for small amounts of data, you'll find that it is always available to a user. Where there are data conflicts in synchronization, that solution is quite simple: the latest value wins. The user is usually not involved.

You'll see how you can enter data on one device and have it appear on another device automatically. In Round Trip solutions, those devices can be running both on iOS and OS X. The time lag for iCloud updates and synchronization is noticeable: you are not dealing with a direct connection such as when you are updating a local document or even a web page. Particularly as you start to test what happens as data automatically moves from your iPhone to your Mac and to your iPad (along with your modifications to it), it is remarkably easy to get confused. In fact, it is almost impossible not to. Precisely because of the time lag, if you blink, you may miss the moment of the update. You may start by looking at two screens: one has `Test 1` on the screen and the other has `Test 2` on the screen (or whatever you want to type in). Blink, look away for a moment, or take a sip of coffee, and they may both have the same text on their screens. Continue with your testing by typing something new into one device and repeat the process. Before very long, you'll find yourself confused about which device received the update and which generated it.

Of course, you may say, it's easy to be organized and keep track of where you are entering data. However, that doesn't solve the problem: much of your testing of synchronization must rely on *not* repeating patterns. In a very controlled testing environment, you can create a list of synchronization tests to perform, but for many developers (particularly independent developers without a support staff), this is impractical. One way in which you can help yourself keep track of synchronization testing is to use a set of cards to remind you of what data has been entered on what devices.

Thus, consider purchasing four packs of colored cards (3- × 5-inch cards are fine for this purpose). (Know that this is not a craft project even though you're buying materials often used in that way.) Line up your devices on your desk and write down the initial values you're setting on each one (if any) using different colors. As the values change, just move the cards. The different colors help you keep track.

As noted, there is a definite lag in the synchronization process, but the problem arises particularly when you're trying to cause collisions and conflicts (an issue that affects other storage techniques more so than KVC). You need a way to quickly change data and keep a record of what the values were before it was changed. The colored card technique may work for you: it works for many developers.

Implementing KVC

KVC is implemented with an informal protocol, `NSKeyValueProtocol`. Default implementations are provided by `NSObject`. The elements of KVC are keys and values—hence the name. The keys are `NSString` objects (they begin with a lowercase letter and contain no spaces), and the values are of type `id`. Thus, the KVC design pattern is powerful and flexible because it can accommodate any kind of Objective-C class.

For iCloud, KVC is implemented in a limited way—in fact, it is implemented with the same limits as property lists, the subject of Chapter 9, "Using Preferences, Settings, and Keychains with iCloud." The objects that can be used with iCloud KVC are simple objects including

- `NSNumber`
- `NSDate`
- `NSString`
- `NSData`
- `NSArray`
- `NSDictionary`

`NSArray` and `NSDictionary` objects themselves can contain any of these objects, so you can construct complex structures. Before you do so, however, bear in mind that for a given app on a given user's device, there are limits to the available space. (Check on developer.apple.com for the latest values: storage is getting faster and devices are gradually getting more of it.)

iCloud synchronization of key-value data succeeds or fails atomically. Keep that in mind as you design your data. If you store multiple values in an `NSArray` or `NSDictionary` all—or none—of them will be synchronized at the same time through iCloud.

KVC as implemented for iCloud lends itself to preferences and settings. If you look at the full documentation of KVC, you'll see that it can handle to-many relationships to groups of properties. For all intents and purposes, the iCloud implementation of KVC is a to-one representation, such as the single value for a user's highest score in a game or the user's player name in a game. (KVC is not designed for secure storage of passwords. For a discussion of secure storage in the context of iCloud, see Chapter 9, "Using Preferences, Settings, and Keychains with iCloud.")

KVC has become a major component of AppleScript support in OS X. It can provide AppleScript support with minimal effort on the developer's part.

Following are the two primary methods of the protocol that implements KVC:

```
- (void)setValue:(id)value forKey:(NSString *)key
- (id) value: forKey:(NSString *)key
```

Testing iCloud on iOS Simulator

Until Xcode 5, iCloud was one of the technologies that couldn't be tested on iOS Simulator. It is now implemented there. You use it just as you would use it on an iOS device. On iOS Simulator, go to Settings and set up your iCloud testing account. To properly test, you should be using that account on at least one iOS device and also on a Mac.

The one difference from deployment on a device is that on iOS Simulator, there are no automatic syncs. Once you have logged into iCloud using Settings on your simulator, choose Trigger iCloud Sync from the Debug menu to force a sync.

Preparing Your Project for Testing

Begin by creating your projects. As noted previously, they will be based on Utility Application (iOS) and Cocoa Application (OS X). On iOS, create a universal app. Make certain that at the very least you have one OS X device and one iOS device ready to be used for testing. (It's better to have both an iPad and iPhone for iOS testing.) Do not use the option for Core Data (that is covered in Chapter 10, "Managing Persistent Storage with Core Data").

If you haven't read Chapter 2, "Setting Up iCloud for Development," review the steps in that chapter. You'll need them in order to proceed. As pointed out there, it is usually best to create your signing identities and certificates on developer.apple.com and set up your devices there. Use Xcode 5 to add capabilities to your app ID, and to manage your profiles.

Here's a quick summary of the steps to take:

1. Create the iOS and OS X projects.

2. Before making any changes, run them to make certain they run. If they don't run, don't expect magic to happen. Recreate the projects and try again. If you're still in trouble, you may need to spend one of your DTS (Developer Technical Support) incidents to resolve the matter: it will be worth it.

3. Select the project and go to the Capabilities tab, as shown in Figure 8.1.

Figure 8.1   Opening Capabilities

4. Begin to turn on iCloud. You may be asked to choose which development team you have listed in your Xcode Preferences under Accounts you want to use, as shown in Figure 8.2.

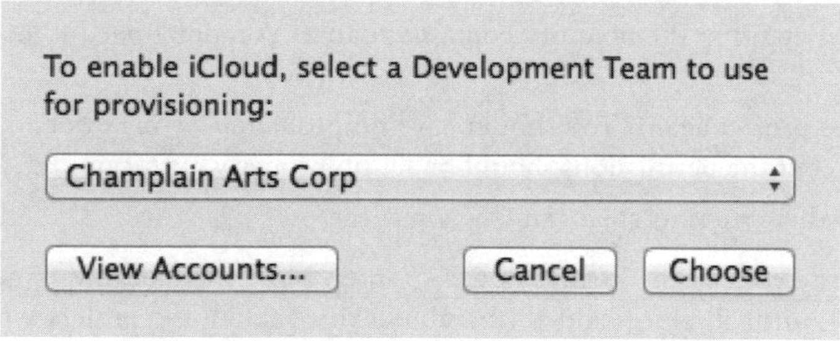

To enable iCloud, select a Development Team to use for provisioning:

Champlain Arts Corp

View Accounts...   Cancel   Choose

Figure 8.2   Selecting a development team

Xcode will turn on iCloud as shown in Figure 8.3. If it encounters errors, it will give you the option to have them fixed automatically.

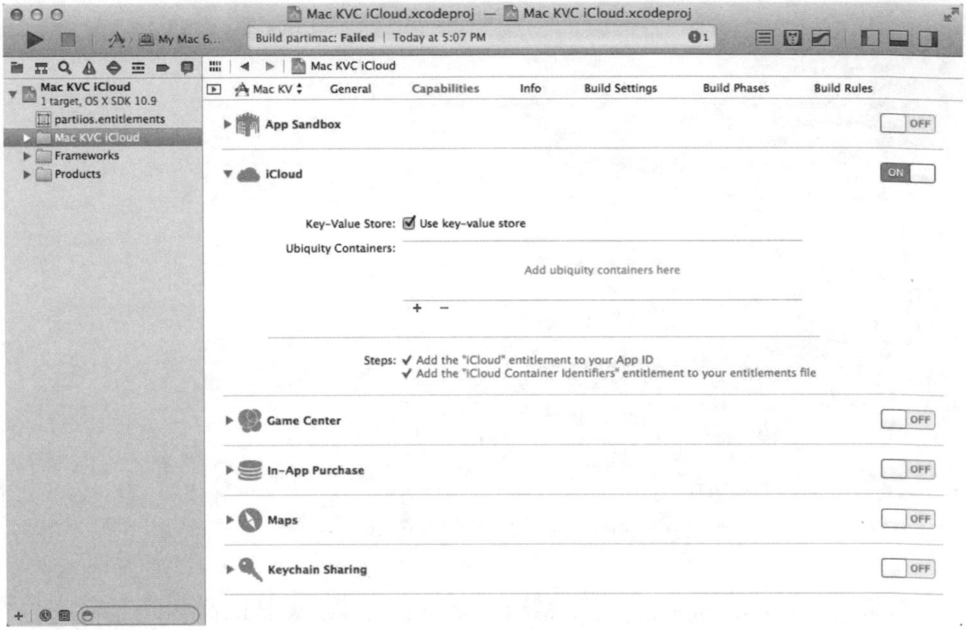

Figure 8.3   Turning on iCloud

5. Turn on the checkbox for the key-value store.

   Xcode may fill in the ubiquity container name. You don't need it for key-value coding.

6. Run the project again. You should have no problems—you're not actually using iCloud, but the permissions should be set up properly at this point.

7. Repeat these steps to create an OS X project.

Now add the code in the listings in this chapter. Note that because some of the code is interrelated, until all of it is added (there's not that much), the project won't build and run.

Sharing the Key-Value Store for the Round Trip

In order to implement the Round Trip, both your iOS and OS X apps need to share the same key-value store. When you turn on iCloud, an entitlements file is created for you (you can find it in the Project navigator). It will have a dictionary called Entitlements

File. Find the key called `iCloud Key-Value Store` (it may be the only key in the dictionary if you've just created the project).

By default, this key is set to the following value:

```
$(TeamIdentifierForPrefix)$CFBundleIdentifier)
```

This concatenates the team ID with the app's bundle identifier, but you can change it if you want to—and you do want to for a shared store. Take one of your apps (either the iOS app or the OS X app) and locate the bundle identifier on the General tab of the project. In that location, you will be able to see the bundle identifier. It will typically be in the following form:

```
com.champlainarts.iOS-KVC-iCloud
```

That is what `$CFBundleIdentifier` is set to now. Leave the bundle identifier as it is in that project, but copy it from the bundle identifier field.

Now, go to the entitlements file in the other project and find the iCloud key-value store. Change it from its default value to a shared value. This means that instead of something like

```
$(TeamIdentifierForPrefix)$(CFBundleIdentifier)
```

you will have something like this in the second file:

```
$(TeamIdentifierForPrefix)com.champlainarts.iOS-KVC-iCloud
```

If you prefer, you can explicitly set the store in both projects, but it's only necessary to change the default values in one of the projects to match the other. (You don't want to change the bundle identifier; just change the `iCloud Key-Value Store` value.)

Setting Up and Using NSUbiquitousKeyValueStore

In your app, you interact with `NSUbiquitousKeyValueStore`. This is the KVC for your app and the user. Each key that you use is unique to this combination of app and user, and that's why you are limited to small amounts of data. However, one of the types that you can store is an `NSDictionary`. Thus, you can build in a second level of data with a dictionary. (In fact, you can go several levels of data deep as long as you stay within the 1 MB limit.)

Looking at the Methods

If you explore the class reference for `NSUbiquitousKeyValueStore`, you'll see that there are six groups of methods (most of the methods have only one method):

- There is a class method that returns the default store. You almost always use it as shown in the code that follows:
  ```
  + (NSUbiquitousKeyValueStore *)defaultStore
  ```

- You can explicitly synchronize your local disk store (maintained automatically) with your in-memory data using the following code. You should do this when your app launches and when it returns to the foreground. As part of the sync process, iCloud is informed of new data, but it may not update the local data at that time. Don't call this method frequently because it's unnecessary and can slow down your app.
  - (BOOL)synchronize
- You can remove an object for a key with the following code. You may want to synchronize the data after you do so, depending on your app and what the data involved is.
  - (void)removeObjectForKey:(NSString *)aKey
- There is a set of eight getters for the eight types of values that can be stored (NSArray, BOOL, NSData, NSDictionary, double, long long, id, and NSString). You use them as needed. They all share the same syntax:
  - (NSArray *)arrayForKey:(NSString *)aKey
- There is a corresponding set of eight setters for the same eight types. You use them as needed, as follows:
  - (void)setArray:(NSArray *)anArray forKey:(NSString *)aKey
- Finally, you can convert all keys and data in the store to a dictionary for further processing (or debugging), as follows:
  - (NSDictionary *)dictionaryRepresentation

Working with the Store

There are four basic interactions that you have with the NSUbiquitousKeyValueStore:

- **Preparing the User Interface:** These are standard Cocoa and Cocoa Touch techniques to add interface elements and connect them to your code.
- **Setting Up the Store at Runtime:** These are the steps you perform when your app launches.
- **Monitoring Store Changes:** As you saw in Chapter 7, you use notifications to keep track of store changes and update interface items.
- **Monitoring Interface Changes:** In addition to updating the interface from store changes, you need to update the store in the other direction from interface changes.

Preparing the User Interface

The user interfaces of these apps are very simple so you can focus on the iCloud functionality. Each has a text field into which you can type data. On iOS, this field has a delegate that implements textFieldDidEndEditing:. In order to fire that message, there is a second text field on iOS that does nothing itself: it just serves as a field you can tap to force the main text field to send `textFieldDidEndEditing:`.

On OS X, instead of a delegate there is a Save button. It is wired to an action called `saveData:`. The action as well as the delegate execute the same code. They move the value out of the text field into a local property (`_editedValue`). Then, they store that value both in local user defaults or settings and in the iCloud key-value store. This means that in the event that iCloud is unavailable, there is a local value for the next time the app runs.

There is another difference between the two apps. On OS X, the setup for iCloud is done in the app delegate; it also manages notifications and updates. Furthermore, in this example, the app delegate manages the text field and button. In a production app, a window controller or other object handles all of these interface elements and tasks, but this app is simplified down to the iCloud basics, so the window controller is not involved.

In the iOS app, the view controller handles the text fields, and it receives iCloud notifications. It is the view controller that then manages updates from iCloud data inside the view controller. In order to make that code a little clearer, the setup of iCloud is also done in the view controller. Just as with the OS X sample, in a production version it is likely that the iCloud setup and notification receiving would be done in the app delegate and the interface elements would be handled by a view controller.

On iOS, add two editable text fields to the storyboard in the main view controller. Wire one of them up to the class extension in MainViewController.m (in the Assistant, control-drag from a text field to the class extension). The other one isn't wired up to anything: it's simply there so that you can tap it to force the main field to stop editing. Do this for both the iPhone and the iPad storyboards. In the storyboard, link the main text field's delegate to `MainViewController`. The new properties are shown in Listing 8.1. Manually add the `editedValue` property—it will contain the value that is shown in the field.

Listing 8.1   **New Declarations in MainViewController.m on iOS**

```
#import "MainViewController.h"

static NSString* kEditableFieldKey = @"editableField";            //1

@interface MainViewController ()

@property (weak, nonatomic) IBOutlet UITextField *editableField;   //2
@property NSString *editedValue;                                   //3

@end
```

1   The static `NSString` is the key you will use.

2   `editableField` is a text field you add to your storyboard. Make sure to connect it to the declared property here.

3   `editedValue` is the value that is entered or retrieved from iCloud.

Listing 8.2 shows the corresponding code on OS X. Note that the only difference is that this is in the app delegate rather than in a view controller. Add a text field to MainMenu.xib along with a button. Wire up the text field to the class extension in the app delegate, and wire the button to a new action in app delegate that you can call `saveData`. Listing 8.2 shows the new properties in the app delegate.

Listing 8.2   New Declarations in AppDelegate.m on OS X

```
#import "JFAppDelegate.h"

static NSString* kEditableFieldKey = @"editableField";           //1

@interface JFAppDelegate ()

@property NSString *editedValue;                                 //2
@property (weak) IBOutlet NSTextField *editableField;            //3

@end
```

1   The static `NSString` is the key you will use.

2   `editedValue` is the value that is entered or retrieved from iCloud.

3   `editableField` is a text field you add to your storyboard. Make sure to connect it to the declared property here.

Setting Up the Store at Runtime

Early in your app's processing, you set up the store; you only do it once when the app runs. Depending on the structure of your app, the precise location in your code may vary, but it should be before any user input is permitted. (In the listings that follow, some comments from the templates are included to help you find the right location to insert the code.)

Listing 8.3 shows the code on iOS (based on the Utility application template). The notification fires whenever changes are made to the store in the future. As noted previously, to simplify the code, it is placed in MainViewController.m rather than in AppDelegate.m.

Listing 8.3   **Setting Up the Store and UI on iOS**

```
- (void)viewDidLoad
{
  [super viewDidLoad];
    // Do any additional setup after loading the view, typically from a nib.
  [[NSNotificationCenter defaultCenter]
      addObserver:self
        selector:@selector(updateCloudItems:)
            name:NSUbiquitousKeyValueStoreDidChangeExternallyNotification
          object:[NSUbiquitousKeyValueStore defaultStore]];        //4

    [[NUbiquitousKeyValueStore defaultStore] synchronize];         //5

    _editedValue = [[NSUbiquitousKeyValueStore defaultStore]
      stringForKey:kEditableFieldKey];                             //6

    _editedValue = [[NSUserDefaults standardUserDefaults]
      stringForKey: kEditableField];                               //7

    _editableField.text = _editedValue;                            //8
}
```

4   updateCloudItems is the name of the method you will write. Everything else is usually boilerplate.

5   Synchronize the store to catch changes made since the last time you ran. You don't need to sync continually.

6   Overlay the local value with the value from iCloud. A breakpoint on this line for debugging is also a good idea.

7   Retrieve the value from the local user defaults. This is a good line on which to place a breakpoint to observe the local value.

8   Depending on your app, you may place the value in a UI element. Note that this syntax varies between iOS and OS X. UITextField uses the text property starting in iOS 6. Compare the syntax to line 13 in Listing 8.4. This is a difference between Cocoa and Cocoa Touch.

On OS X, the corresponding code often goes into AppDelegate.h in the applicatonDidFinishLaunching: method. Listing 8.4 shows the code for AppDelegate.m on OS X.

Listing 8.4   **OS X Code to Initialize the Key-Value Store**

```
- (void)applicationDidFinishLaunching:(NSNotification*)aNotification
{
  // Insert code here to initialize your application

  [[NSNotificationCenter defaultCenter]
      addObserver: self
        selector: @selector (updateCloudItems:)                  //9
          name: NSUbiquitousKeyValueStoreDidChangeExternallyNotification
          object: [NSUbiquitousKeyValueStore defaultStore]];
  [[NSUbiquitousKeyValueStore defaultStore] synchronize];        //10

  editedValue = [[NSUserDefaults standardUserDefaults]
    stringForKey: kEditableField];                                //11

  _editedValue = [[NSUbiquitousKeyValueStore defaultStore]
    stringForKey:kEditableField];                                 //12

  [_editableField setStringValue: _editedValue];                  //13
}
```

9   `updateCloudItems` is the name of the method you will write. Everything else is usually boilerplate.

10   Synchronize the store to catch changes made since the last time you ran. You don't need to sync frequently.

11   Retrieve the value from the local value. This is a good line on which to place a breakpoint to observe the local value.

12   Overlay the local value with the value from iCloud. (You can elaborate on this to compare the two; you may also choose to use the iCloud value. This is safer with KVC than with ubiquity storage containers for documents.) A breakpoint on this line for debugging is also a good idea.

13   Depending on your app, you may place the value in a UI element. `NSTextField` in OS X uses `setString`. Compare this syntax to line 8 in Listing 8.3. This is a difference between Cocoa and Cocoa Touch.

Monitoring Store Changes

Monitoring changes in the key-value store is the same in both versions. Listing 8.5 shows the code. This method is called from the notification that you registered to observe in Listing 8.3 (iOS) or 8.4 (OS X). Both of them register `updateCloudItems` as the selector to be called with the notification. Here is the code that will run at that time. You use this code without alteration most of the time, except for lines 6 through 9. The rest of the code simply unpacks the notification and loops through the changed keys. You test for whatever keys you care about. In this case, an `if` statement is used, but you could use a `switch` statement.

In the example code, this goes in AppDelegate.m on OS X and in MainViewController on iOS.

Listing 8.5   Updating Data from iCloud on iOS and OS X

```
#pragma mark - Cloud support

- (void)updateCloudItems:(NSNotification *)notification
{
    NSDictionary *userInfo = [notification userInfo];                        //1

    NSNumber* reasonForChange = [userInfo
      objectForKey:NSUbiquitousKeyValueStoreChangeReasonKey];               //2
    if (reasonForChange)                                                    //3
    {
      NSInteger reason = [[userInfo
        objectForKey:NSUbiquitousKeyValueStoreChangeReasonKey]
        integerValue];
      if (reason == NSUbiquitousKeyValueStoreServerChange ||
        reason == NSUbiquitousKeyValueStoreInitialSyncChange)
        {
          NSArray *changedKeys = [userInfo
            objectForKey:NSUbiquitousKeyValueStoreChangedKeysKey];          //4

          for (NSString *changedKey in changedKeys)                         //5
          {
            if ([changedKey isEqualToString:kEditableFieldKey])             //6
            {
              editedValue = [[NSUbiquitousKeyValueStore defaultStore]
                objectForKey:kEditableFieldKey];                            //7
              [[NSUserDefaults standardUserDefaults]
                setObject:_editedValue forKey:kEditableFieldKey];           //8
              //ONLY USE ONE OF THE FOLLOWING
              [_editableField setStringValue: _editedValue];                //9
              _editableField.text = _editedValue                           //10

            }
          }
        }
    }
}
```

1   Unpack the userInfo dictionary from the notification.

2   Get the reason for the change.

3   There may not be a reason, so test for it.

4   Move the changed keys into a local array.

5   Fast enumerate through the keys.

6   Check to see if this is a key you care about (customize this line of code).

7   Store the changed value in a local variable or property (customize this line of code).

8   Store the value in user defaults (if relevant, customize this line of code).

9, 10   Use only one of these. In iOS 6 and later, `UITextField` uses the `text` property. `NSTextField` on OS X uses the `setStringValue` accessor.

Monitoring Interface Changes

You have to be able to go in the other direction—from the user interface to the store. This is done by setting the delegate for the text field to one of your classes if you use the delegate structure. If you use a button to save changes, you wire the button up to an action. In this section, you will see how to do both, and you will also see that whether you use a delegate or a button to end editing, the same code will need to be invoked. Note that although one technique is used in this example for OS X and the other for iOS, either technique can be used for either operating system.

If you use the delegate structure as in the iOS code here, add the `UITextField Delegate` to the `MainViewController` declaration as shown in Listing 8.6.

Listing 8.6   **Adopting the `UITextFieldDelegate` Protocol on iOS**

```
#import "FlipsideViewController.h"

@interface MainViewController : UIViewController
  <FlipsideViewControllerDelegate,
  UIPopoverControllerDelegate, UITextFieldDelegate>

@property (strong, nonatomic)
  UIPopoverController *flipsidePopoverController;

@end
```

In the storyboard, set the delegate of the first text edit field to the Main View Controller.

If you use the button structure as in OS X in this example, add the button to the MainMenu.xib file and wire it up to a new action in the app delegate (you can call it `saveData`).

Now implement either (or both) the saveData method and the textFieldDid-EndEditing: method.

Listing 8.7 shows the saveData method that will be wired up to the Save button if you use it.

Listing 8.7   **Storing Data with a Save Button on OS X**

```
- (IBAction)saveData:(id)sender {
  _editedValue = [_editableField stringValue];        //11
  [[NSUserDefaults standardUserDefaults]
    setObject:_editedValue
      forKey:kEditableFieldKey];                       //12
  [[NSUbiquitousKeyValueStore defaultStore]
    setString: _editedValue
      forKey:kEditableFieldKey];                       //13

}
```

11   Take the value from the text field and store it in _editedValue.

12   Store the value in standardUserDefaults locally.

13   Store the value in the ubiquitous key-value store.

On iOS, you can use a delegate of the text field to save the data, as shown in Listing 8.8.

Listing 8.8   **Storing Data with a Delegate on iOS**

```
#pragma mark - textfield delegate
- (void)textFieldDidEndEditing:(UITextField *)textField {
  self.editedValue = [textField text];                           //14
  [[NSUserDefaults standardUserDefaults] setObject:self.editedValue
                                forKey:kEditableFieldKey];        //15
  [[NSUbiquitousKeyValueStore defaultStore]setString: self.editedValue
                                forKey: kEditableFieldKey];       //16
}
```

14   Take the value from the text field and store it in self.editedValue.

15   Store the value in standardUserDefaults locally.

16   Store the value in the ubiquitous key-value store.

Chapter Summary

Key-value storage in iCloud is the simplest use of iCloud. The data consists of tuples—a key and a value. Because it is simple data, it's used often for settings and preferences; it also is always there. In this chapter, you have seen how to set up key-value stores in iCloud and how to use them in OS X and iOS. You can change values on your iPhone and watch them appear on your iPad—and on your Mac (and, of course, any other sequence or combination).

Exercises

1. Work with your apps to get a better feel of the latency in iCloud updates. Turn off WiFi in your devices (turn on Airplane mode on iOS), and make changes. Then, as quickly as possible, reverse the settings and watch the changes appear.

2. Make a list of the kinds of settings and preferences that would require you to involve the user to resolve inconsistencies. Sometimes the wording of the setting or preference can minimize inconsistencies by pushing the user to thinking very specifically about the setting or preference. (As an example, consider replacing a high/low security setting with explicit settings that govern different values.)

3. In the sample apps for this chapter, you synchronized a single field and its data. Add another field, which is to be the title of the single field. Both should be synced together (title and value). Experiment with multiple devices to see if you can get the title and the value out of sync. (Hint: The next chapter shows you how to prevent this.)

Using Preferences, Settings, and Keychains with iCloud

Both Cocoa and Cocoa Touch provide a *user defaults system* that you can use to let users configure their app's behavior. You may have used it on various projects, but in the era of iCloud, user defaults need a bit more thought. You can easily use iCloud to synchronize defaults across devices, and with that possibility, you now have to think about defaults in a multi-device world. For example, a user might be reading or writing a document that is stored in iCloud. In this case it may be a good idea to keep track of the current location in the document so that when the user picks up another device, reading (or writing or viewing or listening) can continue without interruption.

On the other hand, if the user has chosen an arrangement of document windows on a Mac, you may not want to save those as preferences. One reason not to synchronize the arrangement of windows across devices is that on iOS devices, there is only one window visible at a time. Even with multiple Macs, users may not want the arrangement of windows they use on a large-screen monitor to be replicated on a smaller MacBook screen.

This chapter explores user defaults in general as well as how you can work with them in iCloud-enabled apps. It's worthwhile to note that the general topic is referred to as *user defaults*. On OS X, these defaults are often managed with System Preferences, and they often are called *preferences* in user-facing materials. On iOS, the Settings app manages what is often the same type of data, and the term *settings* is often used.

You'll explore the main components of user defaults, including property lists and the preferences and settings API.

Working with Legacy Preferences and Settings

You can implement user defaults in any way that you want. There is no need to add a pane to System Preferences on OS X and no need to use Settings on iOS. You can write them out in your own format in a file that your app maintains. A surprisingly large number of apps do just this. It's not recommended, but the practice is prevalent. It is particularly common with legacy systems and systems that were originally written for other platforms where the OS X or iOS version attempts to try to reuse code that might have been written originally for something as long-ago as a VAX.

The heart of the user defaults settings for iOS and OS X is a set of tools and technologies that work efficiently with structured data. There are two basic tools for doing this: property lists and key-value coding (KVC). They often are used together (property lists rely on KVC, for example).

When you start thinking about converting legacy systems that don't use the Cocoa and Cocoa Touch tools (and standards!) to iCloud synchronization across devices, take the opportunity to seriously consider changing your structure. It may be more work at the beginning, but by the time you add in the cost of maintaining nonstandard code in what is, after all, a fairly complex new technology (iCloud), it may be worth the investment to use System Preferences and Settings.

Using Property Lists

One way or another, property lists are at the heart of preferences and settings in most cases. They are a fast and efficient way of storing limited amounts of structured data in any of the property list classes (NSNumber, NSData, NSDate, NSString, NSArray, and NSDictionary).

Property lists are pervasive in the Cocoa and Cocoa Touch environments. Considering their importance, you may be surprised to learn that there is no such thing as a property list class. The six property list classes just referenced (that is, the six types of objects that can appear in a property list) comprise all of the classes that you need. Most property lists have a root that is a dictionary (sometimes an *array*). Thus, the class of such a property list is NSDictionary or NSArray rather than a hypothetical (and nonexistent) NSPropertyList class.

Looking at Property Lists

Developers are used to working with property lists: we use them all the time in Xcode. Figure 9.1 shows the Info tab of a project. (Note that the project itself is selected at the top of the project navigator.)

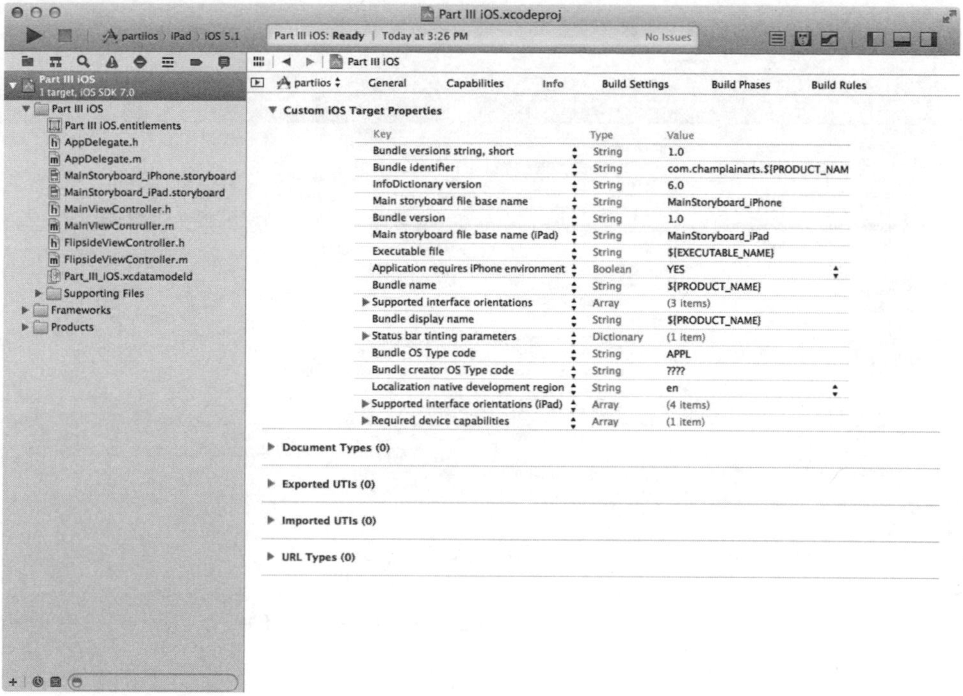

Figure 9.1   Adjusting the Info property list

As you can see, the property list consists of a number of entries. In the center of each line, you see the type of the entry. Many are strings, but there is also a Boolean, a dictionary, and two arrays. Disclosure triangles let you open the dictionary and array items to reveal their contents. You can often type in values for strings. In some cases, Xcode provides a pop-up menu of choices so that you don't have to type in a value (and so you won't type in an illegal value). Xcode also provides pop-up menus to name new entries that you may create.

This is familiar to most developers, but now start to delve more deeply into the property list. You'll soon see how to integrate property lists with iCloud.

Figure 9.2 shows the same property list, but this time it is opened by selecting the <project name>-Info.plist file in the project navigator.

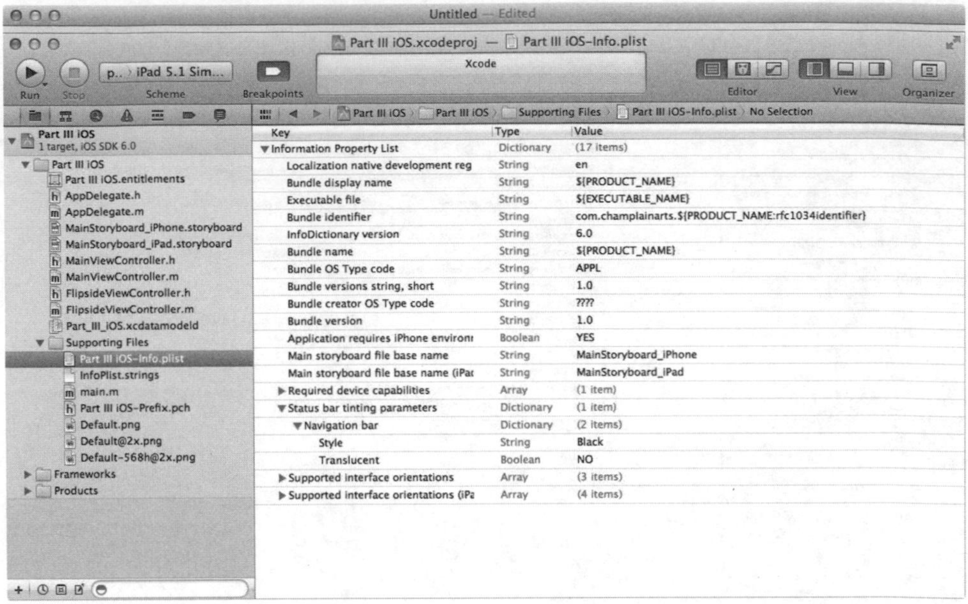

Figure 9.2   Looking inside the property list file

There are two major differences between the two figures. In Figure 9.1, which is part of the display of the project, the property list is embedded in an interface containing other information about the project. In Figure 9.2, you're looking just at the property list. In addition to the added information in Figure 9.2, look at the very top of the property list: you can see that the entire property list is inside a dictionary called Information Property List. You can experiment if you want to prove that, if you close the Information Property List dictionary, you have only a single item in the property list.

The fact that the property list as formatted in Figure 9.1 seems to have a number of separate entries and the same property list as formatted in Figure 9.2 clearly shows a root-level container (the dictionary) matters for iCloud synchronization using KVC. Because the array and dictionary collection classes are eligible for KVC, synchronizing a property list as complex as this one with several layers of embedded data is exactly the same process you saw in Chapter 8, "Using Key-Value Coding (KVC)."

Specifically, you retrieved a value from the store with this code:

```
_editedValue = [[NSUbiquitousKeyValueStore defaultStore]
  stringForKey:kEditableField];
```

You set the value with this code:

```
[[NSUbiquitousKeyValueStore defaultStore]setString:
  self.editedValue forKey:kEditableField];
```

Thus, you already know how to store and retrieve a property list to and from the ubiquitous KVC store.

Looking Inside a Property List

There is more to consider as you look at the property list shown in Figures 9.1 and 9.2. If you open it with a text editor such as BBEdit, you can see what is actually inside the file. It is shown in Listing 9.1. As you can see, it is XML. When Xcode displays the property list as part of a project's details, it formats it as shown in Figure 9.1. When a file with the plist extension is opened in Xcode, it is formatted as shown in Figure 9.2. And when you open the file using a text editor, you can see the XML shown in Listing 9.1.

Listing 9.1   **Info Property List File**

```
<?xml version="1.0" encoding="UTF-8"?>
<!DOCTYPE plist PUBLIC "-//Apple//DTD PLIST 1.0//EN"
"http://www.apple.com/DTDs/PropertyList-1.0.dtd">
<plist version="1.0">
<dict>
  <key>CFBundleDevelopmentRegion</key>
  <string>en</string>
  <key>CFBundleDisplayName</key>
  <string>${PRODUCT_NAME}</string>
  <key>CFBundleExecutable</key>
  <string>${EXECUTABLE_NAME}</string>
  <key>CFBundleIdentifier</key>
  <string>com.champlainarts.${PRODUCT_NAME:rfc1034identifier}</string>
  <key>CFBundleInfoDictionaryVersion</key>
  <string>6.0</string>
  <key>CFBundleName</key>
  <string>${PRODUCT_NAME}</string>
  <key>CFBundlePackageType</key>
  <string>APPL</string>
  <key>CFBundleShortVersionString</key>
  <string>1.0</string>
  <key>CFBundleSignature</key>
  <string>????</string>
  <key>CFBundleVersion</key>
  <string>1.0</string>
  <key>LSRequiresIPhoneOS</key>
  <true/>
  <key>UIMainStoryboardFile</key>
  <string>MainStoryboard_iPhone</string>
  <key>UIMainStoryboardFile~ipad</key>
  <string>MainStoryboard_iPad</string>
```

```
<key>UIRequiredDeviceCapabilities</key>
<array>
  <string>armv7</string>
</array>
<key>UIStatusBarTintParameters</key>
<dict>
  <key>UINavigationBar</key>
  <dict>
    <key>Style</key>
    <string>UIBarStyleBlack</string>
    <key>Translucent</key>
    <false/>
  </dict>
</dict>
<key>UISupportedInterfaceOrientations</key>
<array>
  <string>UIInterfaceOrientationPortrait</string>
  <string>UIInterfaceOrientationLandscapeLeft</string>
  <string>UIInterfaceOrientationLandscapeRight</string>
</array>
<key>UISupportedInterfaceOrientations~ipad</key>
<array>
  <string>UIInterfaceOrientationPortrait</string>
  <string>UIInterfaceOrientationPortraitUpsideDown</string>
  <string>UIInterfaceOrientationLandscapeLeft</string>
  <string>UIInterfaceOrientationLandscapeRight</string>
</array>
</dict>
</plist>
```

In practice, you almost never look at the XML representation of a property list. And, for preferences or settings, you commonly use the user defaults API described in the following section. Property lists have been a part of Cocoa from its very earliest days, which means that the code used to read and write them has been tested and optimized over time. (Yet, even today, there are some people who believe that the overhead of converting from a text-based format like XML to objects in memory adversely affects performance. Most people disagree except for very large property lists and very slow processors.)

Another consequence of the long history of property lists is that if you search for information on the web, you may get misleading results. Today, you can store property lists in XML or in binary. Many years ago, another format (ASCII) was available, but it has not been supported for years. If you consider that KVC ubiquitous storage for a single app is limited to 1 MB, you can get an idea for a reasonable upper limit of a property list's size. Yes, not every property list needs to fit into KVC ubiquitous storage, but if you observe that limit, you won't have to remember which of your property lists are eligible for iCloud and which aren't.

Reading and Writing Property Lists

Because property lists are usually dictionaries or arrays (at least in terms of their root object), those are the methods you use to read and write them. Both `NSDictionary` and `NSArray` have these instance methods:

```
- writeToFile:atomically
- writeToURL:atomically
```

There are class methods to read the data back in. `NSDictionary` has the following class methods:

```
+ dictionaryWithContentsOfFile:
+ dictionaryWithContentsOfURL:
```

For `NSArray`, here are the relevant class methods:

```
+ arrayWithContentsOfFile:
+ arrayWithContentsOfURL:
```

There are other ways of accomplishing the same goal (such as `alloc` followed by a class `init` method).

Using **NSData** Objects in Property Lists

An `NSData` object can be a binary representation of anything. By using `NSData` objects in a property list, you can take an object in your app and serialize it for storage in a property list. Apple advises against using `NSData` objects in ubiquitous KVC stores because they can become quite large. If they do become large, the overhead of synchronizing them across a user's devices can be serious.

It's not that they don't work, it's that the temptation to use them may be too great. If you want to save an app's state and synchronize it, before you use an `NSData` object, consider whether Core Data (the topic of Chapter 10, "Managing Persistent Storage with Core Data") is a better solution.

Using Scalars in Property Lists

There is one further point to remember about property lists. You can store scalars in them, but you need to convert the scalar to one of the property list types—usually an `NSNumber`. You can use the `NSNumber` class methods to do this. These are the class methods to use:

```
+ numberWithBool:
+ numberWithChar:
+ numberWithDouble:
+ numberWithFloat:
+ numberWithInt:
+ numberWithInteger:
+ numberWithLong:
```

```
+ numberWithLongLong:
+ numberWithShort:
+ numberWithUnsignedChar:
+ numberWithUnsignedInt:
+ numberWithUnsignedInteger:
+ numberWithUnsignedLong:
+ numberWithUnsignedLongLong:
+ numberWithUnsignedShort:
```

Working with User Defaults

The user defaults system wraps up the technologies described earlier in this chapter so that you can manage them at a high level of abstraction. The fact that property lists and property-list objects are at the heart of the system does not normally affect the way in which you use the user defaults system as a developer (or the ways in which users use it).

As a developer, you decide what defaults you want to use. There are four key issues to consider in setting up your defaults:

- Can the user set them?
- How frequently are they changed?
- Where should the defaults and settings be located—inside the app or in System Preferences (OS X) or Settings (iOS)?
- How do you use iCloud with them?

Can the User Set Defaults?

When it comes to a default such as the default font to use for new documents (if you have such a default), you may want to make this settable by the user. The more defaults a user can set, the more the user's experience with your app can be enhanced. On the other hand, the more customization you allow, the more complex the app can become for both the developer and user. Depending on your app, you need to find a comfort area for both yourself and your users. (You may also be thinking about the difference between a Lite and a Pro version of your app.)

In the case of a hypothetical default for a font in new documents, you have three basic choices:

- You can make the default your choice and allow users to change fonts as they want, but they would always start from your choice.
- You can let users set the default.
- You can recast the question to provide a simpler user interface if possible. For example, in this case you could use the font of the previous document. Creating a new document and setting its font would reset the unseen preference. (For documents that allow multiple fonts, you would have to make some decisions striking the balance between ease of use and mysterious behavior.)

How Frequently Are Defaults Changed?

Some defaults are set frequently, while others are set-and-forget defaults. Sometimes, they work in pairs. For example, in an app that presents text, movies, or music, you might want to automatically store the last location the user has visited. On the other hand, you might want to always start from a known location (the beginning, perhaps). You can have it both ways by having a user-settable default to allow users to choose which strategy they prefer. Then you can pair it, if necessary, with a default that is the last location.

Where Should the Defaults and Settings Be Located?

Should the defaults and settings be located inside the app or in System Preferences (OS X) or Settings (iOS)?

Users are used to two basic UI approaches for defaults: control from within your app or control from another app. If you implement control of defaults from within your app on OS X, users will expect to find it in a Preferences command in the app menu. What you place there is up to you.

On iOS, a common icon to open a preferences UI is the gear wheel. Again, the layout of the interface is up to you. (See "Registering Defaults" later in this chapter for the code you'll use to implement the defaults.)

On OS X, you can add a pane to System Preferences to let users manage your app's preferences. In a similar vein, you can use a Settings bundle on iOS so that users manage your defaults with Settings.

How Do You Use iCloud with Your User Defaults?

This section walks you through some of the synchronizing concerns that you have to consider with iCloud. This is pretty much the process you have to go through with any sync strategy. It's a step-by-step process in which you look at every permutation and variation that you can think of. You may think you should be writing code, but without this type of painstaking analysis, your code won't be very usable.

As you saw in Chapter 8, you can use the KVC ubiquity store to keep track of defaults. Listing 8.3 showed you how to load existing defaults on iOS, and Listing 8.4 showed you how to load existing defaults on OS X. Thereafter, you monitor changes in iCloud as shown in Listing 8.5.

Defaults that are device-specific are usually poor candidates for iCloud, but behaviors that provide a comparable user experience across devices are good candidates. What is not handled in Chapter 8 is what you do if the values are inconsistent. One approach is to load the local values as shown in Chapter 8, and then overwrite them with iCloud values if they exist. This has the virtue of getting a default value in place as quickly as possible, but the cost is that a default that has been changed on another device may take longer to be set. Furthermore, if iCloud is unavailable now or when the other device changed the default, you can wind up with a value that is not the most recent value that the user set.

If the values are inconsistent, you may be able to add logic to resolve the problem. The classic example given is a default value that represents the user's highest score in a game that can be played on any of the devices for that iCloud account. That value should only go up over time, so the automatic choice may be the higher of two inconsistent values.

Of course, you may allow the user to reset the highest score. Factoring that issue into the mix means that the value you want would be either the highest value or zero, which would be the default value for the case in which no score has yet been achieved—the case of a reset to the highest score.

Does that sound right? Is your default synchronization strategy complete?

The flaw in the logic is that you can't distinguish between a zero that represents a reset of the highest score and a zero that represents a new device. Sometimes with iCloud you do have to ask the user to step in. It is a best practice to minimize user intervention with iCloud synchronization, but if you can formulate a simple question to pose in an alert, let the user choose.

Registering Defaults

As you saw in Chapter 8, you typically get to your app's defaults by using the `NSUserDefaults` class method:

```
myDefaults = [NSUserDefaults standardUserDefaults];
```

Once you have it, you can then set or get any individual defaults. If no default value has been set yet, zero or nil is returned when you ask for the value. This is often not the best choice. The best way to handle default defaults (that is, default values that the user has not set) is to use `registerDefaults:` when your app starts up. Pass in a dictionary with keys and values to use as the defaults for unset defaults:

```
- (void)registerDefaults:(NSDictionary *)dictionary
```

Thus, in `applicationDidFinishLaunchingWithOptions:` (iOS) or `applicationDidFinishLaunching:` (OS X), you might use code such as that shown in Listing 9.2. Note that Listing 9.2 uses the literals syntax introduced in Xcode 4.4 (OS X) and Xcode 4.5 (iOS). One of the advantages of this syntax is that the order of the keys and values are reversed from the `NSDictionary` class method `dictionaryWithObjectsAndKeys:`. Now you don't have to wonder which comes first—the key or the value. Keys come first just as they do in the name: key-value coding.

Listing 9.2   **Registering Default Values**

```
// Insert code here to initialize your application

NSDictionary *defaultDefaults =@{
  @"saveIntervalInMinutes" : @"10",
  @"playerName" : @"Player",
  @"opponentName" : @"Computer"
};


[[NSUserDefaults standardUserDefaults] registerDefaults: defaultDefaults;
```

Chapter Summary

In this chapter, you have seen how property lists and property-list objects implement settings and preferences. The user defaults system provides a high-level interface to them that you can use to synchronize settings where appropriate across devices. You have seen the issues you must consider in providing a consistent and logical customization environment for your users as well as when you should consider iCloud synchronization.

Exercises

1. If you haven't used the new literals syntax shown in Listing 9.2, this is a good time to bring yourself up to speed. It's a simpler way of building arrays and dictionaries than the previous technique. Using the Xcode Organizer or developer.apple.com, check out the comparable syntax for NSArray.

2. For the types of apps that you are most interested in (games, productivity, or whatever) read the reviews on the App Store and search for comments on the web. Pay particular attention to the comments, suggestions, and complaints about settings. You'll find plenty of them in many cases. Use your research as you plan your settings and preferences. What do people really like or dislike? What annoys them?

3. Try out your proposed settings and preferences on users. As developers, we tend to understand the settings and preferences in a different way from users.

10

Managing Persistent Storage with Core Data

Synchronizing data successfully and efficiently often means structuring the data. Once the data is structured in some way, software can keep track of changes to the structures within the data and synchronize those instead of the entire data store. That is how you can easily sync thousands (or even hundreds of thousands) of addresses: you sync the relatively few that have changed since the last sync.

iCloud and the Cocoa frameworks use a variety of tools and techniques to structure data. For relatively small amounts of data (<1MB), key-value coding (KVC) fits the bill. Property lists and the user defaults system are built on top of KVC to provide you with abstractions and tools that you need to support the data.

As you will see in Part IV, "Using iCloud Documents and Data," you have tools on both OS X and iOS to synchronize documents across a user's iCloud-enabled devices. But first, in this chapter, it is time to look at Core Data, which is perhaps the ultimate data management tool in Cocoa and Cocoa Touch. As such, it is the ultimate iCloud synchronization tool. The structuring of data in Core Data is tightly integrated with iCloud.

This chapter provides you with an overview of Core Data and iCloud integration at a high level. After that, you'll delve into Core Data itself to see how the runtime Core Data stack is created with its persistent stores, data model, and managed objects. Then, you'll see how to build your data model in Xcode.

Some developers loudly proclaim that they have no interest whatsoever in Core Data in particular or databases in general. Among developers who work with both databases and code, there is sometimes an anecdotal and informal feeling that the two processes "feel" different. Certainly, it does make sense that looking for patterns and organizing data is, in some ways, a different type of mental process than writing code to implement a process. That said, there is no reason to think that writing code and working with databases are two incompatible skills. Many, many people do both, and there is really no excuse to ignore the fact that both skills are needed in software development. There is room in a large company for compartmentalization, but many app developers work on their own or in very small organizations. If you are not comfortable with databases, this chapter provides an overview of what you need to know to work with Core Data in iCloud.

Understanding the Goals of Core Data

In 1967, Simula 67, generally considered the first object-oriented programming language, was released. It was built on Algol, which itself was made possible (some would say necessary) by the series of Burroughs mainframe computers that started with the Burroughs 5000. Object-oriented programming caught on and today is the programming style of choice for many projects.

In June of 1970, Edgar Codd from IBM's San Jose Research Laboratory first proposed the relational model of databases. Until that time, there were a number of other database structures in play. Advances in hardware and software (particularly disk access) made new ways of storing and finding data possible at this time. Today, the relational model is used for most major database systems.

From the start, people dreamed of merging the two concepts. There were a number of hardware solutions as well as several software solutions. Why can't we store and retrieve objects from databases in the same way we can store and retrieve common data? There was no clear answer to that question for some time.

In 1994, NeXT released Enterprise Objects Framework (EOF) in conjunction with its WebObjects application server software. The union of objects and relational databases seemed to be achieved. With Apple's purchase of NeXT, EOF arrived at Apple and, with a number of revisions (including a complete rewrite in Objective-C), it became Core Data.

Understanding Object Graphs

Core Data is sometimes referred to as an *object graph management system*. It is not a database, and it is not a query language. As just described, Core Data can be considered in broad terms as the merging of relational databases and object-oriented programming. However, remember that "broad terms" is as far as you can take that point. Fortunately, for most people working with Core Data on iOS and OS X, that is far enough. It provides a high-level overview that is sufficient to get you up and running.

Introducing Faulting

One of the key aspects of Core Data that you should be aware of as a developer is its use of *faulting*. Core Data can retrieve data from a database in two ways. In the first way, it retrieves only enough information to know what the data will be like in terms of name and data type when it is fully retrieved. When you try to access the incomplete data, a *fault* is issued, and the object is fully created with its data. Much of the time, you do not worry about the faulting process: it just works. Of course, whenever you are developing a database application in any language or framework, the more you know that performance demands will be high, the deeper you have to go in performance issues.

The journey of EOF from its first Objective-C implementation to its Java version and then back to Objective-C is relevant, because it demonstrates that its basic structure that abstracts database and language access is robust. Core Data is not a database manager itself. In iOS, it can use a binary representation of the stored data, or it can use the built-in SQLite library. (There are other possibilities for the back-end, but they are beyond the scope of this chapter.) In OS X, it can also use an XML representation of the data. From your perspective as a developer, you do not need to worry about the representation of the data. (In its original incarnation, EOF could use other databases such as Oracle and OpenBase.)

The only point that may be relevant to you is that SQLite is a single-user product. For a multiple-user database, you need other technologies. Exploring the FileMaker iOS and OS X options may be useful if you need a multiuser database. (FileMaker is a wholly owned subsidiary of Apple.)

Introducing the Data Model

You use the data modeling tool in Xcode to graphically create your data model. (In today's world, graphical editors for database designs are very common.) If you are using SQLite to store your data, Core Data routines convert that data model into a SQLite database. Other Core Data routines manage the interaction between your app and the actual SQLite database. You rarely look at the SQLite database itself.

Structuring Data

The relational model for databases is built on *tables* that contain *rows* and *columns*. If this sounds like a spreadsheet, that, indeed, is what it looks like. However, a relational database goes beyond the spreadsheet design by implementing a rigorous metadata structure that helps you define the data you are dealing with. The overall design of the database is specified in a database *schema* which defines the tables, rows, and columns.

With Core Data, you directly work with the data model, and, as noted, Core Data routines handle the creation and management of the underlying persistent store—Core Data in most cases.

Properties

In a single table, each column represents a data item such as a name or address. Each row within that column represents a single value: Shen, Vincent, or Rex, for example. Together, the rows and columns comprise the table. In the relational model, columns are named and the type of values they can contain is set. (This is not a formatting setting: the data itself must be of the specified types.) Each column is formally called an *attribute*.

A table contains logically connected data such as names and addresses, inventory items, or topics to be discussed in a meeting. Often, the data is a digital representation of a physical object, but it can also be a digital representation of an idea (such as a discussion topic).

> **Note**
>
> Sometimes, people refer to columns as *fields*. This is a carry-over from older database models, as is the use of *record* for row.

Switch over to the terminology of Objective-C and objects. In that world, the object that contains logically connected data is a class. (It also can contain methods, which are instructions for using the data, but right now the focus is on data.)

Within a class, the items the class contains are organized into *properties*. For a given class, you can have multiple *instances*; each instance has its own value for each of the properties. You can think of Core Data as the glue that converts tables, rows, and columns back and forth to classes, instances, and properties.

> **Note**
>
> *Property* is used in an inclusive sense and is meant to include instance variables (ivars) if you use them.

Relationships

Simple two-dimensional tables manage simple sets of data. What makes the relational model so powerful is *relationships*. A relationship is a declarative statement of how two tables can relate to one another. Instead of a names and addresses table, you might have two tables—a names table and an addresses table. A relationship is defined so that, for example, a name in the names table is related to a row in the addresses table where the name field matches the name in the names table. In modern relational databases, relationships can be complex. In SQL, the most widely used language of relational databases, it is SQL queries that implement relationships. As you will see, in Core Data you can specify relationships in the database schema itself.

This description of relationships is fine as far as it goes. In order to actually use relationships, you need to adhere to some best practices and conventions. Most important, if you relate a name in a names table to a name in an addresses table, precisely how do you do it? Names change for various reasons. What happens to your database?

Records in tables often have a unique identifier, which can be used to retrieve that record. The unique identifier should not only be unique: it also should be meaningless. As soon as meaningful data is used for all or part of an identifier, it is subject to the problems that occur when a supposedly unique identifier changes. Even if you believe you have meaningful data that is unique and will never change, chances are your assumptions are wrong. It is not unheard of for an adult to learn that his or her birthday was actually one day earlier or later than was supposed. You can often spot identifiers that are likely to cause problems. As soon as you spot an identifier such as M-0805-20130224-pink, you should be able to tell that you're looking at data, not a unique and meaningless identifier.

If you make it a practice to have a unique and meaningless identifier in each record, you can use those identifiers in relationships. The relationship will then be immune to changes in the relationship being changed by data changes. Of course, you do need to decide what the relationship that you desire is. Do you want to relate this object to that object in all cases? Or do you want to relate this object to that object based on a data value (which could be a nonunique name)?

Many database designers make it a practice to include a field in every record for a unique identifier. Sometimes it is called `id`; sometimes it is called `zzID`. (The latter convention means that when you look at fields in alphabetical order, maintenance fields such as this one sort at the bottom of the list. Furthermore, using `zzID` rather than `zID` means that your unique identifier won't show up next to a valid field such as `zipCode` that is not a maintenance field.)

Whatever it is called, your unique and meaningless identifier is also called a *key*; in fact, it is called a *primary key*. Any field that is used to retrieve rows from a database table is a key. A primary key is always present and is unique.

When you use this style of database design, it is easy to create a relationship. You relate the primary key in one table (such as names) to a field key in another table (such as addresses). Often, the field that is used in the relationship has a standard name, such as `nameID`. You relate `nameID` in addresses to `id` in names, and the relationship is created. The `nameID` field in the addresses table is a *foreign key*: you use it to find which record in the names table you want to find to complete the relationship.

In Core Data, you draw the relationships in the data model editor. Behind the scenes, the primary keys are created and managed for you.

This describes the simplest kind of relationship. A relationship can also have multiple members. For example, one person (a name) can have multiple addresses or telephone numbers. While each name in the names table has a unique value for its primary key, in the addresses table, several rows can have the same value for `nameID`. That would mean that all of those addresses are related to the same name. This type of relationship is called a *one-to-many* relationship or a *many-to-one* relationship, depending on which side you're looking at.

You can also have *many-to-many* relationships. Perhaps three members of the same family share two addresses (perhaps one is for weekends and the other for weekdays). In this case, a third table is used to implement the relationship (it's called a *join table*). Usually, the join table has two fields (or columns). One is the `nameID` and the other is the `addressID`. To find all the addresses for a given name, you retrieve all of the join table records for that name. That will give you all of the `addressID`s.

There is much more to relationships, but these basics can get you started with Core Data and iCloud.

Normalizing Data

Relationships are frequently used together with *normalization* in a database schema. Some people compare normalized data to the old saw, "a place for everything and everything in its place." The old saw is remarkably applicable to the concept of normalization. For example, if you have a large database, you should be able to find the field in a specific table where a person's address is stored. There should not be two fields in the database where that data is stored for the same person.

But there is more to normalization than this. There are, in fact, three basic forms of normalization. They are implemented in sequence (in other words, third normal form requires compliance with first and second normal forms), and generally, all three are implemented in well-designed databases.

First Normal Form: Eliminate Repeating Groups

If you have a names table and an addresses table, the relationship between them eliminates a potential normalization problem. In many cases, the first try at a database design might be simply a names table. Within that table, you could have an address for the person. So far, that's normalized data.

However, if you decide that you want to allow a person to have two addresses (home and work, perhaps), you would add fields such as `workAddress` and `homeAddress`. These are both address fields: that's the repeating group referred to in first normal form. There are many problems with this structure. For starters, if a person has only one address, you're wasting space for the second address in every record. (Modern databases often have internal code to minimize the waste, but it still is present to one degree or another.) Perhaps more significant is that as soon as you decide you need two addresses, you preclude a third or fourth address.

Thus, the way to achieve first normal form is to split a table into two and use a relationship so that names are in one table and addresses are in a related table.

Second Normal Form: Eliminate Redundant Data

The second normal form is the "place for everything" rule. If you have a names table and an addresses table, you would not store the name in both places . . . usually. Sometimes, normalizing a database involves splitting up tables and using relationships, but sometimes it means modifying the data descriptions themselves.

You might decide not to store a person's name in both the names and the addresses table, but perhaps you want to store the name to use in the context of an address. For a work address, the name might be Miss Marmelstein, and for a home address it might be Yetta or Tessye. You can make the database compliant with second normal form by changing the name field in the addresses table to something like `nameToUseForThisAddress`.

Third Normal Form: Eliminate Fields Not Dependent on the Key

The third normal formal is a precise way of saying that you should eliminate fields that can be calculated. For example, if you store a street address, in many environments the postal code is calculable.

Denormalizing Data

Sometimes, you deliberately denormalize data. For purposes of performance, sometimes you want to take a nicely normalized database scheme with separate names and addresses tables and combine them into a nonnormalized table for display purposes.

Understanding How Core Data Works with iCloud

iCloud works differently with Core Data than it does with other technologies. The data is not duplicated on iCloud as well as on the shared devices. Instead, there is a local Core Data store on each device, and the changes made on each device are uploaded to iCloud and then automatically downloaded to each device where they are applied to the local store. This avoids moving large databases back and forth.

Core Data works with a persistent store that is usually a SQLite database. That persistent store can be placed in two types of locations:

- *Shoebox* or *central library* apps place the database out of user sight. On OS X, they are typically in the user's /Library/ApplicationSupport/<your app name> directory. A single database stores all of the app's data on the device. iPhoto is an example.

- For document-based apps, the database is part of a document's package.

iCloud works with shoebox apps on iOS or OS X; it works with document-based apps based on `UIManagedDocument` in iOS. Apple's advice on the matter is, "On Mac OS X, there is no built-in support for document-based apps that want to use Core Data with iCloud, and writing such an app will require a non-trivial amount of work." Accordingly, this book focuses on shoebox apps for both operating systems as well as document-based apps for iOS.

Introducing the Core Data Project

This chapter starts to build the Core Data project. It is the same basic project that has been used in previous chapters, but now it uses Core Data and iCloud syncing. In part because it uses Core Data, it can be much more fleshed out than the previous examples. It does address the same issue. Using this app, you can inspect items in the field, such as swings in a playground or trees in a public garden. You can update their status (OK, needs fixing, needs pruning, and so forth), and you can add notes. This project creates a shoebox app that synchronizes through iCloud with mobile devices and Macs.

> **Note**
>
> As has been pointed out several times, the original implementation of NeXTSTEP did not include document objects in the way in which we think of them today. In part because the NeXT products were geared to higher education and business markets (with a concentration in finance), many users were comfortable with relational databases from their other projects. The model-view-controller (MVC) design pattern fit very well into an implementation with a relational database: for example, Oracle or OpenBase for the model; a view for the view; and a window or view controller for the controller. The contortions necessary to fit a traditional personal computer document into MVC simply aren't necessary when you're using a database. So the implementation of a shoebox app in this chapter is historically accurate as well as relatively simple to create.

The simplest way to add Core Data to a project is to build it in from the start. As you can see in Figure 10.1, you create a new Xcode project using the Cocoa Application template for OS X. Do not create a document-based application, and do choose to use Core Data.

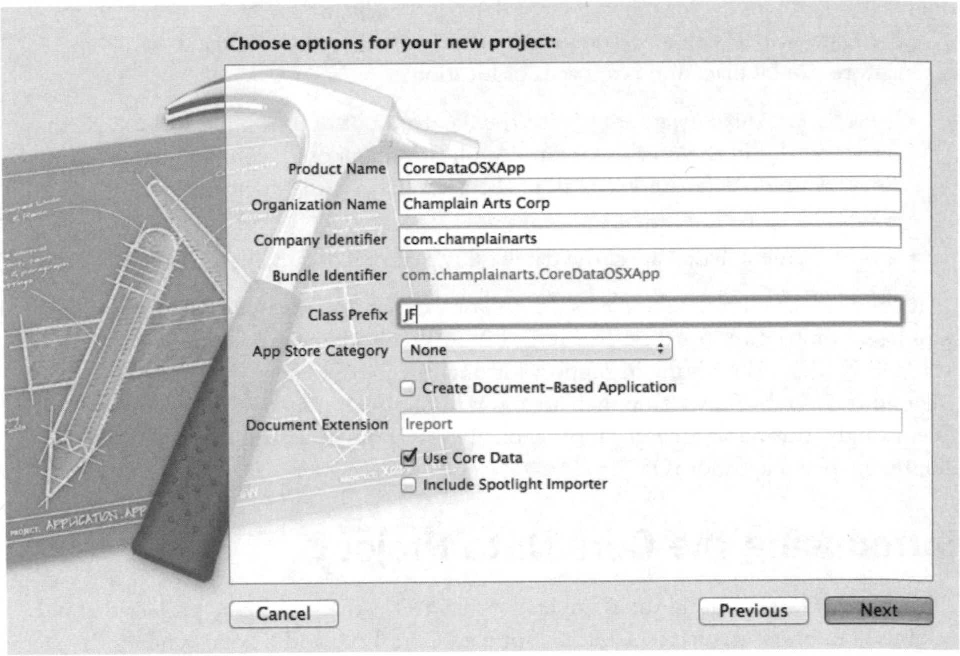

Figure 10.1   Creating the OS X Project

For iOS, choose the Master–Detail Application, make it a universal app, and use Core Data, as shown in Figure 10.2.

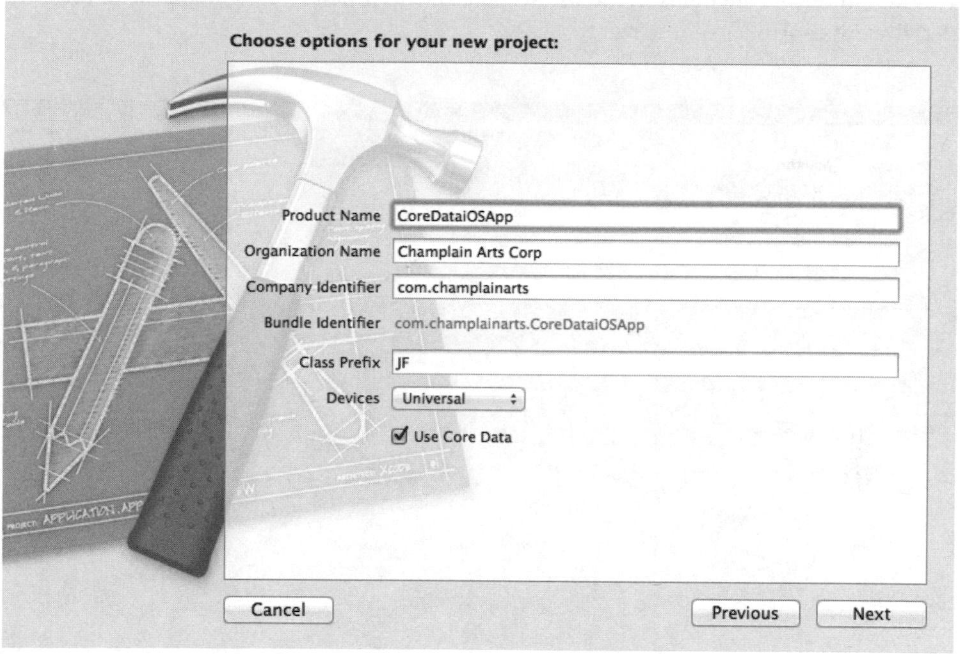

Figure 10.2   Creating the iOS Project

In both cases, build and run the project to verify that it works. Figure 10.3 shows the iOS project running on the iPad simulator. When you click + in the master view controller on the left, a new record with a timestamp will be added to the list. When you tap on one of the items in the list, its details (the timestamp) will appear in the detail view controller on the right.

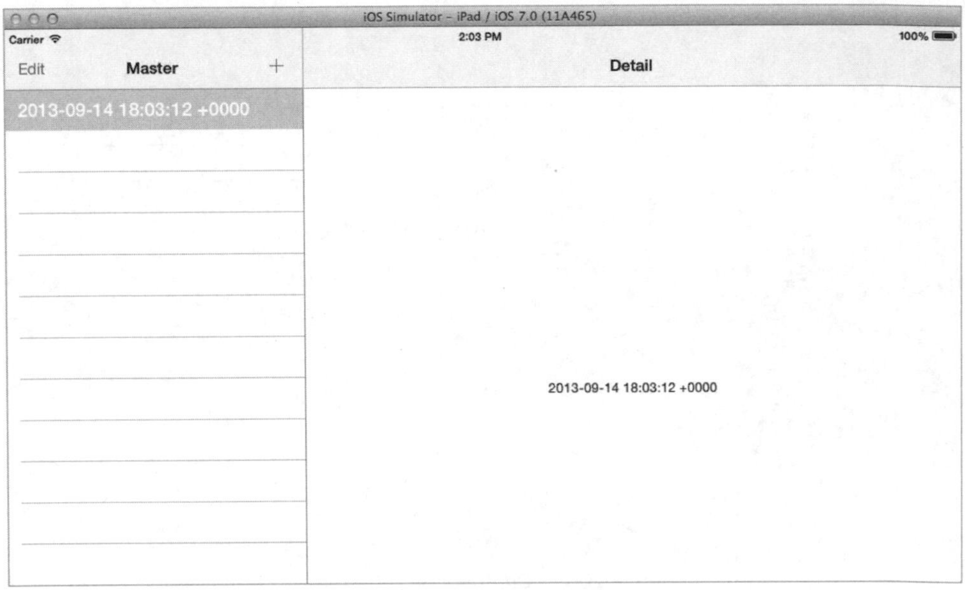

Figure 10.3   Testing the template for the iOS version

Using the Xcode Data Modeling Tool

The remainder of this chapter uses the iOS project shown in Figure 10.3. Open the Xcode project, and locate the data model in the Project navigator. It has the extension xcdatamodeld. Select it, and the Data Model editor will open, as you see in Figure 10.4. Note that if you are building a pair of apps—one for iOS and one for OS X—they will have the same data model.

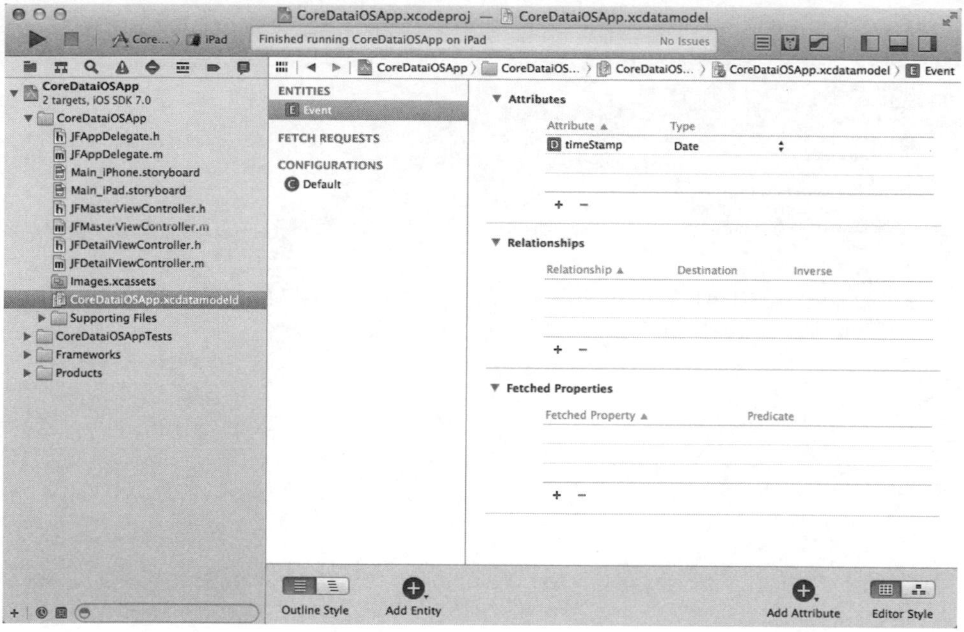

Figure 10.4   Using the Data Model editor

The data model for the Master–Detail App template has one *entity*—this will become a table in the SQLite database, and it will be a class in your app. The entity in the template is called Event (entities always start with a capital letter).

In the lower right of the Data Model editor, you can choose the editor style. Your choices are table and graph styles. In Figure 10.4, you see the table style. Figure 10.5 shows the graph style. Most people switch back and forth depending on what they're doing.

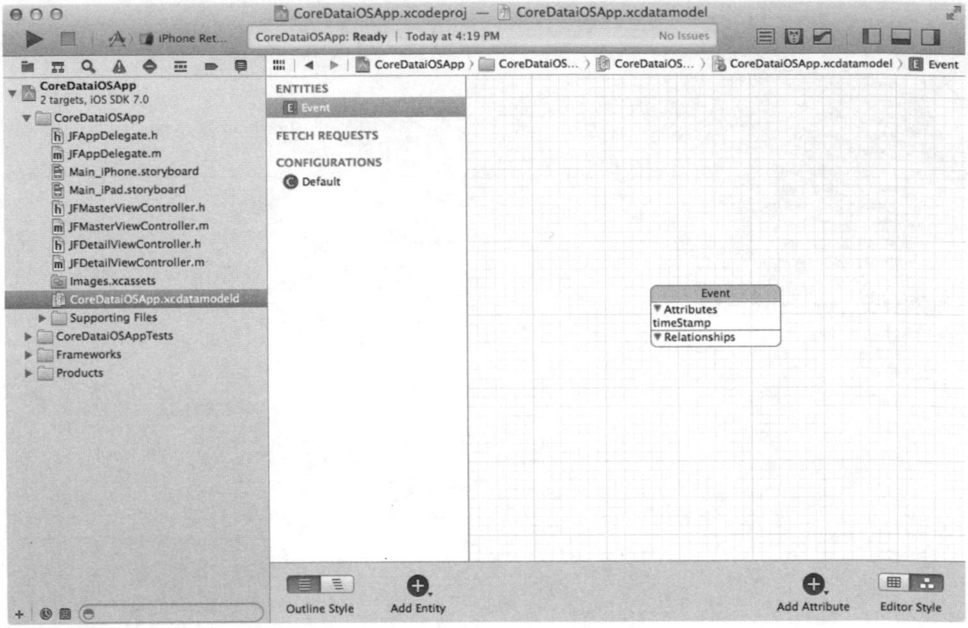

Figure 10.5   Using the graph style

Managing the Data Model

At the left of the Xcode data modeling tool (just to the right of the project navigator) is a list of the items in your data model. They are grouped into three categories:

- Entities in your data model will turn into classes in your project and will turn into tables in the actual database.
- Fetch requests let you define what can become a SQL query.
- Configurations let you manage the persistent store configurations. Most of the time, you leave the default setting.

A button at the bottom of the pane lets you add a new entity, fetch request, or configuration. For this project, you can build on the existing Event entity, or you can create a new one.

Managing Versions

With Core Data, your data model must match the actual database that you open. With the data modeling tool, you can add new versions to your data model. (Note that the icon in the project navigator suggests multiple versions.) Because the data model must match the database, if you make changes to the model, the database must be changed. In the template you are working with, if the database cannot be found, a new one is created from the current data model. Therefore, if you have tested the template, you'll need to delete the existing database so that the next time you run the app it will create a new one. If you're working with the simulator, you'll find the database in /Library/Application Support/iPhone Simulator/<iOS version>/Applications/<app ID>/ Documents/<your target>.sqlite. (Remember, to access the Library folder from the Finder, hold down the Option key.) Just delete the sqlite file. On iOS 7 and OS X Mavericks (10.9) there may be two companion files that have the suffix sqlite-shm and sqlite-wal. If they are there, delete them as well. If you are testing with an iOS device, just remove the app on the simulator. The next time you build and install it, it will be ready to create a new database when you run it. On OS X, the database, by default, will be in /Library/Application Support/<app name>.

Working with Entities

For this project, a reasonable name for the main entity might be Observation. In the template, the entity is called Event; you can change its name just by clicking and typing Observation over Event.

The following might be useful attributes:

- title
- observation
- timestamp
- note
- status
- actionTaken
- dateActionTaken
- personTakingAction

Note that attributes start with lowercase letters. Remember that attributes in Core Data will become columns (or fields) in the database and will become properties in Objective-C.

Each attribute must have a type chosen from the following list:

- Undefined (the initial value; if you leave it, you'll get an error)
- Integer 16
- Integer 32
- Integer 64
- Decimal
- Double

- Float
- String
- Boolean
- Date
- Binary Data
- Transformable

Be careful with binary data: you may have issues with iCloud and, in fact, in all databases. For large amounts of binary data including images and sound, you can store them inside the database itself as binary data, or you can store them elsewhere in the app bundle. If you use that second strategy, you store the name of each file in the bundle in the database. This choice is determined by the size and number of the binary objects as well as by how you are using them. Search Apple Developer Talk and the web for discussions on this topic. You also can view Core Data sessions from WWDC online; they usually include performance issues in one session of Core Data each year.

All of the fields can be strings with the exception of the two dates. Add attributes with the button at the lower right of the data modeling tool or the + at the bottom of the attributes list in table style. As you add attributes, each will initially start with the name `attribute` (or `attribute1`, etc.). Change the name and change the type from Undefined to your desired type, as shown in Figure 10.6.

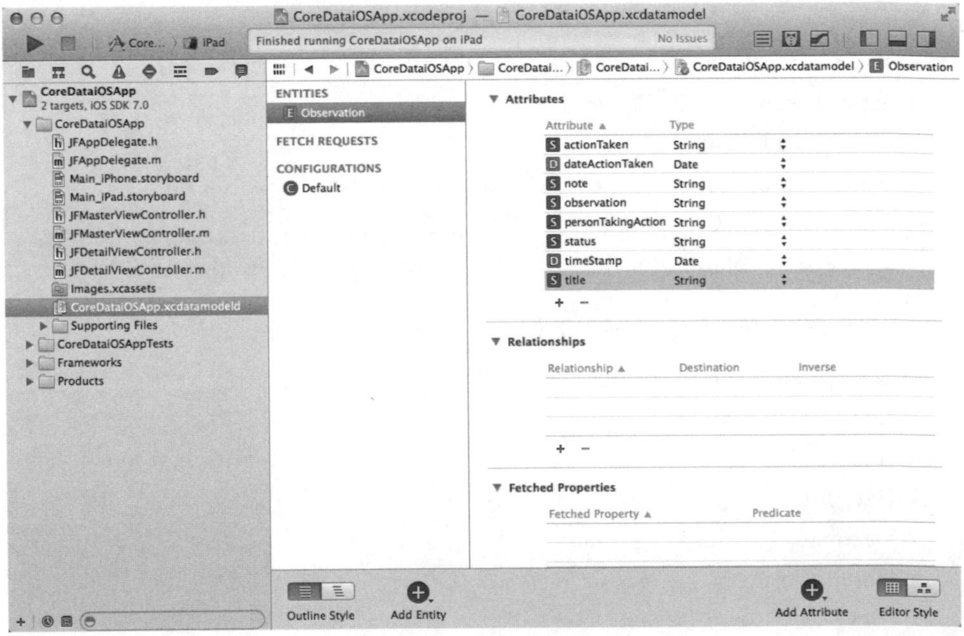

Figure 10.6   Adding attributes

In both table and graph editing styles, the attributes are always shown in alphabetical order. As you can see in Figure 10.7, in graph style, you don't see the types of the attributes.

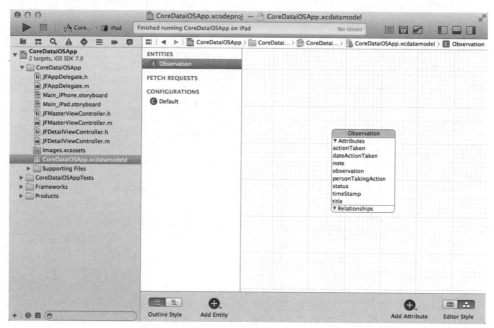

Figure 10.7   Adding attributes in graph style

If you need to change the name or type of an attribute or set other values, open the utility area and use the data model inspector, as shown in Figure 10.8.

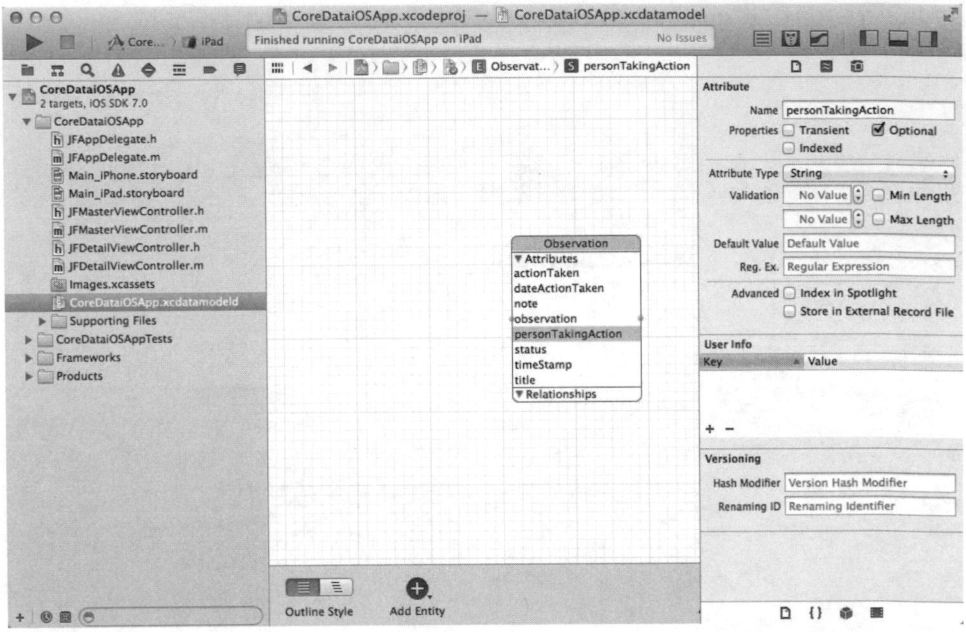

Figure 10.8   Using the data model inspector

If necessary, remove the existing SQLite database from Application Support. If you then try to run the project, you'll find that it is still looking for the Event entity, which you have renamed Observation. (The timestamp attribute is being reused.) The simplest way to resolve the error that is thrown is to search the project for Event. If you have followed the steps here, there is one occurrence. Here is the code you will locate (it's in `(NSFetchedResultsController *)fetchedResultsController` in MasterViewController.m):

```
// Edit the entity name as appropriate.
NSEntityDescription *entity = [NSEntityDescription
  entityForName:@"Event"
  inManagedObjectContext:self.managedObjectContext];
```

You'll notice that there's even a helpful comment inviting you to change the entity name. Change `Event` to `Observation`, and your project should run properly. (If you have already run it from the template before you changed the data model, remember to delete the sqlite, sqlite-shm, and sqlite-wal files from Application Support in the Library.)

Converting Entities to Objects

As the template is written, you are working with an `NSManagedObject` for the Observation entity. At runtime, all entities become objects of that class or subclasses of it. The template displays the data from the instances that you create with + in the master view controller by looking up their attributes with KVC. Listing 10.1 shows the relevant code.

Listing 10.1 **`configureView`** in DetailViewController.m

```
- (void)configureView
{
    // Update the user interface for the detail item.

  if (self.detailItem) {
    self.detailDescriptionLabel.text = [[self.detailItem
      valueForKey:@"timeStamp"] description];
  }
}
```

When the same data is displayed in the table view in the master view controller, the code shown in Listing 10.2 is used.

Listing 10.2 **`configureCell`** in MasterViewController.m

```
- (void)configureCell:(UITableViewCell *)cell
  atIndexPath:(NSIndexPath *)indexPath
{
  NSManagedObject *object = [self.fetchedResultsController
    objectAtIndexPath:indexPath];
  cell.textLabel.text = [[object valueForKey:@"timeStamp"] description];
}
```

KVC is very useful in these cases, but it is less efficient than accessing properties in a class instance. Both for reasons of efficiency as well as to implement other Core Data features, it makes sense to convert an entity in the data model to a subclass of `NSManagedObject`.

Select the entity in the data modeling tool (Observation in this case), and then choose Create NSManagedObject Subclass from the Editor menu. You may be asked to select the data model with entities you want to manage, as shown in Figure 10.9.

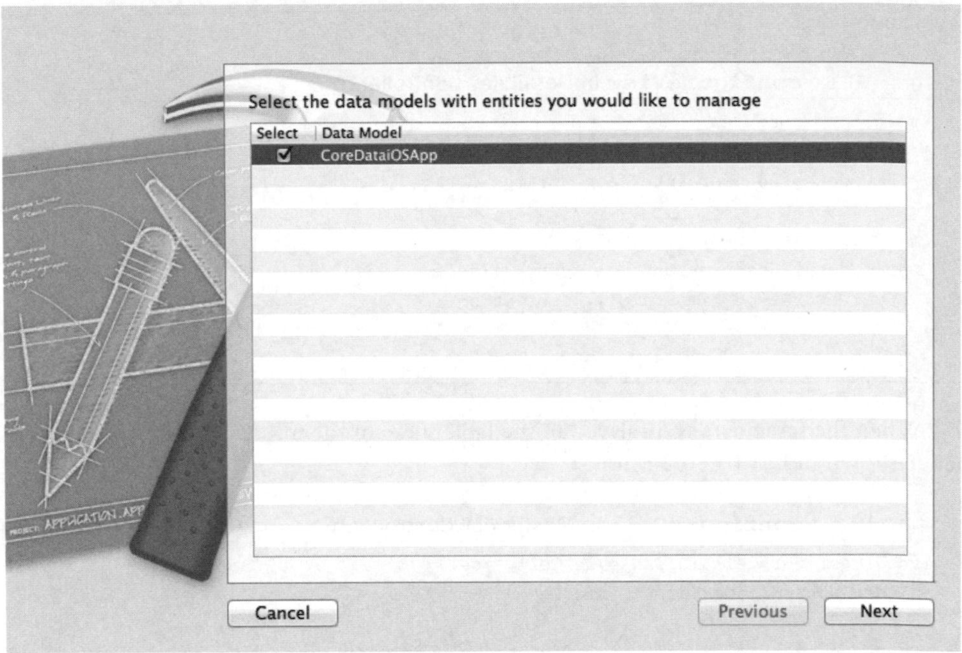

Figure 10.9   Selecting the data model to manage

Next, you can choose the entities within the chosen data model to manage, as shown in Figure 10.10.

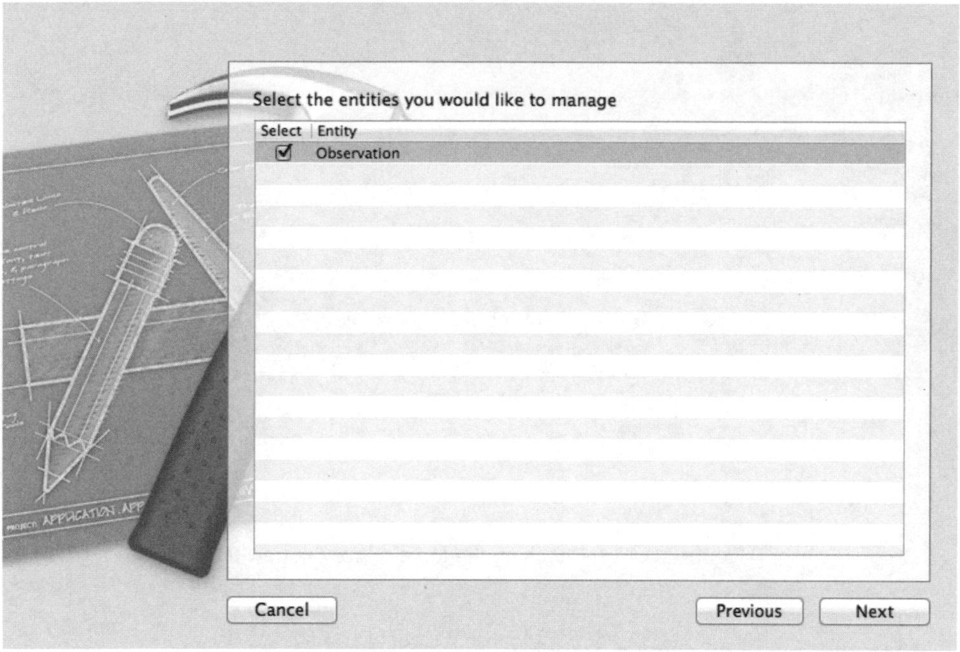

Figure 10.10   Selecting the entities to manage

Finally, select the location to store the new data model file, as shown in Figure 10.11. (The default is usually best.)

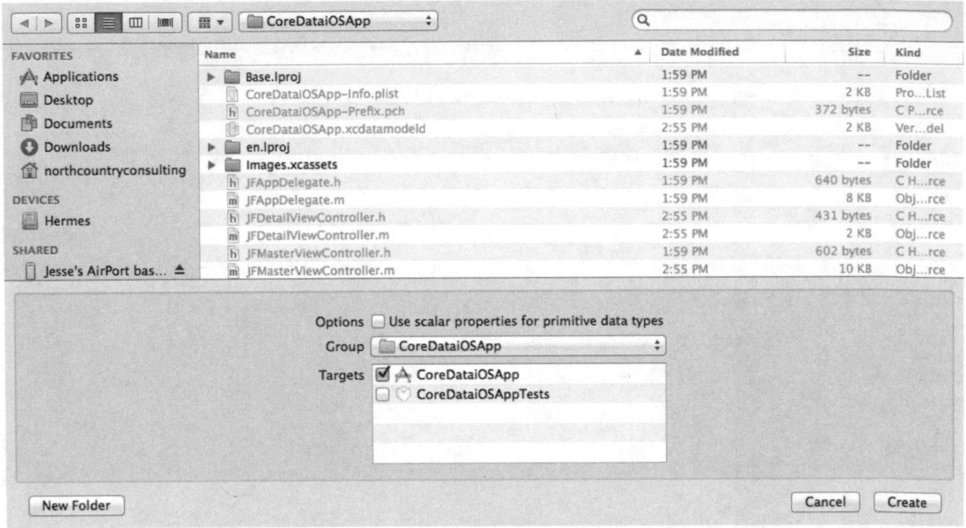

Figure 10.11   Choosing the location for the new file

At the bottom of the window, you have three choices:

- You can use scalar instance variables (ivars) instead of instance variables.
- You can assign the files that will be created to a group. Often, people create a group called Data Model or a similar name for these files; then you can select it when you create the subclass. You can also create a Data Model group later on when you clean up the Project navigator. This is the setting that you most often change.
- You can select which targets to use.

Click Create, and your subclasses are created for you. Listing 10.3 shows the .h file.

Listing 10.3   **Observation.h**

```
//
//  Observation.h
//  CoreDataiOSApp
//
//  Created by Champlain Arts Corp on 11/1/12.
//  Copyright (c) 2012 Champlain Arts. All rights reserved.
//
```

```
#import <Foundation/Foundation.h>
#import <CoreData/CoreData.h>


@interface Observation : NSManagedObject

@property (nonatomic, retain) NSDate * timeStamp;
@property (nonatomic, retain) NSString * title;
@property (nonatomic, retain) NSString * observation;
@property (nonatomic, retain) NSString * status;
@property (nonatomic, retain) NSString * note;
@property (nonatomic, retain) NSString * actionTaken;
@property (nonatomic, retain) NSDate * dateActionTaken;
@property (nonatomic, retain) NSString * personTakingAction;

@end
```

The .m file is shown in Listing 10.4. Note that instead of @synthesize commands, you use a @dynamic command. You don't have to worry about this (or about creating the accessors for your new properties): Xcode has done the work for you.

Listing 10.4   Observation.m

```
//
//  Observation.m
//  CoreDataiOSApp
//
//  Created by Sams Publishing on 11/1/12.
//  Copyright (c) 2012 Champlain Arts. All rights reserved.
//

#import "Observation.h"


@implementation Observation

@dynamic timeStamp;
@dynamic title;
@dynamic observation;
@dynamic status;
@dynamic note;
@dynamic actionTaken;
@dynamic dateActionTaken;
@dynamic personTakingAction;

@end
```

Using the Object

Now that you have your class set up, you can modify the KVC you used previously. Compare Listing 10.5 to Listing 10.1. The KVC line is replaced by direct access to the property of the object. Note that you have to cast `self.detailItem` to be an `Observation`. There are several ways to do this. Because you know that it will be an Observation, you can change its property from `id` to `Observation`. Wherever you do it, you'll need to import Observation.h.

Listing 10.5   Using the Object in `configureView` in DetailViewController.m

```
- (void)configureView
{
    // Update the user interface for the detail item.

  if (self.detailItem) {
    self.detailDescriptionLabel.text =
      [[self.detailItem timeStamp] description];                        //1
}
}
```

1   This line replaces the KVC from Listing 10.3.

You make a similar change to MasterViewController.m, as shown in Listing 10.6.

Listing 10.6   Using the Object in MasterViewController.m

```
- (void)configureCell:(UITableViewCell *)cell
  atIndexPath:(NSIndexPath *)indexPath
  {
  Observation *object = [self.fetchedResultsController
    objectAtIndexPath:indexPath];
  cell.textLabel.text = [[object timeStamp] description];              //1
}
```

1   This line replaces the KVC from Listing 10.3.

Examining the Core Data Stack

The heart of Core Data is the Core Data stack, which consists of the following:

- **The data model:** In database terms, this is the schema, but remember that Core Data is not a database—you pair it with a persistent store, which itself has a schema.

- **Persistent stores and persistent store coordinator:** The persistent store coordinator coordinates all of your persistent stores. Many Core Data apps have a single persistent store, so the need for coordination is minimal, but they still have a persistent store coordinator. You or your Xcode template instantiate an instance of NSPersistentStoreCoordinator, which is frequently named psc.

- **Managed objects:** These are the Objective-C objects that are created from a persistent store at runtime in accordance with the data model. You create subclasses of NSManagedObject in the Xcode data model editor.

- **Managed objects context:** This is often referred to as a *scratchpad*. It contains the data that has been retrieved from the persistent store and turned into managed objects. You work directly with the objects in the managed objects context. When you make changes, you save the managed object context. You create one or more instances of NSManagedObjectContext. You can use multiple instances so that you can manage two sets of data to be stored. (This is often how undo/redo is implemented.)

When you enable Core Data in the Xcode templates, the components of the Core Data stack and their associated code are generated in your project. Most of the time, you use the code as-is. The only changes that you need to make relate to your data model: you need to identify the file name (and that is done for you by Xcode when you create the project), and you often need to change template entity names and attributes to match your own data model.

There is a great deal of power and flexibility in Core Data, but for many purposes, you can just make these changes as you come to them. They are pointed out in this book so that you can quickly customize the code.

Chapter Summary

Core Data is the most powerful tool on iOS and OS X for data management. In this chapter, you have seen how to work with the data modeling tool in Xcode to manage entities and attributes of the data model. You have also seen how to have the Xcode data modeling tool create a subclass of NSManagedObject with your attributes automatically converted to properties.

Exercises

1. The only data that is displayed in the sample app is the timeStamp property. Modify DetailViewController.m to show other properties as well on iPad (if that's what you've been testing with). This is ordinary iOS programming, so you don't have to worry about iCloud.

2. If you chose Universal for the devices, experiment with both iPad and iPhone. With the newest features of iOS, you should only have to change the storyboards to add the other properties.

3. The MasterViewController works by using a table view to display its data. If you aren't familiar with table views, examine the code and work your way through it to see how the data is displayed in MasterViewController. You really can't be an iOS developer without knowing about and using table views.

11

Using Xcode Workspaces for Shared Development

This book provides a guide to the various data management tools you find in OS X and iOS. It is true that some of them, such as preferences and settings, can affect a single app on a single device, but by and large, when you are talking about iCloud, you are talking about several devices for a single user. And those devices often run different operating systems—iOS and OS X.

That is why in the examples so far in this book, you may find an iOS version of the example and an OS X version of the example. That makes sense: although related and very similar in many ways, they are different operating systems for different types of computers.

If you compare the code for the pairs of examples, you'll find tremendous similarities. Not to put too fine a point on it, you'll find a great deal of duplication. That means duplicated code to type twice. Duplicated bugs (no matter how careful you are) to fix twice. The engineers and developers at Apple obviously are aware of this, and they thought about ways to make your life easier.

Xcode 5 (the integrated development environment—IDE—for iOS and OS X) was released in the fall of 2013. It sported many new features—among them a completely redesigned interface that uses the latest UI techniques from Apple along with integration of developer accounts so that provisioning of projects can be done from Xcode. This major change came about just over 2 years after Xcode 4, which, along with a major rearchitecting of the IDE itself, introduced the concept of *workspaces*. Suggesting that Xcode 4 and its rearchitecting were done solely to address the issue of duplicated code is wrong, but the fact is that, without that rearchitecting, it would have been more difficult to address the issue.

Because Xcode 5 is still new to many developers, workspaces are a new technology in many cases. The uses and benefits of workspaces are particularly important to developers like you who are interested in building apps that use and reuse code (between iOS and OS X versions of an app, for example).

Because of the importance of workspaces for apps that are built for both OSes and because so many developers are not familiar with them, this chapter takes a timeout from the APIs to focus on Xcode and its workspaces. By the end of this chapter, you'll be back to more or less where you were at the end of the previous chapter. But at the end of this chapter, a single Xcode workspace will contain that iOS app along with the shell of an OS X version of that same app The two app projects will be unified into a single workspace, and the code that is shared between the two app projects will be placed—once—in the workspace to avoid the issue of duplication.

The code that is shared in this chapter is the essential shared code: the managed object subclass that instantiates the data model as well as the data model itself. There is no point duplicating this code in two projects, and doing so is dangerous because in order to properly share the data, the same data model must be used in both the iOS and the OS X project. Sharing a single copy of the source code prevents consistency problems.

Building on the Digital Hub

The launch of a new Apple device attracts crowds to Apple stores around the world as well as to websites and blogs with the latest news and rumors. The debut of a new operating system typically attracts less attention, but it is still greeted with excitement by Apple devotees and attention by technology media and, in many cases, more broadly focused media.

Then there are the long-term projects that can wind up changing people's lives far more than a new phone, tablet, or computer can. One of these was Apple's Digital Hub strategy, which Steve Jobs introduced in 2001. In my book about it in 2002, I quoted from Apple's own description of the Digital Hub: "Apple is the only company that makes the hardware, the operating system, and the software—all completely integrated with Apple's ease of use. With the help of some select electronics, Mac OS X and applications like iTunes, iMovie2, iDVD2, and iPhoto, Apple makes your digital lifestyle possible."

As introduced, the Digital Hub had the Mac at its center, and that's how it remained for a number of years. The architecture was simple enough that new components could be added to the basic design—iPod and iPhone on the hardware side and iTunes on the software side. iPhone OS evolved into iOS, and the connections from the Mac to the devices changed from wired to over-the-air.

With the advent of over-the-air updates, the digital hub could move from the Mac into the cloud—iCloud in many ways is this decade's digital hub. If you think of the changes that occurred in the decade after the announcement of the Digital Hub at MacWorld in 2001, in retrospect you can see that while there were some blockbuster attention-getting moments (the release of iPod, for example), many small steps moved the architecture forward. How many of these were planned from the start and how many developed as Apple engineers enhanced the broad design of the Digital Hub, we don't know. What we do know is that a clear vision of an overall architecture helps hardware and software developers as well as user experiences move to a new paradigm of usability.

The Digital Hub is a good concept to remember. Not only is it a clear predecessor to iCloud today, but as you look back, you can see that it took many years for all of the pieces to fall into place. When it was first announced, the Digital Hub was often derided as nothing more than a marketing gimmick. People said it didn't work and wouldn't work. The commitment to the architecture and its evolution was a key part of Apple's strategy during the first decade of the 21st century.

iCloud is a remarkably similar architecture, and its evolution is playing out in the same way. Just as with the Digital Hub, small changes and improvements often contribute to the evolution of the concept as a whole. So think about this little bit of history, and bear in mind that a change in Xcode (workspaces) fits very neatly into one particular part of the iCloud architecture.

The pattern is being repeated.

Reviewing Xcode File Management

In Xcode, you normally work on *projects*. A project usually winds up being an app. For example, if you create a new project based on the Xcode iOS Master-Detail Application template for iOS, Figure 11.1 shows you the settings to create the project.

In Figure 11.2, you see the project that is created. Navigate to AppDelegate.h and, in the utility area at the right, choose the file icon at the top.

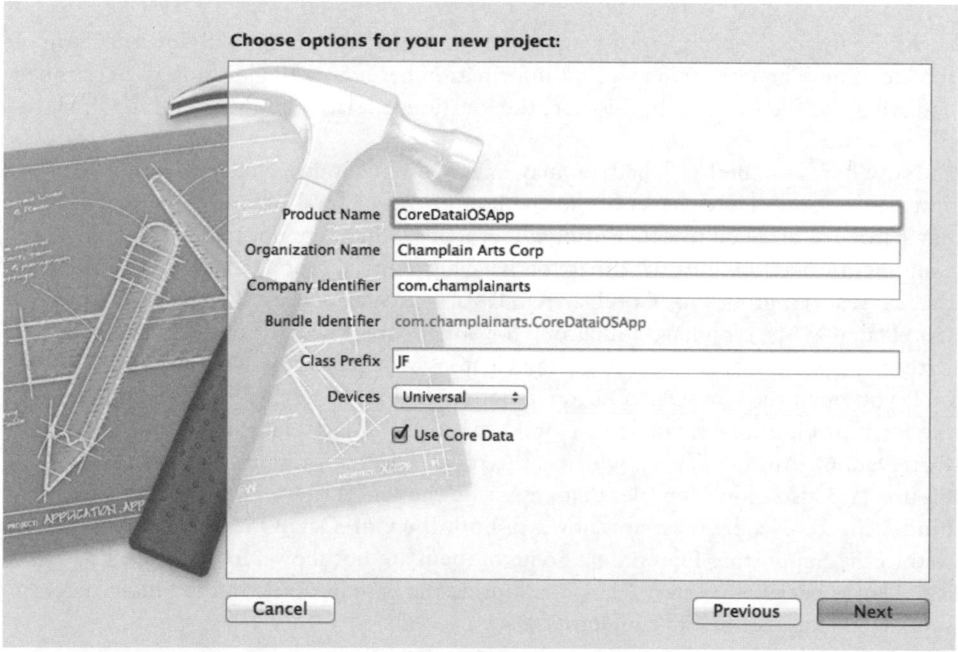

Figure 11.1   Creating a new project

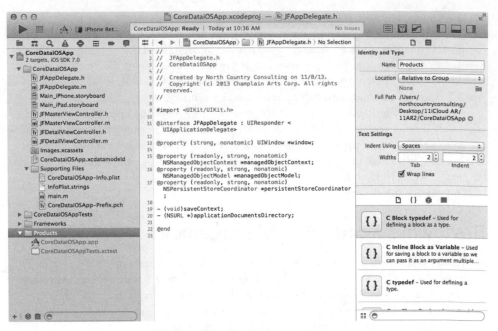

Figure 11.2   Looking at the project

At the top of the utility area, you see the file name and file type. Below that, you see the location. There are two pieces of information here: how the location is determined and what the file name is. In this case, the location is relative to the group in which the file is located.

Now here is something that you may have known about Xcode projects, but you may very well have never bothered about it. The files shown in the project navigator are grouped together using folder icons. These are not folders on disk. For example, notice in Figure 11.2 that you have a group for CoreDataiOSApp, and, at that same level, groups for CoreDataiOSTests, Frameworks, and Products. Within CoreDataiOSApp, you have a subgroup for Supporting Files. All of these groups are within the project itself in the project navigator at the left of the window.

If you open the CoreDataiOSApp folder created by Xcode after you complete the form in Figure 11.1, you see a CoreDataiOSApp folder alongside a file called CoreDataiOSApp.xcodeproj, which is the project file, as shown in Figure 11.3. Figure 11.3 also shows the files that are inside the CoreDataiOSApp folder in the Finder. Inside Xcode, these are shown in both the CoreDataiOSApp group and within the Supporting Files group. Some of them are not shown in the project navigator. That is because interface files are all inside the base.lproj file in the Finder. Every supported language has its own lproj file.

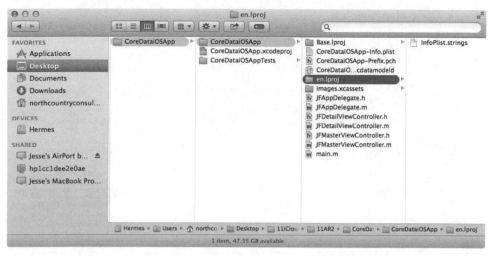

Figure 11.3   Comparing files and folders in the Finder with files and
groups in the project navigator

You can associate a new file on disk with a file in the project. Do so by clicking the small button to the right of the filename in the Location section. That will open the sheet shown in Figure 11.4, which lets you pick a new file on disk for the file in the project.

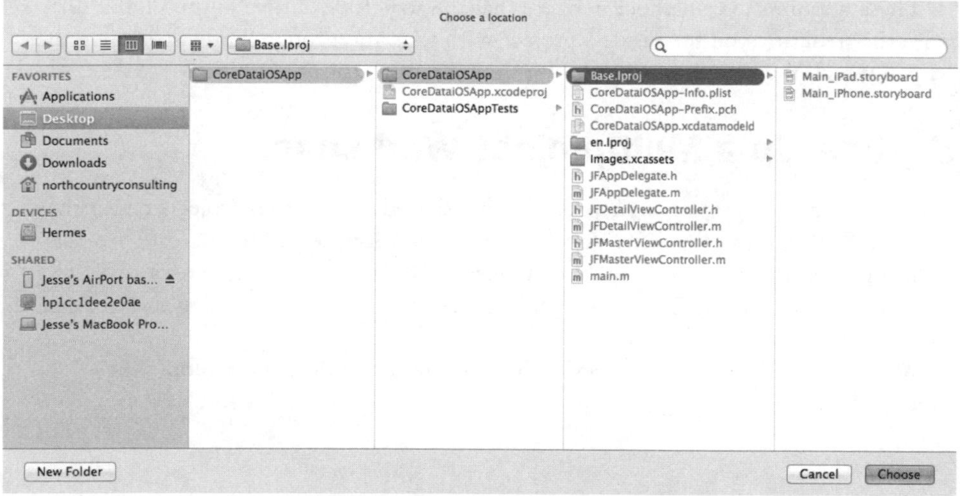

Figure 11.4   Associating a new disk file with the
file in the project navigator

Beneath the location, you see the full path to the file. The small arrow to the right of the path will reveal the file in the Finder, as you see in Figure 11.5.

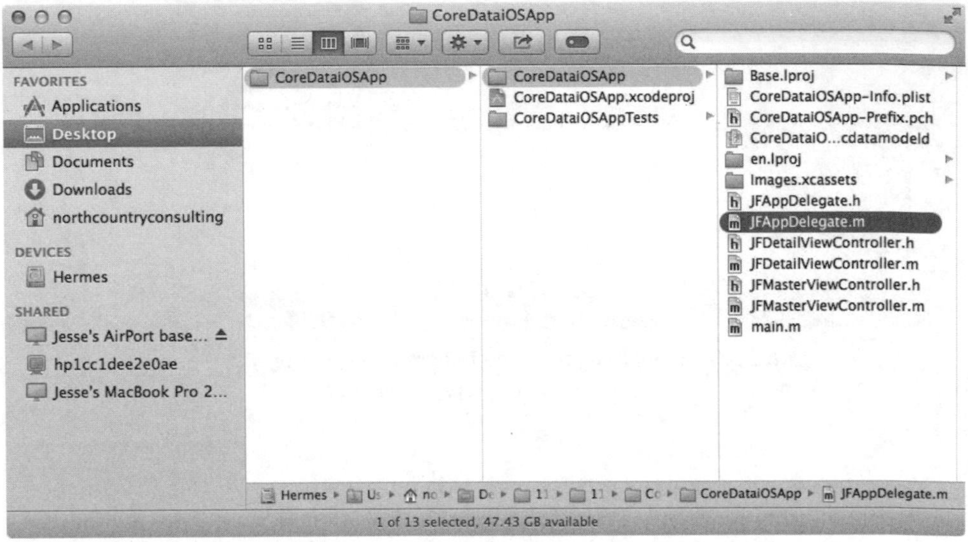

Figure 11.5   Revealing the file in the Finder

The key points to remember here are that the structure of files in the Finder differs from the structure you see inside a project with files and groups. You can change the way in which the mapping occurs using the File inspector in the Utility area.

Setting Up a Multiproject Workspace

The goal of a multiproject workspace is to use shared files in two projects rather than duplicated files in two projects. You can set up a workspace and then create projects within it. You can also add projects to a workspace. What is shown here is a way to add projects to a workspace in a way that makes the project navigator in the workspace particularly usable.

When you are finished, the files in the workspace window should look like Figure 11.6.

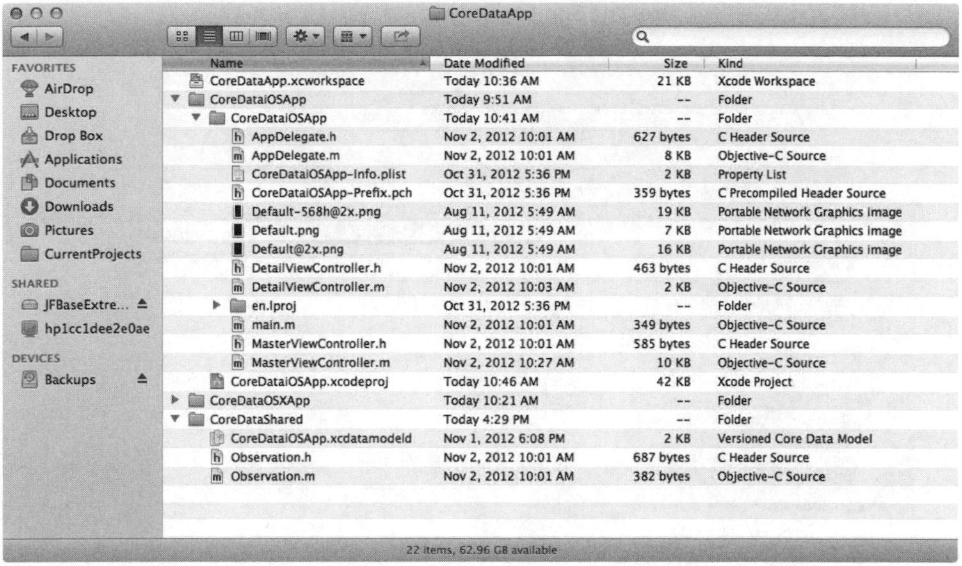

Figure 11.6   Creating a workspace window for two projects
and a shared folder as its own group

Within an enclosing folder (CoreDataApp), you can see the workspace file itself. There are three main folders within it:

- CoreDataiOSApp is the project as you built it in Chapter 10, "Managing Persistent Storage with Core Data." This folder is open in Figure 11.6.

- CoreDataOSXApp is a companion project for OS X.

- CoreDataShared, which is also opened, contains the data model and the two class files. These files will be used by both of the projects without the need for duplication.

There are several ways to set this up. The steps that follow are those that I prefer to use. At the end of this section, I'll show you another way of doing this.

Creating a Multiproject Workspace

The following steps work when you have one or more projects that you want to add to a workspace:

1. Create a new folder in the Finder for the combined project—in this case, it's called CoreDataApp.

2. Drag two existing projects into the folder. You can drag both CoreDataiOSApp (from Chapter 10) as well as a new CocoaDataOSSXApp, if you want.

3. Launch Xcode and create a new workspace from File, New, Workspace.

4. Place it inside the CoreDataApp folder, as shown in Figure 11.7.

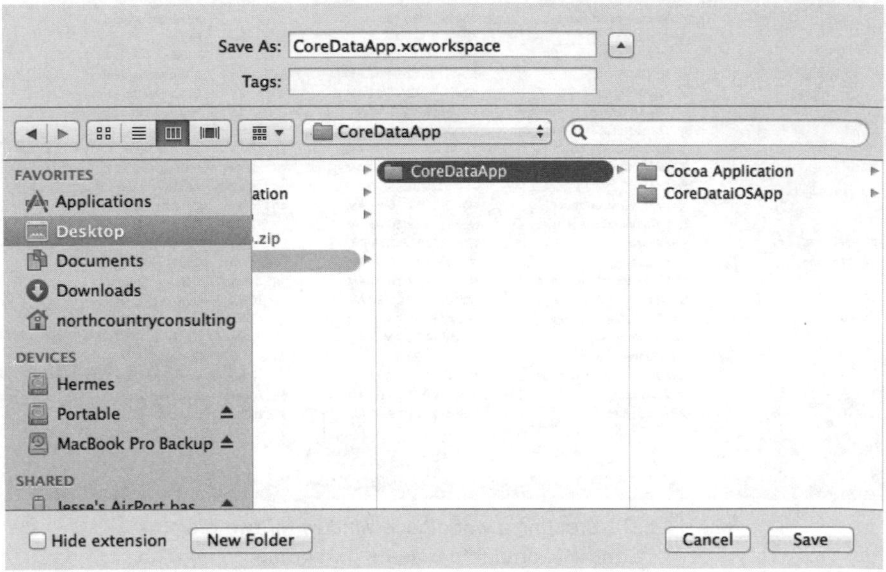

Figure 11.7   Placing the two projects in the same folder

5. Now that the two projects are in the same Finder folder, it's time to put them both in the same Xcode workspace. Control-click in the workspace window to bring up the shortcut menu, as shown in Figure 11.8. Choose Add Files to CoreDataApp.

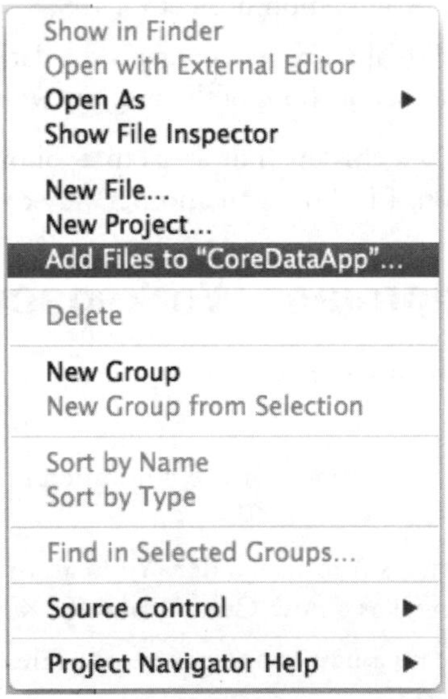

Figure 11.8   Using the workspace window shortcut menu

6. As shown in Figure 11.9, select one of the xcodeproj files from one of the projects that you placed inside CoreDataApp. (Do not use the checkbox to copy files into the destination.) Then click Add.

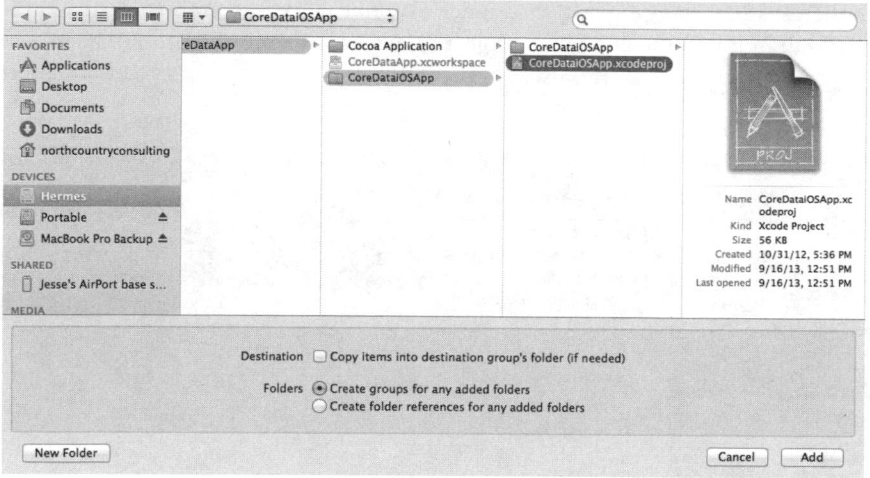

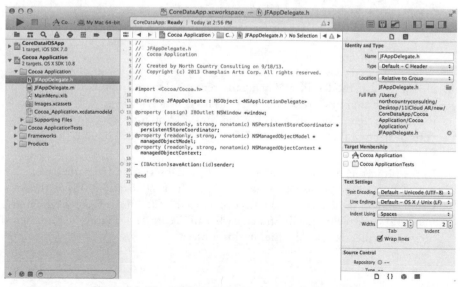

Figure 11.9   Adding a project to the workspace

7. Repeat for the xcodeproj file in the other project.

Your workspace window now has both projects in it, and each project's files are in their own folder in the Finder. Figure 11.10 shows the workspace window now.

Figure 11.10   Both projects are in a single workspace

8. Inside the combined project folder in the Finder, create a new folder called CoreDataShared.

9. Move the Observation.h and Observation.m files as well as the data model from CoreDataiOSApp into this new folder. Because the data model file is actually a file package, dragging it in the Finder may not work, so compress it to a zip file and drag it into the combined project folder, as shown in Figure 11.11.

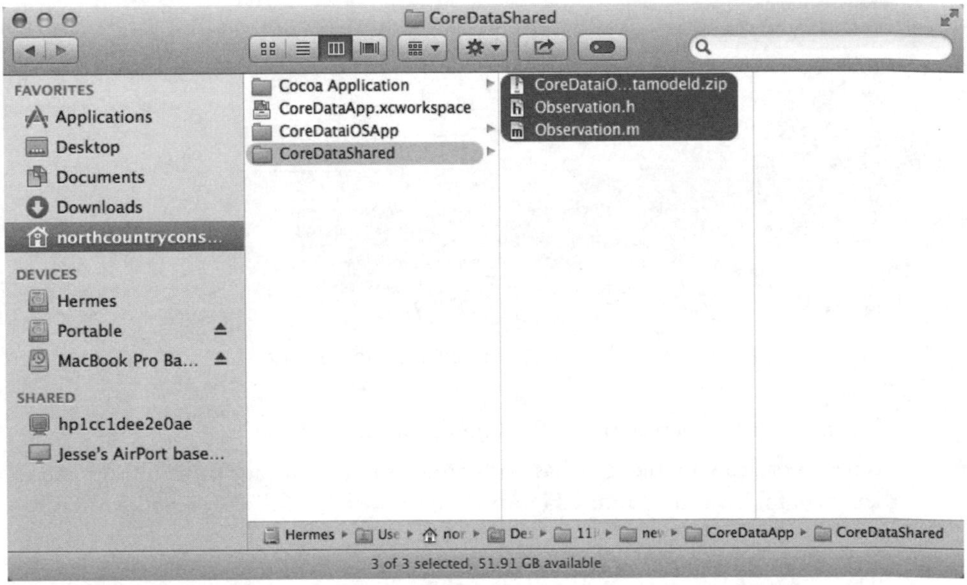

Figure 11.11   Moving the shared files into the shared folder

10. Unzip the data model file and manually remove the uncompressed file from the original location in CoreDataiOSApp. (This is necessary because the data model is a file package.) You can get rid of the zip file. You may want to reorganize your projects in the workspace so that a group in each one contains the shared files.

11. In the project navigator for CoreDataiOSApp, Observation file names are now shown in red because they don't exist in their old locations (inside the CoreDataiOSApp folder). Reconnect them to the files in the CoreDataShared folder. Use the technique illustrated earlier in Figure 11.4. Figure 11.12 shows how that will look with the files in this project.

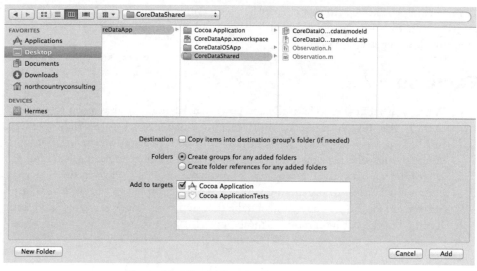

Figure 11.12   Adding the files to the project

You should now be able to build and run the CoreDataiOSApp from the workspace: you're back where you were at the end of the last chapter in terms of code, but you have the common workspace as a way to move on to your shared code base. This will be completed in Chapter 18, "Completing the Round Trip."

Chapter Summary

This chapter showed you how to convert two separate projects that duplicate a data model and other files to a unified project that shares the duplicated code. This is done by using the workspace functionality that was first released in Xcode 4. These shared workspaces can rely in part on the ability to use Xcode's file references so that files can be anywhere. (And remember that those folder-like icons in the project navigator are definitely not Finder folders.) Creating a shared workspace like this can reduce the amount of code you need to maintain and debug. In addition, it can make the structure of your apps clearer.

Shared code and workspaces are not the cure-all for everything. Most of the Xcode templates at this time do not use workspaces, and they're not necessary if you know that you're writing an app that will not need to run on both iOX and OS X. However, if you know you'll need this structure, it's good to set it up from the start.

Nevertheless, the steps in this chapter help you convert separate projects to a shared project using a workspace. That can make your implementation of iCloud on both OSes much easier as you proceed.

Exercise

1. When you adopt this style of file and code structuring, you may need to rethink the way you store your files on disk. Keeping a shared workspace's files organized in a logical way will pay off for you. How you do it depends on the kind of work you're doing, whether you're sharing files with colleagues on the project, and what kinds of backups and shared disks you have available. Devote time—perhaps even a few hours—to organizing your files. And if you haven't been using Git or Subversion for source code control, take that step now. (Both are integrated with Xcode, but the Git integration is more powerful.)

Adding Data to Apps with Bundles and Resources

You have a variety of tools that you can use to manage your app's data: key-value code (KVC), property lists (plists), Core Data, XML, and even unstructured text files. Your app's data falls into two broad categories:

- There is the data that your users create and manipulate. It may be text, photos, video, music, or structured data. It may be stored in documents, or it may be stored in a shoebox-style library.
- There is the data that your app uses. This data includes localized text in your xib files or storyboards as well as a wide variety of graphical data—the images on your buttons, your view backgrounds, and the like.

This chapter focuses on the second category of data. This data is typically stored inside the app itself; as a result, distribution of the app includes this data. Sometimes, this data is transformed into user data (for example, a Core Data persistent store in the app itself may be copied to an area where the user can modify it). You can even combine app-included data with user manipulation and then put the resultant data into an iCloud container so that it can be updated from various devices.

Because of the diverse types of data involved as well as the various ways in which it can be included in your app, this chapter will help you choose what types of data to place where, and it will show you how to use Xcode to get that data into your app.

Furthermore, you'll find an overview of sandboxing on OS X and iOS. You've seen some of the sandboxing features in discussions of iCloud entitlements, but because you often need to take data out of your app and put it somewhere on disk, this chapter gives you an idea of what you can put where.

Packages, Bundles, and Resources

Most apps on OS X and iOS are actually *bundles*—directories with a standard structure that contain executable code and resources that together make up the app. To the user, the app is a simple file that can be moved around on OS X (on iOS, it can be moved around on the Home screen, but its location internally isn't changeable). In addition to compiling your code, one of the key purposes of Xcode is building the bundles for your app and its targets (there are usually separate app bundles for each target).

Bundles are a type of *package*—a directory that appears like a single file. (What sets a bundle apart from other types of packages is the specific directory structure and the specific files that it contains.) You can open a package by Control-clicking on a package icon. The contextual menu includes a Show Package Contents command, as shown in Figure 12.1

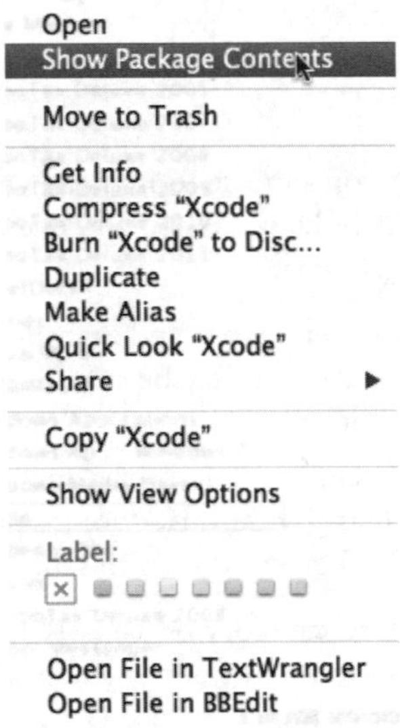

Open
Show Package Contents

Move to Trash

Get Info
Compress "Xcode"
Burn "Xcode" to Disc...
Duplicate
Make Alias
Quick Look "Xcode"
Share   ▶

Copy "Xcode"

Show View Options

Label:
⊠ ▪ ▪ ▪ ▪ ▪ ▪ ▪

Open File in TextWrangler
Open File in BBEdit

Figure 12.1   Opening a package from the contextual menu

Figure 12.2 shows a typical application bundle structure (this is the bundle for the Automator app that's part of the standard OS X installation). If you browse the Resources directory (don't change anything!), you'll see that it includes image files (generally .icns, .pdf, .tiff, and .png) as well as localization folders (.lproj) that contain .strings and .nib files.

Figure 12.2   Looking inside the Automator bundle

Xcode handles the creation of the bundle almost automatically. If you add files to your project (generally with File, Add File or File, New, New File), they show up in the project navigator. Many of them are automatically included in the bundle, but others need to be added manually in Build Phases.

Adding Files to Your App's Bundle

Here are the steps to use in adding files to your App's bundle. Start by creating a new project. For the figures in this section, the iOS Master-Detail Application template is used with the option for Core Data, as shown in Figure 12.3.

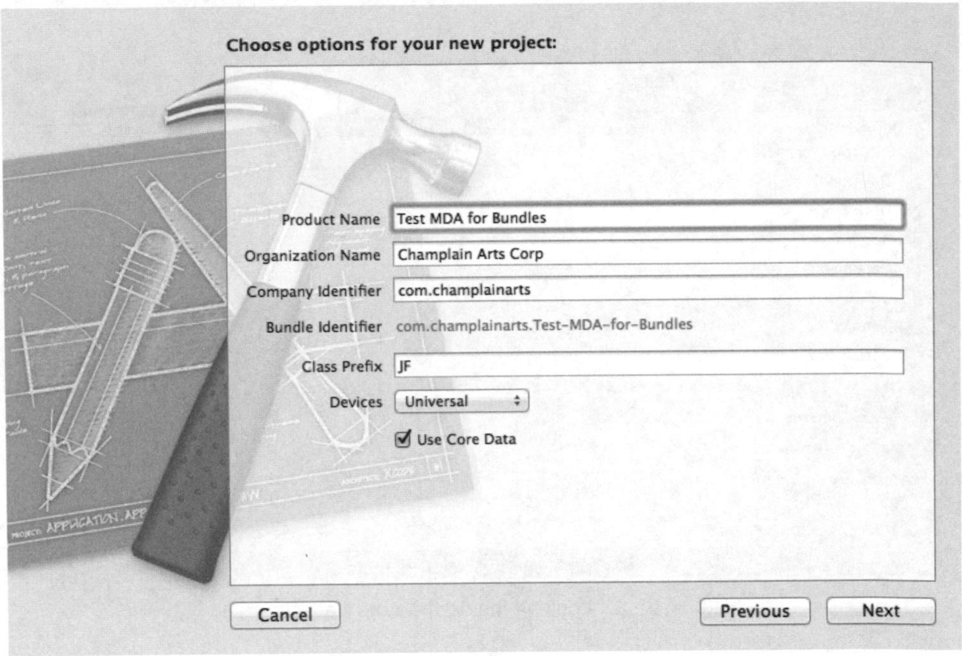

Figure 12.3   Creating a new project

1. Open Copy Bundle Resources in Build Phases, as shown in Figure 12.4. You'll see that the included files include the storyboards and some of the files in the Supporting Files group. Notice that files such as the precompiled header (.pch) are used during the build process and are not brought into the bundle. Note, too, that although the project has Core Data enabled, the data model is not included in the bundle. Rather, it is among the files to be compiled, as you see in Figure 12.4.

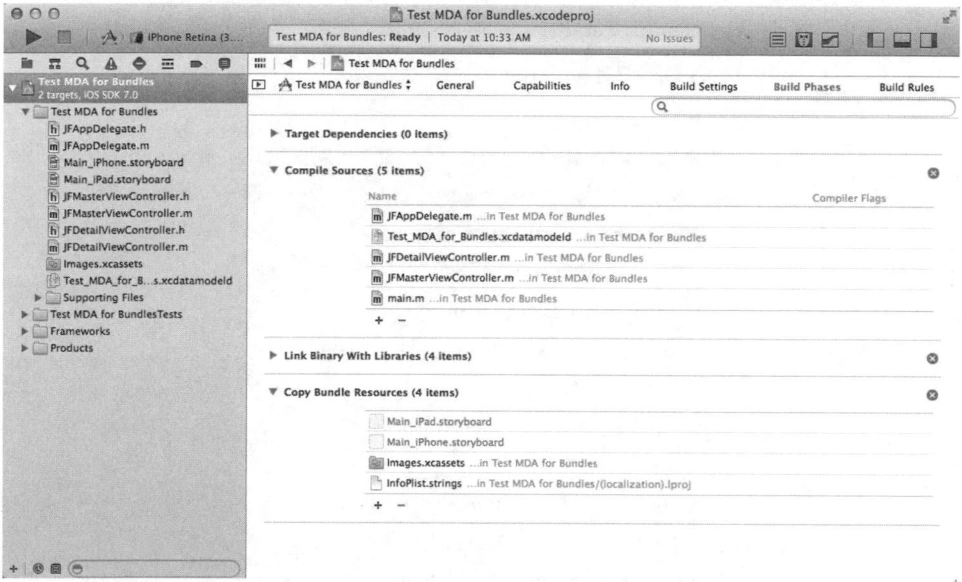

Figure 12.4   Comparing the bundle resources to the project navigator files

2. To add another file to the bundle, click + at the bottom left of Copy Bundle Resources. Choose the file from the project's files, as shown in Figure 12.5.

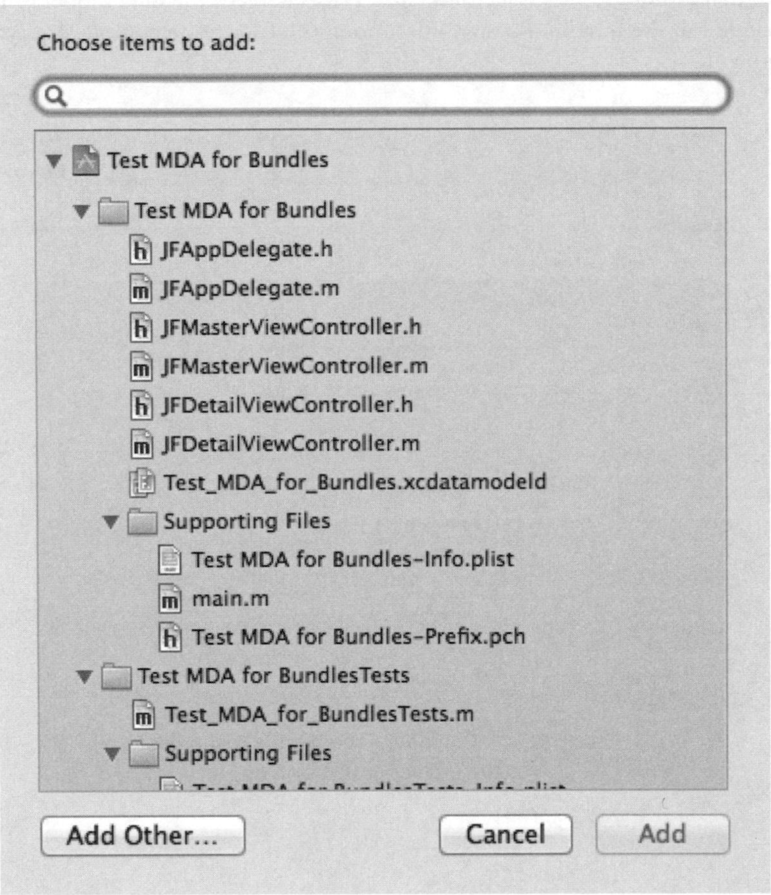

Figure 12.5   Adding another file to the bundle

3. To add a new file to the project and the bundle, click Add Other at the bottom left of Figure 12.5. A standard file open dialog will let you choose the file. After you choose a file, decide whether or not to add it to the project, as shown in Figure 12.6. Normally you do so and copy it into the project.

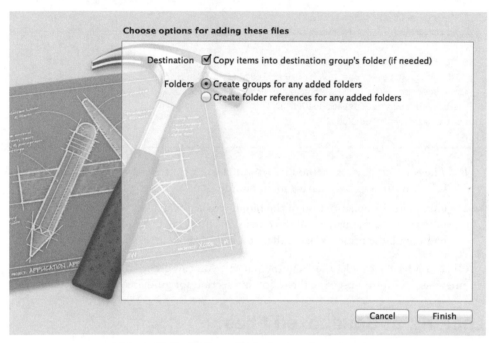

Choose options for adding these files

Destination   ☑ Copy items into destination group's folder (if needed)

Folders   ⦿ Create groups for any added folders
          ◯ Create folder references for any added folders

Cancel   Finish

Figure 12.6   Adding a file to the bundle and project

Getting Files Out of the Bundle

Some of the files in the bundle are used in the interface; you typically set the image for a button or other interface element to one of the graphics files in your project using the Attributes inspector for the storyboard. For these files, the Attributes inspector is all you need to worry about.

Other files that add to the bundle may be used to create your app's environment, and they may need to be extracted from the bundle to be used at runtime. In some cases, they need to be installed on the computer so that the app can use them in the future. Listing 12.1 shows how to get files out of the bundle. This code is part of the Master-Detail Application template: it's the `managedObjectModel` getter from `AppDelegate.m`.

Listing 12.1   AppDelegate `managedObjectModel`

```
// Returns the managed object model for the application.
// If the model doesn't already exist, it is created from the application's
// model.
- (NSManagedObjectModel *)managedObjectModel
{
  if (_managedObjectModel != nil) {
      return _managedObjectModel
  }
  NSURL *modelURL = [[NSBundle mainBundle]                            //1
    URLForResource:@"Test_MDA_for_Bundles" withExtension:@"momd"];    //2
  _managedObjectModel = [[NSManagedObjectModel alloc]
    initWithContentsOfURL:modelURL];
  return _managedObjectModel;
}
```

1   The NSBundle class method mainBundle returns the primary bundle's URL. Most apps only have a main bundle.

2   Complete the construction of the bundle for the managed object model by providing the file name and the extension. By default, Xcode creates a file-name with the project's name that you have provided.

Once you have located a file from the bundle, you can use it, as shown here, or place it somewhere for future use. See the following section for guidance on how to do that.

Looking at Sandboxed Files

If you are a developer experienced with OS X, you are used to an environment that consists of standards and best practices so that your software fits into users' expectations of how apps, files, and their computer in general behave. Each user has an account (often there is a single account on a given Mac, but there can be many). Applications are normally placed in the Applications folder either at the root of the hard disk (/Macintosh HD/Applications in many cases) or within the user's home directory (~/Applications). There's a Library folder at the root of the hard disk that all users share, and there are separate Library folders in each user's home directory.

Beginning in OS X Lion (10.7) the ~/Library folder is hidden, but it's easy to get to it. In the Finder, hold down Option and open the Go menu—you'll see that Library is now enabled and you can open it. You'll find many standard folders in there that apps can create and use. Advanced users may use them, but they are always cautioned to make certain they know what they're doing.

Although the hidden user ~/Library folder is the most visible change, other changes on OS X have been implemented in recent versions to tighten security on the Mac. *Sandboxing* is one of the important tools in that effort. (In its most general form, sand-boxing provides an environment in which an app runs and outside of which the app has limited—if any—access.) On the first personal computers, security was not a major concern, but over the decades, as personal computers have moved into the mainstream, it has been necessary to retrofit security onto the major operating systems.

On iOS, this retrofitting was not necessary. Probably because the hardware was so much more powerful than the initial personal computers, as well as because security on a phone is obviously a major concern, even the initial security on iPhone OS (now iOS) was much tighter than on OS X.

Note

It's not surprising that people at Apple would be sensitive to security on a phone. In the 1960s and 1970s, self-styled "Phone Phreaks" created "blue boxes" to mimic the tones used for long distance dialing. With such boxes, people could make long distance telephone calls for free. (The telephone companies preferred to use the word "steal" in this context.) Among the phone phreaks who made blue boxes were Steve Jobs and Steve Wozniak, founders of Apple.

Setting Up Sandboxing

Sandboxing is optional on OS X but required on iOS where it is set up automatically. Here are the steps for setting up sandboxing on OS X:

1. In the General tab of your project, set up the type of signing and the team to use as a signer, as shown in Figure 12.7.

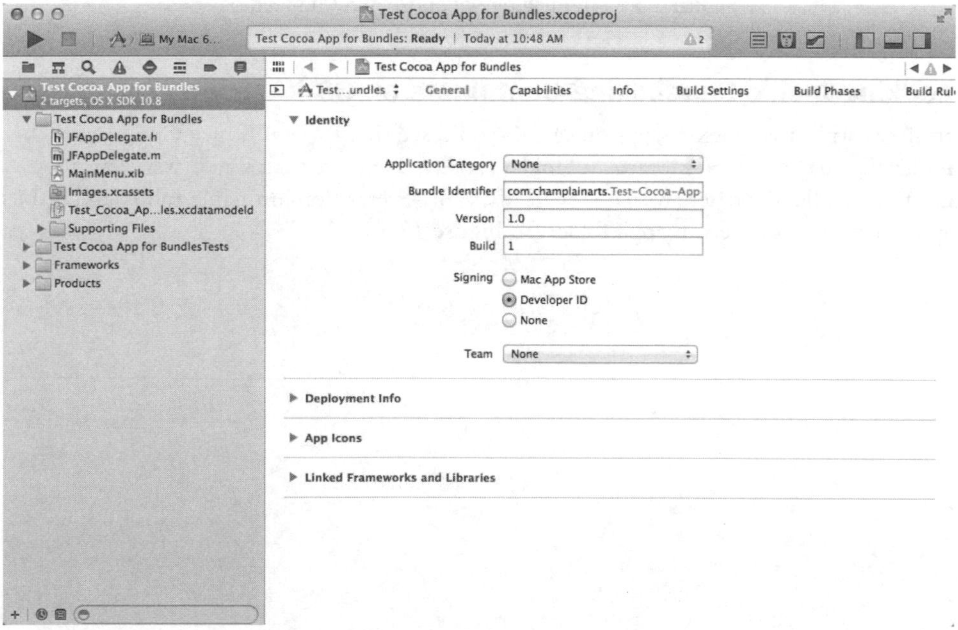

Figure 12.7   Choosing your signing identity

2. From the Capabilities tab, turn on sandboxing, as shown in Figure 12.8.

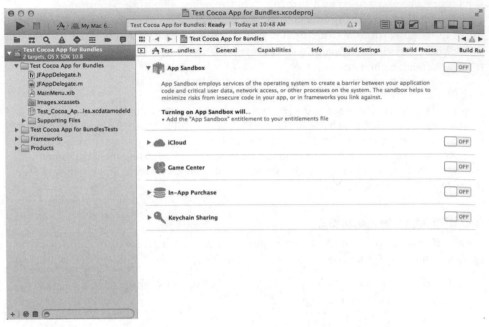

Figure 12.8   Turning on sandboxing in Capabilities

Looking Inside Sandboxing Containers on OS X

In the world of sandboxed apps on OS X, you'll see that there is now a Containers folder inside the user ~/Library. Subfolders are available for each sandboxed app: they use the bundle identifier, which is typically your reverse domain name followed by the app name. You can see an app's folders in Figure 12.9.

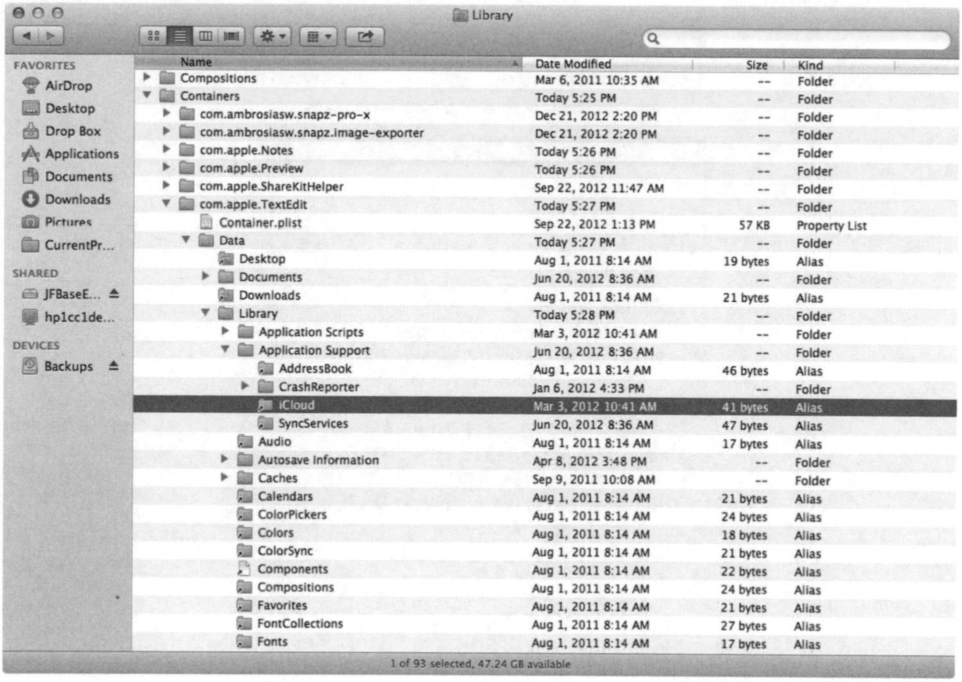

Figure 12.9   A Containers folder in the user ~/Library

Within each app's container, you have a Container.plist file and then a variety of other folders that are under your control. Many apps have a Data folder next to the plist file; all other folders are within it.

As you can see from the TextEdit container shown in Figure 12.9, there's a Library folder, which contains a number of folders that are similar to those that are contained in the ~/Library folder. In fact, if you examine some of the aliases shown in Figure 12.9, you'll see that some of these folders in fact point back to the main ~/Library folder, as shown in Figure 12.10.

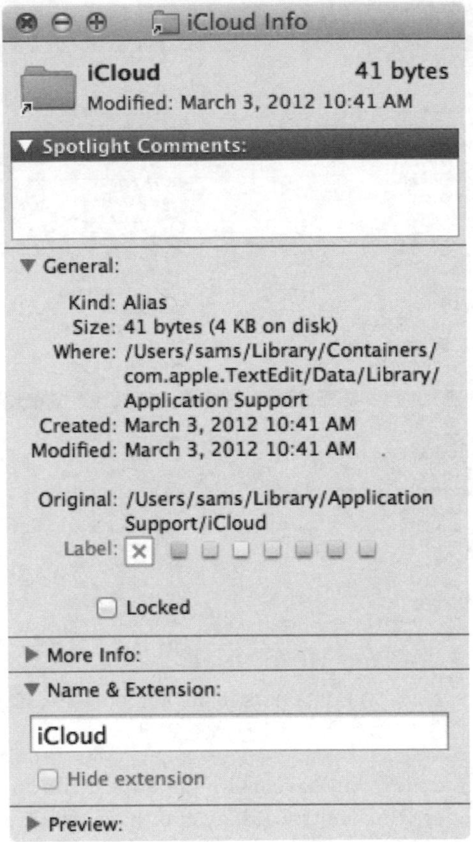

Figure 12.10   Aliases pointing back to ~/Library

If an app saves documents, it's usual to have a Documents folder. On iOS, the Documents folder is visible in iTunes if you have set the Application Supports iTunes File Sharing target property in the Info section (the info.plist) of your project.

Writing to Your Sandbox

On iOS or for sandboxed apps on OS X, you can use the `NSHomeDirectory (void)` function to return the path to the sandbox. For non-sandboxed apps on OS X, this function returns the user's directory as a string.

If you want the URL specifically for the user's document directory, you can use the following code:

```
[[[NSFileManager defaultManager] URLsForDirectory:NSDocumentDirectory
  inDomains:NSUserDomainMask] lastObject]
```

Including Property Lists

Now you have all the pieces so that you can put together a property list that's in your app with your runtime app. One of the most common tasks is to create a property list in your app and then, at runtime, read it into an NSDictionary.

Adding the Property List to Your App

Here are the steps for adding the Property List to your app:

1. Create the property list by using File, New, File.
2. As shown in Figure 12.11, choose the Resource section and then Property List.

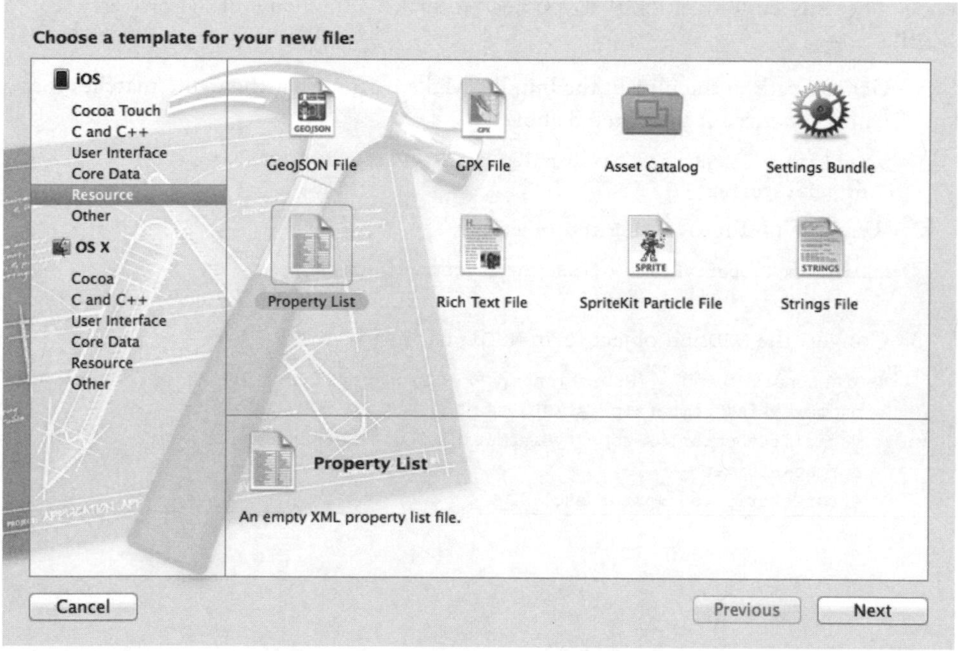

Figure 12.11   Creating a new property list file

3. Click Next and provide a title for the file.

4. Open it from the project navigator, as shown in Figure 12.12. You have the root of the property list; now you use the standard property list editing interface to add more keys and values, as described in "Using Property Lists" in Chapter 9.

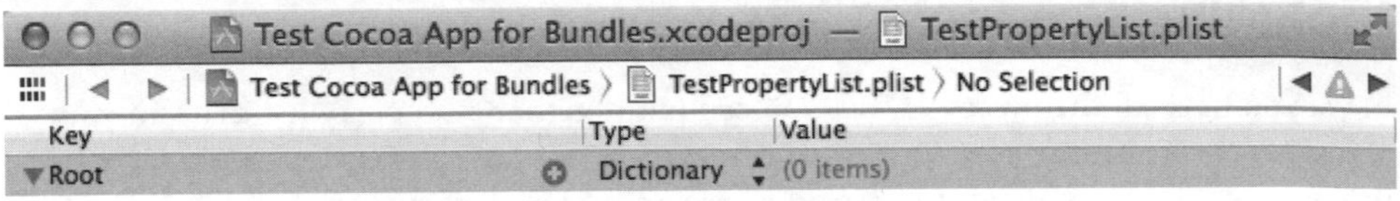

Figure 12.12   Adding your property list data

5. Confirm that it has been added to the bundle, as shown previously in Figure 12.4. If it hasn't been added, add it now.

Reading the Property List into an NSDictionary

Now you need to read the property list into an NSDictionary. This requires standard code. The only customization that you need to make is the name of the property list file.

1. Get the path to the plist in the bundle. Make certain that the name matches the name you saved it as in Step 3 above:

```
plistPath = [[NSBundle mainBundle] pathForResource:@"TestPropertyList"
  ofType:@"plist"];
```

2. Read the plist into an NSData object:

```
NSData *myPropertyList = [[NSFileManager defaultManager]
  contentsAtPath:plistPath];
```

3. Convert the NSData object to an NSDictionary:

```
NSDictionary *temp = (NSDictionary *)[NSPropertyListSerialization
  propertyListFromData:plistXML
  mutabilityOption:NSPropertyListMutableContainersAndLeaves
  format:&format
  errorDescription:&errorDesc];
```

Including a Core Data Store

You can use the same process used above to include a Core Data store with your app. (In fact, just about any file can be included.) The only difference is how you create the included file and where you put it. The Master-Detail Application template puts your compiled data model into the bundle. It will place it in a known location on disk, and if it's not there, it will create a new persistent store based on the data model, as shown in Listing 12.2. (Note that this process should not be used to seed a Core Data database in iCloud. Instead, you should seed the empty database with transactions that will then be synced through the cloud to other devices. This may be as simple as getting them out of a bundled database and then storing them in the new database. In some cases, using a JSON store turns out to be faster as the data source.)

Listing 12.2   **Building a Persistent Store from a Compiled Data Model**

```
- (NSPersistentStoreCoordinator *)persistentStoreCoordinator
{
  if (_persistentStoreCoordinator != nil) {                        //1
    return _persistentStoreCoordinator;
  }

  NSURL *storeURL = [[self applicationDocumentsDirectory]
    URLByAppendingPathComponent:@"Test_MDA_for_Bundles.sqlite"];   //2

  NSError *error = nil;
  _persistentStoreCoordinator = [[NSPersistentStoreCoordinator alloc]   //3
    initWithManagedObjectModel:[self managedObjectModel]];
  if (![_persistentStoreCoordinator
  addPersistentStoreWithType:NSSQLiteStoreType
    configuration:nil URL:storeURL options:nil error:&error]) {   //4

  NSLog(@"Unresolved error %@, %@", error, [error userInfo]);      //5
  abort();
  }

  return _persistentStoreCoordinator;
}
```

1   If you've already found a persistent store coordinator and set the property to it, just return it.

2   Construct the URL for the store. This is the only line you have to change. It's placed in the documents directory. You could place it in its own folder inside the sandbox.

3   Create a new persistent store coordinator using the managed object model in the app's bundle.

4   Add a new persistent store with the URL constructed in Step 2.

5   If an error occurs, provide a more meaningful message (and never use `abort()` in a shipping application except under very special circumstances). Always provide the user with information.

Chapter Summary

This chapter showed you how to package data into your apps. You learned how to add files to your Xcode project for graphics, interface strings, and data in a variety of the formats described in this part of the book. You have seen how to get the files into your app's bundle as well as how to remove them from the bundle and store them in a sandboxed area on disk if necessary.

Exercises

1. If you haven't done so already, test the process for turning the code signing and entitlements on as described in this chapter. Even if you have done this before, do it with Xcode 5 so that you are familiar with the new (and simpler!) way of handling this data.

2. Create a new project (or use the downloadable Test MDA for Bundles project) to experiment with plists and dictionaries as described in this chapter. It's such a common process that you should be comfortable with the conversions back and forth. Display the contents of the info.plist file in a view based on the dictionary that you create from the plist.

IV

Using iCloud
Documents and Data

13

Adding the iCloud Infrastructure

From here on, you'll be building various iCloud-enabled implementations of the Reports app that was mentioned previously. The common core of each of these implementations is the shared iCloud data that at various times will be stored on local devices or on iCloud. The implementations may run on OS X or on iOS. And if you think that you need a bit more complexity, the data will be stored using Core Data, or standard Cocoa and Cocoa Touch documents.

What this means is that you will do the same thing over and over in these various contexts and combinations. This chapter helps you set up the software that makes it possible. The software works for an app that is implemented on OS X as well as a corresponding app on iOS. If you want to build only one of those apps, it will also work: you'll just have an empty folder for the nonsupported operating system. Because it's almost as easy to build this infrastructure as it is to build a single-OS implementation, it is easier to start out this way so that you keep your deployment options open.

After you set up your Xcode project, you'll see how to implement an iOS app that uses iCloud to share a very basic document. The app is built around the "Third iOS App: iCloud" document from developer.apple.com. That document shows you how to build an iCloud-enabled iOS app. The app in this chapter borrows the basic document structure, but it reorganizes the project file structure to make it easier to expand the code so that it runs on both iPad and iPhone. In Chapter 16, "Working with OS X Documents," you'll see how to expand the code again so that it runs on both iOS devices and Macs.

Also in this chapter, you'll see how to implement basic iCloud functionality and how to debug iCloud projects using developer.icloud.com. developer.icloud.com is a critical component of your iCloud testing. You can now use the iOS simulator to test your iCloud code. But, as noted previously, to really test iCloud apps, you need to have multiple devices representing each operating system you want to support. That is true for testing of finished apps, but what can you do if you're just starting out? Do you have to buy lots of new Apple devices?

You can test iCloud with a single iCloud-equipped device. That device can communicate with iCloud, and as a registered developer, you can see your own iCloud container using developer.icloud.com. You can't test as many combinations and permutations of synchronization with a single device and developer.icloud.com as you can with multiple devices, but you can certainly get a feel for the process and complete some basic testing. This chapter focuses on iOS devices, but if you only have a Mac, you may want to jump ahead to Chapter 16 to implement your app and then use developer.icloud.com as described in this chapter to see what happens.

Exploring the Workspace for the App

By using a workspace, as described in Chapter 11, "Using Xcode Workspaces for Shared Development," you can set up an iOS target and an OS X target in the same project. There are many ways to do this, but the design described here is the easiest—at least for the author. What you will work toward is a structure of files and folders, as you see in Figure 13.1.

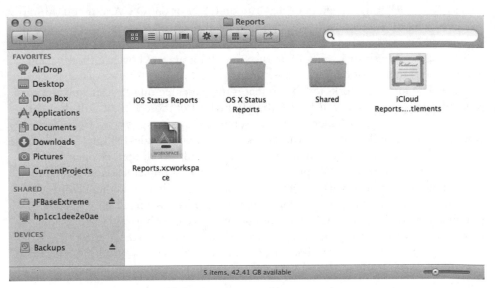

Figure 13.1   Creating a multitarget workspace

There are separate folders for the OS X and iOS projects. A third folder (Shared) contains files that are common to both projects. The workspace itself is placed at the top level of this folder, and the entitlements file, which needs to be part of both targets, is also at the top level of the project folder. (It could also be in the Shared folder.)

That is the structure toward which this chapter is moving. This chapter focuses on what will be the contents of the Shared folder. For simplicity's sake, it is developed here with a single project—iCloudReports—which is the iOS component.

When you open the workspace in Xcode, the project navigator shows you the files and groups at the left of the workspace window, as always, just as you see in Figure 13.2.

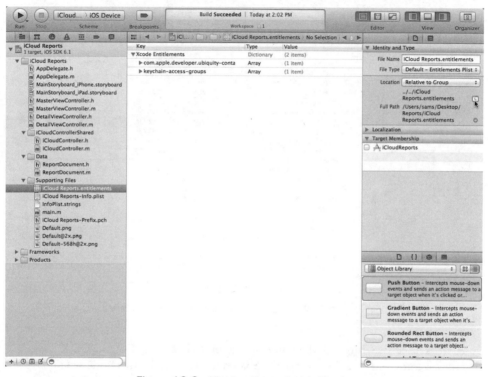

Figure 13.2   Viewing the project in Xcode

Figure 13.2 also shows how you can use the File inspector to check on a file's path or to modify it. Particularly if you are assembling a workspace like this using projects that have already been created, you may at some time need to update file paths (remember that files shown in red have no files associated with them).

When you add files to a project, you have the choice to copy them into the project if needed. One way to assemble a workspace such as the one shown here is to manually add the files to the appropriate folder (or to create a new project using File, New, Project and set the project location to be the appropriate folder). Once the files are in the right place, add the project to the workspace with the shortcut menu by using Add Files to Project. Just make certain not to use the Copy checkbox. If you do use it, you'll find that you've added a group of the added files in addition to the files themselves within the project. This will not necessarily cause problems, but it will annoy some developers.

Figure 13.3 shows the file and folder structure in the Finder. Compare it to the Xcode view shown in Figure 13.2.

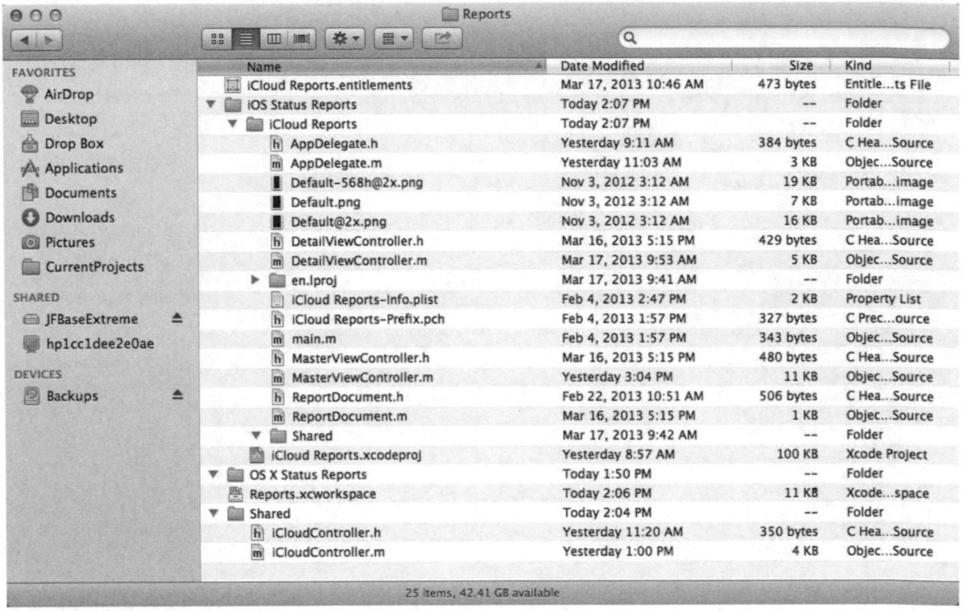

Figure 13.3   Viewing the workspace files in the Finder

A workspace structure like this can help you build both the iOS and OS X apps. The key is knowing what belongs in the Shared folder. Ideally, that code would be used without modifications in both the iOS and OS X versions. Although from time to time you may want to use conditional statements to branch for separate sections for each operating system, many developers feel that the shared code should be "pure" and free of such customizations. You can certainly put the iCloud infrastructure code there. In the case of Core Data, that's where your data model can be along with the code that will implement the Core Data stack.

Two areas to which you do have to pay attention are document and user interface differences in the two operating systems. They are discussed in the following sections.

Exploring iOS and OS X Document Architecture Differences

There are very different architectures for documents on the two operating systems. This means that you have to take care when sharing documents through iCloud. When you use non–document-based storage architectures such as key-value coding (KVC),

Core Data, or property lists, you don't have to worry about the differences between iOS and OS X except for the fact that certain features (telephony and removable storage, to name two) aren't available on both platforms.

Perhaps the most significant user interface difference is that documents are not visible to users through the iOS operating system in the way that users can see and manipulate documents in the Finder on OS X. As noted in Chapter 1, "Exploring iCloud and Its User Experience," iCloud uses apps to organize documents. From the user's point of view, it may mean reversing the steps to open a document. When you're in the iCloud world, you open an app, and then you open or create a document for that app. On OS X, you can go to the Finder to locate the document that you want to open. You select the document and choose Open from the File menu or double-click the icon, and the app will open. (Note that this is a simplification because you can use a shortcut menu to choose among various apps that could open a given document. This is only an overview of the process.)

What is significant is that on OS X the management of opening a document or of saving it is done using standard Cocoa tools. The Finder takes care of showing you the documents that could be opened.

On iOS, because you start by launching the app you want to use, each app is responsible for displaying the files it can open. Thus, managing an app's documents is the app's job rather than the job of the operating system.

Dealing with UI Differences

Although Cocoa and Cocoa Touch have common roots, there are important differences. Also, Cocoa Touch was developed years after Cocoa, so some changes that were difficult to implement on an incremental basis in Cocoa were added from the start in Cocoa Touch (sandboxing is one of these). Among the most important differences are those that stem from document management, as described in the previous section, as well as those that are related to the absence of a menu bar on iOS.

Even when the logic of the interface is the same on both iOS and OS X versions of an app, the mechanics often differ (posing an alert is a good example). Trying to make OS X and iOS versions of an app similar can make life easier for users than having to learn two different interfaces; however, in practice, users seem to prefer interfaces that look "right" for the device over those that look "wrong" on both types of devices.

Designing the Shared App Folder Structure

The challenge for a developer is to create an app structure that allows as much common code as possible but also provides easy implementation of device-specific code. That is the strategy used here. As you have seen, there are two separate projects in the workspace—one for iOS and one for OS X. On disk, each project's files are in a separate Finder folder. A Shared folder contains the files that are shared: these files are added to both of the projects in a Shared group for each of the projects. Although groups in Xcode use folders as icons, remember that they are not Finder folders.

As long as you keep in mind that the shared files exist in a single place on disk (the Shared folder) while they appear in two places in the workspace (the Shared groups in both projects), all will be well. Because these are shared files, editing them from either project edits them in the other.

One prime candidate for the Shared folder will be everything that has to do with iCloud itself. You will share a ubiquity container between the OS X app and the iOS app, so it makes sense to share the code that manipulates it. Unfortunately, that is easier said than done. Apple has an excellent tutorial, "Your Third iOS App: iCloud," that introduces you to iCloud. That app is a great starting point, but it runs only on iPhone. The app shown in this chapter runs on both iPhone and iPad. Furthermore, it is factored so that the common iCloud code can be placed in the Shared folder, while the OS-specific code (mostly UI interactions) is placed in the relevant projects. In addition, the structure of the Shared folder is set up with an eye to expanding the app to OS X, which you'll do in Chapter 16.

Checking Out the End Result

The app in this chapter is built on the Master-Detail Application template for iOS. By the end of the chapter, you'll be able to create documents on an iPhone, as shown in Figure 13.4.

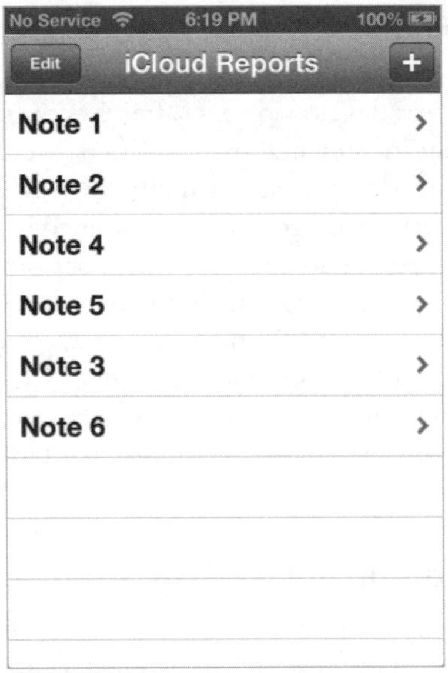

Figure 13.4   Creating and selecting documents on iPhone

You'll also be able to run the same app on an iPad, as shown in Figure 13.5.

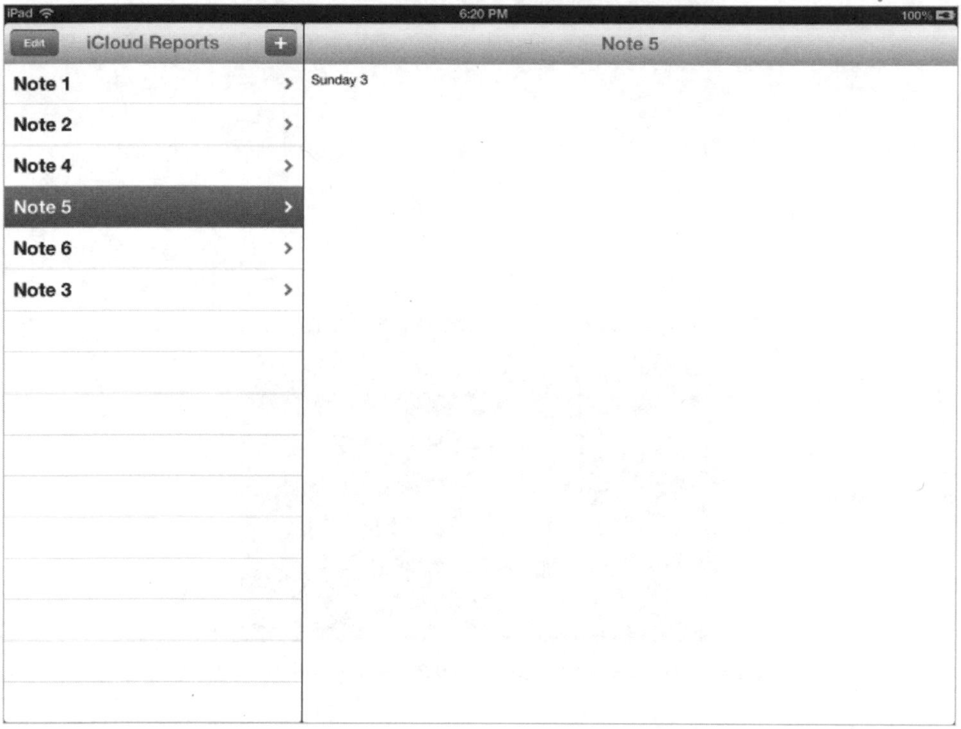

Figure 13.5   Running the app on iPad

One of the biggest differences has to do with the split view controller on iPad: there is no comparable feature on iPhone. Thus, as you see in Figure 13.5, you can see the list of documents as well as the content of the selected document at the same time. On iPhone, a navigation interface lets you move from the list (the master view controller) to a detail controller, as you see in Figure 13.6.

Figure 13.6   The iPhone version uses a navigation interface

Scoping the Project

This chapter's app is not complete: it is designed to get you started with an app that uses iCloud across multiple iOS devices. You'll add OS X functionality in Chapter 16.

Furthermore, it uses the same simplification that is used in "Your Third iOS App: iCloud." It writes the document data directly to iCloud. For a real project, you would probably write to a local directory and then move that local data to iCloud using one of the techniques described in the following chapters. That strategy allows for sharing (through iCloud) as well as continued operation if iCloud is not available.

Managing local and iCloud copies of data is an important part of iCloud development, but it does add a complicating factor, which you don't need at this point. You will see how to help users manage conflicts in versions of their data, but that is one of the areas where the differing document structures in OS X and iOS come into play. That is why that discussion is deferred to Chapters 15 and 16.

Behind the scenes in this project, the document data is stored in a UIDocument in the most minimal form possible—a text string.

Debugging iCloud Apps with developer.icloud.com

When you talk about debugging an app on a Mac or an iOS device, you usually talk about running it to make certain it does what you want it to do (and doesn't do what you don't want it to do.) That's very simple, but when you're working with iCloud, you have some additional challenges. Specifically, how do you see what the app is doing when what it is doing is happening in iCloud?

You can examine your iCloud storage using developer.icloud.com if you are a registered developer. Log in with your developer ID, and you'll see your iCloud storage with its Documents folder, as shown in Figure 13.7. There may be some additional folders, but for now Documents is what you are interested in.

Figure 13.7   Viewing your iCloud storage

Open the Documents folder shown in Figure 13.7, and, as you see in Figure 13.8, each of the apps that you use in iCloud has its own folder.

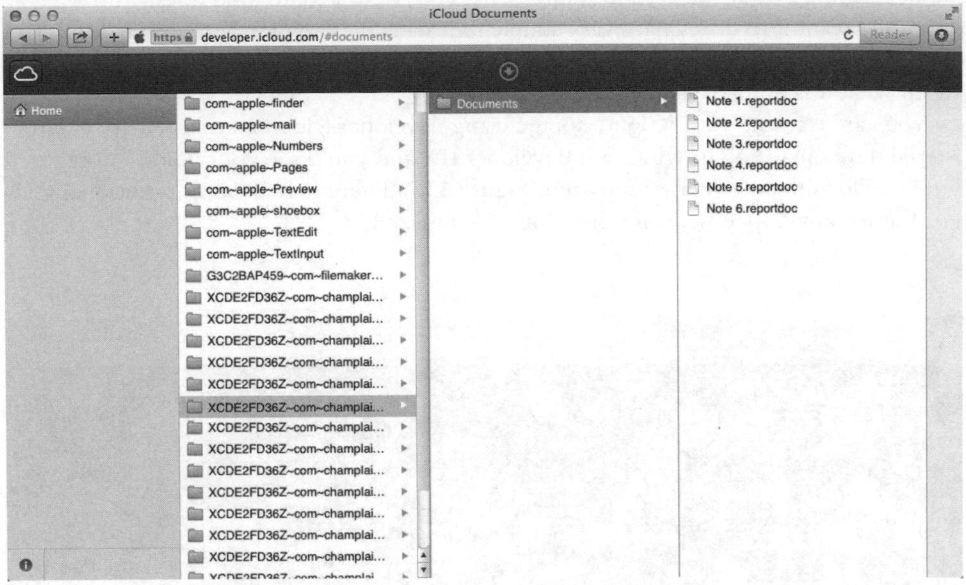

Figure 13.8   Each app has its own iCloud folder

Within the folder for the app that will be developed in this chapter, you can see all of its documents. Compare Figure 13.8 with Figures 13.4 and 13.5 shown previously.

Just as in the Finder, you can select a document and see its size and modification date. Also note that you can use the button at the right of Figure 13.9 or the down-pointing arrow at the top to download a file from iCloud. This lets you open the file on your Mac to check its contents.

Note that these are debugging tools only accessible by a registered developer. Users can't see their iCloud data in this way.

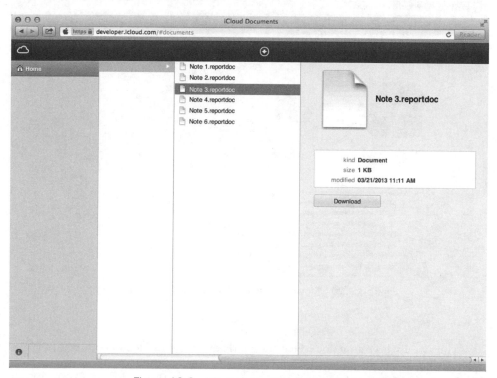

Figure 13.9   Viewing your iCloud documents

As you can see in Figure 13.10, files outside of the Documents folder may or may not be visible to users (it's your choice). You can use the Home button, as shown in Figure 13.10, to move outside the Documents folder to see files and folders you have created inside the app's ubiquity container.

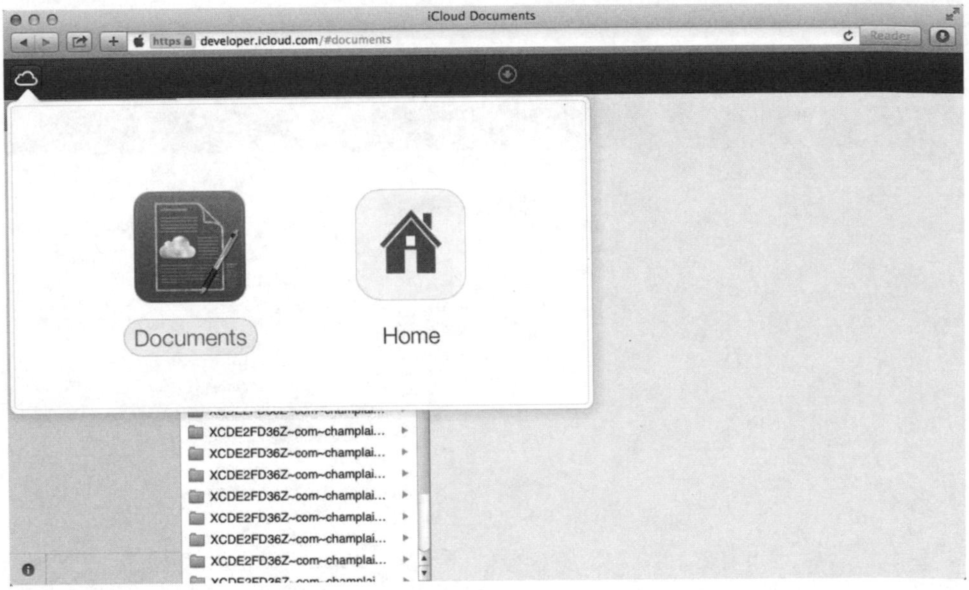

Figure 13.10   Moving outside the iCloud Documents folder

If you already have an iCloud–enabled app that works with documents, you can open developer.icloud.com to see those documents. One of the most important things to learn about iCloud is that it is an asynchronous process. If you have one of the iWork apps, here is an important experiment to conduct:

1. Open developer.icloud.com for your developer ID.

2. Go to the apps list, as shown in Figure 13.8.

3. Run an iWork app and create a new document.

4. Save it to iCloud, as shown in Figure 13.11.

5. Watch to see the document appear in iCloud.

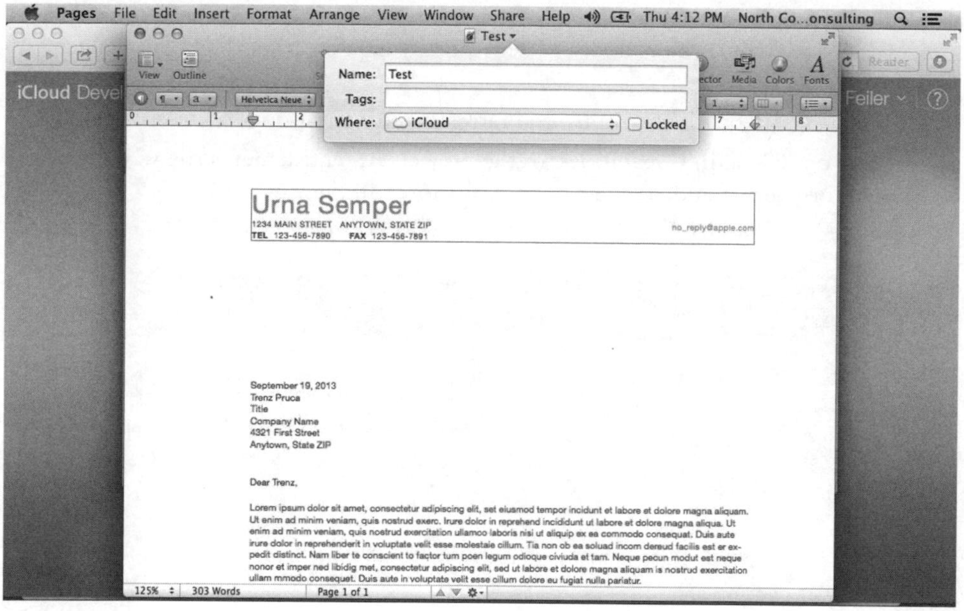

Figure 13.11   Saving an iWork app to iCloud

If this is the first document you've saved in iCloud from this app, the app will be added to the list of apps shown previously in Figure 13.8. Repeat this process periodically to see how the time varies for iCloud updates. Because there is a local copy of your iWork document, it doesn't matter that the upload isn't simultaneous because you can continue working.

Building the App

Before you start to build the app, go to developer.apple.com and create an App ID for iCloud Reports for development on iOS. (Yes, you can build the App ID before you start coding the app.)

Now it's time to build the app. Here are some steps to get started. Because of the shared folder, you may have to do a bit of rearranging, but once it's done, things will be easier to work with.

1. Create a new workspace (see Chapter 11, "Using Xcode Workspaces for Shared Development").

2. Create a new project based on the Master-Detail Application template called iCloud Reports.

3. If you want to use the Shared folder structure described previously, create that folder inside the project folder. (Remember, you're creating the Shared folder using the Finder.)

4. Make certain that it has a universal interface and that it does not use Core Data.

5. Turn on iCloud in Capabilities for the project. An entitlements file will be created for you and added to the project, as shown in Figure 13.12.

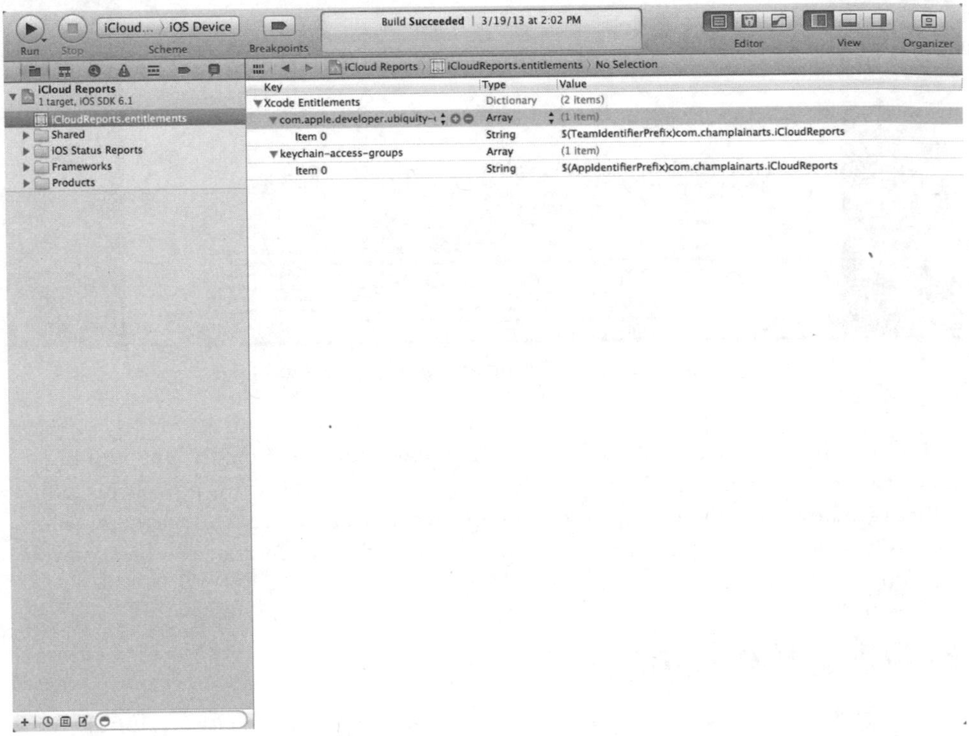

Figure 13.12   Using an entitlements file

6. Depending on your project, you may also want to use iCloud and Key-Value Store.

7. Accept the default ubiquity container.

If you want to look inside the entitlements file, you'll see what Xcode has done for you, as shown in Figure 13.12. There is nothing for you to do, but you might want to see what has been set up.

You will be adding and modifying code in the template classes. The changes are discussed in the following sections.

Creating the Shared Folder

The Shared folder is a good place to start coding with Xcode because it is not dependent on any of the other classes, although other classes are dependent on it. (Notifications make this possible.) There will be two classes in the Shared folder:

- Constants is a convenience class.
- SharediCloudController is just what its name says: it provides iCloud support for both of your projects.

Constants.h

Constants.h is a class containing constants for the project. There are many ways to provide constants across the project. The simplest is an ordinary `#define`. Creating a class is a little more work (but not much), and it can provide some improvements in turnaround time when developing a large project. Once you have declared a constant in the .h file, if you change its value in the .m file, that may require fewer other classes to be recompiled.

You can see the structure of the header in Listing 13.1.

Listing 13.1   **Constants.h**

```
//
//  Constants.h
//  OS X iCloud Reports
//
//  Created by Jesse Feiler on 3/17/13.
//  Copyright (c) 2013 Champlain Arts Corp. All rights reserved.
//

extern NSString *const SharediCloudControllerDidChangeDataNotification;

extern NSString *const SharedReportFileExtension;
extern NSString *const DocumentsDirectoryName;

extern NSString *const DisplayDetailSegue;
extern NSString *const ReportEntryCell;
extern NSString *const KeyForCurrentUbiquityToken;
```

Constants.m

The .m file is shown in Listing 13.2. At this point, you may want to simply create the files (using File, New File and the Objective-C template); you can add the constants as you need them (when their names will make more sense).

Listing 13.2   **Constants.m**

```
//
//  Constants.h
//  OS X iCloud Reports
//
//  Created by Jesse Feiler on 3/17/13.
//  Copyright (c) 2013 Champlain Arts Corp. All rights reserved.
//

#import "Constants.h"

NSString *const SharediCloudControllerDidChangeDataNotification =
  @"iCloudDataChanged";

NSString *const SharedReportFileExtension = @"reportdoc";
NSString *const DocumentsDirectoryName = @"Documents";

NSString *const DisplayDetailSegue = @"DisplayDetailSegue";
NSString *const ReportEntryCell = @"ReportEntryCell";

NSString *const KeyForCurrentUbiquityToken =
  @"com.champlainarts.iCloud.UbiquityIdentityToken";
```

SharediCloudController.h

SharediCloudController.h is the key to the Shared folder: as its name implies, it is a shared iCloud controller (in the sense of model-view-controller). If you compare the code in this section and the following one with "Your Third iOS App: iCloud," you'll notice the code is similar in many places, but it is reorganized so that it can be more easily shared. For example, user interaction is managed by the classes in the iOS project (and, later on, the OS X project). This means that you can't test for a condition and report back immediately. You have to be asked to return a value and then the calling class can report.

One of the consequences of this type of structure that is very common in Cocoa is that you often do not execute code sequentially. iCloud relies heavily on threading to manage its processing. As soon as there are multiple threads, you can't just execute the next line of code, because you can't really tell what the next line of code will be. Thus, you post a notification and another part of your code responds to it. If you aren't familiar with notifications, you will be by the end of the book. Rest assured that one of the reasons they work and are used so extensively is that they really are simple, as you'll see.

Listing 13.3 shows the SharediCloudController.h file. Perhaps the most important thing to take away from the interface is that the controller manages the list of documents stored in iCloud. As noted previously, this is needed only on iOS, but because the shared iCloud controller will be used to manage all iCloud data, it does so here as well.

Listing 13.3   **SharediCloudController.h**

```
//
//  SharediCloudController.h
//  OS X iCloud Reports
//
//  Created by Jesse Feiler on 3/17/13.
//  Copyright (c) 2013 Champlain Arts Corp. All rights reserved.
//

#import <Foundation/Foundation.h>

@interface SharediCloudController : NSObject

- (NSInteger)numberOfDocuments;                             //1
- (NSString*)stringForDocumentNameAt: (NSInteger)index;     //2
- (id)documentURLAt: (NSInteger)index;                      //3


- (NSString *)newUntitledDocumentName;                      //4
- (void)addDocumentURL: (NSURL *)newDocumentURL;            //5
- (void)deleteDocument: (NSURL *)deleteDocumentURL;         //6


- (void)checkOnQuery;                                       //7


- (void)manageiCloudIdentityChange;                         //8
- (void)deleteDocumentsFromUI;                              //9


@end
```

1   Although documents are managed by the controller, certain aspects of them are exposed in the controller's interface. The number of documents is one such aspect.

2   Once documents are loaded, they can be identified by number (this number can change over time). This lets you get the name of the *n*th document. You'll see why it needs to be exposed in Listing 13.4.

3   You can get the URL for the *n*th document.

4   When creating a new document, you need to give it a name that, by default, includes a number (as in Document 2, Document 3).

5   When a document is created, you can add its URL to the documents list even though you can't see the list.

6   You need to be able to delete a document as well as add it.

   7   checkOnQuery is a debugging method. Particularly when you're dealing
        with asynchronous processing, you can't step through code with a break-
        point, so it sometimes helps to put in a debugging method in which you
        can place a breakpoint.

   8, 9   These methods will be used to respond to a notification or the app enter-
        ing or leaving the active state.

SharediCloudController.m

As you can see in Figure 13.13, the methods in this file are separated into five sections
as well as a class extension at the top of the file.

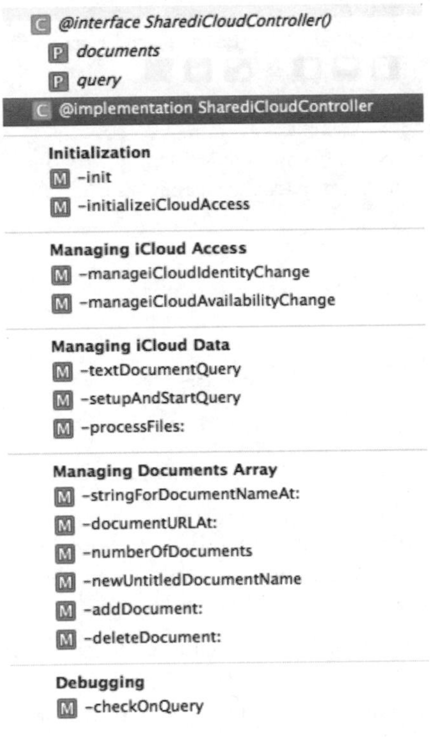

Figure 13.13   SharediCloudController.m has five sections.

The sections of code are:

- **Initialization:** This is standard initialization for any class along with starting iCloud access. You will probably reuse this code pretty much as-is in other

projects. The customization that you will need is done in the Xcode Capabilities tab when you specify the entitlements file and the ubiquity container.

- **Managing iCloud Access:** This is the code that manages access to iCloud, changes to iCloud availability, and changes to the iCloud account. It, too, is fairly generic.

- **Managing iCloud Data:** This code also is fairly generic. You search your iCloud container for the data you're interested in using a query that observes changes. Reusing this code generally requires specifying the objects you're looking for in your container. When they're found, they are added to a local array (documents).

- **Managing Documents Array:** This is pretty much specific to your app as you add and remove items to and from the array.

- **Debugging:** This is a debugging method that is placed in its own section to help you debug the multithreaded code.

Listing 13.4 shows the initialization section. initializeiCloudAccess is the key component here. It makes the connection to iCloud from your app. Because that can take some time, it is critical that you do not call it from your main thread where it could block your app's processing. In this code, messages are written out to the log about iCloud status. You'll see in Chapters 15 and 16 how to create more user-friendly messages.

Following the block, you see the registration for NSUbiquityIdentityDidChange-Notification, which lets you know that the iCloud account has changed (possibly to no account if the user has signed out). In addition, you need to keep track of when the app enters and leaves the active state. There are stub methods in AppDelegate.m that you can use to capture this information. In this section, you will see the methods of the shared iCloud controller that are used to react to those changes.

The reason for tracking the active status of the app is to be able to handle what is a rare but critical occurrence. If the user is running with one iCloud account (call it A), it's easy to log out of account A and log in to account B. On an iOS device, you do that by switching to Settings and making the change. When the user switches to Settings, by definition your app becomes inactive. By tracking the active status of the app in the app delegate, you can capture that account change when the app becomes active again.

Many users do not change their iCloud accounts at all, but you as a developer are likely to change iCloud accounts fairly frequently during testing, so you definitely need this code to function properly. The strategy employed here is very simple: when the app becomes inactive, the list of iCloud documents is emptied, and when it becomes active, it is reloaded with whatever iCloud account is in use at that moment. Depending on your app, you may have other strategies you can use, but you have to prepare for account changes that may happen out of your view.

Listing 13.4 **Class Extension and Initialization**

```objc
//
//  SharediCloudController.m
//  OS X iCloud Reports
//
//  Created by Jesse Feiler on 3/17/13.
//  Copyright (c) 2013 Champlain Arts Corp. All rights reserved.
//

#import "SharediCloudController.h"
#import "Constants.h"

@interface SharediCloudController ()                              //1
  @property NSMutableArray *documents;
  @property NSMetadataQuery *query;
@end

@implementation SharediCloudController

#pragma mark - initialization

-(id)init {
  if ( self = [super init] ) {
    [self initializeiCloudAccess];                                //2

    if (!_documents)
      _documents = [[NSMutableArray alloc] init];                 //3

    [self setupAndStartQuery];
  }
  return self;
}

- (void)initializeiCloudAccess {                                  //4
  dispatch_async (dispatch_get_global_queue
    (DISPATCH_QUEUE_PRIORITY_DEFAULT, 0),
    ^{
      if ([[NSFileManager defaultManager]
        URLForUbiquityContainerIdentifier:nil] != nil)
        NSLog (@"Got iCloud with URLForUbiquityContainerIdentifier %@ \n",
          [[NSFileManager defaultManager]
            URLForUbiquityContainerIdentifier:nil]);
      else
        NSLog (@"No iCloud");
    });
```

```
[[NSNotificationCenter defaultCenter]                                    //5
  addObserver:self
    selector:@selector (manageiCloudIdentityChange)
       name:NSUbiquityIdentityDidChangeNotification
      object:nil];

[self manageiCloudIdentityChange];
}
```

1   The class extension declares two properties. The use of class extensions in this
    way is a fairly recent development. Declaring properties instead of instance
    variables is even more recent. As in the interface, the property declaration
    causes the backing variable to be created (the property name is prefixed by an
    underscore). You can access the backing variable directly with its name or by
    using dot syntax as with any property.

2   The app delegate creates an instance of `SharediCloudController` if
    necessary when a client asks for it (the code is shown later in this chap-
    ter in the AppDelegate.m section). The first request for it comes from
    `MasterViewController` in the `initWithCoder:` method. Thus, the
    instance of `SharedCloudController` is created at the beginning of the
    app's processing.

3   Create `_documents` if necessary. It remains present even if all entries are
    removed from it (as when the iCloud account changes).

4   This is the connection to iCloud and your ubiquity container. This code can
    generally be used as-is without further customization. By passing in nil for
    `URLForUbiquityContainerIdentifier`, you cause Cocoa to pick the first
    ubiquity table from the `com.apple.developer.ubiquity-container-`
    `identifiers` array. That is set automatically when you set up your ubiquity
    container in your project (see Figure 13.10).

5   Register for `NSUbiquityIdentityDidChangeNotification` and call
    `manageiCloudIdentityChange` to get started.

Managing iCloud Access

As part of the initialization of the shared iCloud controller, it registers for notification
of changes in the iCloud account, as you saw in Listing 13.4. Listing 13.5 shows the
code that handles such notifications.

This is standard code that you can reuse. It relies on obtaining the iCloud token
and storing it in `NSUserDefaults`. The first step is to get the previous token out of
defaults, and then you obtain the new token. (Remember that, unlike the code in
Listing 13.4 that gets the ubiquity container URL, you can get the token on the main
thread because it's a very fast operation.

The heart of the method is a nested `if` statement that results in the following actions depending on the values and existence of the current and previous tokens:

- **No current token:** Remove previous token so that there is now no token for the `KeyForCurrentUbiquityToken` key in user defaults. If you support non-iCloud processing, you should capture changes so they can be uploaded at a later time.

- **Current token that doesn't match previous token:** Update the user interface and the _documents array with current token's iCloud data. This is done with `setupAndStartQuery`, shown later in Listing 13.6.

- **Current token does match previous token:** This means the user is continuing with the same account. This case is also handled in `setupAndStartQuery`.

Listing 13.5 **Responding to a Change in iCloud Identity**

```
- (void)manageiCloudIdentityChange {
  id previousiCloudToken = [NSKeyedUnarchiver
    unarchiveObjectWithData:[[NSUserDefaults standardUserDefaults]
            objectForKey:KeyForCurrentUbiquityToken]];
  id currentiCloudToken = [[NSFileManager defaultManager]
    ubiquityIdentityToken];
  BOOL sameAccount  = [previousiCloudToken isEqual: currentiCloudToken];
  NSLog (@" %hhd %@ %@", sameAccount, previousiCloudToken,
    currentiCloudToken);
  if (currentiCloudToken) {
    if (!sameAccount) {
      NSData *newTokenData = [NSKeyedArchiver
        archivedDataWithRootObject: currentiCloudToken];
      [[NSUserDefaults standardUserDefaults]
        setObject: newTokenData
          forKey: KeyForCurrentUbiquityToken];
    }
    [self setupAndStartQuery];                         //6
  } else {
    [[NSUserDefaults standardUserDefaults]
      removeObjectForKey: KeyForCurrentUbiquityToken];
    [self deleteDocumentsFromUI];
  }
}
```

6 This method finds iCloud documents and updates the interface. See List-ing 13.6 for the code.

Managing iCloud Data

The documents array in this app contains the names of all the documents in the ubiquity container. Those names are NSURL object instances. Given the NSURL, you can then open a specific document and retrieve its data (the data is an NSString for simplicity's sake in this case).

The process of managing iCloud data consists of three related methods that are shown in Listing 13.6. They use the NSMetaDataQuery class that was introduced in OS X Tiger (10.4) as part of Spotlight in 2005. You create the query in one method. You then start the query in another method and register to be notified of its status—either a batch of updates or completion. The third method fires when one of the notifications—updates or completion—is triggered. This structure is common when you are managing iCloud data.

You can see the evolution of NSMetaDataQuery in the constants you use to set the scope of the query. Here are the five current constants; the last two were added recently to support iCloud. They refer to the Documents folder in the app's container or to all files outside the Documents folder:

```
NSString *const NSMetadataQueryUserHomeScope;
NSString *const NSMetadataQueryLocalComputerScope;
NSString *const NSMetadataQueryNetworkScope;
NSString *const NSMetadataQueryUbiquitousDocumentsScope;
NSString *const NSMetadataQueryUbiquitousDataScope;
```

You start the query from the main thread, and it continues processing until you stop it (by default it checks once a second). Queries like this are called *live queries*. You can also run *static queries*, which run the query and then finish. When the iCloud account changes (either to another account or by turning off iCloud), the query is set to nil. It will be recreated as needed with the new account. Both for your own testing as well as for user support, it's important to note that Airplane mode will leave the existing iCloud account in place but simply turn off the radio. You can simplify your testing as well as users' experiences with your app if you remind yourself and them that signing out of iCloud isn't necessary to turn off the radio.

Listing 13.6   Managing iCloud Data with NSMetaDataQuery

```
#pragma mark - managing iCloud data

-(NSMetadataQuery *)textDocumentQuery {
  NSMetadataQuery *aQuery = [[NSMetadataQuery alloc] init];
  if (aQuery) {
    // search
    [aQuery setSearchScopes: [NSArray arrayWithObject:
      NSMetadataQueryUbiquitousDocumentsScope]];                    //7
```

```
      // add predicate
      NSString * filePattern = [NSString stringWithFormat:@"*.%@",
        SharedReportFileExtension];                                      //8
      [aQuery setPredicate: [NSPredicate predicateWithFormat: @"%K LIKE %@",
        NSMetadataItemFSNameKey, filePattern]];
    }
    return aQuery;
}


- (void)setupAndStartQuery {
    // create if needed
    if (!_query)
      _query = [self textDocumentQuery];                                 //9


    // register for query notifications
    [[NSNotificationCenter defaultCenter] addObserver:self selector:@selector
      (processFiles:) name:NSMetadataQueryDidFinishGatheringNotification
      object:nil];                                                       //10
    [[NSNotificationCenter defaultCenter] addObserver:self selector:@selector
      (processFiles:) name:NSMetadataQueryDidUpdateNotification
      object:nil];                                                       //11


    // start the query
    [_query startQuery];                                                 //12


}

-(void)processFiles: (NSNotification*)aNotification {
    NSMutableArray *discoveredFiles = [NSMutableArray array];

    // disable updates
    [_query disableUpdates];                                             //13


    NSArray *queryResults = [_query results];                            //14

    for (NSMetadataItem *result in queryResults) {
      NSURL *fileURL = [result valueForAttribute: NSMetadataItemURLKey];
      NSNumber *aBool = nil;

      // don't include hidden files
      [fileURL getResourceValue: &aBool forKey:NSURLIsHiddenKey
      error:nil];                                                        //15
      if (aBool && ![aBool boolValue])
        [discoveredFiles addObject: fileURL];
    }
```

```
// update list
[_documents removeAllObjects];                                          //16
[_documents addObjectsFromArray: discoveredFiles];

//reenable updates
[_query enableUpdates];                                                 //17

[[NSNotificationCenter defaultCenter]
    postNotificationName: SharediCloudControllerDidChangeDataNotification
    object:nil userInfo:nil];                                          //18

}
```

7   Create the query and set the search scope. Take care with Xcode code completion: NSMetadataQueryUbiquitousDocumentsScope can easily be completed as NSMetadataQueryUbiquitousDataScope or something like that if you're not careful.

8   Create a string to use in the predicate to search for all files with the Shared-ReportFileExtension constant. If you haven't added it to Constants.h and Constants.m, do so now. Its value in this example is reportdoc and set the predicate for the query. If you follow this structure, you customize the file extension in line 7 and then use this line of code without modification.

9   If needed, create the query using the textDocumentQuery method.

10 Observe NSMetadataQueryDidFinishGatheringNotification with a selector for the processFiles method (which follows).

11 Similarly, observe NSMetadataQueryDidUpdateNotification with the processFiles method.

12 Start the query.

13 When processFiles is run as a result of a notification, you must disable updates to the query until processFiles is complete. At that point, you enable updates. (See line 17.)

14 Load query results into a local array so you can iterate through it.

15 For each file, check to see if it should be hidden. In getResourceValue:forKey:error, note that &aBool will return the key value for you to check. If it is not hidden, add it to another local array, discoveredFiles.

16 Replace _documents with discoveredFiles. Note that this process simply replaces all the objects. This means that you don't have to worry about deletes—you just take what the query has discovered and use it going forward.

17   Enable updates. (See line 13.)

18   Post a notification that you have found updates using `SharediCloud-`
`ControllerDidChangeDataNotification`. If you haven't yet declared it
in Constants, add it now.

As you can see in Listing 13.6, the query is created and started as necessary when
the iCloud account changes (see Listing 13.5). It's important that it be created properly after an account change, and the easiest way to do that is to set it to nil when the
account logs out. This is handled at the end of the `if` statement in Listing 13.5. If there
has been a change to the account—either by logging out of iCloud or choosing a new
account—the method shown in Listing 13.7 is called to update the UI. It sets the query
to nil and empties the documents array, which will be refilled the next time a query is
created and run. More details on this process are found later in this chapter in the discussion of the master view controller.

Listing 13.7   **Turning Off the Query**

```
- (void)deleteDocumentsFromUI {
  _query = nil;

  [_documents removeAllObjects];                                      //19
  [[NSNotificationCenter defaultCenter]
    postNotificationName: SharediCloudControllerDidChangeDataNotification
    object:nil userInfo:nil];
}
```

19   Empty _documents and post a notification to update the interface.

Managing the Documents Array

At this point, you have discovered the objects in the ubiquity container. The methods
shown in Listing 13.8 let you manage them. There is no iCloud-specific code in this
section, so the methods are not annotated because you have probably seen this code
(or code much like it) many times. Remember that _documents is an array of the
NSURL objects representing the actual documents.

Listing 13.8   **Managing the Documents Array with Names and URLs**

```
#pragma mark - managing documents array

-(NSString*)stringForDocumentNameAt: (NSInteger)index {              //20
  if ([_documents count] > 0)
    {
    NSURL *theURL = [_documents objectAtIndex: index];
    NSLog (@" %@", theURL);
```

```
    return [[theURL lastPathComponent] stringByDeletingPathExtension];
    }
  return nil;
}


-(NSURL *)documentURLAt: (NSInteger)index {                              //21
  //NSLog (@" %ld", (long)index);
  if ([_documents count] > 0)
    {
    NSURL *theURL = [_documents objectAtIndex: index];
    //NSLog (@" %@", theURL);
    return theURL;
    }
  return nil;
}


- (NSInteger)numberOfDocuments {                                        //22
  return [_documents count];
}


- (NSString *)newUntitledDocumentName {                                 //23
    NSInteger docCount = 1;
    NSString *newDocName = nil;

  newDocName = @"new doc";
  BOOL done = NO;
  while (!done) {
    newDocName = [NSString stringWithFormat: @"Note %d.%@", docCount,
      SharedReportFileExtension];
    // check for dups
    BOOL nameExists = NO;
    for (NSURL *aURL in _documents) {
      if ([[aURL lastPathComponent] isEqualToString: newDocName]) {
        docCount ++;
        nameExists = YES;
        break;
      }
    }

    // if not found, exit WHILE
    if (!nameExists)
      done = YES;
  }
  return newDocName;
}
```

```
- (void)addDocumentURL: (NSURL *)newDocumentURL {              //24
    [_documents addObject: newDocumentURL];
}
- (void)deleteDocument: (NSURL *)deleteDocumentURL  {

    dispatch_async (dispatch_get_global_queue
        (DISPATCH_QUEUE_PRIORITY_DEFAULT, 0), ^{              //25
        NSFileCoordinator *fc = [[NSFileCoordinator alloc]
            initWithFilePresenter:nil];
        [fc coordinateWritingItemAtURL:deleteDocumentURL
            options:NSFileCoordinatorWritingForDeleting error:nil
            byAccessor:^(NSURL *newURL) {
            NSFileManager *fm = [[NSFileManager alloc] init];
            [fm removeItemAtURL: newURL error:nil];
        }];
    });

    [_documents removeObject: deleteDocumentURL];              //26

}

#pragma mark - debugging

- (void)checkOnQuery {                                        //27
    if (_query) {
        NSLog (@" %lu", (unsigned long)[_query resultCount]);
        NSLog (@" %lu", (unsigned long)[_query isStarted]);
        NSLog (@" %lu", (unsigned long)[_query isGathering]);
        NSLog (@" %lu", (unsigned long)[_query isStopped]);
        [_query startQuery];
    }
```

20   Get a document name.

21   Get a document URL.

22   Get the number of documents.

23   Get a unique name for a new document.

24   Add a new document to the array. Note that this only happens when you create a new document. If someone else creates a new document in iCloud, you get it in processFiles the next time it runs.

25   Switch off the main queue for the file handling steps to actually delete the document.

26   Delete the document from the _documents array.

27   This is only for debugging. You can comment it out or delete it. You can invoke it as the last line in `processFiles`. Set a breakpoint on the first line of this method if you want to track your query's progress.

The shared iCloud controller is the major piece of code you need for this app. The sections that follow show how you'll use it.

Creating the App's Classes

There are three basic classes in the Master-Detail Application:

- `AppDelegate`
- `MasterViewController`
- `DetailViewController`

Along with the storyboards, they are discussed in this section. The emphasis throughout is on the iCloud features rather than the basic Objective-C and the Master-Detail Application template.

`AppDelegate`

There's not much to do with the `AppDelegate` class. You need to instantiate a `SharediCloudController` instance and assign it to a property in the app delegate.

AppDelegate.h

You need a forward reference to the `SharedCloudController` class, and you need to declare a property for the instance you use in the app. The top of AppDelegate.h is shown in Listing 13.9.

Listing 13.9 **AppDelegate.h**

```
#import <UIKit/UIKit.h>

@class SharediCloudController;                                      //1

@interface AppDelegate : UIResponder <UIApplicationDelegate>

@property (strong, nonatomic) UIWindow *window;
@property (nonatomic, readonly) SharediCloudController *iCloudController;//2

@end
```

1   Forward reference for the controller class.

2   Declare a property for the app delegate to use for the iCloud controller.

AppDelegate.m

You need to instantiate an instance of the iCloud controller. Listing 13.10 shows AppDelegate.m. As you saw in the previous section, the `init` method of `Shared-iCloudController` handles the startup processing for iCloud that often is placed in the app delegate directly. The unused stubs of methods that are found in the template are omitted from Listing 13.10.

Listing 13.10   **AppDelegate.m**

```
#import "AppDelegate.h"

#import "SharediCloudController.h"

@interface AppDelegate
@property  SharediCloudController *_iCloudController;          //1
@end

@implementation AppDelegate

#pragma mark - iCloud

- (SharediCloudController *)iCloudController {
  if (!iCloudController) {                                     //2
    iCloudController = [[SharediCloudController alloc] init];
  }
  return _iCloudController;

- (void)applicationWillResignActive:(UIApplication *)application {    //3
  [_iCloudController deleteDocumentsFromUI];
}

// stub code omitted

- (void)applicationDidBecomeActive:(UIApplication *)application {     //4
  [_iCloudController manageiCloudIdentityChange];
}

// stub code omitted


}
```

1   In the class extension, `SharediCloudController` can be declared as a property. Xcode will create the backing variable, and you'll be able to use dot syntax or the underscore name of the backing variable (`_iCloudController`) when referencing it from this file.

2   This syntax is very common. If a necessary object isn't found, create it.

3   Clear out user interface in case the iCloud account will be changed.

4   Check for a new iCloud account and, if necessary, update the token in user defaults and the UI.

MasterViewController

The master view controller manages the list of detail objects. That list is the major focus of the iCloud integration.

MasterViewController.h

There are four main tasks in managing the list of documents:

- **Initializing the master view controller:** As always, you need to set up the instance of a class at the beginning.

- **Creating a new document:** This is where you will create a new document and store it both in iCloud and in the private documents array. In practice, you will probably also store a local copy in the app's sandbox, but that is covered in Chapters 15 and 16.

- **Deleting an existing document:** You need to be able to delete documents at will. They will need to be deleted from iCloud as well as from the private documents array. In Chapters 15 and 16, you'll see how to also delete them from the local store.

- **Displaying the list of documents:** You need to be able to display new and old documents. (Remember, that's the main function of the master view controller.)

Initializing the master view controller means storing a reference to the app delegate's instance of the iCloud controller as well as registering for necessary notifications. Listing 13.11 shows the header file (MasterViewController.h).

Listing 13.11   **Setting Up the Master View Controller Header**

```
#import <UIKit/UIKit.h>

@class DetailViewController;

@interface MasterViewController : UITableViewController

@property (strong, nonatomic) DetailViewController *detailViewController;
@property (weak, nonatomic) IBOutlet UIBarButtonItem *addButton;

- (IBAction)addDocument:(id)sender;                          //1

@end
```

1   This will implement the button to add a new document to the master view controller.

MasterViewController.m

The beginning of MasterViewController.m is shown in Listing 13.12.

Listing 13.12   **Implementing the Master View Controller**

```objc
#import "MasterViewController.h"
#import "Constants.h"
#import "DetailViewController.h"
#import "ReportDocument.h"
#import "AppDelegate.h"
#import "SharediCloudController.h"

@interface MasterViewController ()

@property (weak,nonatomic) SharediCloudController* iCloudController;     //1

@end

@implementation MasterViewController

- (id)initWithCoder:(NSCoder*)aDecoder                                   //2
{
  if(self = [super initWithCoder:aDecoder])
    {
      AppDelegate *delegate =
        (AppDelegate*)[[UIApplication sharedApplication]
        delegate];
      _iCloudController = [delegate iCloudController];                   //3
    }

  [[NSNotificationCenter defaultCenter] addObserver:self               //4
    selector:@selector (reloadData)
    name:SharediCloudControllerDidChangeDataNotification object:nil];

  return self;
}

- (void)awakeFromNib                                                    //5
{
  [super awakeFromNib];

  self.navigationItem.leftBarButtonItem = self.editButtonItem;

  [self.tableView reloadData];                                          //6

}
```

```
- (void)reloadData {
    [self.tableView reloadData];                                    //7
}
```

1   The the shared iCloud controller is declared as a property inside the class extension.

2   The method to override is `initWithCoder` rather than a basic `init` method. This method is used to initialize an object from a stored (or coded) value. This enables the instantiated object to have the various values that have been set in another file—typically a nib, xib, or storyboard file. `initWithCoder` is how all of your settings for your object move from the storyboard to the runtime instance.

3   Set the value of the property to the app delegate's instance of the shared iCloud controller.

4   Register for notifications that may be sent from the shared iCloud controller. If they are received, `reloadData` will be called to update the list of documents in the master view controller. Note once again the message-based coupling of asynchronous processes.

5, 6   `awakeFromNib` is a standard method to make certain that the app and its interface are up to date. Remember, changes to the list of documents may have happened in iCloud, so it is worthwhile to reload the data.

7   This is the standard way to reload data in a table view. Note that the view controller just hands off the reloading to its table view.

Several methods are omitted from this listing because they are common split view controller methods that are well documented on developer.apple.com. They are `viewDidLoad` and `didReceiveMemoryWarning`, as well as the Table View section with methods such as `numberOfSectionsInTableView`. They are in the downloadable code.

You need to create a method for adding a new document to the Master-Detail Application template for your app. That's the focus of this section. The document will be added directly to iCloud as well as to the internal documents array. (As noted previously, in real life you would usually add the new document to a local persistent store of some kind, but this is a simplification for the first example.) The method is exposed in the .h file. The implementation code is shown in Listing 13.13.

Listing 13.13   Wiring the Add Button

```
#import <UIKit/UIKit.h>

@class DetailViewController;

@interface MasterViewController : UITableViewController
```

```
@property (strong, nonatomic) DetailViewController *detailViewController;
@property (weak, nonatomic) IBOutlet UIBarButtonItem *addButton;

- (IBAction)addDocument:(id)sender;                                    //1

@end
```

1   Create the declaration of the new addDocument method. The easiest
    way is to edit your storyboard with the Assistant in Xcode. Use the exist-
    ing add button in the template, but rewire it by dragging from it to the
    MasterViewController.h file and creating the action. This line of code will
    be generated for you automatically.

In the .m file, you implement addDocument as well as the other methods that manage the list of documents. In Listing 13.14, you see the process of adding the file.

As is so often the case with iCloud, you're dealing with asynchronous processing
in several threads. You start by sending the basic processing to a background queue
(this created the new document). You then send a block to the main queue to update
the user interface. (The user interface cannot be updated from a background queue.)
As you'll notice in Listing 13.14, the code in the background queue sets up some variables that are then dispatched to the main queue (such as newDocumentURL). Thus,
although you have two queues in action, the second doesn't get scheduled until the
first has set the variables. This is the common structure for this type of work. (This is
basically the same code used in "Your Third iOS App: iCloud" on developer.apple
.com; however, in this version, SharediCloudController manages the documents
array instead of having it managed by the master view controller. This can provide for
greater flexibility in reusing the code.

Listing 13.14 **Creating a New Document**

```
- (NSString *)newUntitledDocumentName {                               //1
  return [_iCloudController newUntitledDocumentName];
}


- (IBAction)addDocument: (id)sender {

  self.addButton.enabled = NO;                                        //2

  dispatch_async(dispatch_get_global_queue(DISPATCH_QUEUE_PRIORITY_DEFAULT,
    0),
    ^{                                                                //3
    NSFileManager *fm = [NSFileManager defaultManager];               //4
    NSURL *newDocumentURL = [fm URLForUbiquityContainerIdentifier:nil]; //5
    newDocumentURL = [newDocumentURL
      URLByAppendingPathComponent:DocumentsDirectoryName isDirectory:YES];
```

```
newDocumentURL = [newDocumentURL URLByAppendingPathComponent:
  [self newUntitledDocumentName]];

dispatch_async (dispatch_get_main_queue(), ^{                     //6
  // update documents
  [_iCloudController addDocumentURL: newDocumentURL];

  // update UI                                                    //7
  NSIndexPath *newCellIndexPath = [NSIndexPath
    indexPathForRow:([_iCloudController numberOfDocuments] - 1)
    inSection:0];
  [self.tableView insertRowsAtIndexPaths:
    [NSArray arrayWithObject:newCellIndexPath]
    withRowAnimation: UITableViewRowAnimationAutomatic];
  [self.tableView selectRowAtIndexPath: newCellIndexPath animated:YES
    scrollPosition:UITableViewScrollPositionMiddle];

  UITableViewCell *selectedCell = [self.tableView
    cellForRowAtIndexPath: newCellIndexPath];
  if ([[UIDevice currentDevice] userInterfaceIdiom] ==
    UIUserInterfaceIdiomPad) {                                    //8
    // set selectedItem for iPad
    NSIndexPath *cellPath = [self.tableView indexPathForSelectedRow];
    NSURL *theURL = [_iCloudController documentURLAt:[cellPath row]];
    _detailViewController.detailItem = theURL;                   //9
  } else if ([[UIDevice currentDevice] userInterfaceIdiom] ==
    UIUserInterfaceIdiomPhone) {
    // start segue for iPhone
    [self performSegueWithIdentifier: DisplayDetailSegue
      sender: selectedCell];                                     //10
  };

  //re-enable add button
  self.addButton.enabled = YES;                                  //11

}); // main queue
}); // background queue
}
```

1   Ask the shared iCloud controller to create a new document name. It will
    be used in line 4.

2   Disable updating while the original update is being processed.

3   This is the beginning of the block being sent to the background queue.

4   Get the default file manager. This and the following two lines could be
    merged into a single, rather inscrutable statement.

5   Build the new file name using the ubiquity container name, the documents directory name (from Constants.h), and the document name created in line 1. To place the document somewhere else, replace Documents-DirectoryName with another location.

6   Move back to the main queue.

7   Update the UI.

8, 9   For the iPad, set the detail item.

10   On the iPhone, the detail item is set in performSegueWithIdentifier: sender.

11   Re-enable updating (see Note 2 for disabling it).

Whether you have just created a new document or are looking at existing documents, the master view controller is responsible for handling the tap in the list of documents and setting the correct detail item.

This is one difference between the iPad and iPhone versions. On iPad, there is no segue from one view to another: the detail view is always visible. (It's the master view that is sometimes hidden when the device is rotated to a portrait position.) Thus, on iPad, you handle the tap in a row in the table view by setting the detail item in MasterViewController.m, as you see in Listing 13.15.

Listing 13.15   Responding to a Tap in the Table View

```
- (void)tableView:(UITableView *)tableView
  didSelectRowAtIndexPath:(NSIndexPath *)indexPath
{
  if ([[UIDevice currentDevice]
    userInterfaceIdiom] == UIUserInterfaceIdiomPad) {
    NSURL * theURL = [_iCloudController documentURLAt: [indexPath row]]; //1
    self.detailViewController.detailItem = theURL;                       //2
    self.detailViewController.navigationItem.title =
      theCell.textLabel.text;                                            //3
  }
}
```

1   Ask the shared iCloud controller for the object at the table row.

2   Set the detailViewController detailItem to the object. Remember that this statement will invoke the setter for the property. As you'll see in Listing 13.16, the default setter has been overridden.

3   Set the title of the navigation item.

tableView didSelectRowAtIndexPath: isn't called when you're running on iPad if you're using a storyboard (as this project does). That's all handled when you set up the standard segue. This means that you set the detail item in prepareForSegue:, as shown in Listing 13.16.

Listing 13.16   **Handling the Segue**

```
- (void)prepareForSegue: (UIStoryboardSegue*)segue sender:(id)sender {
  NSLog (@" %@ %@", segue.identifier, DisplayDetailSegue);
  if ([segue.identifier isEqualToString: DisplayDetailSegue]) {        //1

    DetailViewController *destVC =
      (DetailViewController *)segue.destinationViewController;          //2

    NSIndexPath *cellPath = [self.tableView indexPathForSelectedRow];
    UITableViewCell *theCell = [self.tableView
      cellForRowAtIndexPath: cellPath];
    NSURL * theURL = [_iCloudController documentURLAt: [cellPath row]];
    destVC.detailItem = theURL;
    destVC.navigationItem.title = theCell.textLabel.text;              //3
  }
}
```

1 Even if you're certain there's only one possible segue, check the identifier so that if and when you extend this code, it will work properly.

2 Whether you assume that the destination view controller in the segue is the same as the destination view self.detailViewController is up to you. They should be—and you may even want to test that.

3 Set the title of the navigation item.

Deleting a document is a collaboration between the master view controller and the shared iCloud controller. As in the case of adding a document (see Listing 13.14), you need to delete it from the shared iCloud controller's list of documents as well as from the user interface. This is done in your override of tableView:commitEditing-Style:forRowAtIndexPath:, as shown in Listing 13.17.

Listing 13.17   **Deleting a Document**

```
- (void)tableView:(UITableView *)tableView
    commitEditingStyle:(UITableViewCellEditingStyle) editingStyle
    forRowAtIndexPath:(NSIndexPath *)indexPath
{
  if (editingStyle == UITableViewCellEditingStyleDelete) {             //1
    NSURL *fileURL = [_iCloudController documentURLAt: [indexPath row]]; //2

    [_iCloudController deleteDocument:fileURL];                        //3

    [tableView deleteRowsAtIndexPaths:[NSArray arrayWithObject:indexPath]
      withRowAnimation:UITableViewRowAnimationAutomatic];             //4
  }
}
```

1   Check to see if you are deleting a row from the table.

2   Get the document URL for the row from the iCloud controller.

3   Ask the iCloud controller to delete the row.

4   Delete the row from the interface yourself.

DetailViewController

Whether you are arriving at the detail view controller through a navigation interface on iPhone or with a split view controller on iPad, now you have to worry about displaying the data. As noted previously, this is a minimal document that simply contains a text string. The code you need to worry about is simpler than the shared iCloud controller and the master view controller.

DetailViewController.h

First of all you need to update the template for DetailViewController.h, as shown in Listing 13.18.

Listing 13.18   **DetailViewController.h**

```
#import <UIKit/UIKit.h>

#import "ReportDocument.h"                                        //1

@interface DetailViewController : UIViewController
  <UISplitViewControllerDelegate, ReportDocumentDelegate>        //2

@property (weak, nonatomic) IBOutlet UITextView *textView;       //3
@property (strong, nonatomic) id detailItem;

@end
```

1   You'll need to import your custom document class. If you know you'll be using this in advance, you can import it now. Often, in the real world, you decide to implement a custom class and come back to add your import statements later on.

2   When you implement the custom document class, it will have a delegate protocol that you'll need to adopt.

3   The Master-Detail Application template uses a UILabel to display its data. Remove that from the storyboard and add a text view. Make sure to connect it to this property.

DetailViewController.m

In DetailViewController.m, you'll need to manage setting the detail item (the document), as well as handling notifications when the detail view appears and disappears.

Listing 13.19 shows the top of DetailViewController.m with the class extension and the setter for the detail item.

Listing 13.19   **Class Extension and Setter for the Detail Item**

```
#import "DetailViewController.h"

@interface DetailViewController ()

@property (strong, nonatomic) UIPopoverController *masterPopoverController;
@property (strong, nonatomic) ReportDocument *document;                 //1

@end

@implementation DetailViewController

#pragma mark - Managing the detail item

- (void)setDetailItem:(id)newDetailItem                                 //2
{
  if (_detailItem != newDetailItem) {
    _detailItem = newDetailItem;
    _document = [[ReportDocument alloc] initWithFileURL:self.detailItem];//3
    _document.delegate = self;

    // open or create
    NSFileManager *fm = [NSFileManager defaultManager];                 //4
    if ([fm fileExistsAtPath: [self.detailItem path]])
      [_document8:nil];
    else
      //save
      [_document saveToURL:self.detailItem
        forSaveOperation:UIDocumentSaveForCreating completionHandler:nil];
  }
}
```

1 This is the document for the custom document type that you'll use.

2 Override the default setter for the detail item so that you can do additional processing.

3 Create the new document and initialize it with the detail item, which is its URL.

4 Get the default file manager and use it to see if the new document exists. If it does, open it. If it doesn't, create it.

Listing 13.20 shows you the code to manage the document when the view appears and disappears. Compare the document handling code with Listing 13.19, and you'll find some duplication. This is because views appearing and disappearing happens on the iPhone in this app. With a split view controller on iPad, the split view appears at the beginning and then remains visible with changing data as needed.

Listing 13.20   Handling Notifications When View Appears and Disappears

```
- (void)viewWillAppear:(BOOL)animated {                              //5
  [super viewWillAppear:animated];

  self.textView.text = @"";

  if (self.detailItem) {
    _document = [[ReportDocument alloc] initWithFileURL:self.detailItem];
    _document.delegate = self;

    // open or create
    NSFileManager *fm = [NSFileManager defaultManager];
    if ([fm fileExistsAtPath: [self.detailItem path]])
      [_document openWithCompletionHandler:^(BOOL success) {         //6
        if (!success) {
          NSLog(@"ERRROR: cannot open %@", _document.fileURL);
        }
      }];
    else
      //save
      [_document saveToURL:self.detailItem
        forSaveOperation:UIDocumentSaveForCreating completionHandler:nil];
  }

  // register for keyboard notifications                            //7
  [[NSNotificationCenter defaultCenter] addObserver:self selector:@selector
    (keyboardWillShow:) name:UIKeyboardWillShowNotification object:nil];
  [[NSNotificationCenter defaultCenter] addObserver:self selector:@selector
    (keyboardWillHide:) name:UIKeyboardWillHideNotification object:nil];

}

- (void)viewWillDisappear:(BOOL)animated {                          //8
  [super viewWillDisappear: animated];

  NSString *newText = self.textView.text;
  _document.documentText = newText;

  [_document closeWithCompletionHandler: ^(BOOL success) {          //9
      if (!success) {
```

```
      NSLog(@"ERROR: Can't close %@", _document.fileURL);
    }
  }];
  [[NSNotificationCenter defaultCenter] removeObserver:self
    name:UIKeyboardWillShowNotification object:nil];          //10
  [[NSNotificationCenter defaultCenter] removeObserver:self
    name:UIKeyboardWillHideNotification object:nil];

}
```

5 You can optimize this code by checking to see if the app is running on an iPad. If so, you can omit the code that's already been executed in Listing 13.19. On both, you need to register for keyboard show and hide events.

6 You can pass in nil for the completion handler, but, particularly during debugging, it's often useful to pass in a block that reports an error if it occurs. You can add diagnostics to the message; also, if you set a breakpoint within the completion handler block, you'll be able to inspect data to help with troubleshooting.

7 Register for keyboard notifications

8 Remember, this will not be executing on iPad.

9 You can use nil for the completion handler, but a block such as this can help with debugging.

10 Remove notification observer.

ReportDocument

The most basic type of document is used in this example: it contains nothing but a text string and its title. As you will see in Chapters 15 and 16, there are two types of documents—NSDocument for OS X and UIDocument for iOS. You will build on this framework in the following chapters. For the purpose of getting started in this chapter, you just need these basics.

As you have seen, much of the communication between threads and with asynchronous processes such as iCloud is facilitated by notifications. This document is no exception. When its text is changed, a notification is posted, and any observers can then update their interface displays.

ReportDocument.h
The brief header to ReportDocument.h is shown in Listing 13.21.

Listing 13.21 **ReportDocument.h**

```
#import <UIKit/UIKit.h>

@class ReportDocument;                                        //1
```

```
@protocol ReportDocumentDelegate <NSObject>                              //2
@optional
- (void)documentContentsDidChange: (ReportDocument *)document;
@end

@interface ReportDocument : UIDocument                                   //3

@property (copy, nonatomic) NSString* documentText;
@property (weak, nonatomic) id<ReportDocumentDelegate> delegate;
@end
```

1   Although this is the header to ReportDocument.h, you need a forward class declaration to the ReportDocument class in order to declare the protocol (see line 2).

2   The ReportDocumentDelegate protocol has one optional method—documentContentsDidChange. An interface class (DetailView-Controller in this app's case) can adopt the protocol and be notified of changes.

3   This is the basic class declaration. Two properties are declared: one for the document text and the other for the delegate.

ReportDocument.m

There are only three methods in this file; none of them is visible in the header, so they can only be invoked by this class itself. Methods in DetailViewController, which is the delegate for ReportDocument instances, also serve to manipulate the document data.

You'll notice that undo is implemented (at line 2 in Listing 13.22). That may surprise you because this is a very bare-bones implementation that focuses on iCloud. Undo may seem like an advanced topic for sophisticated users and developers. It isn't with the current document architecture. A document's undo manager keeps track of changes when they are done, undone, and redone. It sends notifications to the document itself, which, in turn, updates its change count and arranges to save the document automatically as needed. Without the undo manager, the document won't know that it has changes that need to be saved.

The code for ReportDocument.m is shown in Listing 13.22.

Listing 13.22   ReportDocument.m

```
#import "ReportDocument.h"

@interface ReportDocument ()

@end

@implementation ReportDocument
```

```objc
- (void)setDocumentText: (NSString *)newText {                          //1

  NSString *oldText = _documentText;
  _documentText = [newText copy];

  [self.undoManager registerUndoWithTarget:
     selector:@selector (setdocumentText:) object:oldText];            //2

}


- (id)contentsForType: (NSString *)typeName error: (NSError **)outError {//3
  if (!self.documentText) self.documentText = @"";
  NSData *docData = [self.documentText
     dataUsingEncoding: NSUTF8StringEncoding];                         //4
  return docData;
}

- (BOOL)loadFromContents:(id)contents ofType:(NSString *)typeName
     error:(NSError *__autoreleasing *)outError {                      //5
  if ([contents length] > 0)
    self.documentText = [[NSString alloc] initWithData: contents
       encoding: NSUTF8StringEncoding];
  else
    self.documentText = @"";


  if (self.delegate && [self.delegate                                 //6
    respondsToSelector: @selector(documentContentsDidChange:)])
      self.delegate documentContentsDidChange: self];

  return YES;
}

@end
```

---

1 This method, which is usually called from an interface class or from
   `loadFromContents:ofType:error` (line 3), sets the text from a string.

2 Set up the undo manager to undo `setDocumentText:`.

3 `contentsForType:error` is a standard `UIDocument` class that is used to
   load data.

4 Notice in the code here that the string that is stored is converted to an
   `NSData` object.

5 This is the basic `UIDocument` code to load a document's content.

6 This is standard code to first check if there is a delegate, and then, if so, check
   whether the delegate responds to the signature.

Storyboards

You might need to make a few changes to storyboards. The code is described in this chapter, but here is a summary of the storyboard changes to support it:

- `addDocument` needs to be added. Use the Assistant editor to control-drag from the + in the master view controller to MasterViewController.h. A blank definition will be created in MasterViewController.m, and you can add the code there.

- The segue from the master view controller to the detail view controller in the iPhone storyboard may need to be renamed to `DisplayDetailSegue` to match the code here.

- On both storyboards, remove the `UILabel` detail item and replace it with a text view, as described in the `DetailViewController` section.

> **Note**
> If you have any warnings about certificates or provisioning profiles, handle them now.

Chapter Summary

This chapter gave you a basic structure for managing iCloud documents on iOS. It built on and extended Apple's "Third iOS App: iCloud." In this version, you have a structure that combines the Master-Detail Application template with a new class—`SharediCloud Controller`—that manages iCloud interactions. The controller not only manages the basic interface with iCloud but also manages the list of app documents that are stored on iCloud. You saw how adding and deleting documents requires them to be added and deleted from the user interface (mostly in the master view controller) as well as from the list of documents maintained by the controller.

Exercises

1. If you have followed along with the app, build and run it. Use developer.icloud.com to inspect your iCloud storage as you add and delete documents. Experiment with downloading documents from developer.icloud.com to check their contents with what you can examine with the Xcode debugger and breakpoints.

2. Make a copy of the app and modify it so that it includes features from projects you're working on. In other words, build your app on top of the iCloud app from this chapter. As soon as it's your app and your app's language, it will look very different.

3. If you have two iOS devices, try to break the app. Using Airplane mode and Settings, turn iCloud on and off and try to get the two devices to create duplicate document names. Get a feel for how long the documents list takes to rebuild when you turn a device on with Airplane mode.

14

Working with File Wrappers in iCloud

Part IV of the book gets to the heart of iCloud—the APIs for managing documents and data. You have to go back to the basics and understand how common terms you are familiar with have very specific meanings in iCloud. In particular, you may be among the many people who use "document" and "file" interchangeably. There has always been a distinction between those terms, but it hasn't mattered too much until iCloud. Now it matters.

This chapter introduces the distinctions between these terms and then explores the APIs you need to use to manage files and file wrappers. The remaining chapters in this part delve into the APIs for managing documents on iOS (Chapter 15) and on OS X (Chapter 16). The Core Data API that was described in Chapter 10 comes into play again in Chapter 17 when it is merged with iCloud and the concept of documents.

The focus in this chapter is on files and file wrappers and how you use them with iCloud. The chapter looks for the iCloud ubiquity container and, if it finds it, uses it. That's a good start for looking at files and file wrappers, but as you move into chapters 16 and 17, you'll see how to manage iCloud accounts, availability, and options. Those features are necessary in a shipping app.

As is the case with the other chapters in this part of the book (as well as many chapters in previous parts), this chapter contains an annotated example; you can download it from the author's website as well as from www.informit.com/title/9780321889119. The project in this chapter is code-named Placid. (The project code names are taken from the names of lakes in northern New York's Adirondack mountains.) In this chapter, Placid is implemented only for iOS. Chapter 16 explores an OS X version.

Exploring Files, File Wrappers, and Documents

This section explores the distinctions between files and documents and introduces the file wrapper structure. You may be familiar with these topics, and in that case feel free to skim this section or to skip over it entirely. The challenge for both reader and author is that although these and many other iCloud concepts are not particularly new (the NSFileWrapper class goes back to the first release of OS X), you may not have needed to pay attention to them before now.

This is actually a common situation with iCloud. iCloud has been implemented by making changes—often relatively small changes—to existing APIs across the two operating systems. Along the way, many recommendations and best practices have become required. That's the reason it is necessary to occasionally backtrack to some basics.

Looking at Files

On almost all operating systems, files contain data. They are stored on disks and other storage devices. Users and developers generally access them by name and location—the directory in which they are stored. (Note that *folder* is the user-facing term for what is technically a *directory*.)

Files can be of various types; in general, a file of a specific type is linked in some manner to apps that can be used to edit or display it. Typically, this linkage has been accomplished with a *file extension* that is appended to the file's name.

As you may have learned (the hard way), this structure is a bit fragile, especially when moving files across platforms. (Is it JPEG or JPG? TEXT or TXT?) Over the last several iterations of Apple's operating systems and Xcode, a more robust mechanism has been implemented—the Uniform Type Identifier (UTI). It is more robust and flexible, but it also is a little more complicated. Fortunately, much of that complexity has been removed with Xcode 5, as you will see later in this chapter.

As you saw in Chapter 1, "Exploring iCloud and Its User Experience," iCloud introduces a new file storage structure. No longer are files visibly stored on disks in whatever structure the user wants using folders such as My Projects, Trail Maps, Pictures, Soccer Games, and the like. Instead, as described in Chapter 1, files are stored in areas reserved for individual apps. Within that area, there can be any number of files or directories (subject, of course, to device storage limitations).

In fact, the description in Chapter 1 is the common description presented to users, but it is an oversimplification. The storage area for files is not specific to an app; rather, it is specific to a bundle identifier. In most cases, apps have unique bundle identifiers; however, several apps may share one bundle identifier. Thus, they share a storage area and the files and directories within it.

Exploring File Wrappers

File wrappers (instances of NSWrapper or a subclass thereof) provide a means of working with file-system nodes, which are files, directories, or symbolic links using a common interface. (In the context of iCloud, you typically work only with files and directories.) A file wrapper has a name and a set of file-system attributes (as described in the NSFile Manager Class Reference). If a file wrapper wraps a file, the file's content is available through the `regularFileContents` method, which returns an `NSData` object. Thus, file wrappers provide a mechanism that lets you work with files and directories using a common interface for both of them. (In fact, you can argue that this common interface for files and directories is one of the key roles of the Finder on OS X.)

If a file wrapper wraps a directory, that directory itself is a file wrapper within the overall directory file wrapper. You can access the items within a directory file wrapper using the `fileWrappers` method, which returns an `NSDictionary`. Where the user sees a folder within a folder, the developer sees a dictionary within a dictionary, and, when using file wrappers, the developer sees a file wrapper within a file wrapper.

File wrappers become very important in the iCloud world. As noted previously, synchronizing data is easiest when the data is structured so that it can be disassembled and reassembled on demand. If it is structured in this way, the sync process can be run only for those specific parts of the data that have changed since the last sync. A file wrapper provides an excellent example of this. What appears to be a single file can actually be multiple files and file wrappers, each of which can be synced separately by iCloud if that is desired.

Exploring Documents

On OS X and iOS, *document* refers to a specific class of object—either `UIDocument` on iOS or `NSDocument` on OS X. A document almost always contains data that can be stored in a file wrapper, in a single file, or in a Core Data persistent store that is part of the document. Both document classes implement a robust and complex user experience for the platform. The document is not the file (or file wrapper). They are related but different.

The differences between `UIDocument` and `NSDocument` are significant in many areas, which is why they are discussed in separate chapters. For example, `NSDocument` builds in an Open dialog, which lets users select files to open from any disk or folder to which access is provided. On iOS, it is the responsibility of the app to display the list of documents that can be opened. Fortunately, that is not too difficult to accomplish.

How Users Manage iCloud Files

In Chapter 13, "Adding the iCloud Infrastructure," and this chapter, you see what you do to manage files. It's time to switch roles for a moment and see what the users see as they work with your file management code.

With OS X Mavericks (10.9), users have direct access to their iCloud containers just as you do with developer.icloud.com. This access comes through the iCloud System Preferences pane, as shown in Figure 14.1. Click Manage in the lower right to begin the process.

Figure 14.1   Managing iCloud storage

Next, you see the list of apps in your iCloud container just as you do in developer .apple.com, as shown in Figure 14.2.

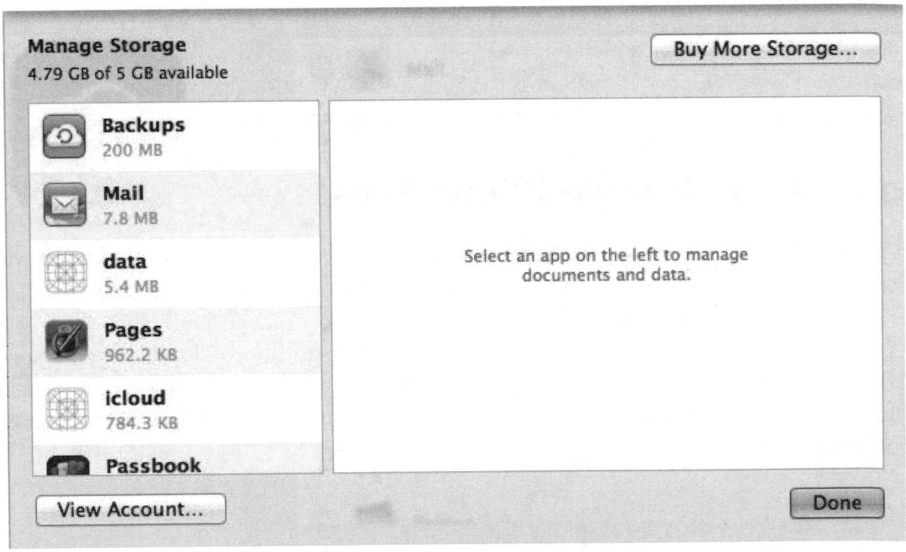

Figure 14.2   Listing apps in iCloud storage

In developer.icloud.com, you have the ability to download a file from the iCloud container, but the user does not have that feature. There is another difference: users can remove files from their iCloud container, but you can't do that with developer.icloud .com. (There are Delete and Delete All buttons at the bottom of the pane that shows the containers. You reach it with the Manage button at the bottom of Figure 14.1.) Figure 14.3 shows the developer.icloud.com display.

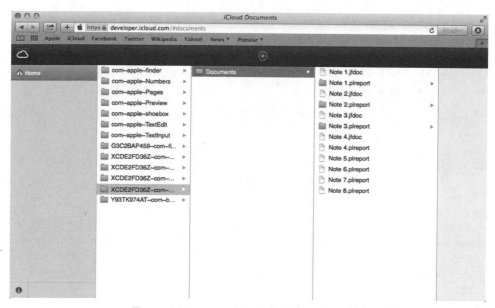

Figure 14.3   Accessing developer.icloud.com

If you download a document from developer.icloud.com, it appears as a single file on your desktop. If it is a file wrapper, control-click the file and you'll see a contextual menu containing the Show Package Contents command. (This command never appears in the menu bar.) If you use the command, the file will open, as shown in Figure 14.4, and you can see the files contained within the file wrapper (a .png image, a property list, and a text file).

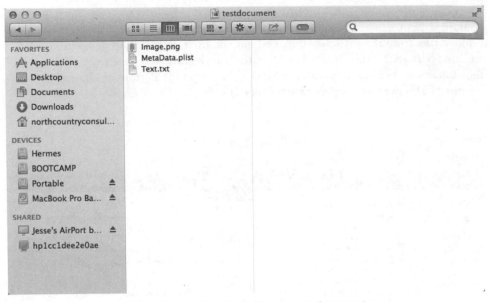

Figure 14.4   Opening a file wrapper document

In this case, the file wrapper contains three files: an image, a plist, and a text file. It could also contain one or more file wrappers. Thus, in various contexts a file wrapper can appear as a single file (the basic Finder display), a package of embedded files and folders (Show Package Contents), or in other formats that your app may implement.

Starting the Placid Project

Like many other iOS projects, Placid starts from the Xcode built-in Master-Detail Application template. It's always a good idea to build and run a new project as soon as you have created it. The Master-Detail Application template should run at this point. If it doesn't, backtrack to check your various installations (operating system, Xcode, and developer program). At this time, you can run it in the simulator.

In order to focus on building an iCloud-enabled file wrapper–based app, the version of Placid used in this chapter omits many of the features that you need in a shipping application, such as error messages, and even the basic user choice of whether or not to use iCloud—iCloud is the only data storage that is implemented. Much of the iCloud infrastructure described in the previous chapter is omitted to focus on the file wrapper code.

Like previous examples, Placid is a simple app that lets people keep track of issues that need attention. For each entry in the app, there will be a description (a text field) and a location (another text field). You can expand this model to include more data, including images. Each entry will wind up as a document whose data is stored in a file wrapper. (It is a simplification that the text document contains only a single field.) In practice, you often have a variety of fields as well as data in the overall file wrapper itself in addition to within the inner file wrappers.

This section lists the steps you need to go through to set up your new project. Some are specific to all iCloud projects, and others are not. It may seem as if you're jumping around, but these steps involve settings that are entered out in various places inside your Xcode project and on developer.apple.com. So if you're chomping at the bit to get started writing code, just hold on for a little bit. You may be able to carry out these steps in a different sequence, but remember that cutting corners by skipping steps will often come back to haunt you. As many developers have found out the hard way, tracking down configuration issues can be very time consuming.

Here are the sections that follow:

- **Certificates, Identifiers, Devices, and Profiles on developer.apple.com:** These settings are configured on developer.apple.com.

- **Certificates, Identifiers, Devices, and Profiles on Xcode 5:** Some of these can be configured directly from Xcode 5.

- **Adjusting the General Settings:** These settings are mostly as they were in Xcode 4, but the interface is drastically different in Xcode 5.

- **Setting Images:** One of the major features of Xcode 5 is its ability to manage images as assets without having to worry about file naming conventions.

- **Configuring Capabilities:** This is where you set up iCloud access and other capabilities for your app.

- **Setting Document and Universal Type Identifiers:** If you are going to be using your own documents and importing or exporting them, this is the section where you do so.

- **Checking Build Settings:** This is a final review before you move on to writing the code.

Certificates, Identifiers, Devices, and Profiles on developer.apple.com

Now is a good time to check your provisioning profiles and to create one for Placid. It may seem as if you're skipping the basic project setup steps, but you'll get back to them shortly. The reason for focusing on the certificates, identifiers, devices, and profiles is that they must be set up on your developer account. (Provisioning profiles can be set up either on the developer website or on Xcode 5.) Particularly if you have not done this before or if you have not done it for a while, that process may require a little time (and it might require one of your technical support incidents the first time). So it is a good idea to get these steps out of the way right at the start. If there is a delay in sorting out your developer account, you can move on to configure your app, as described in the next section, while you wait for the resolution.

To recap, following are the documents and certificates you need to create a provisioning profile. You create them on developer.apple.com. For both iOS and OS X, you access them at the right side of the page in the Developer Program section. They are under the link named Certificates, Identifiers & Profiles.

- **Signing certificates:** As a developer, you should have at least one of these. You should not have any duplicates—that is one of the root causes of problems in setting up provisioning profiles. For Placid, you must have at least an iOS Development certificate. You may also have an iOS Distribution certificate (this is for the App Store).

- **Identifiers:** You need to add an App ID for your app. This is another area that has changed recently. If you search the web for information on how to delete an App ID from your account, you will find many references to the fact that you can never delete an App ID. That is not the case today. The rule is that you cannot delete an App ID for any app that has been submitted to the App Store—that is *submitted*, not necessarily *accepted*. You can see the reason for this. The App Store software does let you revoke an app or even not resubmit an app that has been rejected. In both cases, the app is not on the App Store after the revocation or rejection. However, to keep the App Store records straight, the App ID must continue to exist for these previously submitted apps. If you are creating an App ID for a test app and have no intention of submitting it to the App Store, you should have no qualms about creating a new App ID and then deleting it. For now, add an App ID for Placid.

- **Devices:** Here is where you add devices to your account for testing. You can have up to 100 devices. You may need to add a device for testing if you don't already have one in your developer account. (The simulator is a special "device," so don't worry about adding it.)

- **Provisioning profiles:** This is where you combine a signing certificate, an App ID, and one or more device IDs. (Don't worry, you just use checkboxes off your list of up to 100 devices.) Add a provisioning profile for Placid on developer .apple.com, or use the steps in the following section with Xcode 5 on your Mac.

Certificates, Identifiers, Devices, and Profiles on Xcode 5

Once you have everything set up on developer.apple.com, you can use the new Accounts preferences on Xcode 5 to manage that end of things. Choose Xcode, Preferences and select the Accounts tab as shown in Figure 14.5.

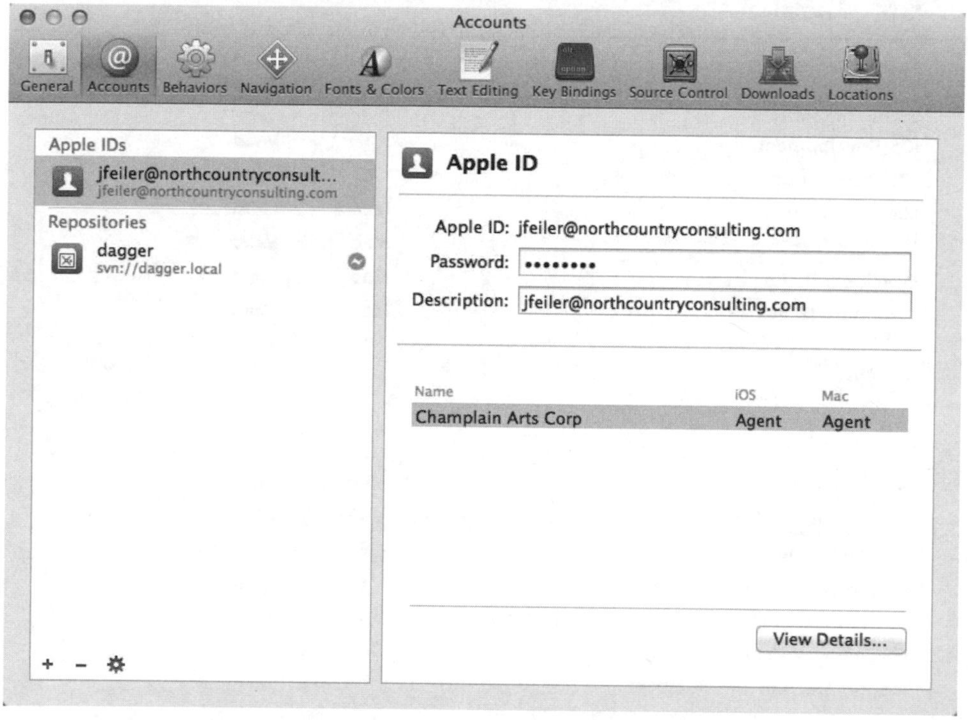

Figure 14.5   The Accounts tab of the project

You can add any number of developer accounts to Xcode as long as you have the proper credentials. Select an account and click View Details to see the information shown in Figure 14.6.

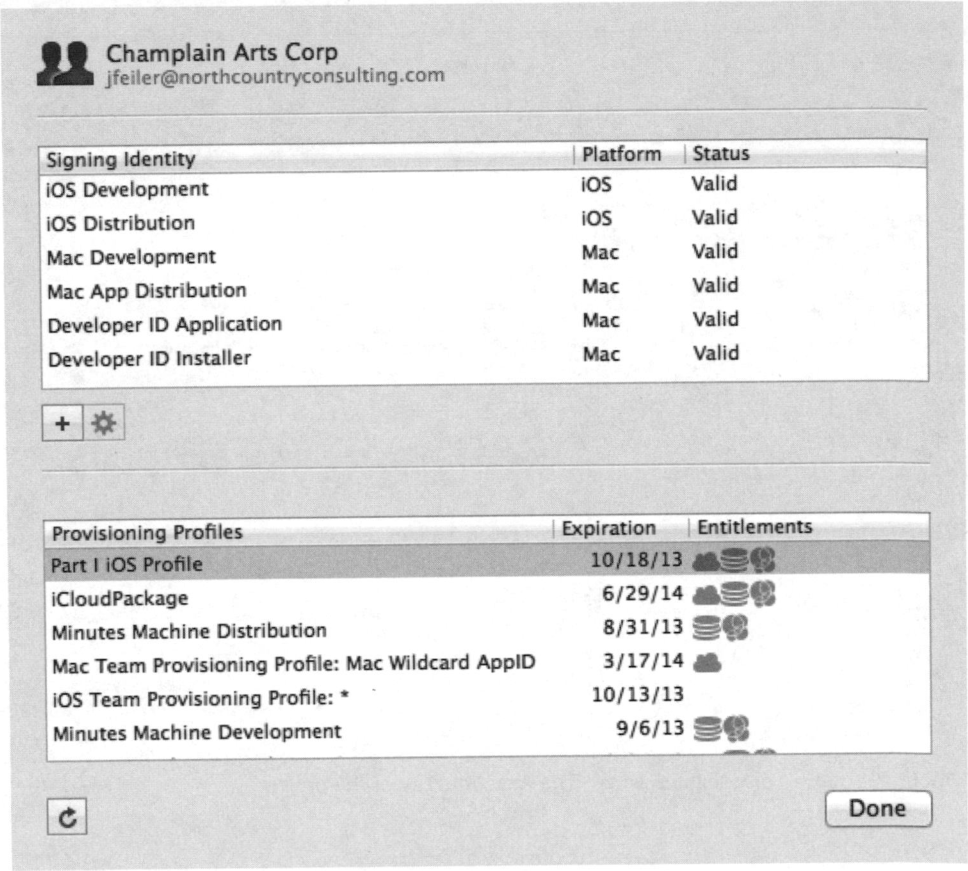

Champlain Arts Corp
jfeiler@northcountryconsulting.com

Signing Identity	Platform	Status
iOS Development	iOS	Valid
iOS Distribution	iOS	Valid
Mac Development	Mac	Valid
Mac App Distribution	Mac	Valid
Developer ID Application	Mac	Valid
Developer ID Installer	Mac	Valid

Provisioning Profiles	Expiration	Entitlements
Part I iOS Profile	10/18/13	
iCloudPackage	6/29/14	
Minutes Machine Distribution	8/31/13	
Mac Team Provisioning Profile: Mac Wildcard AppID	3/17/14	
iOS Team Provisioning Profile: *	10/13/13	
Minutes Machine Development	9/6/13	

Figure 14.6   Viewing details for a selected account

It is a good idea to compare the account details as shown in Xcode with the details for the same account shown on developer.apple.com. As this system has evolved over the years, many developers have discovered some anomalies that have crept into their account. These are not bugs; rather, they are the result of various misunderstandings some developers have had over time. Now that everything is laid out clearly, get rid of those before you find yourself locked out of the App Store at a crucial moment.

Adjusting the General Settings

Once you have created the project, built it, and run it on your testing device, it's time to adjust some of the settings in the project. As noted in the Preface, this book is based on Xcode 5, OS X Mavericks (10.9), and iOS 7. Xcode 5 brings some extraordinarily significant improvements to the process of setting up and configuring a project: they are described in this section. If you are using an earlier version of Xcode, your best choice is to update to Xcode 5 (Xcode is free). If you need Xcode 4 to maintain legacy projects, rest assured that you can have both versions installed on a single computer. The only issue you must remember is that opening an Xcode 4 project in Xcode 5 may reformat some storyboard or nib files to the Xcode 5 format. If you want to be doubly safe, create a separate user account on your Mac for your Xcode 5 and Xcode 4 projects and install the appropriate Xcode version in each.

The basic setup for the project is the same process you're used to. The general information is collected during the process of creating the project as always. In Xcode 5, there are some new features, which are described in this section. In every case, they simplify your work (in some cases, dramatically so). Figure 14.7 shows the General tab of the project settings.

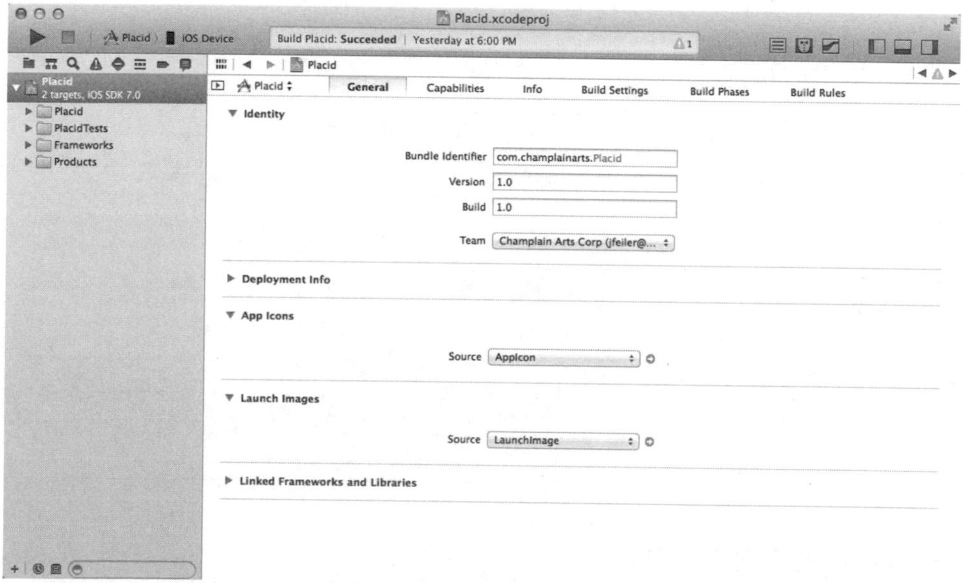

Figure 14.7   The General tab of the project

Setting Images

One of the changes in Xcode 5 is the addition of the xcassets file type for managing assets such as images in *asset catalogs*. The easiest way to work with assets is to experiment with them yourself. Figure 14.8 shows the editor for the app's Images.xcassets file. Gone are the days when we relied on dedicated file names to identify what file is what. Furthermore, as you can see in Figure 14.8, critical dimensions for specific files are shown right there on the editor. Note that the dimensions are given in points rather than pixels. Points are and have been measures of length (1/72 of an inch). As you can see in Figure 14.8, you can supply Retina (2x) and non-Retina (1x) versions of your images. Try not to think about how much time you have spent tracking down this information in the past. (And, in all fairness, remember that some of the difficulties in setting up apps before Xcode 5 occurred because the entire app universe is only a few years old now and was evolving as Xcode was evolving.)

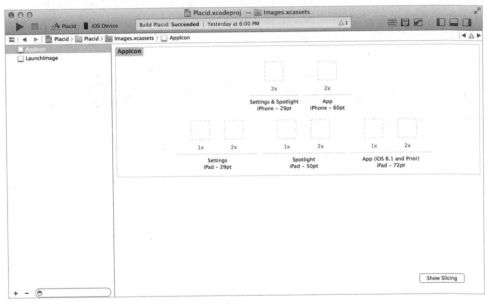

Figure 14.8   Using Images.xcassets

Configuring Capabilities

You really have to have gone through the pre-Xcode 5 process of configuring your app's capabilities to appreciate the new process of configuring the capabilities in Xcode 5. Here are the capability configuration steps in Xcode 5:

1. Verify your certificates, identifiers, devices, and profiles on developer.apple.com as described previously.

2. Verify them on Xcode, Preferences, Account as described previously. (If the versions on developer.apple.com and those on Xcode don't match, resolve the conflicts and/or create missing certificates, identifiers, and profiles.)

3. Select your project in the Xcode navigator and choose the target you want to configure.

4. In the Capabilities tab, click to turn iCloud on. That's it—one mouse click (as long as you've done the preparatory work).

Xcode adjusts your App ID to add the iCloud entitlement (this used to be a manual process you had to do), and it updates or creates an entitlements file in your project. Figure 14.9 shows the Capabilities tab.

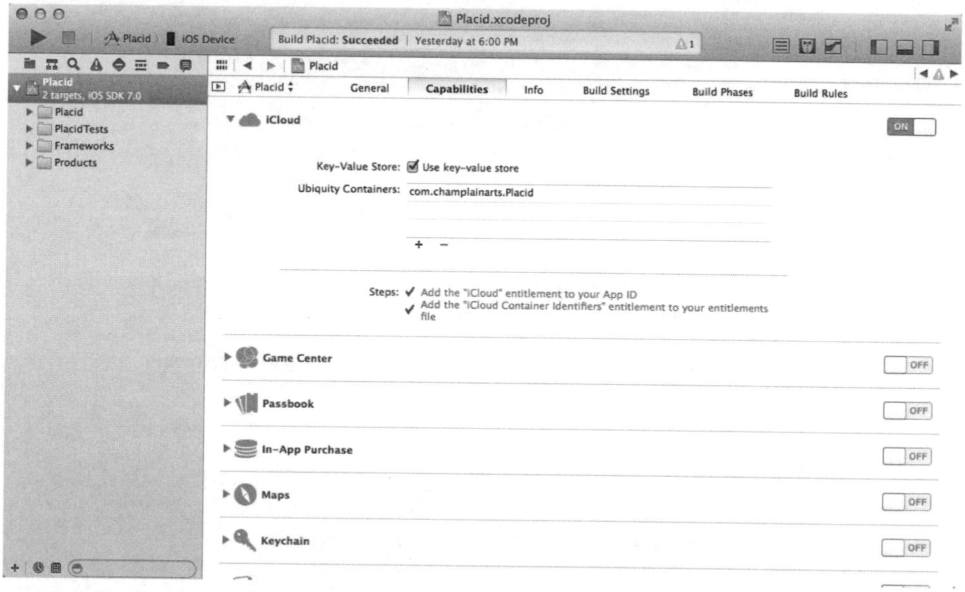

Figure 14.9   Configuring the iCloud capabilities

Note that Capabilities has an extra feature that can come in very handy. If there's a problem with your credentials, you may have had the experience of tracking down which document is wrong or missing. This is often somewhat a trial-and-error process; more than one developer has managed to cause further difficulties in attempting to rectify the initial problem in this way.

Now, if you have issues such as missing profiles or anything else that prevents compilation or running on a device, your immediate action should be to click Capabilities. If you have already turned on iCloud or any of the other options, you may see a message indicating what is wrong. (This alone can save hours for work.) Even better, you may find a Fix button that you can click to resolve the issue automatically.

Setting Document and Universal Type Identifiers

As described previously, the distinction between files and documents is sometimes not important to users, but it's critical to developers. In the Info tab of the project's target(s), you describe the documents with *document* types. UTIs describe the files your app deals with; you have separate UTIs for imported and exported files—that is, files from other apps that you read and those that you write for other apps to read. UTIs and document types are linked by a common value—*type* in a document type and *identifier* in a UTI.

If you use documents in your app, you declare a *document type* in the Info tab of your project's target, as shown in Figure 14.10.

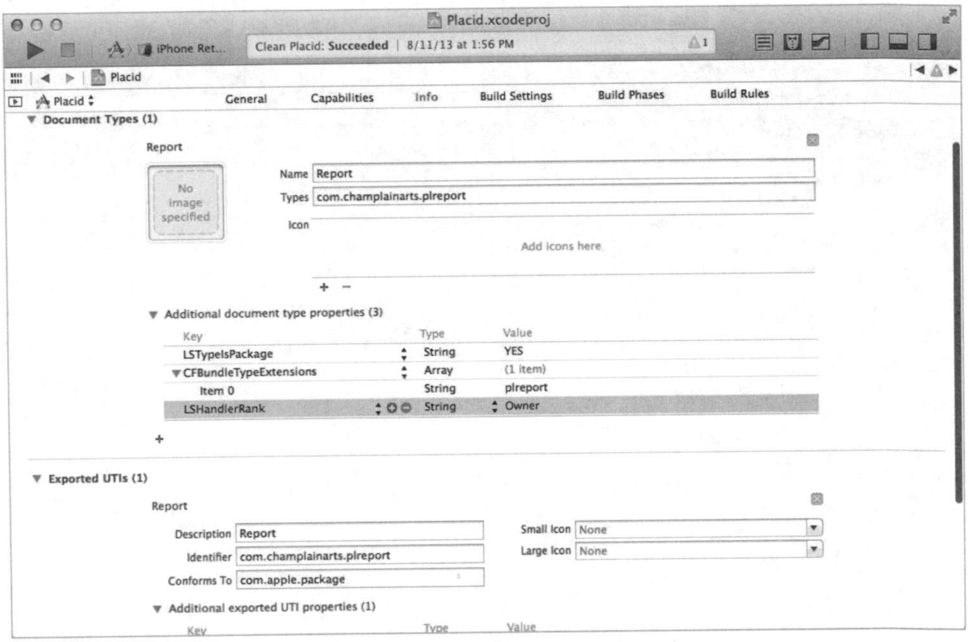

Figure 14.10   Setting up a UTI

Setting Up Document Types

Here are the steps to follow to create a document type:

1. Create a new document type with + in the document types section.

2. Provide a name for the document type. This is a name for you to use in Xcode.

3. Provide a type using reverse-domain name notation. You can provide several types, but you commonly only provide one.

4. Add icons for the document.

5. Open additional document type properties and add three of them, as shown in Figure 14.10:

   - LSTypeIsPackage: For file wrappers or packages (as described in this chapter), add this string and set its value to YES.

   - CFBundleTypeExtensions: Add an array with the file extensions used for this document type. As you see in Figure 14.10, the extensions are strings; it doesn't matter what their names are.

   - LSHandlerRank: This string's value is usually either Editor or Owner depending on how your app will be using the document.

Setting Up UTIs

The UTIs provide information about files you read and write. Here are the steps to follow to set up a UTI either for importing or exporting:

1. Set the description. This is a user- and developer-oriented description. It is not used internally.

2. Provide a unique identifier. Follow the practice of using your reverse-domain name and appending a final term that makes sense to you. This should match a type in a document type.

3. Provide the name of the UTI to which your new UTI conforms. For a file wrapper–based document, you want com.apple.package. The UTI structure is a hierarchical one in which you can specify your own object or inherit from a higher-level one such as com.apple.package.

4. Add icons for a production version of your app. Use the Images.xcassets file to store them and then select them in defining the UTI.

5. Add a new UTI property called UTTTypeSpecification as a dictionary. Within the dictionary, create an array called public.filename-extension. Within that array, create at least one string, which will be the file extension (it doesn't matter what the name of it is).

Checking Build Settings

As you can see in Figure 14.11, if you have followed the steps for setting up a UTI, your code signing settings have been set up for you by Xcode. If you need to adjust them, the Build Settings tab is where you do it.

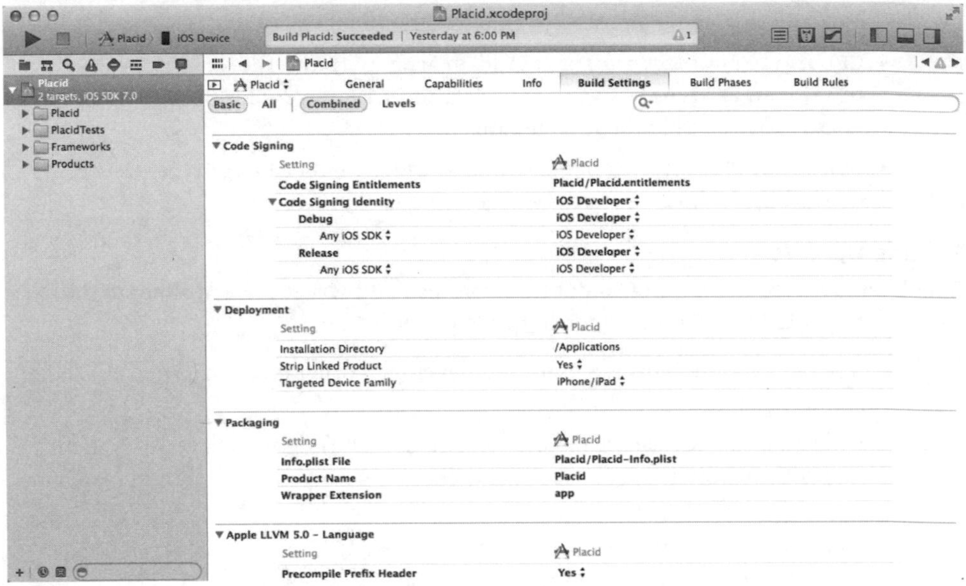

Figure 14.11   Code signing set up automatically

If you have resolved an issue using the Fix button in Capabilities, you may need to revisit your build settings for them to match your new capability settings.

Writing the Code

Now it's time to move on to the code. As you have seen before, much of the code that you write is a small snippet here and perhaps a tweak to the template code there. Often, the biggest single chuck of "writing" the code is designing the user interface and functionality with Interface Builder in Xcode, as shown in Figure 14.12.

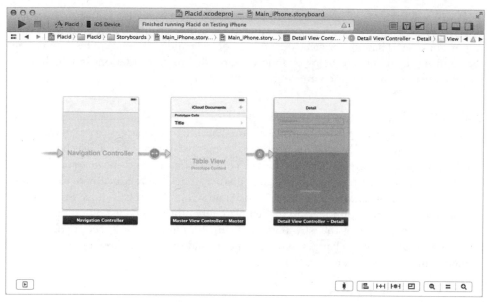

Figure 14.12   The basic app interface

In general these are the sections of code that you will customize or create:

- `AppDelegate`: This is part of the template. You need to add some minor iCloud housekeeping code.

- `MasterViewController`: The master view controller will display the list of documents from iCloud. As is always the case in Master-Detail Application apps, it will allow you to add new documents to the list, so it must have the supporting code to create them, read them, and write them.

- `DetailViewController`: As always, this displays the detail information for a selected item in the master view.

- `WrappedDocument`: This is the document that contains the file wrapper that stores the data for each document created by the app. All of this code is new.

Note that in the examples, the file prefix has been set to JF in setting up the project. You can use your own initials if you want to keep your files separate. You may also want to compare the code in this chapter with the code in Chapter 13. Although both start from the same template, they have different approaches to the overall structure of the app.

There are two projects on developer.apple.com that you can explore to see other approaches to using file wrappers and iCloud:

- Your Third iOS App: iCloud (this is under documentation)

- Document Package with iCloud (this is an OS X project under sample code)

Placid and these two projects accomplish basically the same goal, but there are some implementation differences. The code annotations in this chapter point out the most important ones. These differences are a matter of style and preference. The only reason for pointing them out is to help you follow the parallel implementations in which different names are used for the same logical elements.

AppDelegate

There are just two changes to AppDelegate.m. There are no changes to AppDelegate.h. Listing 14.1 shows AppDelegate.m. As always, some spacing in the code has been adjusted to the book layout. Most of this file consists of comments in the template reminding you of features you can use and enhance. They are retained here to remind you of what is missing: the focus in this book is on iCloud, so if you move this code to production, check the comments in the template for additional code you might write. Also note that this code is the bare-bones implementation of iCloud access: you will need to monitor account changes, Airplane mode, and the like as shown in the shared iCloud controller in Chapter 13.

Listing 14.1   **AppDelegate.m**

```
//
//  JFAppDelegate.m
//  Placid
//
//  Created by Jesse Feiler on 7/3/13.
//  Copyright (c) 2013 Champlain Arts. All rights reserved.
//

#import "JFAppDelegate.h"

@implementation JFAppDelegate

#pragma mark - launch and background

- (BOOL)application:(UIApplication *)application
    didFinishLaunchingWithOptions: (NSDictionary *)launchOptions
{
  //iCloud
  [self initializeiCloudAccess];                                    //1

  // Override point for customization after application launch.
  if ([[UIDevice currentDevice] userInterfaceIdiom] ==
    UIUserInterfaceIdiomPad) {
      UISplitViewController *splitViewController =
        (UISplitViewController *)self.window.rootViewController;
      UINavigationController *navigationController =
        [splitViewController.viewControllers lastObject];
```

```objc
    splitViewController.delegate =
      (id)navigationController.topViewController;
  }

  return YES;
}


- (void)applicationWillResignActive:(UIApplication *)application
{
  // Sent when the application is about to move from active to inactive
  // state. This can occur for certain types of temporary interruptions
  // (such as an incoming phone call or SMS message) or when the user quits
  // the application and it begins the transition to the background state.
  // Use this method to pause ongoing tasks, disable timers, and throttle
  // down OpenGL ES frame rates. Games should use this method to pause the
  // game.
}


- (void)applicationDidEnterBackground:(UIApplication *)application
{
  // Use this method to release shared resources, save user data, invalidate
  // timers, and store enough application state information to restore your
  // application to its current state in case it is terminated later. If
  // your application supports background execution, this method is called
  // instead of applicationWillTerminate: when the user quits.
}


- (void)applicationWillEnterForeground:(UIApplication *)application
{
  // Called as part of the transition from the background to the inactive
  // state; here you can undo many of the changes made on entering the
  // background.
}


- (void)applicationDidBecomeActive:(UIApplication *)application
{
  // Restart any tasks that were paused (or not yet started) while the
  // application was inactive. If the application was previously in the
  // background, optionally refresh the user interface.
}


- (void)applicationWillTerminate:(UIApplication *)application
{
  // Called when the application is about to terminate. Save data if
  // appropriate. See also applicationDidEnterBackground:.
}

#pragma mark - iCloud                                              //2
```

```
- (void)initializeiCloudAccess {                                      //3
  dispatch_async(dispatch_get_global_queue(DISPATCH_QUEUE_PRIORITY_DEFAULT,
    0), ^{
  if ([[NSFileManager defaultManager]
      URLForUbiquityContainerIdentifier:nil] != nil)
    NSLog (@"Got iCloud\n");                                           //4
  else
    NSLog (@"No iCloud\n");                                            //5
  });
  //async
}

@end
```

1   This code is used to initialize iCloud. Make sure it's called when the app launches. It calls a method that you add at line 2. The name of this method is up to you.

2   It's always a good practice to create a pragma for an API you're using in your app if you can do so. Some pragmas have been added to the basic template.

3   This is the method called from `applicationDidFinishLaunching-WithOptions:`. It uses the ubiquity container set up in Capabilities, so you don't need to do any customization there.

4, 5   Log whether you have gotten iCloud or not. This is important for debugging. Note that this call is an async process, so you can't be certain that the user interface has already been totally created. If you have a problem with iCloud, you'll have to set a flag and then check it at the end of the launch sequence and display an alert if necessary.

MasterViewController

As always, the master view controller handles the list of items that are shown by the detail view controller. It also handles reading and writing the items. The code is a combination of standard Master-Detail Application code from the template and iCloud-specific additions. Listing 14.2 shows MasterViewController.h

Listing 14.2   **MasterViewController.h**

```
#import <UIKit/UIKit.h>

@class JFDetailViewController;

@interface JFMasterViewController : UITableViewController

@property (strong, nonatomic) JFDetailViewController *detailViewController;
@property (weak, nonatomic) IBOutlet UIBarButtonItem *addButton;       //1

@end
```

1   This is the add button on the master view controller. When you create your storyboard, add the button to the scene. Then, with the Assistant, show the storyboard and this file at the same time. Control-drag from the button in the storyboard to this file, and this line of code will be generated automatically after you respond to the request to provide the name.

The beginning of MasterViewController.m is shown in Listing 14.3.

Listing 14.3   MasterViewController.m Declarations

```
#import "JFMasterViewController.h"
#import "JFDetailViewController.h"
#import "JFWrappedDocument.h"

NSString *JFDocFilenameExtension = @"plreport";            //1
NSString *DisplayDetailSegue = @"showDetail";              //2
NSString *JFDocumentsDirectoryName = @"Documents";         //3
NSString *DocumentEntryCell = @"DocumentEntryCell";        //4

@interface JFMasterViewController () {

NSMutableArray *_objects; //template                        //5
NSMutableArray *documents; //TE3                            //6
NSMetadataQuery *_query;
}
@end
```

1   This is the file extension. It must match one of the tags in your exported UTI section.

2   In the storyboard, this will be the identifier of the segue from the master view controller to the detail view controller. You set it by selecting the segue in the storyboard and showing the Attributes inspector.

3   This is the directory in the sandbox for the app's data. You can name it anything you want. If you use Documents, you can make it visible to users with the `Application supports iTunes file sharing` setting in the Info pane of your project data.

4   This is the identifier of the prototype table cell in the master view controller scene. You can use any name, but it must be the same in this define and in the Attributes inspector for the scene.

5, 6   In the Master-Detail Application template, the individual items are stored in `_objects`. In Your Third iOS App, they're stored in `documents`. In Placid, `documents` is used. You can delete `_objects`.

At the beginning of the implementation, standard methods are implemented. There are a number of modifications you need to make but, as you can see in Listing 14.4, they're not really iCloud issues. You're just setting up the interface for the app.

Listing 14.4   **Master View Controller View Setup**

```objc
@implementation JFMasterViewController

#pragma mark - load and memory

- (void)awakeFromNib
{

  [super awakeFromNib];

  if ([[UIDevice currentDevice] userInterfaceIdiom] == UIUserInterfaceIdiomPad) {
    self.clearsSelectionOnViewWillAppear = NO;
    self.preferredContentSize = CGSizeMake(320.0, 600.0);
  }

  if (!documents)
    documents = [[NSMutableArray alloc] init];                        //7

  self.navigationItem.leftBarButtonItem = self.editButtonItem;        //8

  [self setupAndStartQuery];                                          //9
}

- (void)viewDidLoad
{
    [super viewDidLoad];
    // Do any additional setup after loading the view, typically from a nib.
    self.navigationItem.leftBarButtonItem = self.editButtonItem;

    UIBarButtonItem* addButton = [[UIBarButtonItem alloc]
      initWithBarButtonSystemItem:UIBarButtonSystemItemAdd
      target:self
      action:@selector(addDocument:)];                               //10
    self.navigationItem.rightBarButtonItem = addButton;              //11
    self.detailViewController = (JFDetailViewController *)
      [[self.splitViewController.viewControllers lastObject]
        topViewController];
}

- (void)didReceiveMemoryWarning
{
    [super didReceiveMemoryWarning];
    // Dispose of any resources that can be recreated.
}
```

7   Create the mutable documents array. It must be mutable because you need to be able to add and remove documents. An alternative structure uses an immutable array, which is temporarily copied into a mutable array when you need to add or remove a document. After the operation, the mutable array is copied back into an immutable array.

8   Add an Edit button at the left.

9   You need to implement a method to run a query to find changes in the list of documents. This will be implemented at line 33 later in this chapter.

10   Create an add button.

11   Add the button to the navigation item.

The next section of the code deals with managing documents. As always, it's a good idea to use a pragma to set off sections like this. These are the standard document management methods with customization for the Placid app. Only addDocument uses the iCloud APIs.

As you will see in Listing 14.5, addDocument uses two blocks. One runs on the priority queue, and the other one runs on the main queue. The priority queue is used to construct the NSURL for the new document. When that is done, it fires off another block on the main queue that actually adds the document and updates the interface. Frequently, the actual iCloud calls are handed off to another queue rather than the main queue.

Listing 14.5   **Master View Controller Managing Documents**

```
#pragma mark  - documents

/*
 - (void)insertNewObject:(id)sender
{
    if (!_objects) {
        _objects = [[NSMutableArray alloc] init];
    }
    [_objects insertObject:[NSDate date] atIndex:0];
    NSIndexPath *indexPath = [NSIndexPath indexPathForRow:0 inSection:0];
    [self.tableView insertRowsAtIndexPaths:@[indexPath]
      withRowAnimation:UITableViewRowAnimationAutomatic];
}
*/
- (IBAction)addDocument:(id)sender {                              //12
  self.addButton.enabled = NO;

  dispatch_async (dispatch_get_global_queue(DISPATCH_QUEUE_PRIORITY_DEFAULT,
    0), ^{                                                       //13
    NSFileManager* fm = [NSFileManager defaultManager];
    NSURL *newDocumentURL = [fm URLForUbiquityContainerIdentifier:nil]; //14
```

```
      newDocumentURL = [newDocumentURL
        URLByAppendingPathComponent:JFDocumentsDirectoryName
          isDirectory:YES];                                       //15
      newDocumentURL = [newDocumentURL URLByAppendingPathComponent:
        [self newUntitledDocumentName]];                          //16


      dispatch_async(dispatch_get_main_queue(), ^{                //17
        [documents addObject:newDocumentURL];


        // Update table                                           //18
        NSIndexPath* newCellIndexPath =
          [NSIndexPath indexPathForRow: ([documents count] - 1) inSection: 0];
        [self.tableView insertRowsAtIndexPaths:
          [NSArray arrayWithObject: newCellIndexPath]
          withRowAnimation:UITableViewRowAnimationAutomatic];


        [self.tableView selectRowAtIndexPath:newCellIndexPath animated:YES
          scrollPosition:(UITableViewScrollPositionMiddle)];
        UITableViewCell *selectedCell = [self.tableView
          cellForRowAtIndexPath: newCellIndexPath];
        [self performSegueWithIdentifier:DisplayDetailSegue
          sender:selectedCell];


        self.addButton.enabled = YES;                             //19
      });
    });
  }


- (NSString *)newUntitledDocumentName {                            //20

    NSInteger docCount = 1;
    NSString *newDocName = nil;

    // Manage document list updates
    BOOL done = NO;

    while (!done) {
      newDocName = [NSString stringWithFormat: @"Note %d.%@", docCount,
        JFDocFilenameExtension];

      // Search for first unused docCount value
      BOOL nameExists = NO;
      for (NSURL *aURL in documents) {
        if ([[aURL lastPathComponent] isEqualToString: newDocName]) {
          docCount++;
```

```
        nameExists = YES;
        break;
      }
    }

    if (!nameExists)
      done = YES;
  }


  return newDocName;


}
```

12 This is a new method to add a document. For comparison, the template version `insertNewObject:` is shown in the commented-out section just above. While you are adding a new document, disable the add button.

13 This block is sent to the priority queue.

14 The file manager is asked to find the ubiquity container NSURL.

15 You then add the directory name set earlier at line 3. You also note that this will be a directory.

16 You get the new document name. The code for this message appears later at line 20.

17 Switch back to the main queue to add the document.

18 Here you do standard table view maintenance.

19 On completion, re-enable the add button.

20 This is the code that finds the next document name. It uses fast iteration to run through documents. It hard-codes the name Note and appends a number to it as it iterates through. If it doesn't find a match, it returns that string as the new document name. This code enables you to reuse numbers for documents that have been deleted. There is more on document naming in Chapters 15 and 16.

Now that you have created a new document, you'll need to update the table view in the master view controller. Listing 14.6 shows that code. It is standard table view code with no iCloud features.

One important point to note is that the name of the document is displayed in the table view at line 24 in Listing 14.6. You don't have to do that. You can modify this code so that the file name is only used internally and the display name is something else.

Listing 14.6   **Master View Controller Updating the Table View**

```
#pragma mark - Table View

- (NSInteger)numberOfSectionsInTableView:(UITableView *)tableView
{
  return 1;                                                    //21
}


- (NSInteger)tableView:(UITableView *)tableView
  numberOfRowsInSection:(NSInteger)section
{
    return documents.count;                                    //22
}
- (UITableViewCell *)tableView:(UITableView *)tableView
  cellForRowAtIndexPath:
  (NSIndexPath *)indexPath
{
  UITableViewCell *newCell = [tableView
    dequeueReusableCellWithIdentifier: DocumentEntryCell
    forIndexPath:indexPath];

  if (!newCell)
    newCell = [[UITableViewCell alloc] initWithStyle:
    UITableViewCellStyleDefault \
      reuseIdentifier: DocumentEntryCell];

  if (!newCell)
    return nil;

  NSURL *fileURL = [documents objectAtIndex:[indexPath row]];   //23

  newCell.textLabel.text = [[fileURL lastPathComponent]
    stringByDeletingPathExtension];                            //24

  return newCell;
}

- (BOOL)tableView:(UITableView *)tableView
    canEditRowAtIndexPath:(NSIndexPath *)indexPath
{
    // Return NO if you do not want the specified item to be editable.
    return YES;
}
```

```
- (void)tableView:(UITableView *)tableView commitEditingStyle:
  (UITableViewCellEditingStyle)editingStyle
  forRowAtIndexPath:(NSIndexPath *)indexPath
{
  if (editingStyle == UITableViewCellEditingStyleDelete) {

  NSURL *fileURL = [documents objectAtIndex: [indexPath row]];        //25

      dispatch_async (dispatch_get_global_queue(DISPATCH_QUEUE_PRIORITY_DEFAULT, 0),
        ^{                                                              //26
      NSFileCoordinator *fc = [[NSFileCoordinator alloc] initWithFilePresenter:nil];
      [fc coordinateWritingItemAtURL:fileURL
        options:NSFileCoordinatorWritingForDeleting error:nil
        byAccessor: ^(NSURL *newURL) {
          NSFileManager *fm = [[NSFileManager alloc] init];
          [fm removeItemAtURL:newURL error:nil];
        }];
      });

      [documents removeObjectAtIndex:[indexPath row]];                 //27

      [tableView deleteRowsAtIndexPaths:[NSArray arrayWithObject:indexPath]
        withRowAnimation:UITableViewRowAnimationAutomatic];            //28
    }
}
```

21 There's one section (column) in the table view.

22 The number of rows in the column is the number of documents.

23 Get the appropriate object from documents.

24 Get the last item in the path. (That means you don't show the directory name.) Set the text of the appropriate cell.

25 Get the filename of the object to delete.

26 Do the deletion on the priority queue. Note that this code asks the file coordinator to delete the file.

27 Now delete the file from the documents array.

28 And delete the row from the table.

The sequence in which you write this code depends on your preferences and style. Somehow or other, you'll need to have a segue from a selected cell in the master view controller to the detail view controller. You'll need to implement prepareForSegue: sender: to pass the selected object into the detail view controller. Listing 14.7 shows that code. If you want, you can jump ahead to the storyboard before you write the code. It doesn't matter in which order you implement these as long as you have the appropriately named segue on the storyboard and in your code.

Listing 14.7   Master View Controller Preparing for the Segue

```
#pragma mark - Segue

- (void)prepareForSegue:(UIStoryboardSegue *)segue sender:(id)sender
{

  if (![segue.identifier isEqualToString:@"showDetail"])
      return;

  JFDetailViewController *destVC = (JFDetailViewController *)
    segue.destinationViewController;

  NSIndexPath *cellPath = [self.tableView indexPathForSelectedRow];
  UITableViewCell *theCell =
    [self.tableView cellForRowAtIndexPath: cellPath];
  NSURL *theURL = [documents objectAtIndex: [cellPath row]];       //29

  destVC.detailItem = theURL;                                      //30
  destVC.navigationItem.title = theCell.textLabel.text;            //31

}
```

29   Get the URL from the documents array. Remember that the objects in the documents array are actually NSURL objects.

30   Pass the NSURL object into the detailItem of the destination view controller (DetailViewController in this case).

31   Set the title of the destination view controller appropriately. theCell was set in tableview cellForRowAtIndexPath: at line 24.

Now it's back to your iCloud data. You create a NSMetadataQuery that runs on its own. This class provides the functionality of MDQuery that was originally used for Spotlight. You set up a query and start it. Remember that we're in an asynchronous world much of the time. After you start the query, it will get back to you using notifications. The code in Listing 14.8 references your ubiquity container, but other than that, it's not iCloud-specific code.

Listing 14.8   **Working with the Query**

```
#pragma mark iCloud query

- (NSMetadataQuery *)wrappedDocumentQuery {                              //32
  NSMetadataQuery *aQuery = [[NSMetadataQuery alloc] init];
  if (aQuery) {
    [aQuery setSearchScopes: [NSArray arrayWithObject:
      NSMetadataQueryUbiquitousDocumentsScope]];                        //33
    NSString *filePattern = [NSString stringWithFormat: @"*.%@",
      JFDocFilenameExtension];
    [aQuery setPredicate: [NSPredicate predicateWithFormat:@"%K LIKE %@",
      NSMetadataItemFSNameKey, filePattern]];
  }

    return aQuery;
}


- (void)setupAndStartQuery {                                            //34
  if (!_query)
    _query = [self wrappedDocumentQuery];
  [[NSNotificationCenter defaultCenter] addObserver: self selector:@selector
    (processFiles) name: NSMetadataQueryDidFinishGatheringNotification
                object: nil];
  [[NSNotificationCenter defaultCenter] addObserver: self selector:@selector
    (processFiles) name: NSMetadataQueryDidUpdateNotification
                object: nil];

  [_query startQuery];

}

- (void)processFiles {                                                  //35

  NSMutableArray *discoveredFiles = [NSMutableArray array];            //36

  [_query disableUpdates];                                            //37

  NSArray *queryResults = [_query results];
  for (NSMetadataItem *result in queryResults) {
    NSURL *fileURL = [result valueForAttribute: NSMetadataItemURLKey];
    NSNumber *aBool = nil;
    [fileURL getResourceValue: &aBool forKey: NSURLIsHiddenKey error: nil];
    if (aBool && ![aBool boolValue])                                   //38
      [discoveredFiles addObject: fileURL];
  }
```

```
[documents removeAllObjects];                                    //39
[documents addObjectsFromArray: discoveredFiles];
[self.tableView reloadData];

[_query enableUpdates];                                          //40

}

@end
```

32   You create the query. You use this code as-is in your project pro-
      vided that you have set your file extension that in this code is stored in
      `JFDocFilenameExtension`.

33   Set the scope of the query to documents.

34   This is the code that was called from `AwakeFromNib`. If necessary, it creates
      the query. It then registers to receive notifications about the query. If one
      arrives, `processFiles` will be invoked.

35   This is the method that will be invoked by the notifications.

36   `discoveredFiles` will store the files that the query finds.

37   Stop the query while we process.

38   Add files to `discovered` files unless they are marked as hidden. (This
      might be skipped for debugging.)

39   Move `discoveredFiles` to documents.

40   Re-enable the query updates.

DetailViewController

The master view controller does most of the work, so the detail view controller is typical boilerplate code. You may want to jump ahead to the storyboard to see what it will
look like. What matters is that you have two text fields (one for description and one for
location).

The detail view controller displays data from a specific instance of `WrappedDocument`,
which is described next. What matters about `WrappedDocument` is that it contains the
data, and it also has a protocol that manages updates.

Listing 14.9 shows the header file. Note that it imports `WrappedDocument` and
conforms to the `WrappedDocumentDelegate` protocol. The interface views are
declared. (Remember that the easiest way to do this is to add them to the storyboard
and use the Assistant to control-drag from the views to this file.)

Listing 14.9   **DetailViewController.h**

```
#import <UIKit/UIKit.h>
#import "JFWrappedDocument.h"                                   //1

@interface JFDetailViewController : UIViewController
  <UISplitViewControllerDelegate, JFWrappedDocumentDelegate>

@property (strong, nonatomic) NSURL *detailItem;

@property (weak, nonatomic) IBOutlet UITextField *textField;
@property (weak, nonatomic) IBOutlet UITextField *locationField;
@end
```

1   You need to import the WrappedDocument header file because it declares
the protocol that is adopted in the interface.

Listing 14.10 shows the detail view controller code. Most of it is standard code with
customizations for specific classes such as WrappedDocument.

Listing 14.10   **DetailViewController.m**

```
#import "JFDetailViewController.h"

@interface JFDetailViewController ()
@property (strong, nonatomic) UIPopoverController *masterPopoverController;
- (void)configureView;
@end

@implementation JFDetailViewController {                        //1
  JFWrappedDocument *_document;
}

#pragma mark - Managing the detail item

- (void)configureView
{
  // Update the user interface for the detail item.
}

- (void)viewDidLoad
{
    [super viewDidLoad];
    // Do any additional setup after loading the view, typically from a nib.
    [self configureView];
}
```

```objc
- (void)viewWillAppear:(BOOL)animated {

  [super viewWillAppear:animated];

  _document = [[JFWrappedDocument alloc ]
    initWithFileURL: self.detailItem];                        //2

  _document.delegate = self;

  NSFileManager *fm = [NSFileManager defaultManager];

  if ([fm fileExistsAtPath: [self.detailItem path]])
    [_document openWithCompletionHandler:nil];
  else
  {
    [_document saveToURL: self.detailItem
        forSaveOperation: UIDocumentSaveForCreating
      completionHandler:
      ^(BOOL success) {
        if (success) _textField.text = _document.documentText;
    }];
  }
}

- (void)viewWillDisappear:(BOOL)animated {

  [super viewWillDisappear:animated];


  NSString *newText = self.textField.text;                    //3
  NSString *newLocation = self.locationField.text;

  _document.documentText = newText;
  _document.documentLocation = newLocation

  [_document closeWithCompletionHandler:nil];                 //4


}

- (void)didReceiveMemoryWarning
{
    [super didReceiveMemoryWarning];
    // Dispose of any resources that can be recreated.
}
```

```
- (void)documentContentsDidChange: (JFWrappedDocument *)document {          //5
   dispatch_async (dispatch_get_main_queue(), ^{
     self.textField.text = document.documentText;
     self.locationField.text = document.documentLocation;
   });
}


#pragma mark - Split view

- (void)splitViewController:(UISplitViewController *)splitController
   willHideViewController:(UIViewController *)viewController
        withBarButtonItem: (UIBarButtonItem *)barButtonItem
    forPopoverController:(UIPopoverController *) popoverController
{
    barButtonItem.title = NSLocalizedString(@"Master", @"Master");
    [self.navigationItem setLeftBarButtonItem:barButtonItem animated:YES];
    self.masterPopoverController = popoverController;
}


- (void)splitViewController:(UISplitViewController *)splitController
        willShowViewController:(UIViewController *)viewController
    invalidatingBarButtonItem:(UIBarButtonItem *)barButtonItem
{
    // Called when the view is shown again in the split view, invalidating
    // the button and popover controller.
    [self.navigationItem setLeftBarButtonItem:nil animated:YES];
    self.masterPopoverController = nil;
}

@end
```

---

1   In the class extension, declare a local wrapped document.

2   Create the document for the view. Then, either open it or create it.

3   When the view will disappear, move data from the interface views into local variables and then into the document for storage.

4   Close and save.

5   This is the `WrappedDocumentDelegate` protocol implementation.

WrappedDocument

Finally, we get to the data for the app. It is stored in instances of `WrappedDocument`. Listing 14.11 shows the header file. It has properties for the three data items, and it declares setters that will be implemented for them. It also has a delegate, which is normally set to the detail view controller.

Listing 14.11   **WrappedDocument.h**

```objc
#import <UIKit/UIKit.h>

@protocol JFWrappedDocumentDelegate;                              //1

@interface JFWrappedDocument : UIDocument

@property (strong, nonatomic) NSFileWrapper *fileWrapper;

@property (strong, nonatomic) NSString *documentText;
@property (strong, nonatomic) NSString *documentLocation;
@property (strong, nonatomic) UIImage *documentImage;

@property (weak, nonatomic) id <JFWrappedDocumentDelegate> delegate;    //2

-(void)setDocumentText: (NSString*)newText;
-(void)setDocumentLocation: (NSString*)newText;
-(void)setDocumentImage:(UIImage *)image;

@end

@protocol JFWrappedDocumentDelegate <NSObject>                    //3
@optional

- (void)documentContentsDidChange: (JFWrappedDocument *)document;

@end
```

1. You need a forward reference to the protocol because you'll need it in the interface declaration.
2. This is the line of code that requires the forward reference to the protocol.
3. This is the protocol itself. It contains the `documentContentsDidChange` method that you saw implemented in the detail view controller at line 5.

Listing 14.12 shows you the beginning of WrappedDocument.m. These are standard declarations of fields, views, and strings. Use your own names if you want, or just reuse these to get started.

Listing 14.12   **WrappedDocument.m**

```objc
#import "JFAppDelegate.h"
#import "JFWrappedDocument.h"

NSString *UbiquityDirectoryComponentForDocuments = @"Documents";    //1
```

```objc
NSString *TextFileName = @"Text.txt";                              //2
NSString *LocationFileName = @"Location.txt";


NSStringEncoding kTextFileEncoding = NSUTF8StringEncoding;         //3


@interface JFWrappedDocument ()                                    //4

@property (strong, nonatomic) NSFileWrapper *wrapperText;
@property (strong, nonatomic) NSFileWrapper *wrapperLocation;

@end

@implementation JFWrappedDocument

+ (BOOL)autosavesInPlace
{
    // This gives us autosave and versioning for free in 10.7 and later
    return YES;
}

- (id)init
{
    self = [super init];
    if (self)
    {

    }
    return self;
}
```

1　This is the name of your top-level directory. It must match `JFDocument-DirectoryName` in `MasterViewController`. Alternatively, you can pull both declarations out into a shared file called Constants.h and include it.

2　These are the names of the files you will be putting inside the document wrapper.

3　This is the text encoding you will use for text files.

4　The class extension declares properties for each of the data types.

In Listing 14.13, you see the code that works with fields and views. Most of this is fairly standard, but the accessors for the text and location data show you how to work with data that is enclosed in a wrapper.

Listing 14.13   **WrappedDocument Using the Fields and Views**

```
-(void)setDocumentText: (NSString*)newText {                              //5
  NSLog (@" %@ %@ %@", newText, self.documentText, _fwText);

  if (newText != _fwText )//self.documentText)
  {
    NSString *oldText = _fwText;
    _fwText = newText;

    //register undo and cause autosave
    [self.undoManager setActionName: @"Text Change"];
    [self.undoManager registerUndoWithTarget:self
                              selector: @selector(setDocumentText:)
                                object: oldText];
  }
}


-(void)setDocumentLocation: (NSString*)newLocation {                      //6
    if (newLocation != _fwLocation)
  {
    NSString *oldLocation = _fwLocation;
    _fwLocation = newLocation;

    [self.undoManager setActionName: @"Location Change"];
    [self.undoManager registerUndoWithTarget:self
                              selector: @selector(setDocumentLocation:)
                                object: oldLocation];


  }


}

-(NSString*)documentText {                                                //7
  if (_fwText)
    return _fwText;

  NSDictionary *fileWrappers = [_fileWrapper fileWrappers];               //8

  if (!_wrapperText) {
    _wrapperText = [fileWrappers objectForKey: TextFileName];             //9
  }

  if (_wrapperText != nil)
  {
    NSData *textData = [_wrapperText regularFileContents];                //10
    _fwText = [[NSString alloc] initWithData:textData
      encoding:kTextFileEncoding];                                        //11
```

```
  } else {
    // handle error
  }

  return _fwText;
}

-(NSString*)documentLocation {                                    //12
  if (_fwLocation)
    return _fwLocation;

  NSDictionary *fileWrappers = [_fileWrapper fileWrappers];

  if (!_wrapperLocation) {
    _wrapperLocation = [fileWrappers objectForKey: LocationFileName];
  }

  if (_wrapperLocation != nil)
  {
    NSData *locationData = [_wrapperLocation regularFileContents];
    _fwLocation = [[NSString alloc] initWithData:locationData
      encoding:kTextFileEncoding];
  } else {
    // handle error
  }

  return _fwLocation;
}
```

5, 6   These are the custom setters for text and location. Note that undo support
       is added. This is standard code, but it's important here. That's because it is
       the undo registration that enables auto save, which this app relies on.

7   This is the custom getter for text.

8   The document-level `fileWrapper` declared in WrappedDocument.h is
       asked to return its own file wrappers into a dictionary.

9   If we don't have _wrapperText, get it from the file wrapper dictionary
       created in line 8.

10   Get the content of the wrapper as `NSData`.

11   Extract the text as an `NSString`.

12   This is a similar getter for location.

Finally, Listing 14.14 show the ins and outs of file wrapper support. You have
to implement these two methods in order to access your own data. Testing note:
`contentsForType:error:` is dispatched asynchronously. Particularly when testing

on Xcode with debugging code, it is very easy to get ahead of the dispatch. Set a break-point at the beginning of this method and wait for it to stop before you try to inspect variables. It is not uncommon for it to take a minute to get here.

Listing 14.14 WrappedDocument File Wrapper Support

```
#pragma mark - File Wrapper/ Package Support

- (BOOL)loadFromContents:(id)contents ofType:(NSString *)typeName
                error:(NSError *__autoreleasing *)outError {        //13

  self.fileWrapper = (NSFileWrapper *)contents;                     //14

  if ([_delegate respondsToSelector: @selector(documentContentsDidChange:)])
  {
    [_delegate documentContentsDidChange: self];                   //15
  }

  return YES;
}

- (id)contentsForType:(NSString *)typeName error:
  (NSError *__autoreleasing *)outError {
  if ( _documentFileWrapper == nil)                                //16
  {
      self.fileWrapper = [[NSFileWrapper alloc]
        initDirectoryWithFileWrappers:nil];                       //17
  }

  NSDictionary *fileWrapperDictionary = [_documentFileWrapper
                                   fileWrappers];                 //18

  if (self.documentText != nil)                                   //19
  {
    NSData *textData = [self.documentText
      dataUsingEncoding: kTextFileEncoding];

    NSFileWrapper *textFileWrapper = [fileWrappers
      objectForKey:TextFileName];
    if (textFileWrapper != nil) {
      [_documentFileWrapper removeFileWrapper: textFileWrapper];
    }
    textFileWrapper = [[NSFileWrapper alloc]
      initRegularFileWithContents:textData];
    [textFileWrapper setPreferredFilename: TextFileName];
    [self.fileWrapper addFileWrapper: textFileWrapper];
  }
```

```
    if ( self.documentLocation != nil)                              //20
    {
      NSData *locationData = [self.documentLocation
        dataUsingEncoding: kTextFileEncoding];

      NSFileWrapper *locationFileWrapper = [fileWrappers
        objectForKey:LocationFileName];
      if (locationFileWrapper != nil) {
        [self.fileWrapper removeFileWrapper: locationFileWrapper];
      }
      locationFileWrapper = [[NSFileWrapper alloc]
        initRegularFileWithContents:locationData];
      [locationFileWrapper setPreferredFilename: LocationFileName];
      [self.fileWrapper addFileWrapper: locationFileWrapper];
    }

      return self.fileWrapper;
}


@end
```

13 You must implement this method to get data out of the file wrapper. Set a breakpoint here (details in the next section).

14 Get the `contents`, which is the top-level file wrapper for the document.

15 If this document's delegate responds to `documentContentsDidChange`, call it. This is the method in the protocol that is declared in DetailViewController.h.

16, 17 If there is no top-level file wrapper for the document (`self.file-wrapper`), create one.

18 Get the subsidiary file wrappers out of the top-level file wrapper. If this code looks familiar, you're right. You saw it in Listing 14.13 at line 7 in the implementation of the `documentText` getter. Now you're using it to go through the file wrappers and their data in order to create the snapshot of your content for storage.

19 Check to see if there's data to store.

20 Do the same for location.

The `if` statement at line 18 is problematic and requires customization. You have several tests you can make. Certainly, testing whether or not you have data to be included in the content snapshot is a valid test to make in all cases. However, you need to apply your knowledge of the data to determine the other part of that test.

The code here works just fine for a new document. The issue comes up when you have an existing document that already has a file wrapper for text or any other wrapped data. Do you want to remove it and create a new one? Or do you want to just always write out a new one with the current data?

Also, note that the breakpoint that is suggested at line 13 is very important. In order to simplify this example, it uses iCloud and only iCloud. When there's something to store, you call `closeWithCompletionHandler:` (line 4 in Listing 14.10). This is all done asynchronously. To really appreciate what's going on, set a breakpoint there as well as at line 18 in this file. You'll see that there can be a very significant gap in time. File operations in general take time, and iCloud operations generally take even more so.

Working with the Storyboard

The storyboard from the template is basically set up for you. You just need a few customizations. The template storyboard was shown previously in Figure 14.12.

Here are the steps to customize the storyboard:

1. Add whatever fields you need in the detail view controller.

2. With the Assistant, control-drag from each one to create and connect the property in DetailViewController.h.

3. If you are using Xcode 5, make certain that any constraint warnings are taken care of. (In previous versions of Xcode, constraints were automatically inserted for you, which turned out to make extra work much of the time.)

4. Make certain that the segue name matches the name in MasterViewController.m.

Chapter Summary

This chapter showed you how to save a wrapped document in iCloud. It provided a simplified example that uses no local storage. This not only simplified things but also demonstrated the time delays that you have to work with.

You also saw how to use developer.apple.com to inspect your iCloud documents and other files; you have also seen how to use iCloud in System Preferences to delete files. If you are supporting a production application, you may be called on to guide users through this process.

Exercises

1. After you have built this project, run it and track it using developer.iCloud.com as well as System Preferences on OS X and Settings on iOS. Experiment with adding and deleting documents, paying particular attention to the time lags.

2. Add more fields to the project. Remember that in this example there's one field per wrapped file, but you can have many—and they can be different types. Particularly on iPhone and iPod touch, it may be useful to make a single screen's data correspond to a wrapped file.

3. There are no error messages in this sample, although there are some comments. What is the best way to implement those messages? Remember that this is not specifically an iCloud issue. One point to remember is that if you're dealing with an error in an asynchronous process, you may deal with it after the fact, so you'll need to keep the relevant information in your app until it is time to talk to the user.

15

Working with iOS Documents

The word *document* has a number of meanings, so a few words about its use in the title of this chapter and Chapter 16, "Working with OS X Documents," are in order. In this chapter, *document* means a class that you create as a subclass of UIDocument, which is part of the Cocoa Touch framework. In Chapter 16, *document* means a subclass of NSDocument that you create. NSDocument and UIDocument are similar but different, just as are Cocoa and Cocoa Touch. Fundamentally, the differences are between laptop and desktop computers with keyboards and trackpads on the one side and mobile devices with touchscreens on the other side.

This distinction is important for developers but is not even noticed by most users. Most of those users also make no distinction between the file (or files) that provides the storage for a document's data and the runtime representation of that data that is visible on their screen. However, for developers, that runtime representation of a document that is provided by a subclass of UIDocument or NSDocument is what we work with. Among the functions that the document classes provide are interaction with the file system for saving and reading document data from a file, the ability to undo and redo commands, and the basic tools for working with iCloud and app sandboxes on both OS X and iOS.

In this chapter, you will see how to work with UIDocument and related classes in iOS. With local storage of data, you work with the app sandbox on iOS, and with iCloud storage, you work with iCloud itself. Part of working with iCloud consists of keeping track of the notifications of changes in iCloud account or preferences, and those changes may entail moving all of the app's documents to or from the sandbox or iCloud. Those topics are covered in Chapter 18, "Completing the Round Trip." This chapter focuses primarily on what you have to do to implement your UIDocument subclass.

The biggest difference between Chapter 14's Placid project and this chapter's Loon project is that Placid stores data only in iCloud. Loon stores data either in iCloud or in the app's local sandbox depending on a user's preference setting. This is the standard way in which Apple suggests apps use iCloud—either everything in iCloud or everything locally.

This distinction—all in iCloud or both in iCloud and on the device—is the primary difference. Both apps (as well as the apps in chapters 16, 17, and 18) let you record a series of observations. Two demonstration fields are provided where users can enter a description of an issue (a broken streetlight, for example) and the location of the issue. These can obviously be expanded to cover many more types of data, but these apps focus on the basics and the iCloud implementation.

Among the topics covered in this chapter are

- Creating a new document
- Saving a document
- Storing data into a document
- Retrieving data from a document

Those topics are addressed for both iCloud and local documents.

Planning the App's Structure

Apple's primary reference for working with documents on iOS is "Document-Based App Programming Guide for iOS." This chapter organizes the information differently from Apple's reference. This alternative organization helps you understand your options and choose one approach, the other, or a hybrid. If you talk to developers, you will see that there are still other ways of approaching documents on iOS.

Choosing between Navigation and Split View Controller on iPad

The first issue you have to address is whether or not the Loon app will use a split view controller on iPad. On iPhone, chances are it will use a navigation controller to manage a list of documents and then open a specific one when a document is selected. That's a job for a master view controller (the list) and a detail view controller (the selected document). You can combine the architectures with a master view controller that itself contains a navigation controller; when you drill down far enough, you can open your selected object in a detail view controller.

On iPad, because the screen is larger, you can keep your master view controller visible either onscreen or in a popover alongside the detail view controller. In fact, the Master-Detail Application template presents exactly these architectures—a split view controller on iPad and a navigation controller on iPhone.

If you want this interface, you have to do a little bit of refactoring to accommodate the different structures. Specifically, you cannot use `viewWillAppear` or `viewWillDisappear` to drive your interactions with document data: they are called every time a detail view controller appears or disappears in a navigation controller, but in a split view controller, they are called only at the beginning and end of the app. In between, the data in the detail view controller is updated as needed, but these methods aren't called.

That is why if you compare the structure of this app to some other apps, you'll see that the code to manage interactions between the interface and its objects is pulled out into its own methods such as `configureView`. In this way, the same code is used on both iPhone and iPad, but it is triggered in different ways in the two environments.

Deciding on a Structure

The refactoring described in the previous section is not just a matter of managing views and their data. The structure of Loon is a common approach to managing iCloud functionality. When you first look at the code, it may seem as if it is scattered all over the place. However, there is a logic behind it, and that logic rests on two concepts: managing iCloud availability and working with the Model-View-Controller design pattern.

Managing iCloud Availability

The advice from Apple is that the user should be given a choice between storing app data in iCloud or locally. (Some apps, such as the iWork apps from Apple and other iOS document-based apps, allow users to make that choice on a document-by-document basis.) That is one of the reasons for using a document-based structure. When an app's data is stored in a single repository—the *library* or *shoebox* pattern—it all should reside in one place or another.

However, if you are using iCloud, you need to prepare for the possibility that at any given moment it will be unavailable. As you will see in Chapter 18, "Completing the Round Trip," using iCloud may mean also using local storage when iCloud is unavailable. Yes, that's more work than simply writing out to a file that the user can manipulate directly (for good or bad), but the value to the user is much greater.

Confronting the Models in Loon

When you think about iCloud and the fact that it may or may not be available at any given moment regardless of the user's preference, the structure of iCloud–related functionality in Loon (and many other projects) falls into place. (It is not the only such structure, but it's the one used in Loon.) Here is an overview of what goes where:

- `AppDelegate` manages the basic iCloud interactions. It determines if iCloud is available, for example.

- `MasterViewController` manages the list of documents that the app will deal with. (This is how it works in most projects of this type.) `MasterViewController` constructs that list, and it reflects the availability of iCloud and the user's storage preference. The job of `MasterViewController` is to manage that list appropriately. Managing the list includes updating it for new documents as needed. As part of updating the list for new documents, `MasterViewController` creates them appropriately. `DetailViewController` manages a single document that has been selected in `MasterViewController`. (Again, this is typical of this kind of project.) Managing a single document includes moving the data to and from interface elements.

- `WrappedDocument` is a single document that manages its data. It is a subclass of `UIDocument`, and it is basically the same document class you created in Chapter 14.

- `FileRepresentation` is a lightweight object that represents a file. It contains the NSURL for the document as well as the document name (that is, the last part of the URL such as Note 1).

You may be wondering where the reading and writing of documents takes place. Mostly, that's not done in your code: it's part of Cocoa Touch provided that you set things up properly. If you have provided a filename and URL for the document, the system knows how to read and write it, so your work is confined to calling `closeWithCompletionHandler:`, which does the work.

You'll see the code that is used in "Writing the Code" later in this chapter.

Starting the Loon Project

This chapter's project, like all the projects in this book, is named after a lake in the Adirondack Mountains of New York—Loon. Set it up as you set up Placid in Chapter 14 in the "Starting the Placid Project" section. After you create the project (using the Master-Detail Application template as in Chapter 14), you select the project at the top of the project navigator; the tabs across the top of the editor are where you configure the project.

Setting Project General Info

As you see in Figure 15.1, the general info is set by default based on the project name you entered when you created the project. Don't worry that in Figure 15.1 the project name is capitalized and that it has carried through to the first target and then to the default bundle name. The names are case-sensitive, so you can mix upper- and lowercase as long as you are consistent. (In other words, the bundle identifier for this project is com.champlainarts.Loon; com.champlainarts.loon can be used for another project, but most developers avoid that situation.) Typically, developers leave the beginning of the bundle identifier (the reverse domain name section such as `com.champlainarts`) in lowercase. The name that follows the reverse domain is going to appear in some user-facing contexts such as System Preferences for iCloud, so it will look better if it starts with a capital letter. (Note that Figure 15.1 shows the Loon project after files have been added to it, so if you are just starting out with a new project, not all of these files will be present. They will be present when you have worked through this chapter.)

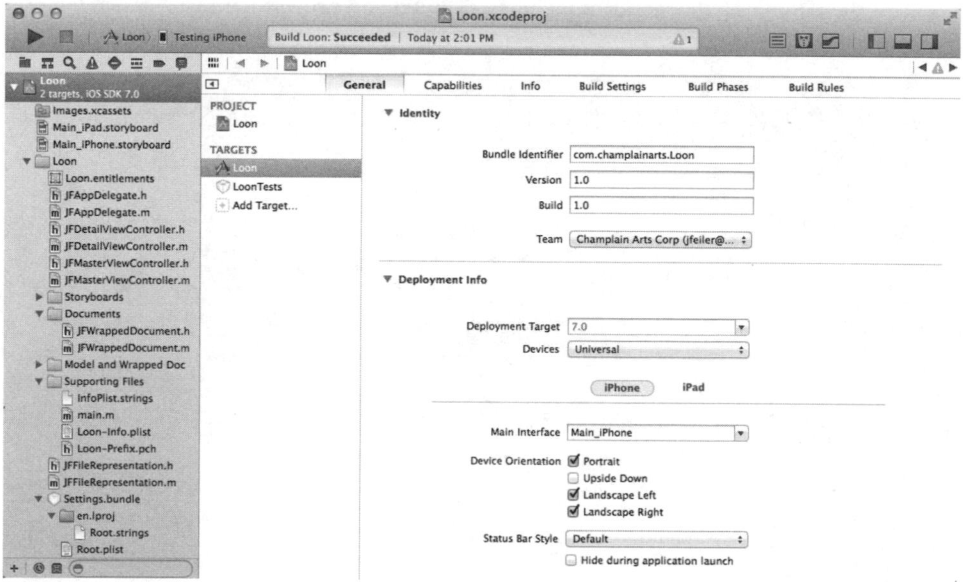

Figure 15.1   Using upper- and lowercase letters in your bundle name

You can usually leave the general info as it is set by Xcode. If you need to change it later, you can do so. However, note that changing names and identifiers can be a bit of a chore once the project has been created. If you need to do so, try selecting the name in question and using Edit, Factor, Rename to do a smart renaming. Not all names can be changed in this way—you may need to actually retype the name or use a standard find/replace command, but Edit, Factor, Rename should be your first choice.

Give some thought to the name you'll use for your project. It should normally be short and descriptive because in some cases it will be seen by users. It is true that you can customize the string that the user sees, but the project name is used in a number of places in your project's configuration, and changing it later on can break some settings.

Setting Project Capabilities

You need to turn on iCloud in the Capabilities section, as you see in Figure 15.2. You don't need a key-value store, but you do need to add a ubiquity container with the + at the bottom of the ubiquity containers section, as you see in the figure. Again, you can go with the default name even if it includes a capitalized project name.

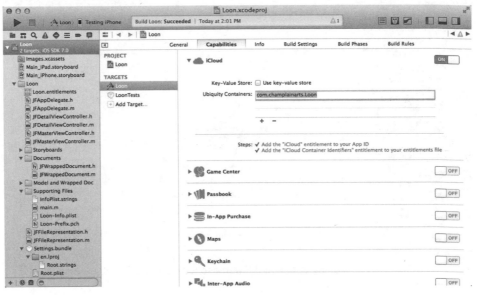

Figure 15.2   Configuring iCloud

The steps section at the bottom of the iCloud section changes as you set up the project. When you first turn iCloud on, the steps describe what will happen. As you configure iCloud, the steps normally change to have checkmarks indicating what has been done. If an error occurs, it will be marked in red. (If you have configured iCloud in Xcode before Xcode 5, you will be very pleasantly surprised. Many manual steps in previous versions of Xcode have been replaced in the Xcode 5 interface.)

An entitlements file will be automatically created after you have configured iCloud. You can find it in the project navigator and view it as you see in Figure 15.3. Normally you don't need to make any changes to it.

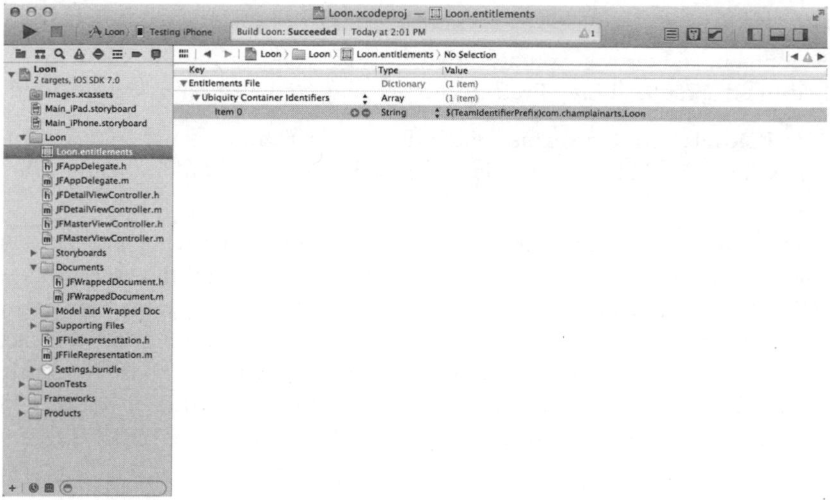

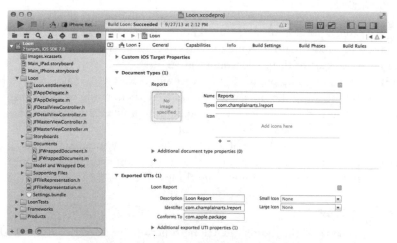

Figure 15.3   Automatically created entitlements file when you enable iCloud in Xcode

Setting Up Documents

In the Info tab, set up your documents just as you did in Chapter 14. You can use the same settings as you did in Chapter 14, but for learning and testing, it can be easier to use a separate document name and extension so that the documents in the two chapters are separate even if their contents and structure are the same. Figure 15.4 shows the Info settings for Loon.

Figure 15.4   Setting up your documents

Adding Settings

For development and testing, you need two settings; you can add them now, as described in Chapter 9, "Using Preferences, Settings, and Keychains with iCloud":

- **Use iCloud:** This is a yes/no switch that the user can use to choose whether or not iCloud should be used for document storage. This should remain in the finished app.

- **First Time:** This is a yes/no switch that is designed for testing. For production, the first time the app is run, you should ask whether or not the user wants to use iCloud for document storage. The answer should be stored in the Use iCloud preference so that the user can later come back and turn it on or off. The actual code for determining the first time the app runs may make it hard to test this logic. Adding a switch that you can use to determine whether or not you should take the first-time path makes testing easier. Note that this is only for testing.

Writing the Code

With your project set up from the template and configured as described in the previous section, it's time to write the code. As noted previously, the iCloud functionality is spread among a number of classes in the project. You may wind up jumping around in the code in order to implement the app. For that reason, the example code presented here contains some diagnostics that may be helpful in tracking down bugs.

Don't spend much time trying to follow the flow of the code presented here. As is true of so much of iCloud (and many other technologies these days), there is no flow in a traditional sense. Notifications fly around, starting some processes and reporting that other processes are complete. If you run the code with breakpoints set at key points (a number of breakpoints are set in the downloadable code), you'll see these jumps from one part of the code to another part. Particularly when blocks are used as completion handlers, it's often a good idea to set a breakpoint on the first line within the block because you will almost never execute that line of code after the line above it. It will be executed at the start of the asynchronous process.

Even if you are not going out to iCloud, you will encounter what appear to be lengthy gaps in processing. If you want, you can time them, and you'll see that they are actually not as long as they may appear to you, although when running a debug version of your app, there are moments when a delay of half a minute or more may occur. More than one developer has wasted a lot of time wondering why some method or another wasn't firing when the reality was just that the notification hadn't gotten through yet. Be patient until you get a sense of how long things take.

AppDelegate

`AppDelegate` manages the most basic iCloud functionality: determining whether the user wants to use it and whether or not it is available. Listing 15.1 shows AppDelegate.h.

Listing 15.1   **AppDelegate.h**

```
#import <UIKit/UIKit.h>

@interface JFAppDelegate : UIResponder <UIApplicationDelegate,
  UIAlertViewDelegate>                                          //1

@property (strong, nonatomic) UIWindow *window;                //2
@property (readonly) BOOL documentsIniCloud;                   //3

@end
```

1   This code is almost the same as it was in Placid. You'll need to conform to `UIAlertViewDelegate` because you'll have an alert that asks the user about using iCloud or local storage on the app's first launch.

2   `window` is a property that is part of the Master-Detail Application template. It is used to set up the split view.

3   `documentsIniCloud` is added in Loon. Properties and methods generally start with a lowercase letter and capitalize each word in a multiword name. In example code, Apple tends to leave iCloud as lowercase, which is why this is not `documentsInICloud`.

You can get to `documentsIniCloud` directly from elsewhere in the project with the following code:

```
BOOL usingiCloud = ((JFAppDelegate *)[[UIApplication sharedApplication]
  delegate]).documentsIniCloud;
```

You can also write an accessor. The choice depends on your style and, probably, the number of times you need to get the value.

The implementation in AppDelegate.m falls neatly into two pieces. Listing 15.2 shows the first part. It is followed by stubs and comments that show you what you might want to implement. The code for Loon then follows in Listing 15.3.

Right at the beginning, you see the use of a *ubiquity token*. This is a lightweight object that you can request from the system when the app starts up. The ubiquity token represents the current active iCloud account for the user (it is not the account itself). You don't care about the value of a ubiquity token in most cases. Rather, you care about whichever of these situations apply:

- If there is no ubiquity token when you ask for it, the user does not have an active iCloud account.

- If the ubiquity token matches a ubiquity token that you have previously stored, the user is using the same iCloud account.

- If the ubiquity token does not match a previously stored ubiquity token, the user is using a different iCloud account, and you will need to update stored data accordingly (this is addressed in Chapter 18).

Notice that nowhere is it mentioned that iCloud is or is not available. If the user is running in Airplane mode but had an active iCloud account before turning on Airplane mode, the ubiquity token is still returned. A key part of the iCloud architecture is that the availability of iCloud is a separate issue from the current account identifier. You can have an iCloud account identifier when iCloud is not available.

The code in Listing 15.2 is fairly standard. You need to customize it for your own identifiers, but the processing is used in many iCloud apps.

Listing 15.2   **AppDelegate.m Part I**

```objectivec
#import "JFAppDelegate.h"

@interface JFAppDelegate ()

@property id ubiquityToken;                                       //1
@property NSURL *ubiquityContainer;
@property (readwrite) BOOL documentsIniCloud;                     //2

@end

@implementation JFAppDelegate

#pragma mark - launch and background
- (BOOL)application:(UIApplication *)application didFinishLaunchingWithOptions
   (NSDictionary *)launchOptions
{

   if (![[NSUserDefaults standardUserDefaults]
     boolForKey: @"com.champlainarts.Loon.hasLaunched"]) {        //3
     [[NSUserDefaults standardUserDefaults] setBool:YES
     forKey: @"com.champlainarts.Loon.hasLaunched"];
     [[NSUserDefaults standardUserDefaults] synchronize];
     NSString *msg = @"Should documents be stored in iCloud and
       available on all your devices?";                           //4

     UIAlertView *alert = [[UIAlertView alloc]                    //5
                            initWithTitle: @"Choose Storage Option"
                                  message: msg
                                 delegate: self
                        cancelButtonTitle: @"Local Only"
                        otherButtonTitles: @"Use iCloud", nil];
   [alert show];

   }
```

```
dispatch_async(dispatch_get_global_queue(DISPATCH_QUEUE_PRIORITY_DEFAULT,
  0), ^{
_ubiquityContainer = [[NSFileManager
  defaultManager]URLForUbiquityContainerIdentifier:nil];              //6
if (_ubiquityContainer != nil) {
  NSLog (@"Got iCloud\n");
  dispatch_async (dispatch_get_main_queue(), ^(void) {              //7
  });
}
else
  NSLog (@"No iCloud\n");
});


_documentsIniCloud = [[NSUserDefaults standardUserDefaults]
  boolForKey: @"com.champlainarts.Loon.documentsIniCloud"];         //8

NSLog (@" %s, %hhd", __PRETTY_FUNCTION__, _documentsIniCloud);       //9

if (_documentsIniCloud){
  [self initializeiCloudAccess];                                    //10
};

if (!_documentsIniCloud) {                                          //11
}

// Override point for customization after application launch.
if ([[UIDevice currentDevice] userInterfaceIdiom] ==
  UIUserInterfaceIdiomPad) {
  UISplitViewController *splitViewController =
  (UISplitViewController *)self.window.rootViewController;
  UINavigationController *navigationController =
    [splitViewController.viewControllers lastObject];
  splitViewController.delegate =
    (id)navigationController.topViewController;
}

  return YES;
}
```

_____

1 `AppDelegate` will take care of the ubiquity token and container.

2 Note that the class extension redefines `documentsIniCloud`. In `AppDelegate` it is `readonly`, but here it is `readwrite` so that only `AppDelegate` can write to it.

3   This is the code for the first-time launch. It does not use the switch for
     testing that was discussed in "Adding Settings" previously in this chapter.
     This is the code you would use in production. The issue it addresses is that
     if the setting is off, that can mean that the user turned it off or that there is
     no value. That is why defining a setting so that it is only used if its value is
     "Yes" is sometimes useful.

4   The string for the alert is stored in its own variable simply to make spacing
     of the code more readable.

5   This is the alert for the first launch that asks the user to choose a storage
     location. It can subsequently be changed in Settings.

6   Look for the ubiquity container to find out if iCloud is available. Do this off
     the main thread because it can be a lengthy process. This is a good place to
     log the results for testing.

7   Once you have determined the ubiquity container, switch back to the main
     thread to set up the interface.

8   Get the user storage setting from Settings.

9   Log diagnostic message to console.

10   To use iCloud, send `initializeiCloudAccess` to `self`. (The code is in
     Listing 15.3.)

11   Check again because `initializeiCloudAccess` may have turned
     `documentsIniCloud` off. This code will be completed in Chapter 18.

After the stubs and comments that are always part of the AppDelegate.m template,
you add three methods to `AppDelegate` that are specific to iCloud. These three are
fairly common because they deal with iCloud itself. Once you get into the two main
view controllers, you'll deal with your subclass of `UIDocument`, its data, and the user
interface. Listing 15.3 shows those methods.

Listing 15.3   **AppDelegate.m Part II**

```
#pragma mark - iCloud

- (void)initializeiCloudAccess {
  _ubiquityToken = [[NSFileManager
                  defaultManager]ubiquityIdentityToken];          //12
      // Check for icloud avail and store token

  if (_ubiquityToken) {                                            //13
    NSData *newTokenData = [NSKeyedArchiver archivedDataWithRootObject:
    _ubiquityToken]; // archive
    [[NSUserDefaults standardUserDefaults] //defaults
      setObject:newTokenData
      forKey: @"com.champlainarts.Loon.UbiquityIdentityToken"];
```

```
      [[NSUserDefaults standardUserDefaults] synchronize];
    } else {
      [[NSUserDefaults standardUserDefaults]                          //14
        removeObjectForKey: @"com.champlainarts.Loon.UbiquityIdentityToken"];
      [[NSUserDefaults standardUserDefaults] synchronize];

    }

    [[NSNotificationCenter defaultCenter] addObserver:self             //15
                        selector:@selector(manageUbiquityIdentityChange)
                          name: NSUbiquityIdentityDidChangeNotification
                        object:nil];
}

#pragma mark - NSUbiquityIdentityDidChangeNotification

- (void) manageUbiquityIdentityChange {                               //16

}

#pragma mark - UIAlertViewDelegate

- (void)alertView:(UIAlertView *)alertView
    didDismissWithButtonIndex:(NSInteger)buttonIndex {
  if (buttonIndex == [alertView firstOtherButtonIndex]) {    // other button
    _documentsIniCloud = YES;
  } else {
    _documentsIniCloud = NO;
  }

  NSLog (@" %hhd", _documentsIniCloud);


  [[NSUserDefaults standardUserDefaults]                             //defaults
    setBool:_documentsIniCloud
    forKey: @"com.champlainarts.Loon.documentsIniCloud"];
}

@end
```

12   Get the ubiquity token. Unlike getting the ubiquity container, this is a fast operation, so it can happen on the main thread.

13   If there is a ubiquity token, store it in user defaults. Chapter 18 will show you how to check if it is different from the last-used token, but for now, this is the basic processing you should be familiar with.

14   If there isn't a ubiquity token, remove one that exists. Remember that in Airplane mode, there is still a ubiquity token, but there is no iCloud access.

15   Register for notification of a changed iCloud user.

16   In order to register, you need to provide at least the shell of the method to receive the registration. You may want to set a breakpoint at this time so that when you start testing, you'll be reminded that the method needs to be implemented (you'll see that in Chapter 18).

MasterViewController

As is always the case with a master view controller, its primary function is to manage the master view. In the Master-Detail Application, that view is presented in a UITableView. Typically, the elements of the master view controller are stored at runtime in an array. That master view controller lets you create new detail elements; they need to be added to the runtime array and stored appropriately.

MasterViewController.m is the longest file in the app, and because of its central role, it touches on just about every aspect of the app. As noted previously, because control does not flow in a linear way through the app, some of the aspects of MasterView-Controller will not become clear until you drill down into the other classes. You may want to skip around in this chapter, but you may also want to read through quickly to get an overview and then come back to specific parts as they become relevant.

Listing 15.4 shows the header file.

Listing 15.4   **MasterViewController.h**

```
#import <UIKit/UIKit.h>

@class JFDetailViewController;

@interface JFMasterViewController : UITableViewController

@property (strong, nonatomic) JFDetailViewController *detailViewController;
@property (weak, nonatomic) IBOutlet UIBarButtonItem *addButton;          //1

@end
```

1   This is a button that is used to add new elements to the list. You can create it either by control-dragging from the storyboard to the .h file or by explicitly typing the code. A third way, which is used here, is to programmatically create the button. You need to expose it because, as you will see, you need to disable adding new items during a part of the iCloud discovery of existing items.

MasterViewController.m is a fairly long file. You can use `pragma mark - ` to divide it into seven sections:

- **Load and Memory:** These are standard methods to manage the view. There is minimal customization here.

- **Documents:** Two methods handle the actual adding of a new document and obtaining a name for it. You will learn that these are the basic methods for working with `UIDocument` and its subclasses.

- **Table View:** Six familiar methods let you manage the `UITableView`. There is basically nothing about iCloud here.

- **Segue:** This is `prepareForSegue:sender:`. Note that it is used in the navigation interface for the iPhone version. It sets the detail item for the new detail view controller. For iPad, that is done elsewhere.

- **iCloud Query:** This is the heart of the iCloud code. It locates documents in the cloud and keeps that local `_documents` array up to date.

- **Local Sandbox:** This is the code used when iCloud is not being used. Like iCloud Query, it keeps the local `_documents` array up to date.

Before looking into each of those sections in detail, take a look at the beginning of the implementation file, which is shown in Listing 15.5.

Listing 15.5   **MasterViewController.m Part I**

```
#import "JFMasterViewController.h"
#import "JFDetailViewController.h"
#import "JFWrappedDocument.h"
#import "JFAppDelegate.h"
#import "JFFileRepresentation.h"

static NSString *JFDocFilenameExtension = @"lreport";          //1
static NSString *DisplayDetailSegue = @"showDetail";           //2
static NSString *JFDocumentsDirectoryName = @"Documents";      //3
static NSString *DocumentEntryCell = @"DocumentEntryCell";     //4

@interface JFMasterViewController () {
  NSMetadataQuery *_query;                                      //5
}

@property (strong, nonatomic) NSMutableArray *documents;       //6

@end

@implementation JFMasterViewController
```

1   This is the file extension.

2   For the navigation interface on iPhone, you need a named segue from the prototype cell in the iPhone storyboard to the detail view controller. This name must match the name you set in Interface Builder.

3   This is the name of the documents directory in the local sandbox and in iCloud.

4   This is the name of the reusable prototype cell in the master view controller.

5   The heart of the iCloud discovery process is a query that runs asynchronously to check for new documents. This is that query. You'll set it up once and then send it off. It is described further in "iCloud Query" later in this chapter.

6   This is the array of documents obtained either from the local sandbox or from iCloud in the "iCloud Query" section. It can be a mutable array, as it is here, because it needs to be modified. Depending on your data and how much it is updated, you may want to use an NSArray (which is immutable) and copy it into a mutable array and then back when needed. You use arrayWithArray: for this. You have to balance whether the faster performance of an immutable array outweighs the cost of the copy, and that depends on your data and particularly how much there is of it. This array stores the names and paths for the documents but not the document contents, so there usually isn't much of it.

Load and Memory Section

Listing 15.6 is standard code from the template with very few customizations. The one difference is at the end of viewDidLoad where the documents array is filled either from iCloud or from the local sandbox.

Listing 15.6   **Load and memory**

```
#pragma mark - Load and memory

- (void)awakeFromNib
{

  [super awakeFromNib];

  if ([[UIDevice currentDevice] userInterfaceIdiom] ==
    UIUserInterfaceIdiomPad) {
    self.clearsSelectionOnViewWillAppear = NO;
    self.preferredContentSize = CGSizeMake(320.0, 600.0);
  }


}
```

```
- (void)viewDidLoad
{
  [super viewDidLoad];
  // Do any additional setup after loading the view, typically from a nib.

  self.navigationItem.leftBarButtonItem = self.editButtonItem;        //7
  UIBarButtonItem* addButton = [[UIBarButtonItem alloc]
    initWithBarButtonSystemItem:UIBarButtonSystemItemAdd target:self
    action:@selector(addDocument:)];                                  //8
  self.navigationItem.rightBarButtonItem = addButton;                 //9
  self.addButton = addButton;                                         //10
  self.detailViewController = (JFDetailViewController *)
    [[self.splitViewController.viewControllers lastObject]
    topViewController];

  BOOL usingiCloud = ((JFAppDelegate *)[[UIApplication sharedApplication]
    delegate]).documentsIniCloud;

  if (!_documents)
    _documents = [[NSMutableArray alloc] init];                       //11

  if (usingiCloud) {
    [self setupAndStartQuery];                                        //12
  } else {
    [self fillDocumentsForLocalStorage];                             //13

  }

}


- (void)didReceiveMemoryWarning
{
    [super didReceiveMemoryWarning];
    // Dispose of any resources that can be recreated.
}
```

7 Create an edit button at the left of the navigation bar.

8 Create an add button.

9 Place the add button at the right of the navigation bar.

10 Store a reference to the add button. (This is a property that was added to the template in the header file.)

11 If necessary, create the _documents array and then fill it.

12 Set up and start the query if using iCloud.

13 If not using iCloud, fill the Documents array locally.

Documents

The section for documents consists of two methods: the first adds a new document in response to a user command, and the second calculates the name of the new document. The basics of adding a new document are shown in the default `insertNewObject` code in the Master-Detail Application template; it is shown in Listing 15.7.

There are two tasks involved in inserting a new object:

- Insert the object into the array of objects.
- Update the `UITableView` interface.

This is exactly what the code in Loon does, but it also does a number of other things specific to the project. Don't let that distract you from the fact that the main purpose is to update the array as well as the table view. You don't need to actually insert the object into the table view: `tableView:cellForRow:` takes care of getting data from the mutable array on demand. (Remember also that instead of a mutable array, you can use an immutable array, which is faster, and then use `arrayWithArray:` to switch the mutable and immutable arrays when you need to.)

Note that the template code to create a new object is provided in Listing 15.7 for comparison purposes. Don't worry that the method name is different: the functionality is comparable. In Listing 15.7, letters rather than numbers are used to identify the lines of code to underscore the point that this is template code that is separate from the Loon code.

Listing 15.7   **Adding a New Object in the Template**

```
#pragma mark  - Documents

 - (void)insertNewObject:(id)sender
{
  if (!_objects) {
    _objects = [[NSMutableArray alloc] init];            //A
  }
  [_objects insertObject:[NSDate date] atIndex:0];        //B

  NSIndexPath *indexPath = [NSIndexPath indexPathForRow:0 inSection:0];  //C
  [self.tableView insertRowsAtIndexPaths:@[indexPath]     //D
    withRowAnimation:UITableViewRowAnimationAutomatic];
}
```

A   If the mutable array of objects doesn't exist, create it.

B   Insert the new object at the beginning of the array. This completes the first task.

C   Create `indexPath` for row 0 in section 0.

D   Insert a new row in the table view using `indexPath`.

Now it's time to look at the Loon implementation of the comparable insertNewObject: code from the template with addDocument:, which is shown in Listing 15.8. A number of NSLog statements are left in the code so that you can follow what's happening as you test the code. They are useful because a major chunk of the processing happens asynchronously off the main thread, so control jumps around in the code.

You can now see why a property for the add button was added to the template. In many cases, you simply add buttons to the navigation bar at runtime and don't worry about them. You set them up with the appropriate selectors, and they just work.

In this case, however, you need to disable the add button while you are processing the addition of a new item. Because of the asynchronous processing, there could come a moment in which the add button could be pushed in the middle of an add operation, and the results of that would be at the least undefined. Thus, in order to be able to enable or disable the add button, you need to be able to get to it with a property.

When you are working with UIDocument and subclasses of it, remember that the sequence of steps you may be used to as a user or developer changes. You may be used to creating a blank and untitled document, working with it, and then saving it either with a default name or a name that you provide.

Now, you first name the document (even though this may be a temporary name, such as Untitled-1). The document's location is determined by the name and by its path. With those pieces of information, the document is savable. The reason for making a distinction between the file name and the path is that the path differs for files in iCloud and files stored locally. When you need the complete location, you often need to construct it from the known location (iCloud or the local sandbox) and the file name.

Thus, a key aspect of adding a new document is constructing its name and assembling an NSURL that combines the appropriate location with the file name. The _documents array actually contains the file name and location for each document: given those, you can retrieve the document itself any time you want it. In order to make this easier, a lightweight class, FileRepresentation, is created later in this chapter. It contains the NSURL and the file name. You'll see it used in Listing 15.8.

Listing 15.8 **Managing Documents**

```
#pragma mark - Documents
- (IBAction)addDocument:(id)sender {                          //14
  NSURL *newDocumentURL;

  BOOL usingiCloud = ((JFAppDelegate *)[[UIApplication sharedApplication]
    delegate]).documentsIniCloud;
  if (usingiCloud) {
    self.addButton.enabled = NO;
```

```
dispatch_async                                                        //15

  (dispatch_get_global_queue(DISPATCH_QUEUE_PRIORITY_DEFAULT, 0), ^{

    NSFileManager *fm = [NSFileManager defaultManager];
    NSString *newFileName = [self newUntitledDocumentName];
    NSURL *newDocumentURL =
      [fm URLForUbiquityContainerIdentifier:nil];                     //16
      NSLog (@" %s %@", __PRETTY_FUNCTION__,
      [fm URLForUbiquityContainerIdentifier:nil]);
    newDocumentURL = [newDocumentURL
      URLByAppendingPathComponent:JFDocumentsDirectoryName
      isDirectory:YES];                                               //17
  newDocumentURL = [newDocumentURL                                    //18
    URLByAppendingPathComponent:newFileName];
  NSLog (@" %s %@", __PRETTY_FUNCTION__, newDocumentURL);

    JFFileRepresentation *fr = [[JFFileRepresentation alloc]
      initWithFileName: newFileName fileURL:newDocumentURL];

    [_documents addObject: fr];

    NSLog (@" %s %@", __PRETTY_FUNCTION__, _documents);

    dispatch_async(dispatch_get_main_queue(), ^{                      //19
    // Update table                                                   //20
      NSIndexPath* newCellIndexPath =
      [NSIndexPath indexPathForRow: ([_documents count] - 1)
        inSection: 0];
      [self.tableView insertRowsAtIndexPaths: [NSArray
        arrayWithObject: newCellIndexPath]
        withRowAnimation:UITableViewRowAnimationAutomatic];

      [self.tableView selectRowAtIndexPath:newCellIndexPath animated:YES
        scrollPosition:(UITableViewScrollPositionMiddle)];
      UITableViewCell *selectedCell = [self.tableView
        cellForRowAtIndexPath: newCellIndexPath];
      if ([[[UIDevice currentDevice] userInterfaceIdiom] !=
        UIUserInterfaceIdiomPad) {                                    //21
        [self performSegueWithIdentifier:DisplayDetailSegue
          sender:selectedCell];
      } else {
        [self.detailViewController setDetailItemAndConfigure:fr];
        _detailViewController.navigationItem.title = [fr fileName];

      }
```

```
      self.addButton.enabled = YES;                                //22
    });
  });
} else {
  newDocumentURL = [self localDocumentsDirectoryURL];              //23
  NSLog (@" %s %@", __PRETTY_FUNCTION__, newDocumentURL);
  newDocumentURL = [newDocumentURL URLByAppendingPathComponent:    //24
    [self newUntitledDocumentName]];

  NSLog (@" %s %@", __PRETTY_FUNCTION__, newDocumentURL);
  JFFileRepresentation *fr = [[JFFileRepresentation alloc]
    initWithFileName:
    [self newUntitledDocumentName] fileURL:newDocumentURL];
  [_documents addObject: fr];                                      //25

  NSLog (@" %s %@", __PRETTY_FUNCTION__, _documents);              //26
  NSIndexPath* newCellIndexPath =
  [NSIndexPath indexPathForRow: ([_documents count] - 1) inSection: 0];
  [self.tableView insertRowsAtIndexPaths: [NSArray
    arrayWithObject: newCellIndexPath]
  withRowAnimation:UITableViewRowAnimationAutomatic];

  [self.tableView selectRowAtIndexPath:newCellIndexPath animated:YES  //27
    scrollPosition:(UITableViewScrollPositionMiddle)];
  UITableViewCell *selectedCell = [self.tableView
    cellForRowAtIndexPath: newCellIndexPath];

  if ([[[UIDevice currentDevice] userInterfaceIdiom] !=
    UIUserInterfaceIdiomPad) {                                     //28
    [self performSegueWithIdentifier:DisplayDetailSegue
      sender:selectedCell];
  } else {
    [_detailViewController setDetailItemAndConfigure: fr];         //29
    _detailViewController.navigationItem.title = [fr fileName];
  }

  self.addButton.enabled = YES;
}
}
```

14 Start by declaring newDocumentURL. If using iCloud, disable the add button. (You only need to worry about it if you're going to be using iCloud and asynchronous processing.) If you are working in iCloud, continue. There's an else later on at line 23.

15 Switch off the main queue to search iCloud.

16   Call `newUntitledDocumentName` to get the file name for the new document (it is described in the following section). Combine it with the ubiquity container URL (this is the part that may take time).

17   Append a directory if you use it (see the static declaration at the top of the file).

18   Append the file name. Create a file representation and add it to _documents.

19   Switch back to the main queue.

20   Update the table view.

21   Set the detail view controller detail item explicitly (iPad) or as a result of the segue (iPhone).

22   Enable the add button. You can test if you need to, but it's easier just to enable it in all cases.

23   For local sandbox storage, get the local documents directory. (This method is described in the section that follows.)

24   Add the file name. .

25   Create a file representation and add it to _documents.

26   Insert a new row in the table view.

27   Select the new row.

28, 29   Set the detail view controller with the segue (iPhone) or explicitly (iPad).

Listing 15.9 is the method that gives you a new document name—the name, not the full NSURL or path. This is basic C code with only two lines that even use Objective-C features. It attempts to construct file names such as Note 1, Note 2, and so forth. For each one, it uses fast enumeration to see if that name is used in _documents. If it is not, it returns that name. This technique, which is used in Apple examples (and other places), fills in the gaps as you remove documents. For instance, if you have Note 1, Note 2, and Note 3 and then delete Note 2, the next time you ask for a name, you'll get Note 2 rather than Note 4. "Note" is hard-coded here; it should be a constant or define for better maintainability in a production system.

Listing 15.9 **newUntitledDocumentName**

```
- (NSString *)newUntitledDocumentName {

  NSInteger docCount = 1;
  NSString *newDocName = nil;

  BOOL done = NO;
```

```
  while (!done) {
    newDocName = [NSString stringWithFormat: @"Note %d.%@",
      docCount, JFDocFilenameExtension];                      //30

    BOOL nameExists = NO;
    for (JFFileRepresentation *fr in _documents) {             //31
      if ([[[fr fileName] lastPathComponent] isEqualToString: newDocName]) {
        docCount++;
        nameExists = YES;
        break;
      }
    }

    if (!nameExists)
      done = YES;
  }

  NSLog (@" %s %@", __PRETTY_FUNCTION__, newDocName);

  return newDocName;

}
```

30 Construct the next document name.

31 Check to see if it exists in `_documents`.

Listing 15.10 shows the delegate methods for `UITableViewDelegate`, which is adopted by `UITableViewController`. There are few customizations you'll need to make to reuse this code. (Note that it is not yet complete: there are some additions you'll find in Chapter 18.)

Listing 15.10   **Table View**

```
#pragma mark - Table View

- (NSInteger)numberOfSectionsInTableView:(UITableView *)tableView
{
  return 1;                                                   //32
}

- (NSInteger)tableView:(UITableView *)tableView
  numberOfRowsInSection:(NSInteger)section
{
    return _documents.count;                                 //33
}
```

```objc
- (UITableViewCell *)tableView:(UITableView *)tableView
  cellForRowAtIndexPath:(NSIndexPath *)indexPath

{
  UITableViewCell *newCell = [tableView
    dequeueReusableCellWithIdentifier:DocumentEntryCell          //34
    forIndexPath:indexPath];

  if (!newCell)
    newCell = [[UITableViewCell alloc]
      initWithStyle: UITableViewCellStyleDefault
      reuseIdentifier: DocumentEntryCell];                       //35

  if (!newCell)
    return nil;

  JFFileRepresentation *fr =
    (JFFileRepresentation*)[_documents objectAtIndex:[indexPath row]];  //36

  NSURL *fileURL = [fr fileURL];
  NSLog (@" %s %@", __PRETTY_FUNCTION__, fileURL);
  newCell.textLabel.text = [[[fr fileURL] lastPathComponent]
    stringByDeletingPathExtension];                              //37

  return newCell;
}

- (BOOL)tableView:(UITableView *)tableView
  canEditRowAtIndexPath:(NSIndexPath *)indexPath
{
    // Return NO if you do not want the specified item to be editable.
    return YES;
}

- (void)tableView:(UITableView *)tableView
    didSelectRowAtIndexPath:(NSIndexPath *)indexPath {
  JFFileRepresentation *fr = (JFFileRepresentation *)[_documents
    objectAtIndex: [indexPath row]];                             //38

  [self.detailViewController setDetailItemAndConfigure:fr];      //39
}
```

32 A single column table has only one section.

33 Take the row count out of _documents.

34, 35   Dequeue the reusable prototype cell from the storyboard. This should be a constant or define for easy maintainability.

36, 37   Take the appropriate items out of _documents, get the last path component, and then delete the extension so that you wind up with something like Note 1.

38   On iPad, pick up the file representation for the selected row.

39   On iPad, set the detail view controller detail item. On iPhone, this happens in prepareForSegue:sender:.

On iPhone, prepareForSegue:sender: is where you pass the new detail item to the detail view controller, as shown in Listing 15.11. On iPad, it is done in tableview didSelectRowAtIndexPath:, as you saw in Listing 15.10.

Listing 15.11   **Segue**

```
#pragma mark - Segue

- (void)prepareForSegue:(UIStoryboardSegue *)segue sender:(id)sender
{

  if (![segue.identifier isEqualToString:@"showDetail"])
     return;

  JFDetailViewController *destVC = (JFDetailViewController *)
    segue.destinationViewController;

  NSIndexPath *cellPath = [self.tableView indexPathForSelectedRow];
  UITableViewCell *theCell = [self.tableView
    cellForRowAtIndexPath: cellPath];
  JFFileRepresentation *fr = (JFFileRepresentation *)[_documents
    objectAtIndex: [cellPath row]];                           //40

  destVC.detailItem = fr;                                     //41
  destVC.navigationItem.title = theCell.textLabel.text;       //42

}
```

40   Get the document. Compare to line 28 in Listing 15.8.

41   Set the destination view controller's detail item to the document.

42   Set the navigation bar title to the title of the document.

iCloud Query

A NSMetadataQuery is used to find the iCloud documents. Originally designed for supporting the Spotlight feature on the Mac, these queries are designed to run in the background and report back periodically.

In the class extension, a _query variable was declared (line 5 in Listing 15.5). In viewDidLoad, [self setupAndStartQuery] is sent if iCloud is being used (line 12 in Listing 15.6).

Listing 15.12 shows where that message goes. The first thing that happens is that if _query doesn't exist, you must create it with wrappedDocumentQuery. Register for notifications from the query—a notification for an update to the query and a notification for completion of the query. Then start the query and sit back.

Once one of those notifications is received, control passes to processFiles, which is also in Listing 15.12. Use fast enumeration to run through the query results and store them in a local array called discoveredFiles. On completion, remove all the elements from _documents and replace them with discoveredFiles. This is a place where breakpoints and NSLog messages can help you follow the control sequence.

Listing 15.12   **Working with the iCloud Query**

```
#pragma mark - iCloud Query

- (void)setupAndStartQuery {                                           //43
  if (!_query)
    _query = [self wrappedDocumentQuery];
  [[NSNotificationCenter defaultCenter] addObserver: self
    selector:@selector (processFiles)
    name: NSMetadataQueryDidFinishGatheringNotification
    object: nil];
  [[NSNotificationCenter defaultCenter] addObserver: self
    selector:@selector (processFiles)
    name: NSMetadataQueryDidUpdateNotification
    object: nil];

  [_query startQuery];
}

- (NSMetadataQuery *)wrappedDocumentQuery {                            //44
  NSMetadataQuery *aQuery = [[NSMetadataQuery alloc] init];
  if (aQuery) {
    [aQuery setSearchScopes: [NSArray
      arrayWithObject: NSMetadataQueryUbiquitousDocumentsScope]];      //45
    NSString *filePattern = [NSString stringWithFormat: @"*.%@",
      JFDocFilenameExtension];
    NSLog (@" %s %@", __PRETTY_FUNCTION__, filePattern);
```

```
   [aQuery setPredicate: [NSPredicate predicateWithFormat:@"%K LIKE %@",
      NSMetadataItemFSNameKey, filePattern]];
   }
   return aQuery;
}

- (void)processFiles {                                          //46

   //preserve selection listing 4-4 doc

   NSMutableArray *discoveredFiles = [NSMutableArray array];    //47

   [_query disableUpdates];                                     //48

   NSArray *queryResults = [_query results];
   for (NSMetadataItem *result in queryResults) {
     NSString *fileName =
       [result valueForAttribute: NSMetadataItemFSNameKey];
     NSURL *fileURL = [result valueForAttribute: NSMetadataItemURLKey];
     NSLog (@" %s %@ %@", __PRETTY_FUNCTION__, fileName, fileURL);
     NSNumber *aBool = nil;
     [fileURL getResourceValue: &aBool forKey: NSURLIsHiddenKey error: nil];
     if (aBool && ![aBool boolValue])         {                 //49
       JFFileRepresentation *fr = [[JFFileRepresentation alloc]
          initWithFileName: fileName fileURL:fileURL];
     [discoveredFiles addObject: fr];
     //[discoveredFiles addObject: fileURL];
     }
   }

   [_documents removeAllObjects];                               //50
   [_documents addObjectsFromArray: discoveredFiles];
   [self.tableView reloadData];

   [_query enableUpdates];                                      //51

}
```

43 Create the query and register for the notifications. The only changes you make in this code may be if you use different names for _query or the methods.

44 Here is where you create the query.

45 Confine the query to the ubiquitous documents for your app. This code is usable as-is except that you may change your DocFileNameExtension value.

46 This is the code that is triggered by either notification. It updates `_documents`.

47 Declare a mutable array for the files from the query.

48 Disable updates to the query results so that you don't get into a deadlock.

49 Using fast enumeration, run through the query results, and add each one to `discoveredFiles`.

50 Remove everything from `_documents` and replace with the contents of `discoveredFiles`.

51 Re-enable updates.

Local Sandbox

The last section of the file has to do with managing the local sandbox on the iOS device. Whereas sandboxing on OS X is optional, on iOS, it is not, so you are obliged to use the code if you use any local storage, as shown in Listing 15.13.

Because you can access the sandbox directory directly, you don't have to worry about queries and notifications, so the code is somewhat simpler than the iCloud code. Nevertheless, you're doing the same thing: you're filling the `_documents` array.

Listing 15.13   **Using the Local Sandbox**

```
#pragma mark - Local Sandbox

- (void)fillDocumentsForLocalStorage {
  NSMutableArray *discoveredFiles = [NSMutableArray array];            //52

  NSArray *localDocumentsArray = [[NSFileManager defaultManager]       //53
  URLsForDirectory:NSDocumentDirectory inDomains:NSUserDomainMask];
  NSURL *documentsDirectoryURL = localDocumentsArray[0];
  NSError *error = nil;
  NSArray *properties = @[NSURLNameKey];
  NSArray *documents = [[NSFileManager defaultManager]
    contentsOfDirectoryAtURL:documentsDirectoryURL
    includingPropertiesForKeys:properties
    options:NSDirectoryEnumerationSkipsHiddenFiles error:&error];

  for( NSURL *myFileURL in documents) {                               //54
    NSString *fileName = [myFileURL lastPathComponent];
    NSLog (@" %s %@ %@", __PRETTY_FUNCTION__, fileName, myFileURL);
    NSString *filePath = [[documentsDirectoryURL path]
      stringByAppendingPathComponent:fileName];
    [discoveredFiles addObject: [[JFFileRepresentation alloc]
                                 initWithFileName: fileName
                                 fileURL: myFileURL
                                 ]];
  }
}
```

```
    [_documents removeAllObjects];                                          //55
    [_documents addObjectsFromArray: discoveredFiles];
    [self.tableView reloadData];

}


- (NSURL*)localDocumentsDirectoryURL {                                      //56
    static NSURL *localDocumentsDirectoryURL = nil;

    if (localDocumentsDirectoryURL == nil) {
      NSString *documentsDirectoryPath = [NSSearchPathForDirectoriesInDomains(
        NSDocumentDirectory, NSUserDomainMask, YES ) objectAtIndex:0];
      localDocumentsDirectoryURL =
        [NSURL fileURLWithPath:documentsDirectoryPath];
    }
    return localDocumentsDirectoryURL;
}
@end
```

52 Declare a mutable array for the files you find.

53 This is used to get the local files. You can use it as-is.

54 Use fast enumeration to add each file to the discovered files.

55 Update _documents and reload the table view.

56 This is the routine that gives you the directory to the local sandbox. It is used at line 23 in Listing 15.8. Compare this to lines 16 and 17 in Listing 15.8.

DetailViewController

The detail view controller is much simpler than the master view controller, and it focuses on the user interface. It has relatively little to do with iCloud: the master view controller handles the direct interaction with iCloud at the document level, and the WrappedFile class manages the transfer of data to and from iCloud after a document has been selected.

The header file is shown in Listing 15.14

Listing 15.14   **DetailViewController.h**

```
#import <UIKit/UIKit.h>
#import "JFWrappedDocument.h"                                              //1
#import "JFFileRepresentation.h"                                          //2
```

```
@interface JFDetailViewController : UIViewController
<UISplitViewControllerDelegate,
  JFWrappedDocumentDelegate>                                        //3

@property (strong, nonatomic) JFFileRepresentation *detailItem;

@property (weak, nonatomic) IBOutlet UITextField *textField;
@property (weak, nonatomic) IBOutlet UITextField *locationField;
@property (weak, nonatomic) IBOutlet UIImageView *imageView;

- (void)setDetailItemAndConfigure: (JFFileRepresentation *)fr;
@end
```

1, 2   `WrappedDocument` and `FileRepresentation` are the document and a
lightweight helper class that are discussed later in this chapter.

3   `DetailViewController` conforms to `WrappedDocumentDelegate`,
which will manage content changes.

The code in `DetailViewController` addresses the user interface and two delegate implementations that `UITableViewController` conforms to. As such, they are
not particularly related to iCloud. If you compare the code in Listing 15.15 with other
code, you'll notice that it has been changed in some ways. Other sample code uses
methods such as `ViewWillAppear` and `ViewWillDisappear` to trigger moving of
data between the interface and persistent objects (the documents). As pointed out previously, this works well with navigation interfaces, but with split view controllers on
iPad, the mechanism breaks down.

Accordingly, the code is structured somewhat differently from much of the sample
code. Two new methods are created: `configureView` and `unconfigureView`. They
move data from the document to the user interface and back again. (`configureView`
appears in a number of sample code projects.) With the user interface code in these
methods, they can be called as appropriate for a split view controller interface or a navigation interface.

Listing 15.15   DetailViewController.m Part I

```
#import "JFDetailViewController.h"
#import "JFFileRepresentation.h"

@interface JFDetailViewController ()                               //1
@property (strong, nonatomic) UIPopoverController *masterPopoverController;
@end

@implementation JFDetailViewController {                          //2
  JFWrappedDocument *_document;
  BOOL _createFile;
}
```

```objc
#pragma mark - Managing the detail item

- (void)setDetailItemAndConfigure: (JFFileRepresentation *)fr {          //3
  [self unconfigureView];

  self.detailItem = fr;
  [self configureView];
}


- (void)configureView                                                    //4
{
  // Update the user interface for the detail item.
  if (self.detailItem) {
    NSURL *URLToSave = [self.detailItem fileURL];

    _document = [[JFWrappedDocument alloc ]initWithFileURL: URLToSave];   //5
    _document.delegate = self;

    if (_createFile) {                                                   //6
      [_document saveToURL: _document.fileURL forSaveOperation:
        UIDocumentSaveForCreating completionHandler:^(BOOL success) {
        if (success) {                                                   //7
          NSLog (@" %s %hhd", __PRETTY_FUNCTION__, success);
        }
      }];
      _createFile = NO;
    }

    if (_document.documentState & UIDocumentStateClosed) {               //8
      [_document openWithCompletionHandler:nil];
    }
  }
}


- (void)unconfigureView {                                                //9
  NSString *newText = self.textField.text;                               //10
  NSString *newLocation = self.locationField.text;

  _document.documentText = newText;                                      //11
  _document.documentLocation = newLocation;

  [_document closeWithCompletionHandler:nil];                            //12
}


- (void)viewDidLoad
```

```
{
    [super viewDidLoad];

    // Do any additional setup after loading the view, typically from a nib.
    [self configureView];                                          //13
}

- (void)viewWillAppear:(BOOL)animated {

    [super viewWillAppear:animated];

    [self configureView];                                                   //14

}

- (void)viewWillDisappear:(BOOL)animated {

    [super viewWillDisappear:animated];

    [self unconfigureView];                                                 //15

}

- (void)didReceiveMemoryWarning
{
    [super didReceiveMemoryWarning];
    // Dispose of any resources that can be recreated.
}
```

1   This class extension is from the template.

2   Local variables are the wrapped document and a Boolean indicating whether or not it needs to be created. Remember that the detail item is a `FileRepresentation`, not the document itself.

3   A method such as `setDetailItem` can be confused with a setter. This may be what you want, but if you want to avoid confusion, a more meaningful name that cannot be confused with a setter may be a better choice.

4   This is code that in various samples is in `viewWillAppear`.

5   Create the document from the file representation.

6   If necessary, save the document.

7   Set a breakpoint here. It's part of a block, so if you are stepping through the code, you'll jump right over this unless you explicitly set a breakpoint on a line of code within the block.

8   Open the document if necessary.

9   This moves the code to the document from the user interface. Note that there is no reverse code in line 8. That is handled by the delegate at lines 16, 17, and 18 in Listing 15.16.

10, 11   Move the text to the document itself. (The code for the location is similar.)

12   Close the document.

13, 14, 15   `viewDidLoad`, `viewWillAppear`, and `viewWillDisappear` are changed to call `configureView` and `unconfigureView`.

Listing 15.16 finishes the detail view controller. It contains unchanged code from the Master-Detail Application template along with the implementation of the `WrappedDocumentDelegate`. This is yet another asynchronous process. When the document determines that its contents have changed (in `WrappedDocument`), it posts a notification that responds by running this code. This code is dispatched on the main queue, and it moves the document's data to the user interface.

Listing 15.16   DetailViewCotroller.m Part II

```
#pragma mark - JFWrappedDocumentDelegate

- (void)documentContentsDidChange: (JFWrappedDocument *)document {      //16
  dispatch_async (dispatch_get_main_queue(), ^{                        //17
    self.textField.text = _document.documentText;                     //18
    self.locationField.text = _document.documentLocation;
  });
}


#pragma mark - Split view

- (void)splitViewController:(UISplitViewController *)splitController
  willHideViewController:(UIViewController *)viewController
  withBarButtonItem:(UIBarButtonItem *)barButtonItem
  forPopoverController:(UIPopoverController *)popoverController
{
    barButtonItem.title = NSLocalizedString(@"Master", @"Master");     //19
    [self.navigationItem setLeftBarButtonItem:barButtonItem animated:YES];
    self.masterPopoverController = popoverController;
}

- (void)splitViewController:(UISplitViewController *)splitController
    willShowViewController:(UIViewController *)viewController
    invalidatingBarButtonItem:(UIBarButtonItem *)barButtonItem
```

```
{
    // Called when the view is shown again in the split view,
    // invalidating the button and popover controller.
    [self.navigationItem setLeftBarButtonItem:nil animated:YES];
    self.masterPopoverController = nil;
}

@end
```

16 Implement the `WrappedDocumentDelegate`.

17 Move to the main thread.

18 Move the data.

19 Add a title to the popover button. "Master" is a good default, but it probably should be customized for the items you're managing—Reports, Observations, or the like.

This small method is a good way to observe how blocks work. Here's how to create the demonstration for yourself:

1. Set breakpoints at lines 17 and 18.

2. Change some data so that the notification fires. (You'll have to do this after you have worked through this chapter because the notification isn't wired yet. It saves a bit of jumping around to have these steps listed here next to the code that will run.)

3. When you stop at the breakpoint for line 17, step over it. The line you have executed moves to the main thread and schedules the block.

4. When you get to the end of the method, click run in the breakpoint navigator. Control will stop at line 18.

Remember that to set a breakpoint to debug code in a block, you must set a breakpoint on the code itself: you cannot step into a block.

WrappedDocument

`WrappedDocument` is a continuation of the same class in Placid. The major differences are in the handling of saving and opening because in Placid, the documents were stored only in iCloud. In Loon, documents can be stored either in iCloud or in the local sandbox.

Listing 15.17 shows the header file. It's a bit more complex than files you've seen before; that complexity comes from its use of a protocol and the way in which that protocol is declared. Because this is common, it is worthwhile to look at the issue.

The protocol (`WrappedDocumentDelegate`) is used in the declaration of the delegate property at line 3 in Listing 15.17. In order to use it there, a forward declaration for the protocol is placed at line 17. The protocol itself is declared at line 3 at the bottom of the file. This is a common issue in which you have two declarations (Wrapped Document and WrappedDocumentDelegate in this case), each of which refers to the other. The standard solution is to use a forward declaration for one of them. You can play around with the header file, and you'll see that either WrappedDocument-Delegate or WrappedDocument needs to be declared in a forward declaration. It's a matter of style which one you pick. (In cases like this, use a forward declaration for the protocol so that the overall structure of a header file focuses on the class declaration with other items being declared in forward declarations.)

Listing 15.17   **WrappedDocument.h**

```objc
#import <UIKit/UIKit.h>

@protocol JFWrappedDocumentDelegate;                               //1

@interface JFWrappedDocument : UIDocument

@property (strong, nonatomic) NSFileWrapper *fileWrapper;

@property (strong, nonatomic) NSString *documentText;
@property (strong, nonatomic) NSString *documentLocation;

@property (weak, nonatomic) id <JFWrappedDocumentDelegate> delegate;    //2

-(void)setDocumentText: (NSString*)newText;
-(void)setDocumentLocation: (NSString*)newText;

@end

@protocol JFWrappedDocumentDelegate <NSObject>                     //3
@optional                                                          //4
- (void)documentContentsDidChange: (JFWrappedDocument *)document;
@end
```

1   Declare a forward reference of the protocol.

2   Use the forward reference in the declared property.

3   Declare the protocol.

4   Because documentContentsDidChange triggers saving and user interface interactions, consider if this protocol would ever be used in another context. Making it optional allows this. The choice depends on your preference and app structure. Explicitly indicating which methods are required and which are optional is always a good choice.

`WrappedDocument` is divided into three sections:

- **Accessors, Undo/Redo:** These methods manage moving the data in and out to and from fields.
- **File Wrapper/Package Support:** This code works at the document level rather than the field level.
- **Saving:** This is an override of a single `UIDocument` method that exists for the sole purpose of being able to set a breakpoint to observe the asynchronous saving of the document.

The top of WrappedDocument.m contains declarations and a class extension. It is shown in Listing 15.18.

Listing 15.18 **WrappedDocument.m Declarations and Class Extension**

```
#import "JFAppDelegate.h"
#import "JFWrappedDocument.h"

NSString *UbiquityDirectoryComponentForDocuments = @"Documents";    //1

NSString *TextFileName = @"Text.txt";                               //2
NSString *LocationFileName = @"Location.txt";

NSStringEncoding kTextFileEncoding = NSUTF8StringEncoding;          //3

@interface JFWrappedDocument ()                                     //4

@property (strong, nonatomic) NSFileWrapper *wrapperText;
@property (strong, nonatomic) NSFileWrapper *wrapperLocation;

@property (strong, nonatomic) NSString *fwText;
@property (strong, nonatomic) NSString *fwLocation;

@end
```

1. This is the directory name to be constructed for iCloud.
2. These are the default file names within the file wrapper.
3. This is the encoding for the text file inside the wrapper.
4. The class extension declares properties for the text, location, and image (the image is still a placeholder at this point). `fwText` and `fwLocation` are backing variables for the properties.

The accessors use the private variables declared in the class extension (line 4 in Listing 15.18). On demand, the data is extracted from the wrapped document. Note that the setters are undoable: that causes the document to be autosaved. Also note the comment that error handling needs to be added. That is standard error handling and doesn't deal with iCloud, so it is omitted.

This section of `WrappedDocument` is shown in Listing 15.19.

Listing 15.19   WrappedDocument.m—Accessors, Undo/Redo

```
@implementation JFWrappedDocument

#pragma mark - Accessors, Undo/Redo

-(NSString*)documentText {
  if (_fwText)
    return _fwText;

  NSDictionary *fileWrappers = [_fileWrapper fileWrappers];            //5

  if (!_wrapperText) {
    _wrapperText = [fileWrappers objectForKey: TextFileName];          //6
  }

  if (_wrapperText != nil)
  {
    NSData *textData = [_wrapperText regularFileContents];             //7
    _fwText = [[NSString alloc] initWithData:textData
      encoding:kTextFileEncoding];
  } else {
    // handle error
  }

  return _fwText;
}


-(void)setDocumentText: (NSString*)newText {                            //8

  if (newText != _fwText )
  {
    NSString *oldText = _fwText;
    _fwText = newText;

    //register undo and cause autosave
    [self.undoManager setActionName: @"Text Change"];
    [self.undoManager registerUndoWithTarget:self
                               selector: @selector(setDocumentText:)
                                 object: oldText];
  }
}
```

```objectivec
-(NSString*)documentLocation {                                          //9
  if (_fwLocation)
    return _fwLocation;

  NSDictionary *fileWrappers = [_fileWrapper fileWrappers];             //10

  if (!_wrapperLocation) {
    _wrapperLocation = [fileWrappers objectForKey: LocationFileName];   //11
  }

  if (_wrapperLocation != nil)
  {
    NSData *locationData = [_wrapperLocation regularFileContents];      //12
    NSLog (@" %@", locationData);
    _fwLocation = [[NSString alloc] initWithData:locationData
      encoding:kTextFileEncoding];                                      //13
  } else {
    // handle error
  }

  return _fwLocation;
}

-(void)setDocumentLocation: (NSString*)newLocation {
  if (newLocation != _fwLocation)
  {
    NSString *oldLocation = _fwLocation;
    _fwLocation = newLocation;


    [self.undoManager setActionName: @"Location Change"];
    [self.undoManager
      registerUndoWithTarget:self
                  selector: @selector(setDocumentLocation:)
                    object: oldLocation];
  }

}



- (IBAction)handleUndo:(id)sender {
  [self.undoManager undo];
}

- (IBAction)handleRedo:(id)sender {
  [self.undoManager redo];
}
```

5	Get the file wrappers from the wrapped document.
6	Get the value for the key `TextFileName`.
7	Get the data as `NSData` and store it in the `NSString` that is the backing variable.
8	This is the setter for the text. Note the undo settings that will call this same method for undo.
9	This is the getter for location. It matches the getter for text.
10, 11, 12	Get the file wrappers, the key, and the data.
13	Set the location and register for undo.

The two main methods in Listing 15.20 handle the actual work of reading and writing. `loadFromContents:ofType:error:` loads the data from content that has been received. `contentsForType:error:` moves data into an object. As you can see in Listing 15.20, the content is an `id`, which means any class.

Thus, the sequence from the data store on reading is

1. `configureView` in DetailViewController.m creates and opens the private `_document` instance. It sets `DetailViewController` as the delegate for `_document`.

2. In WrappedDocument.m `loadFromContents:ofType:`, the contents are stored in the `fileWrapper` property of `WrappedDocument`.

3. Then, still in `loadFromContents:ofType:` in WrappedDocument.m, the `_document` delegate's `documentsContentDidChange:` is called. (Remember the delegate was set to `DetailViewController` in step 1.)

4. In `documentsContentDidChange` of DetailViewController.m, the data is moved to the interface fields that are properties of `DetailViewController`.

To appreciate how this process plays out, it's a good idea to set breakpoints at the start of all of these methods. What you'll see is that when the document is created or opened in line 1, control passes to other parts of the app. If you set a breakpoint at the end of that method and then step over it, you'll probably be back at the main event loop. Some time later—perhaps even a minute or two—you'll see that the breakpoint at the start of `loadFromContents:ofType:` is triggered. It is called asynchronously as a result of the opening of a document. There may be another time lapse before line 4 is carried out.

`contents:forType:error:` is the companion method. It moves data from your `_document` object (where it was placed by your user interface fields and storyboard) into an object that is then saved. These two methods are symmetrical: they implement reading and writing.

Listing 15.20   WrappedDocument.m—FileWrapper/Package Support

```objc
#pragma mark - File Wrapper / Package Support

- (BOOL)loadFromContents:(id)contents ofType:(NSString *)typeName
                error:(NSError *__autoreleasing *)outError {        //14

  _fwText = nil;
  _fwLocation = nil;
  self.fileWrapper = (NSFileWrapper *)contents;                    //15

  if ([_delegate respondsToSelector:
    @selector (documentContentsDidChange:)]) {
    [_delegate documentContentsDidChange: self];                   //16
  }

  return YES;
}

- (id)contentsForType:(NSString *)typeName
  error:(NSError *__autoreleasing *)outError {

  if (self.fileWrapper == nil)                                     //17
  {
    self.fileWrapper = [[NSFileWrapper
      alloc]initDirectoryWithFileWrappers:nil];                   //18
  }

  NSDictionary *fileWrappers = [self.fileWrapper fileWrappers];    //19

  if (self.documentText != nil)                                   //20

  {

    NSData *textData = [self.documentText
      dataUsingEncoding: kTextFileEncoding];

    NSFileWrapper *textFileWrapper = [fileWrappers
      objectForKey:TextFileName];
    if (textFileWrapper != nil) {
      [self.fileWrapper removeFileWrapper: textFileWrapper];
    }
    textFileWrapper = [[NSFileWrapper alloc]
      initRegularFileWithContents:textData];
    [textFileWrapper setPreferredFilename: TextFileName];
    [self.fileWrapper addFileWrapper: textFileWrapper];
  }
```

```
  if ( self.documentLocation != nil)                              //21
  {
    NSLog (@" %s locationData %@", __PRETTY_FUNCTION__,
      self.documentLocation);

    NSData *locationData = [self.documentLocation dataUsingEncoding:
      kTextFileEncoding];

    NSFileWrapper *locationFileWrapper = [fileWrappers
      objectForKey:LocationFileName];
    if (locationFileWrapper != nil) {
      [self.fileWrapper removeFileWrapper: locationFileWrapper];
    }
    locationFileWrapper = [[NSFileWrapper alloc]
      initRegularFileWithContents:locationData];
    [locationFileWrapper setPreferredFilename: LocationFileName];
    [self.fileWrapper addFileWrapper: locationFileWrapper];
  }

    return self.fileWrapper;
}

#pragma mark - Saving

- (void)saveToURL:(NSURL *)url forSaveOperation:              //22
    (UIDocumentSaveOperation)saveOperation completionHandler:(
    void (^)(BOOL))completionHandler {
[super saveToURL:url forSaveOperation:saveOperation completionHandler:^(BOOL
    success) {
    if (success) {                                           //23
      NSLog (@" %s %hhd", __PRETTY_FUNCTION__, success);
    }
  }];

}
@end
```

---

14 It's a good idea to set a breakpoint here to see when it's called. It's an asynchronous call, so you can't step into it from the code you normally write.

15 Place the contents passed into the method into the `fileWrapper` property of `WrappedDocument`.

16 Call the delegate's `documentContentsDidChange` method (it is in `DetailViewController` in this implementation, but it need not be if you restructure the code).

17, 18　The _document fileWrapper property is created if necessary.

19　An NSDictionary fileWrappers is created from the fileWrappers within the outer fileWrapper. File wrappers within file wrappers were explained in Chapter 14.

20, 21　If the text and location properties exist, they are placed in the appropriate internal file wrapper, as in Chapter 14

22　This override is for debugging purposes.

23　You can set a breakpoint here so that you can observe the actual save and its status. As with other cases cited in this chapter, it's an asynchronous process, so you can't just step through it: you have to enter it by a breakpoint on the first line that will be executed.

FileRepresentation

FileRepresentation is a lightweight object that stores a fileName and a URL for a file. You could do the same thing with NSURL, but this object allows for future customization and expansion. It was described previously in this chapter. It is shown in Listings 15.21 and 15.22.

Listing 15.21　**FileRepresentation.h**

```
#import <Foundation/Foundation.h>

@interface JFFileRepresentation : NSObject

@property (strong, nonatomic) NSString *fileName;
@property (strong, nonatomic) NSURL *fileURL;

- (id)initWithFileName: (NSString*)fileName fileURL:(NSURL*)URL;

@end
```

Listing 15.22 shows the implementation of FileRepresentation.

Listing 15.22　**FileRepresentation.m**

```
#import "JFFileRepresentation.h"

@implementation JFFileRepresentation

- (id)initWithFileName: (NSString*)fileName fileURL:(NSURL*)URL {
  self = [super init];
  if (self)
```

```
  {
    _fileName = fileName;
    _fileURL = URL;
  }
  return self;
}


@end
```

Chapter Summary

This chapter showed you how to work with the iOS document version of the app. It built on Placid but extended it so that it can use either local or iCloud storage.

In the next chapter, you'll find the OS X companion version of this app.

Exercises

1. Work through a string of tests related to iCloud discovery. Experiment with turning Airplane mode on and off, with signing out of iCloud, and with signing in again. In addition, experiment using the debugging switch to indicate whether or not you want iCloud. Compare the results of setting that switch with the code you write to determine whether or not iCloud should be used.

2. Test the app. If you are building on the code from Placid in Chapter 14, test to make certain that everything still works.

3. Experiment on a device as well as on the simulator. Remember that on the simulator, you have to use the Debug menu to trigger an iCloud sync.

16

Working with OS X Documents

This chapter looks at OS X document–based apps: that is, apps with a document that is managed as a subclass of NSDocument that you create for your specific needs. Just as with UIDocument on iOS, NSDocument takes care of a lot of overhead for you. You wind up writing just the code that differentiates your document from documents in other apps for a very efficient design and development cycle.

That said, it is important to note that although UIDocument and NSDocument have similar roles to play, they are not interchangeable. Many of the differences are due to the major contrasts in OS X, including the presence (or absence) of a menu bar and a tool such as the OS X Finder, which lets users manage files directly. In this chapter, you'll see more information about how these differences arose and why the two document classes are not interchangeable.

You'll then see how to set up an OS X app that uses a subclass of NSDocument. This app (codenamed Chazy—another Adirondack lake) is deliberately structured to be somewhat parallel to Loon in the previous chapter. In this way, it diverges somewhat from the structures described in the major documentation on developer.apple.com: "Document-Based App Programming Guide for Mac." Rest assured that these differences are deliberate.

Evolution of NSDocument and UIDocument Differences

In addition to the differences between NSDocument and UIDocument that arise from the menu bar and the Finder, a less-noticed difference has to do with the evolution of what is now iOS compared to the evolution of OS X. From the beginning, most personal computer operating systems have had open file systems to which the users have access. This has been a mixed blessing because, although it is an important feature for many users, it brings with it some security and stability issues.

Mainframe systems have often been tied to databases rather than documents and user-accessible files. For large-scale systems (particularly multiuser systems), databases provide data storage tools that go far beyond what can be developed in the context of separate documents. With the advent of relational databases on mainframes in the 1970s, application designers embraced that technology and never looked back.

Thus, in the 1970s and early 1980s when personal computers and their operating systems were being developed, some developers understood that as hardware got faster and cheaper (as it always does), eventually they would move to relational databases for storage. A similar understanding took place among some developers when they realized that some of the tried-and-true operating system features they were used to on mainframes would gradually migrate to more-powerful personal computers.

Relational databases were implemented on personal computers, but their use by the operating systems did not occur nearly as quickly as some people had hoped. Perhaps more important, the document model of data storage became a critical part of the user experience. After Apple purchased NeXT and began turning NeXTSTEP/OpenStep into Rhapsody/OS X, there were some heated discussions about whether or not a document object should be added to the document class-less OpenStep. The discussions took a good deal of time, and ultimately NSDocument was born (in Rhapsody Developer Release 2 in 1998).

Part of the issue is that the Model-View-Controller (MVC) design pattern doesn't work intuitively with a traditional personal computer document. MVC works terrifically with database-based apps. The model is the database schema (or model), the view is the view on the user's screen, and the controller is a view controller (on iOS) or a window controller (on OS X).

When documents enter the picture, things can get a little murky. A traditional personal computer document contains aspects of the data model (the document's data) as well as features that could be considered the domain of a controller in the MVC design pattern. You can find detailed discussions of these issues on developer.apple.com. For many people (including the author), MVC is a critically important aspect of Cocoa and Cocoa Touch. However, exactly how it maps to traditional personal computer documents is not on the critical path to developing an app or becoming a proficient Cocoa or Cocoa Touch programmer. What's important is the apps that you design and write. The discussions about the role of documents in the App Kit took place many years ago, and the issue should be considered settled.

Settled it may be, but there is a theory that part of the reason for the difference between NSDocument and UIDocument may come about from an attempt to clarify the document structure. Certainly, from the standpoint of the MVC design pattern, it appears that when the controller is a view controller (as in iOS) rather than a more complex window controller (as in OS X), things get easier to grasp.

The only point you might want to ponder is whether building a document based on what may be an idiosyncratic structure for your app is the best way to go from the long-term standpoint of the app's evolution. It appears that using the file wrapper structure discussed in Chapter 15, "Working with iOS Documents," for iOS and this chapter for OS X, or using the document-based Core Data structure discussed in Chapter 17, "Working with Core Data and iCloud," may be preferable routes to take in many cases. Nevertheless, in many cases, a subclass of UIDocument and/or NSDocument is the best development route to take.

Planning the Project

With Xcode 5, planning and setting up the Chazy project follows the same pattern you used in Chapter 15. The biggest difference, of course, is that you start from the Cocoa Application template under OS X and Application in Xcode rather than from the Master–Detail Application template under iOS and Application. Make sure you choose the option to create a document-based application, and do not use Core Data.

The project will be created for you, and, as always when you create a project from an Xcode template, it's a good idea to build and run it so that you know you have a good starting point. The app should open with a document, as shown in Figure 16.1.

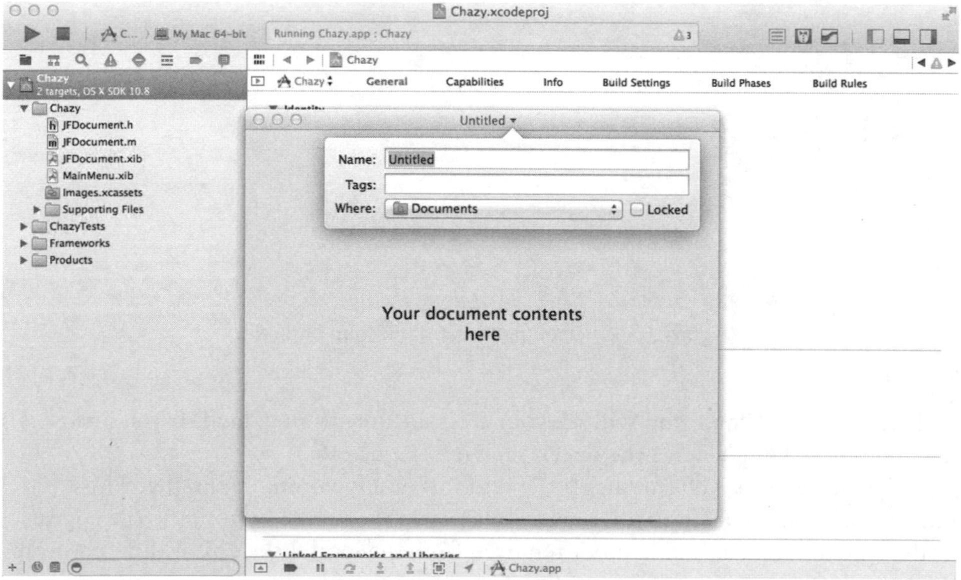

Figure 16.1   Running your new project

As you can see in Figure 16.1, by default your documents will use the OS X Auto Save feature introduced in OS X Lion (10.7) in 2011. Auto Save means less work for users as well as less work for developers. Users can skip saving their documents, and developers can skip supporting a number of user actions that are done behind the scenes by Auto Save.

The template comes with a basic menu bar that already implements basic document functionality. If you choose Open from the File menu, you can browse files locally or in iCloud, as you see in Figure 16.2. (Note that at this point, the actual opening of a document will not happen because the code in the following sections needs to be implemented. This is just a high-level overview of where you will end up by the end of this chapter.)

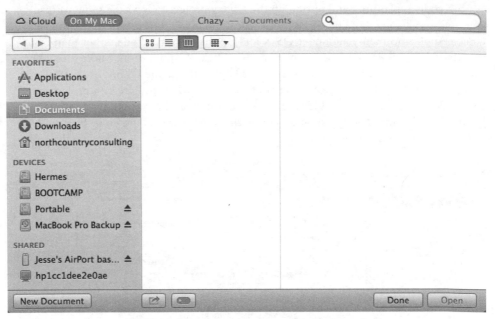

Figure 16.2   Opening files from iCloud or locally

If you choose iCloud, you will see your app's documents in iCloud. If you don't yet have apps in iCloud, you see the screen shown in Figure 16.3.

As the screen says, you can drag a file into this window from the Finder. This built-in behavior is worth noting: when you release the mouse button, the file appears in the iCloud window, and it also is removed from the local disk. This is different from the behavior of copying a file to another disk where the file is copied and remains on both the original disk and the disk to which it was copied.

Figure 16.3   Opening a file from iCloud

Starting the Chazy Project

Once you have verified that your new project runs, you can begin to make it ready to run much as you did with Loon in Chapter 15. The biggest difference is that Loon is an iOS app that uses storyboards. They're not available on OS X, so you work with nib files. Other than that, the process is much the same, so it's summarized here.

There are two primary tasks to get started. First, you can make the template Document class look a bit like the one in Loon. Then, you may need to add an app delegate if it is not in your template.

Setting Up the App in Xcode

The process of setting up the app in Xcode is similar to the processes you've been through for Placid and Loon; it is summarized here.

Select the target in the Project navigator and verify that its name and bundle ID are what you want them to be. You can change them later, but it is easiest to start with them correctly set, as you see in Figure 16.4.

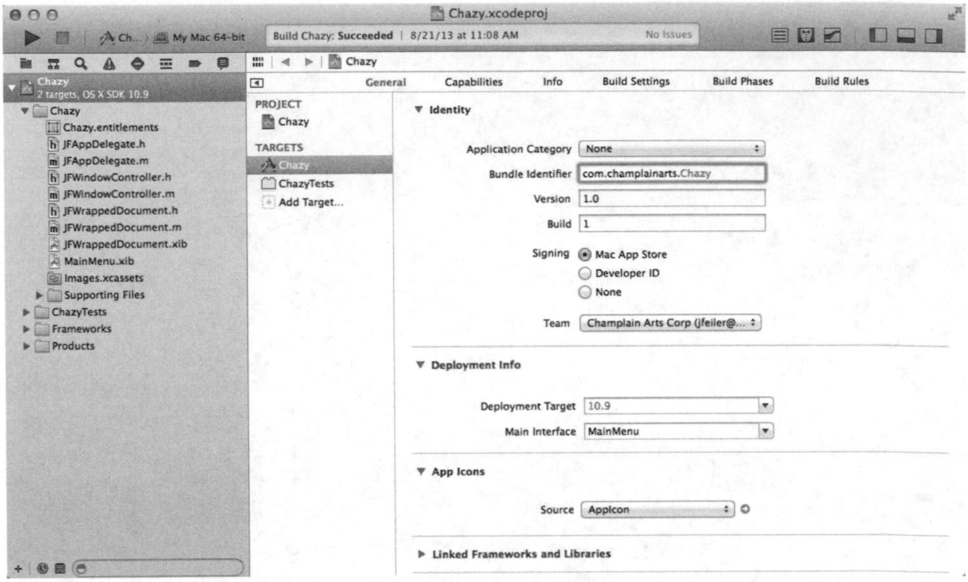

Figure 16.4   Set up the target.

Turn on iCloud in the Capabilities tab, as shown in Figure 16.5. By default, your ubiquity container will be named with your project name—Chazy if you have followed the steps in this section. If you have created Loon in Chapter 15, "Working with iOS Documents," you may want to change the ubiquity container name in Capabilities to use Loon rather than Chazy. This means that when you first launch Chazy, you'll be able to see and update the documents you created in Chapter 15. (It's sort of a sneak preview of the Round Trip.)

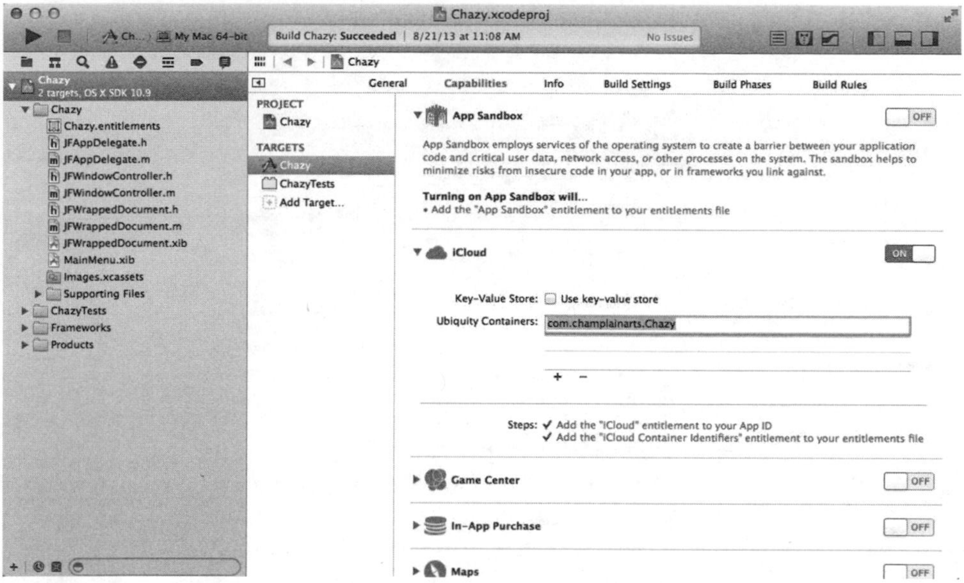

Figure 16.5   Turning on iCloud

Changing Document to WrappedDocument

In Loon, you worked with a new WrappedDocument class rather than a UIDocument. Although you could work directly with NSDocument in Chazy, the code will be easier to compare to Loon if you create WrappedDocument in Chazy. The process is the same except that you're working with a nib file in OS X rather than with a storyboard.

1. Open Document.h (it may have a prefix if you specified one when you created the project).

2. Highlight Document in the @interface section and choose Edit, Factor, Rename. Rename it to be WrappedDocument and use the option to rename the associated files.

3. Delete the text field from the view in the window in WrappedDocument.xib. It has "Your document contents here" as a placeholder.

4. Add a new text field to the view.

5. If necessary, add a class extension at the top of WrappedDocument.m. (It may or may not be there as part of the template.)

6. Control-drag from the text field to the class extension to create a new
   `NSTextField` property, as shown in Figure 16.6. Name it `fieldDescription`.

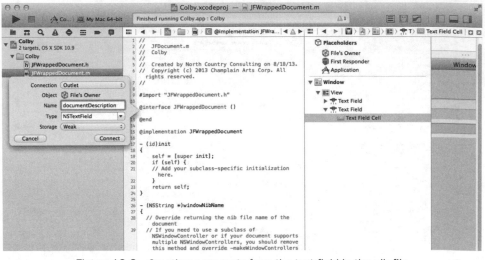

Figure 16.6   Creating a property from the text field in the nib file

7. Repeat steps 3, 4, and 5 for a `fieldLocation` field.

8. These are the properties for the fields in the interface. Create fields for the data as
   well: name them `fieldDescription` and `fieldLocation`.

Listing 16.1 shows the code in WrappedDocument.m at this point.

Listing 16.1   WrappedDocument.m Class Extension

```
#import "JFWrappedDocument.h"
#import "JFWindowController.h"

@interface JFWrappedDocument ()

@property (strong, nonatomic) NSFileWrapper *wrapperDescription;
@property (strong, nonatomic) NSFileWrapper *wrapperLocation;

@property (strong, nonatomic) NSString *fwDescription;
@property (strong, nonatomic) NSString *fwLocation;

@end
@implementation JFWrappedDocument
```

Confirm that the code runs, and then you'll be ready to write the rest of the code.

Adding an App Delegate (If Necessary)

Review the code you have created to see if it has an app delegate. In recent versions of Xcode, the basic template does not always have an app delegate. It's very easy to add it once you know how to do so. The key is to create an `AppDelegate` class that conforms to the `NSApplicationDelegate` protocol. Add it to main.xib and attach it to the delegate for the application itself.

Many developers make it a routine matter to have an app delegate. In the context of iCloud-enabled apps, it can be important because it gives you a place to initiate iCloud functionality during the app's launch process.

Here's how to add the app delegate:

1. To add the new class, choose New, File or command-click on the project in the project navigator and choose Add File.

2. Name the class `AppDelegate`. This is actually not required: you can name it anything you want, but it's easiest to use this name because it's often what people look for.

3. Make the class a subclass of `NSObject`.

4. Choose the appropriate location for the file (the default location is usually best) and create the class.

5. In the AppDelegate.h file, make it conform to the `NSApplicationDelegate` protocol, as you see here:

   `@interface JFAppDelegate : NSObject <NSApplicationDelegate>`

6. In MainMenu, drag a blue Object from the library into the document outline, as you see in Figure 16.7.

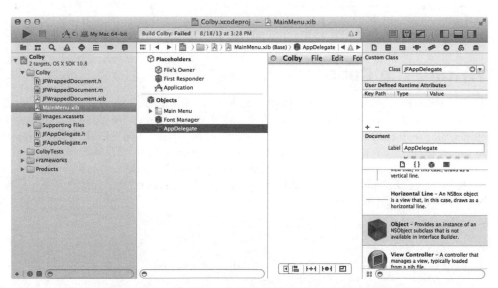

Figure 16.7   Connecting the new `AppDelegate` object to File's Owner

7. With the new object selected, set its class to `AppDelegate` in the Identity inspector.

8. Finally, control-drag from File's Owner to the new object and connect it as the delegate; this is also shown in Figure 16.7. Because File's Owner is the application itself (`NSApplication`), the delegate—your new `AppDelegate` object—will be loaded when the app launches. This is how you add nonvisual objects to your app in Interface Builder.

Implement `applicationWillFinishLaunching:` in AppDelegate.m. It will follow the class extension at the top of Listing 16.1. Note that it is comparable in some ways to `applicationDidFinishLaunchingWithOptions:` in iOS. Its signature is different, and this method is called just before the end of the launch process and before any documents are opened. This might be important for iCloud integration. If you want, you can set a breakpoint in the method to verify that it is being called. Note that this message is part of the `AppDelegate` protocol, so you are not subclassing anything and you do not call `super`. This code is shown in Listing 16.2.

Listing 16.2 Creating the `AppDelegate` Class

```
@implementation JFAppDelegate

- (void)applicationWillFinishLaunching:(NSNotification*) notification
{
}

@end
```

For now, this code is a placeholder. If you want to run your app and set a breakpoint in this method, you'll be able to verify that your app runs and loads the app delegate.

With these two structural additions, you're ready to start writing code.

Writing the Code

The code for the OS X app is a bit simpler than the code for the iOS app. In part, that is because the discovery and opening of files on OS X is managed by the `NSDocument` class rather than the app that you write. In addition, the split view controller, which is so useful on iOS, has no parallel on OS X. Of course, nothing would prevent you from constructing such an interface, but in an environment where multiple windows can easily be created, a split view controller is of less use than it is on iOS. You have three basic files to work with on OS X:

- `AppDelegate`
- `WrappedDocument`
- `WindowController` (rather than a detail view controller on iOS)

You're a bit ahead of the game already because the app delegate has been created in Listings 16.1 and 16.2 to show you how the nib file can be used to link a class to a delegate or other property. Remember that storyboards are the preferred way of managing views and view controllers on iOS, but they don't exist on OS X, so you'll need to use nib/xib files on OS X.

WrappedDocument

As is the case with Loon, there are two data elements in the app—the location and description of whatever it is the user is interested in. WrappedDocument is a subclass of NSDocument. It is designed to be used with file wrappers, but it encapsulates that functionality so that nothing about file wrappers or the implementation of the data structure is visible.

The model consists of the location and description of data elements. They are defined as properties in WrappedDocument.h: documentDescription and documentLocation. Listing 16.3 shows the header file at this time.

Listing 16.3 **WrappedDocument.h**

```
#import <Cocoa/Cocoa.h>
#import "JFWindowController.h"


@interface JFWrappedDocument : NSDocument

@property (strong, nonatomic) NSString *documentDescription;            //1
@property (strong, nonatomic) NSString *documentLocation;

@property (weak, nonatomic) JFWindowController *windowController;

@end
```

1   documentDescription and documentLocation are properties that are exposed to all users of the class. As you will see, they have no direct backing variables in WrappedDocument.m.

The class extension inside WrappedDocument.m declares the basic file wrapper—documentFileWrapper. Also inside the class extension, fwDescription and fwLocation are declared as NSString properties. Thus, within documentFileWrapper, you have the wrapperDescription and wrapperLocation file wrappers, and, as noted, each has a string inside it—fwDescription and fwLocation.

All of this is hidden inside the class extension in WrappedDocument.m as you can see in Listing 16.4.

Listing 16.4 **WrappedDocument** Class Extension

```objc
#import "JFWrappedDocument.h"
#import "JFWindowController.h"

@interface JFWrappedDocument ()

  @property (strong, nonatomic) NSFileWrapper *documentFileWrapper;

  @property (strong, nonatomic) NSFileWrapper *wrapperDescription;
  @property (strong, nonatomic) NSFileWrapper *wrapperLocation;

  @property (strong, nonatomic) NSString *fwDescription;
  @property (strong, nonatomic) NSString *fwLocation;

@end

@implementation JFWrappedDocument
```

The first section of WrappedDocument.m contains initialization and management code, as shown in Listing 16.5. You will note several template methods that are provided as shells that you can implement later on.

Listing 16.5 **WrappedDocument.m Initialization**

```objc
@implementation JFWrappedDocument

NSString *UbiquityDirectoryComponentForDocuments = @"Documents";          //1

NSString *descriptionFileName = @"Description.txt";                       //2
NSString *locationFileName = @"Location.txt";

NSStringEncoding kTextFileEncoding = NSUTF8StringEncoding;                //3

#pragma mark - initialization

- (id)init
{
  self = [super init];
  if (self) {

  // Add your subclass-specific initialization here.
  }

  return self;
}
```

```
/*
 - (NSString *)windowNibName                                        //4
{
  // Override returning the nib file name of the document
  // If you need to use a subclass of NSWindowController or if your document
  // supports multiple NSWindowControllers, you should remove this method
  // and override - makeWindowControllers instead.
    }
 */


- (void)windowControllerDidLoadNib:(NSWindowController *)aController
{
  [super windowControllerDidLoadNib:aController];
  // Add any code here that needs to be executed once the windowController
  // has loaded the document's window.
}

+ (BOOL)autosavesInPlace                                            //5
{
    return YES;
}
```

1   You always set your directory in iCloud. `Documents` is standard and can be seen by users if you set Application Supports iTunes File Sharing in the Info tab of the target.

2   These file names identify the files within the internal file wrappers that are inside `documentFileWrapper`.

3   This is the text encoding for the string content.

4   This is not needed, so it has been commented out. We are using a custom view controller, which will be shown in Listing 16.6.

5   `autoSavesInPlace` must be set to `YES` to get the behavior that will autosave and move the document to iCloud.

The next section of the code manages windows for `WrappedDocument`. Because you are overriding `NSWindowController` with a custom controller, you need to add it to the document, as shown in Listing 16.6.

Listing 16.6 Managing Windows for **WrappedDocument**

```
#pragma mark - windows
- (void)makeWindowControllers {                                    //6
  JFWindowController *myController;
```

```
  myController = [[JFWindowController alloc] init];
  [self addWindowController: myController];
  [myController setDocument: self];
  self.windowController = myController;


}

- (void)showWindows {                                              //7
  [super showWindows];


  [self.windowController documentContentsDidChange:self];


}
```

6   Instantiate the custom window controller and add it to the document.

7   Override showWindows to call the documentContentsDidChange method
    of the window controller for this app.

When it comes to reading and writing, the code is also similar to Loon, as you
can see in Listing 16.7. There are several stubbed methods in the template that
you can remove: you need the readFromFileWrapper:ofType:error: and
fileWrapperOfType:error: methods.

The code for reading relies on *lazy loading*, which is used frequently in Cocoa and
Cocoa Touch. The initial read operation is as fast as possible; details are read only on an
as-needed basis. (If this reminds you of faulting in Core Data, you're right: it's the same
basic idea.) As you can see in Listing 16.7, the document file wrapper is passed into that
method and dumped into a property without being analyzed. See Listing 16.8 later in
this chapter for the accessors that decode it as needed.

As in Loon, you don't worry about writing. What you do is create the file wrapper
for the document that includes the internal file wrappers and the data. Your method is
called as needed, and Cocoa takes care of the actual writing.

Listing 16.7   Reading and Writing

```
#pragma mark - read/write

- (BOOL)readFromFileWrapper: (NSFileWrapper *)fileWrapper
                                                                   //8
                    ofType: (NSString *)typeName
                     error: (NSError **)outError
{

  self.documentFileWrapper = fileWrapper;                          //9

  return YES;
}
```

```
- (NSFileWrapper *)fileWrapperOfType: (NSString *)typeName
    error:(NSError **)outError {
  if (self.documentFileWrapper == nil)                              //10
  {
    self.documentFileWrapper = [[NSFileWrapper alloc]
      initDirectoryWithFileWrappers:nil];                          //11
  }

  NSDictionary *fileWrappers = [self.documentFileWrapper fileWrappers];   //12

  if (self.documentDescription != nil)                             //13

    NSData *descriptionData = [self.documentDescription
      dataUsingEncoding: kTextFileEncoding];

    NSFileWrapper *descriptionFileWrapper =
      [fileWrappers objectForKey:descriptionFileName];
    if (descriptionFileWrapper != nil) {
      [self.documentFileWrapper removeFileWrapper: textFileWrapper];
    }
    descriptionFileWrapper = [[NSFileWrapper alloc]
      initRegularFileWithContents:descriptionData];
    [descriptionFileWrapper setPreferredFilename: descriptionFileName];
    [self.documentFileWrapper addFileWrapper: textFileWrapper];
  }

  if ( self.documentLocation != nil)                               //14
  {
    NSData *locationData = [self.documentLocation
      dataUsingEncoding: kTextFileEncoding];

    NSFileWrapper *locationFileWrapper = [fileWrappers
      objectForKey:locationFileName];
    if (locationFileWrapper != nil) {
      [self.documentFileWrapper removeFileWrapper: locationFileWrapper];
    }
    locationFileWrapper = [[NSFileWrapper alloc]
      initRegularFileWithContents:locationData];
    [locationFileWrapper setPreferredFilename: locationFileName];
    [self.documentFileWrapper addFileWrapper: locationFileWrapper];
  }

  return self.documentFileWrapper;                                 //15
}
```

8   This is the lazy loading read method.

9   In other examples, this property is called contents.

10   Check to see if you already have self.documentFileWrapper.

11   If you don't have self.documentFileWrapper, create it.

12   Extract the internal file wrappers from self.documentFileWrapper and save them in a dictionary.

13   Check for documentDescription in the document (see the accessors later in Listing 16.8). If you have it, encode the data, remove the existing textFileWrapper, and then create and add a new one.

14   Repeat line 13 for documentLocation.

15   Return self.documentFileWrapper.

The final section of the file implements the accessors—the other end of lazy loading. In many cases, a declared property is backed by an instance variable. By default, for a property called myProperty, the instance variable that Xcode creates will be _myProperty. Default accessors called myProperty and setMyProperty are created for you. (You'll find this out if you accidentally forget this fact and declare your own setMyProperty accessor without realizing that it will be invoked automatically. That is why you often will find methods with names like setMyPropertyForXYZ: that are not going to be confused with custom accessors.)

In Listing 16.7, you saw that the document file wrapper is just passed to a WrappedDocument property without being parsed. Within WrappedDocument, you'll find fwDescription and fwLocation properties. In a roundabout way, those are the backing variables for the public WrappedDocument properties documentDescription and documentLocation.

When you set a value with setDocumentLocation: or setDocumentDescription:, _fwLocation or _fwDescription needs to be set and the undo mechanism needs to be set up to reverse that process if necessary. The appropriate getters must check to see if _fwLocation or _fwDescription exists. If it does, it is returned. If it does not exist, the document file wrapper is unpacked, the local variables are set, and the appropriate value is returned. Listing 16.8 shows the accessors.

Listing 16.8 **Accessors**

```
#pragma mark - accessors

-(void)setDocumentDescription: (NSString*)newText {                    //16

  if (newText != _fwDescription )
  {
    NSString *oldText = _fwDescription;
    _fwDescription = newText;
```

```
      //register undo and cause autosave
      [self.undoManager setActionName: @"Text Change"];
      [self.undoManager
        registerUndoWithTarget: self
                      selector: @selector(setDocumentDescription:)
                        object: oldText];
  }
}


-(void)setDocumentLocation: (NSString*)newLocation {                    //17
  if (newLocation != _fwLocation)
  {
    NSString *oldLocation = _fwLocation;
    _fwLocation = newLocation;

    [self.undoManager setActionName: @"Location Change"];
    [self.undoManager
      registerUndoWithTarget: self
                    selector: @selector(setDocumentLocation:)
                      object: oldLocation];

  }

}


-(NSString*)documentDescription {                                      //18
  if (_fwDescription)
    return _fwDescription;

  NSDictionary *fileWrappers = [_documentFileWrapper fileWrappers];    //19

  if (!_wrapperDescription) {
    _wrapperDescription = [fileWrappers
      objectForKey: descriptionFileName];                             //20
  }

  if (_wrapperDescription != nil)
  {
    NSData *descriptionData = [_wrapperDescription regularFileContents]; //21
    _fwDescription = [[NSString alloc] initWithData:descriptionData
      encoding:kTextFileEncoding];                                    //22
  } else {
    // handle error
  }

  return _fwDescription;
}
```

```
-(NSString*)documentLocation {                                          //23
  if (_fwLocation)
    return _fwLocation;

  NSDictionary *fileWrappers = [_documentFileWrapper fileWrappers];

  if (!_wrapperLocation) {
    _wrapperLocation = [fileWrappers objectForKey: locationFileName];
  }

  if (_wrapperLocation != nil)
  {
    NSData *locationData = [_wrapperLocation regularFileContents];
    _fwLocation = [[NSString alloc] initWithData:locationData
       encoding:kTextFileEncoding];
  } else {
    // handle error
  }

  return _fwLocation;
}
@end
```

16, 17   Custom setters set the internal property and set up undo.

18, 23   Custom getters return the appropriate local property if it exists.

19   If the property doesn't exist, create a local dictionary of the file wrappers inside the document file wrapper.

20   If there isn't a wrapper for the description file, create it.

21   Encode the data.

22   Store the encoded data in the _fwDescription property.

23   Repeat lines 18 to 22 for location.

WindowController

The WindowController subclass lets you manage redrawing of the user interface when the text fields change. There are several other ways of accomplishing it, but this method is used because it is reasonably comparable to the structure of the iOS document. Listing 16.9 shows the interface file.

Listing 16.9   **WindowController.h**

```
#import <Cocoa/Cocoa.h>

@class JFWrappedDocument;

@interface JFWindowController : NSWindowController <NSTextFieldDelegate>    //1

@property (weak, nonatomic) IBOutlet NSTextField *fieldDescription;
@property (weak, nonatomic) IBOutlet NSTextField *fieldLocation;

- (void)documentContentsDidChange: (JFWrappedDocument *)document;    //2
@end
```

1   The class adopts the `NSTextFieldDelegate` protocol.

2   `documentContentsDidChange:` must be exposed so that it can be referenced by a notification.

Listing 16.10 shows you the code for the window controller.

Listing 16.10   **WindowController.m**

```
#import "JFWindowController.h"
#import "JFWrappedDocument.h"

@interface JFWindowController ()    //1

@end

@implementation JFWindowController

- (void)setDocument: (NSDocument *)document {    //2
  [super setDocument:document];
}

- (id)init {

  self = [super initWithWindowNibName:@"JFWrappedDocument"];    //3
  if (self) {
    // Initialization code here.
  }
  return self;
}
```

```
- (void)windowDidLoad                                                      //4
{
    [super windowDidLoad];

    // Implement this method to handle any initialization after your window
    // controller's window has been loaded from its nib file.
}

#pragma mark - moving to/from UI
- (void)documentContentsDidChange: (JFWrappedDocument *)document {          //5
    [self.fieldDescription setStringValue: document.documentDescription];
    [self.fieldLocation setStringValue: document.documentLocation];
}

- (void)UIContentsDidChange: (JFWrappedDocument *)document {               //6
    document.documentDescription = [_fieldDescription stringValue];
    document.documentLocation = [_fieldLocation stringValue];
}

#pragma mark - Notifications
- (void)controlTextDidEndEditing:(NSNotification *)aNotification           //7
{
    NSTextField *textField = [aNotification object];
    if (_fieldDescription == textField) {
        ((JFWrappedDocument *)self.document).documentDescription =
            [textField stringValue];
    } else if (_fieldDescription == textField) {
        ((JFWrappedDocument *)self.document).documentLocation =
            [textField stringValue];
    }

    // should check if changed
    [self UIContentsDidChange: self.document];
}

@end
```

1   The class extension may be part of the template, or you may create it. It's empty here, so not needed, but many developers automatically create the class extension because it is frequently needed later on.

2   This method simply calls super, so it is not needed. However, it is a good place to set a debugging breakpoint to examine the state of the variables.

3 To use a custom window controller, override `init` and pass the controller class name as shown here.

4 You need not implement this method, but it, too, is often useful as development proceeds.

5, 6 These methods move data from the document to the UI fields, and vice versa.

7 Because this class implements the `NSTextFieldDelegate` protocol, you can set it as the delegate for your text fields in the nib file. Then register to receive the notification.

Testing the App

The app should now run. With the default Xcode 5 settings, the iCloud report is now visible in the Debug navigator, as you can see in Figure 16.8.

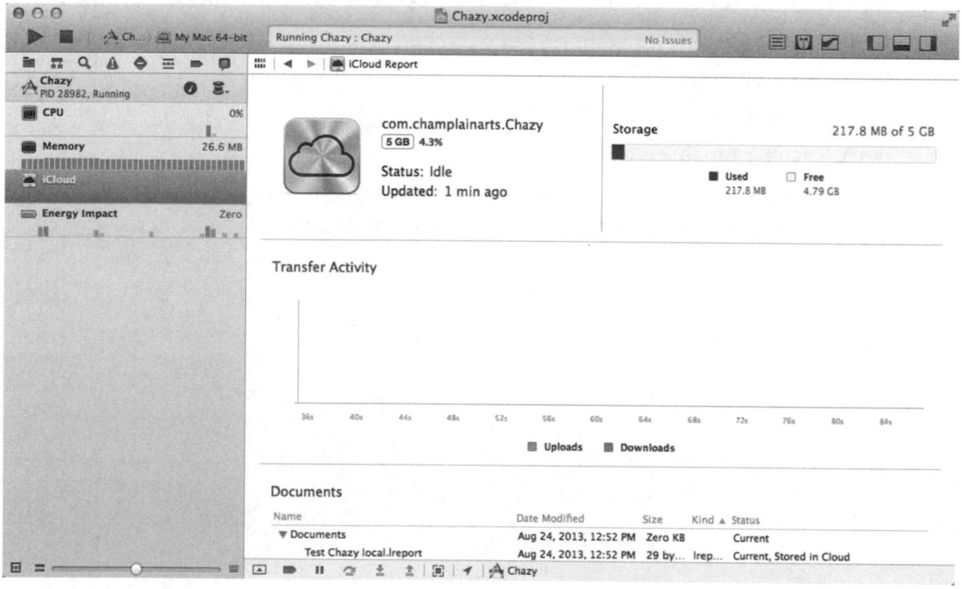

Figure 16.8   Using the iCloud report

You can track the usage of iCloud both in System Preferences and in the iCloud report (only System Preferences is available to users).

Chapter Summary

This chapter completed the sequence that began with Chapter 14, where you worked with an iCloud file wrapper, and continued in Chapter 15, where you worked with an iCloud file wrapper in an iOS document that could be stored either in iCloud or locally. Now you have the final combination: an OS X document.

If you compare the chapters, you'll see that the closer you get to the heart of the document, the more similar the chapters are. The differences are in the user interface and the environment in which the document lives.

Exercises

1. This chapter and its code are significantly shorter than Chapter 15, which does the same thing on iOS. What are the differences in code and capabilities that account for this difference?

2. Use the structure of this chapter to store a more complex wrapped document. You might start by including an image wrapped in a file wrapper.

3. Continue to use a more complex file wrapper. Use a file wrapper that contains the following wrapped files:

   - A wrapper for an image.
   - A wrapper for three text fields.
   - A wrapper for a custom object that you create. (Remember that the object must be able to be serialized to NSData and back again.)

17

Working with Core Data and iCloud

In Chapter 10, "Managing Persistent Storage with Core Data," you saw the basics of Core Data and an overview of relevant database theory. Throughout Part IV of the book, you have seen how to use iCloud in various contexts—with file wrappers (Chapter 14), iOS documents (Chapter 15), and OS X documents (Chapter 16). Core Data can fit into any of those contexts.

For example, you can use a file wrapper to wrap a file that contains a Core Data store and the necessary code for the Core Data stack to access it. You can add the store and Core Data stack support to a subclass of `UIDocument` (it is called `UIManagedDocument`). On OS X, `NSPersistentDocument` is a subclass of `NSDocument` and is functionally comparable to `UIManagedDocument`.

For more information on Core Data itself, see Jesse Feiler's *Sams Teach Yourself Core Data in 24 Hours, Second Edition*.

Looking at the iCloud Core Data Implementation

The basic structure of Core Data needed very little changing to support iCloud. The changes that have been made build on the existing structure. However, it is very important to note that those changes came in two batches. The initial release of iCloud and Core Data was for iOS 6 and OS X Mountain Lion (10.8), both of which were announced at Apple's Worldwide Developers Conference in 2012. The iCloud integration was based on a transactional model (it is described shortly). Over the course of a year, people worked on apps that used iCloud and Core Data; some problems were encountered. In a review of new features at WWDC 2013, it was announced that the Core Data team had devoted the year to strengthening the iCloud implementation and making some revisions (mostly simplifications) to the way it works under the hood.

Also, remember that Core Data and iCloud themselves are a collection of modifications to various frameworks from the addition of new notifications, a few new messages on the basic Core Data classes, and more. For that reason, this chapter may appear to jump around a bit, but that is the nature of the iCloud/Core Data implementation.

Using the Class Extension for the Snippets in This Chapter

The changes that were made to iCloud at WWDC 2013 are significant enough that it's very important to check the dates on any materials that provide Core Data information. Information dated after June 2013 that incorporates the WWDC 2013 revisions is what you should be looking for. (That's the information that's provided in this book.)

Documentation on developer.apple.com is provided when you search on Core Data or coredata; in addition, videos from WWDC 2012 and WWDC 2013 are available to registered developers. Each year, the conference had several Core Data sessions. The overview in WWDC 2013 is Session 207, which is worth watching if you want further information on the topics covered in this chapter.

This chapter focuses on the WWDC 2013 changes and additions. The changes and additions help you manage iCloud and Core Data as they work together at runtime. The code in this chapter consists of targeted snippets to handle the various issues raised in the chapter. Listing 17.1 shows the class extension assumed in this chapter. There is more code depending on your app, but these properties are expected to exist for the code snippets.

Listing 17.1   **Class Extension for This Chapter**

```
@interface JFAppDelegate () {
  id store;                                                    //1
}

@property (readonly, strong, nonatomic) NSURL *storeURL;
@property (readonly, strong, nonatomic)
  NSManagedObjectContext *managedObjectContext;
@property (readonly, strong, nonatomic)
  NSManagedObjectModel *managedObjectModel;
@property (readonly, strong, nonatomic) NSPersistentStoreCoordinator
  *persistentStoreCoordinator;

@end
```

1   The store instance variable can be any object because it is declared as id. This is a typical declaration for something that will be stored in a dictionary, as described in the following section.

Using the Options Dictionary

Many of the Core Data methods take an options NSDictionary as an argument. This is a very efficient way to pass in a number of arguments wrapped in a single message. For example, here is the complete addPersistentStoreWithType: configuration:URL:options:error: declaration:

```
- (NSPersistentStore *)addPersistentStoreWithType: (NSString *)storeType
                                  configuration: (NSString *)configuration
                                            URL: (NSURL *)storeURL
                                        options: (NSDictionary *)options
                                          error: (NSError **)error
```

For a typical use, you would declare the local `error` variable as well as a dictionary to be passed into options:

```
NSError *error;
NSDictionary *userInfo =@{
                    NSAddedPersistentStoresKey: @[store],
                    NSRemovedPersistentStoresKey: @[store]
                    };
```

If you have a persistent store coordinator called `psc`, the full message in your code might be as follows:

```
[psc addPersistentStoreWithType: NSSQLLiteStoreType
              configuration: nil
                        URL: storeURL // something you have set already
                    options: userInfo // the dictionary
                      error: &error];
```

As you will see, there are some new options you can put into your dictionary for various messages.

Fallback Stores

When you design for iCloud, you need to take into consideration the fact that iCloud may not always be available. In some cases, the absence of an Internet connection or an iCloud account is a show-stopper, but in many cases, you need some way to be able to continue without them.

How you do that depends on you and your app. For example, if your app is a multiplayer game, it's hard to imagine that you can manage without another player. However, if the app is a game that requires some skills and strategy, perhaps a fallback approach is a single-user version that focuses on those skills and strategies.

For a great many apps, planning for the absence of the Internet or an iCloud account means storing data locally in one way or another and then synchronizing it with iCloud when it or Internet connectivity is restored.

At WWDC 2012, the synchronization for fallback stores was presented in detail. It is one of two areas that caused problems for developers over the year. (The other was data model migration, which is discussed later in this chapter.) The WWDC 2012 version of synchronization involved synchronizing Core Data transactions with iCloud. The transactions, rather than the entire database, could then be downloaded and reapplied to peer clients (that is, other devices under the same Apple ID iCloud account). Plenty of sample code was provided.

However, the process was reasonably complex, so the Core Data engineers came up with a simple solution: managing the fallback store moved from being the developer's responsibility to being Core Data's responsibility. Of course, this simple change is only conceptually simple—a lot of work from the Core Data team went into realizing the goal.

Core Data now logs console messages so that you can track which store is being used. The fallback store is used when the iCloud store is unavailable for reasons that you typically can't control (the user signs out, the network connection drops, and so forth). The two console messages you may see indicate that local storage is not being used:

```
Core Data: Ubiquity peerID: <StoreName> - Using local storage:0
```

or that local storage is being used:

```
Core Data: Ubiquity peerID: <StoreName> - Using local storage:1
```

Whenever the store changes, you receive one message or the other on the console (viewed via Console app). Note that these are Console messages; for the corresponding notifications, read on.

Setting Up and Managing Persistent Stores

Core Data is now responsible for managing the fallback store, but you are responsible for setting up and managing a persistent store itself.

Setting Up a Persistent Store Asynchronously

With the fallback store maintained by Core Data, it can now be used by Core Data in new ways. Perhaps the most visible is a change to the way `addPersistentStore` functions. When you had to manage the fallback store, adding a persistent store required Core Data to go out to iCloud to find the store (if possible) and then to use it to set up the persistent store. Now that Core Data manages the fallback store, it can assume the fallback store is available. It uses it to add the persistent store: that method now returns quickly. After it returns, Core Data can go out to iCloud and do additional setup processing (usually retrieving updates that have been logged against the iCloud version of the store and that need to be applied against the fallback store locally). Thus, you no longer need to run `addPersistentStore` on a background thread.

Listing 17.2 shows a sample use of `addPersistentStore` on the main thread, which is now safe in WWDC 2013.

Listing 17.2   **Adding a Persistent Store**

```
NSError *error;

_persistentStoreCoordinator = [[NSPersistentStoreCoordinator alloc]
  initWithManagedObjectModel:[self managedObjectModel]];
if (![_persistentStoreCoordinator
  addPersistentStoreWithType:NSSQLiteStoreType
              configuration:nil
                     URL:_storeURL
                  options:nil
                    error:&error]) {
  // handle error
}
```

As part of the asynchronous setup, the processing involved in adding a persistent store is the same as in managing a change in the persistent store, as described in the following section.

Managing Persistent Store Changes

The sequence of events when a persistent store changes has been simplified. There are now five basic steps involved:

1. You receive `NSPersistentStoreCoordinatorsStoresWillChange-Notification`.

2. Save and reset your managed object context. If you use the names shown in Listing 17.1, your code would be similar to the following:
    ```
    [_managedObjectContext save:];
    [_managedObjectContext reset];
    ```
    The argument after `save` is a pointer to an `NSError`.

3. Core Data removes the store.

4. You receive `NSPersistentStoreCoordinatorsStoresDidChange-Notification`.

5. Save the managed object context with the new store:
    ```
    [_managedObjectContext save:];
    ```

If you are used to WWDC 2012, you may be thinking about dropping a persistent store and wiping out a managed object context. You don't need to worry about those steps any more: these are the only steps you need to follow.

Listing 17.3 shows the code to register for the notifications and to handle them. Note that if the code is placed within a single block, you should declare the default notification center (`dc`) only once. In many cases, the code will be in several blocks, so you need declare it in each one.

Listing 17.3 **Handling Persistent Store Changes**

```
- (void)storesWillChange: (NSNotification *)n {
  NSError *error;
  if ([_managedObjectContext hasChanges]) {
    [_managedObjectContext save:&error];
  }

  [_managedObjectContext reset];
  // update UI
}

- (void)storesDidChange: (NSNotification *)n {
  // update UI
}

NSNotificationCenter *dc =[NSNotificationCenter defaultCenter];
[dc addObserver:self
      selector:@selector(storesWillChange:)
          name:NSPersistentStoreCoordinatorStoresWillChangeNotification
        object:nil];

NSNotificationCenter *dc =[NSNotificationCenter defaultCenter];
[dc addObserver:self
      selector:@selector(storesDidChange:)
          name:NSPersistentStoreCoordinatorStoresDidChangeNotification
        object:nil];
```

Managing Account Changes

Many users use a single iCloud account on all of their devices. The only time they change their iCloud account is when they get a new device—and, in many cases, that is handled automatically during setup.

Other people routinely use several iCloud accounts. One may be for home and the other for work. You, as a developer, are likely to have separate iCloud accounts for your personal use, your developer work, and perhaps yet another for your iBooks Author projects.

When you are developing an iCloud app, you have to be able to handle both scenarios. That basically means being able to handle account changes: the situation with a single iCloud account that doesn't change is a dramatic simplification of the multiple account case.

Account changes in WWDC 2012 were handled with `NSUbiquityIdentity-TokenDidChangeNotification`. After receiving that notification, you typically called two methods (again using the properties from Listing 17.1):

```
[_managedObjectContext reset];
[_persistentStoreCoordinator removePersistentStore: <old account store>];
[_persistentStoreCoordinator addPersistentStore: <new account store>];
```

Beginning with WWDC 2013, you respond to a different notification: `NSPersistentStoreCoordinatorStoresWillChangeNotification`. This requires the same process as described in the preceding section for managing persistent store changes. For persistent store changes and account changes, the bulk of the processing is now done asynchronously inside Core Data; you can stay on the main thread.

Database Migration

One of the features of Core Data is its ability to migrate from one database model version to another either automatically or with varying degrees of developer involvement. It appears from discussions on the Apple Developer Forums over the last year that some of the issues involved migration from one data model to another, slightly revised data model.

Putting Data Model Changes in Perspective

Database managements systems (DBMSs) have been in widespread use for decades. Originally a mainstay of mainframe computers, they migrated to personal computers with products such as Paradox, dBase, Access, and FileMaker. On many mainframe installations, there were designated database administrators (DBAs) who managed database schemas and often fine-tuned performance. Software engineers and programmers often created draft versions of schemas, which were then formally implemented by DBAs.

On personal computers, the DBA role often disappeared with the coming of the new breed of databases. Modifying a database schema or its user interface is something that can be done on the fly and often has been done by power users with products such as FileMaker.

Core Data provides wonderful tools to migrate your data model to a new version, but it's worthwhile remembering that changing a data model or database schema is a significant operation. You might want to ratchet up your sensitivity to data model changes. Yes, it's easy to implement them with Core Data, and, yes, when using iCloud, the data model changes can often be implemented without any loss of data. But remember how significant the changes are to your database.

With the WWDC 2013 version of Core Data, migration along with many Core Data features is much improved, but that doesn't mean you should push the limits. Until you (and your users) are comfortable with migration, you may want to experiment with other options. Perhaps the most widely used alternative is to unload the data from the persistent store to a neutral format and then reload it to a new database. That is a more complicated way of approaching migration than using the automated tools, but it's not a bad choice for your first few migrations.

Also note that, depending on your app, the ability to unload data from a Core Data persistent store to a neutral format may be a feature you want to include in your app. It is your user's data, and he or she should be able to access it.

Starting Over

With Core Data now managing the fallback store, it became easier to wipe out a Core Data persistent store that uses iCloud. There are two primary reasons for doing this:

- During development, you often fiddle with your data model and persistent store as you refine your app.
- With some apps, there are moments when a user needs the ability to start over from scratch. A common example of this is a game where a user's best scores and perhaps other information are stored until the slate is wiped clean. It's easy to just reset the scores to zero, but if you're storing a history of moves in the persistent store, it may be easier to start from scratch.

Judging from discussions and comments on Apple's developer discussion boards, it seems that there were some occasions when iCloud synchronization could proceed even while a developer (or, ultimately, a user) was trying to wipe out a persistent store. Now that everything about the fallback store is managed by Core Data, there are tools to simply tell Core Data that you want to start over from scratch. You don't have to do all the work yourself: Core Data wipes the persistent store out.

There are three basic ways to start over:

- Rebuild the local store
- Remove metadata and the local store file
- Remove everything

Rebuilding the Local Store

For a message such as `addPersistentStore`, you can use the new `NSPersistentStoreRebuildFromUbiquitousContentOption` in your options dictionary. This will delete the local store and rebuild it from iCloud. If you use that option, `addPersistentStore` will always return an empty store because it switches over to the fallback store while the local store is being rebuilt from iCloud.

Removing Metadata and the Local Store File

Another new option, `NSPersistentStoreRemoveUbiquitousMetadataOption`, removes the local store file and metadata. By comparison with the previous option, it removes them but doesn't rebuild them. If you are using `migratePersistentStore: toURL:options:withType:error` to create backups, you may want to use this option to remove the metadata from the backup.

Removing Everything

Finally, there is the method for wiping everything out. It is obviously very useful during development and testing. It may also be useful for certain apps even in production. Obviously, the risks of accidentally deleting everything are substantial, so if this option is included in a production version of an app, be certain to protect it from accidental use.

The code for this method is very robust and very fast. Its most critical part is accomplished with a single I/O command. However, you (and your users if you allow them to use it through an interface element) should take every possible precaution, including the following:

- If the app is running on an iOS device, it should be tethered to a Mac for the fastest and surest possible connection.
- Tethering also supplies power to the iOS device. Check the battery level (or have the user do so) before sending the message.

This is a synchronous message: nothing else can be processed until it finishes. Here is the class method you use:

```
+ (BOOL)removeUbiquitousContentAndPersistentStoreAtURL:(NSURL *)storeURLs
                                              options:(NSDictionary *)options
                                                error:(NSError**)error;
```

You need to pass in the name and URL keys in the dictionary, so a typical use with a persistent store coordinator called `psc` might be as follows:

```
NSError *error;
NSDictionary *options = @{
    NSPersistentStoreUbiquitousContentNameKey: @"Store",
    NSPersistentStoreUbiquitousContentURLKey: @"Subdir"
};
BOOL success = [psc removeUbiquitousContentAndPersistentStoreAtURL:storeURL
                                              options:options
                                                error:&error];
```

Chapter Summary

This chapter provided an overview of the WWDC 2013 updates to APIs and architectures for Core Data in iOS 7 and OS X Mavericks (10.9). Efficiency and stability improvements make Core Data and iCloud easier to use together. These improvements directly benefit both users and developers.

The two most significant changes are that Core Data now manages the fallback store itself and that a new class method is available for starting over with a blank slate.

Exercises

1. Create a basic Core Data–based app that uses iCloud and enter some data. Then, remove its stores using `removeUbiquitousContentAndPersistentStore-AtURL:storeURL`. You'll need to use multiple devices to make certain that it is removed properly. This is something you will probably need to do during your testing. The steps and options in this chapter provide a number of ways to handle the removal. Try them all (and, of course, re-create the data store from scratch as needed). Don't wait to learn the removal processes when you are in the middle of debugging a production version of an app.

2. As in the previous exercise, create a Core Data–based app that uses iCloud and enter some data. Turn off one device. (You could use Airplane Mode, but just powering it off is definitive.) Now, remove the stores as you did in Exercise 1. Power all devices back on. Does data automatically propagate from the device that was turned off during your store removal?

18

Completing the Round Trip

In this book, you have seen how to work with iCloud in the apps you develop. You've explored the technologies you can use for easy integration with iCloud as well as the APIs such as Contacts and Calendar that let you access user data that is stored in iCloud. You've also seen how to write apps that store your user's data in iCloud in various types of documents and on both iOS and OS X. Several times, you have seen references to the Round Trip—the ability for you to use iCloud so that data from an iOS app is synchronized to iCloud and thence to OS X where the Round Trip can continue.

This chapter shows you how to put the previous chapters together in a Round Trip of your own. The major topics are

- What the user will see
- What you will see
- Configuring an iOS and OS X app to use a shared iCloud Ubiquity container

> **Note**
>
> Before looking at the figures in this chapter, a word of caution is in order: these figures have been prepared to emphasize what is happening behind the scenes. In an app for the App Store, you would make the different versions of the app look much more alike, but doing that for this chapter's examples might make it harder for you to follow what's going on, so in this chapter the differences are highlighted with different fonts and styles. Also note that there are efficiency and operational improvements you can make. For example, you can separate the testing for iCloud (using tokens) from the locating of the ubiquity container. The former is fast and can run on the main thread, while the latter should be fired off on a separate thread.

How the User Sees the Round Trip

First, it's worthwhile to look at what the Round Trip will look like from the user's point of view. When you successfully implement a Round Trip, it will seem to the user that it's another one of those Apple technologies that "just works." So, paradoxically, your job as a developer is to not have the user notice what you've done: it should just work the way the user expects. If a close friend or relative looks at your finished app and says, "What's so special about that?" you've succeeded. Unfortunately, you may have to abandon your friends and relatives temporarily and find a local developers Meetup group or other forum where the participants will understand what is so special about what you've done.

This section shows you how the user manages files on the Round Trip. The figures in this section show four files in the shared iCloud ubiquity container for the iOS and OS X apps. They have already been created using the techniques you saw in Chapter 15, "Working with iOS Documents" and Chapter 16, "Working with OS X Documents." The four files involved are

- Note 1 and Note 2: These were created on iOS in Chapter 15.
- Colby Test and Test for Colby Shared: These were created on OS X in Chapter 16.

As you will see, regardless of where the files were created, they are all visible in the shared ubiquity container in both the iOS and OS X apps.

Three basic types of displays are discussed in this section:

- On iOS and OS X, users can see their files in the Open dialog on OS X or a developer-written view such as a master-detail view on iOS. These displays are the most user-centric.

- Advanced users can look at and manage their iCloud accounts and storage with System Preferences on OS X and Settings on iOS.

- You as a developer have access to two additional iCloud tools through Xcode and through developer.icloud.com.

Working with the Open Dialog on OS X

On OS X, you start from the Cocoa Application template under OS X in File, New, Project. A great deal of the app is already set up to you. If you build and run the template without making any changes to it, you'll see that it is a basic document with a functioning menu bar. If you choose File, Open from the menu bar in your new app, you'll see the Open dialog, as shown in Figure 18.1. (For a brand new app, you will see an empty Open dialog. As noted previously, four files have already been created to demonstrate what the Open dialog looks like once the app has been used.)

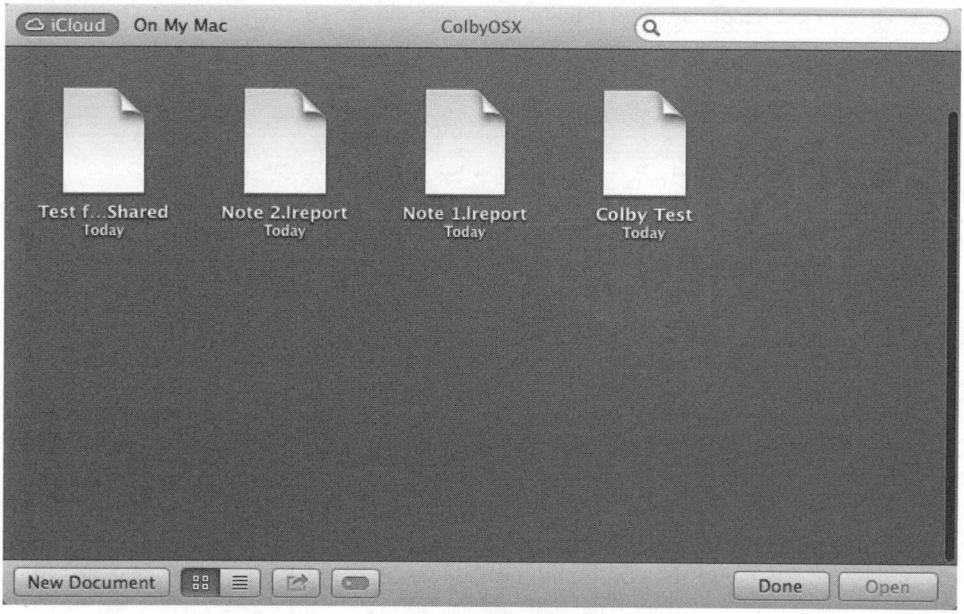

Figure 18.1   Looking at documents on OS X in icon view

Using the buttons at the bottom left, you can switch between the icon view in Figure 18.1 and the list view shown in Figure 18.2.

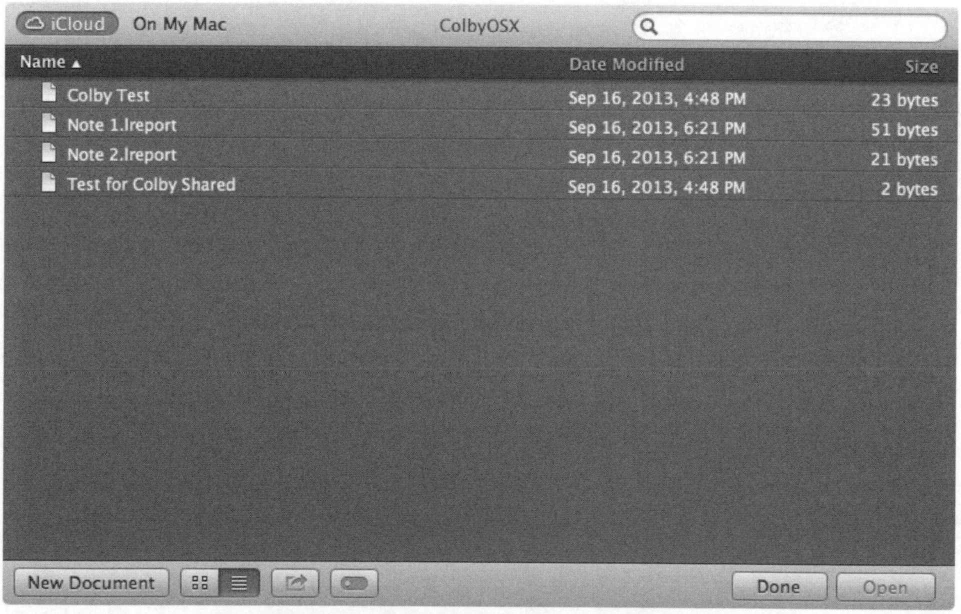

Figure 18.2   Looking at documents on OS X in list view

Table 18.1   **First Responder Commands and Actions in the Template**

Command	Action
New	`newDocument:`
Open	`openDocument:`
Open Recent, Clear Menu	`clearRecentDocuments:`
Close	`performClose:`
Save/Save a Version	`saveDocument:`
Revert Document	`revertDocumentToSaved:`
Page Setup	`runPageLayout:`
Print	`printDocument:`

Provided that you have implemented the code shown in Chapter 16, you'll see that the New Document button works along with the other buttons in the lower left of the dialog. Table 18.1 shows the commands available in the First Responder in the nib file as well as the actions that they trigger.

You generally do not implement or override these actions: the template takes care of that for you. What you do is implement the subactions. Thus, when the user chooses `openDocument` (or double-clicks on a document in the Open dialog), lots of work goes on behind the scenes until Cocoa gets around to the code you need to write. Your job is to implement one of the following methods (they're in `WrappedDocument` in Chapter 16):

- `makeWindowControllers`
- `showWindows`

Also in Chapter 16, you saw how to implement the read/write methods that are needed to support opening and saving of file wrapper documents:

- `readFromFileWrapperOfType:`
- `fileWrapperOfType:error:`

If, instead of using a file wrapper, you use just an `NSData` object, the methods you implement are

- `readFromData:ofType:error:`
- `dataOfType:error:`

Alternatively, you may be reading and writing from and to a specific URL. In that case, you use

- `readFromURL:ofType:error:`
- `writeToURL:ofType:error:`

For further customization of the Open dialog, remember to set your document's icons in the Info tab of your project in Xcode.

Working with a Split View Controller on iOS

On iOS, there is no Open dialog: you have to create whatever you want to use to play that role. Figure 18.3 shows a split view controller based on the Master-Detail Application on iPad. The master view controller is used to display the same documents shown in Figures 18.1 and 18.2.

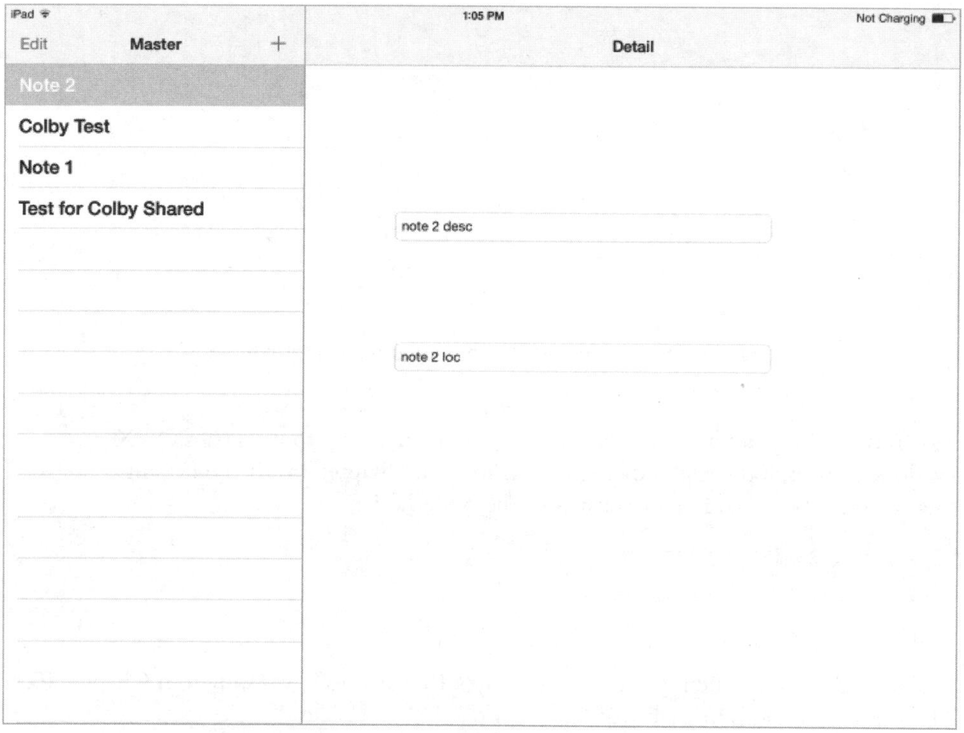

Figure 18.3   Looking at documents on iOS for iPad

In Figure 18.4, you see the same template displaying the same data on iPhone.

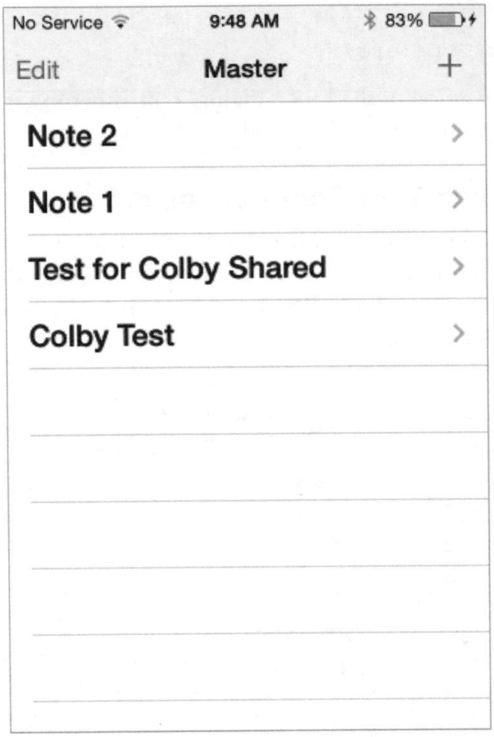

Figure 18.4   Looking at documents on iOS for iPhone

On iOS, the process of discovering the documents is up to you. (On OS X, it's done as part of the Open dialog processing.) In Chapter 15, the code is in `MasterViewController`. It consists of these methods:

- `setupAndStartQuery`
- `wrappedDocumentQuery`
- `processFiles`

The code to implement the views in Figures 18.3 and 18.4 was shown in Chapter 15. The critical methods in `WrappedDocument` are

- `loadFromContentsOfType:error:`
- `contentsForType:error:`

Examining iCloud Files in System Preferences on OS X

In addition to the Open dialog, users can see their iCloud files using System Preferences on OS X. (This is the case for files that are in the Documents directory. Files outside of the Documents directory but within the sandbox are invisible to users through System Preferences.) Users can get to the files by using the iCloud pane in System Preferences. They select the ubiquity container (app name to users in most cases) and click Manage in the bottom right to see the files, as shown in Figure 18.5.

Figure 18.5   Looking at iCloud files in System Preferences

Figure 18.5 actually shows the names of ubiquity containers. It uses a naming convention that some developers adopt. Ubiquity containers under development start with a lowercase letter. When development is done, the initial letter is changed to uppercase, which looks better for users. This enables you to develop and test two versions of your app on the same developer account at the same time.

Notice at the bottom of the list of documents for an application that users can delete one or all of them from the ubiquity container and thus from iCloud.

Examining iCloud Files with Settings on iOS

Similarly, users can examine their iCloud files on iOS using Settings. Here are the steps a user follows to look at the files. You may need to provide this information in your app's documentation: not all users are adept at configuring iCloud. Note that users can delete files from their ubiquity containers and thus from iCloud using their iOS devices. Not everyone knows this because there are several steps involved, as you will see in the following list. (The steps are the same on iPad.)

1. In Settings, select iCloud, as shown in Figure 18.6. You will see the settings for the major apps. You can turn iCloud on or off from here.

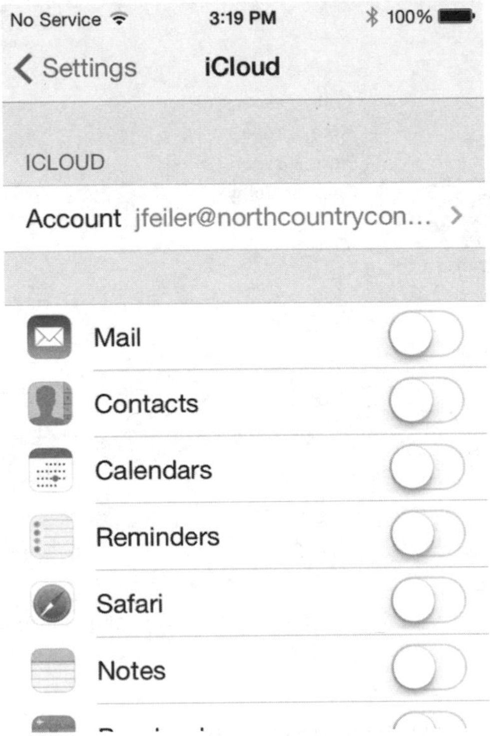

Figure 18.6   Configuring iCloud for apps

2. Scroll down to Documents & Data where you will be able to configure individual apps, such as yours as shown in Figure 18.7.

Figure 18.7   Selecting Documents & Data to configure apps

3. Inside Documents & Data, you can turn iCloud on or off for each app. If a user is experiencing problems, you may recommend that these settings be checked. Users report that these settings mysteriously are turned on or off. (These reports are consistent with various other reports from users about mysterious behavior that they absolutely had nothing to do with, such as the infamous two disks jammed into a single slot on a drive.)

Note that the names in Figure 18.8 are the names of the apps (the product names in Xcode).

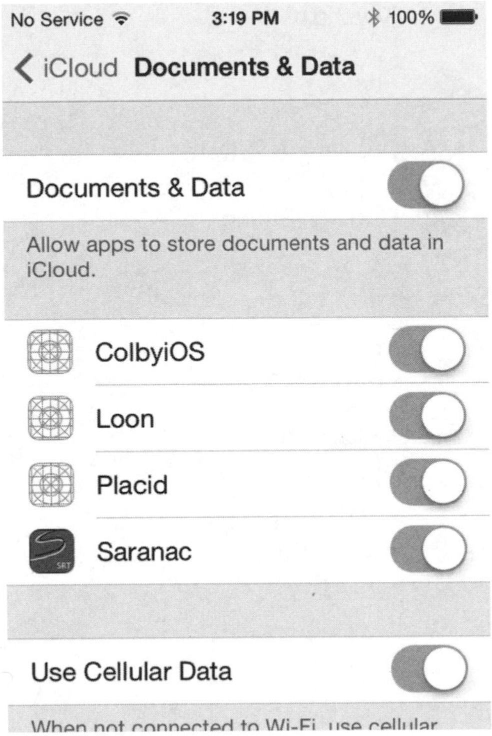

Figure 18.8   Turning iCloud on and off for individual apps

4. Return to iCloud (that is, the screen shown in Figure 18.6), scroll to the bottom, and select Storage & Backup (this was shown previously in Figure 18.7).

5. From Storage & Backup, go to the individual files by tapping Manage Storage, as shown in Figure 18.9.

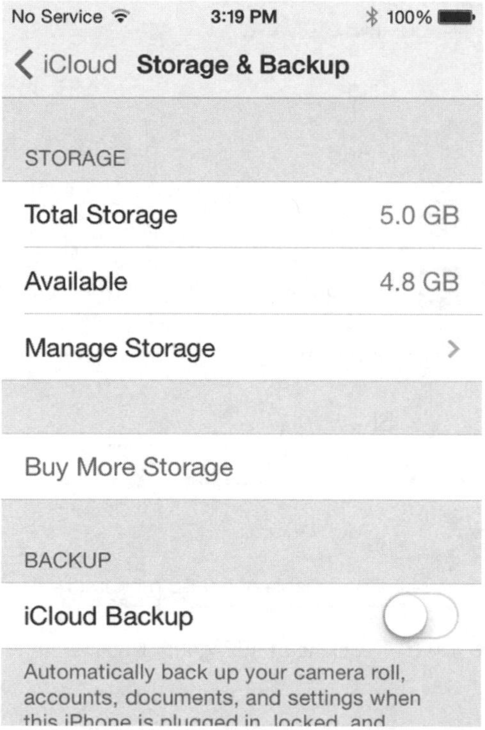

Figure 18.9   Using Manage Storage to see your iCloud storage

6. In Manage Storage, look at the storage you are using, as shown in Figure 18.10.

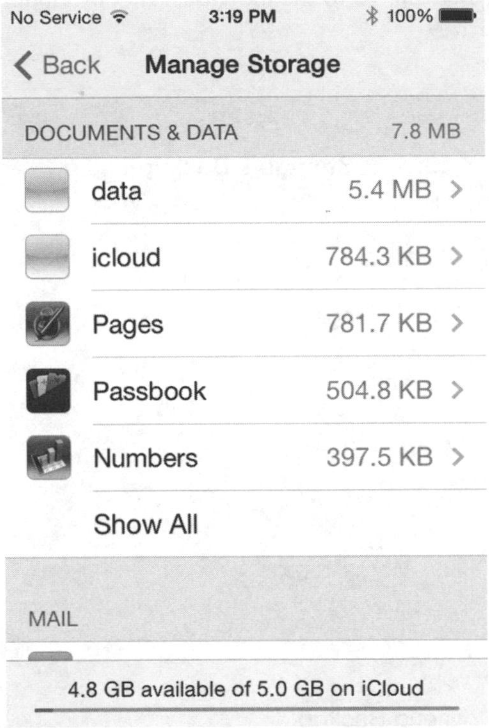

Figure 18.10   Looking at storage for Documents & Data

7. Select Show All to see all of your storage, as shown in Figure 18.11. If you look closely, you'll see that the items in the list shown in Figure 18.11 are the names of ubiquity containers rather than the app names shown in Figure 18.8.

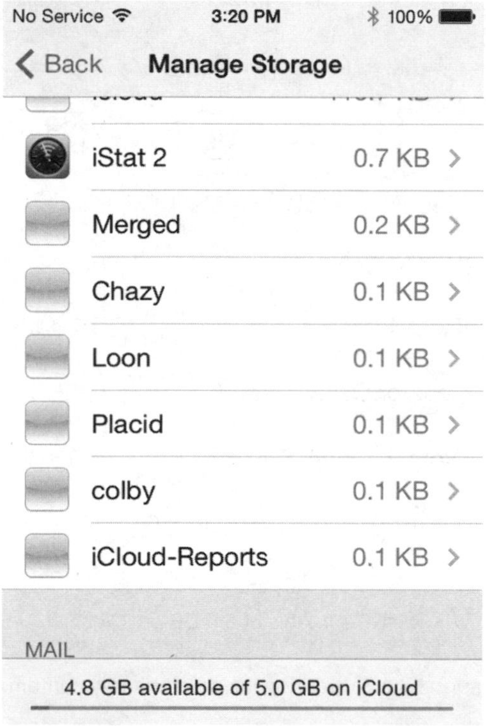

No Service 🛜	3:20 PM	🦷 100% 🔋
‹ Back	**Manage Storage**	
	iStat 2	0.7 KB ›
	Merged	0.2 KB ›
	Chazy	0.1 KB ›
	Loon	0.1 KB ›
	Placid	0.1 KB ›
	colby	0.1 KB ›
	iCloud-Reports	0.1 KB ›
MAIL		
4.8 GB available of 5.0 GB on iCloud		

Figure 18.11   Looking at storage for all apps

8. Tap a ubiquity container to see its files, as shown in Figure 18.12.

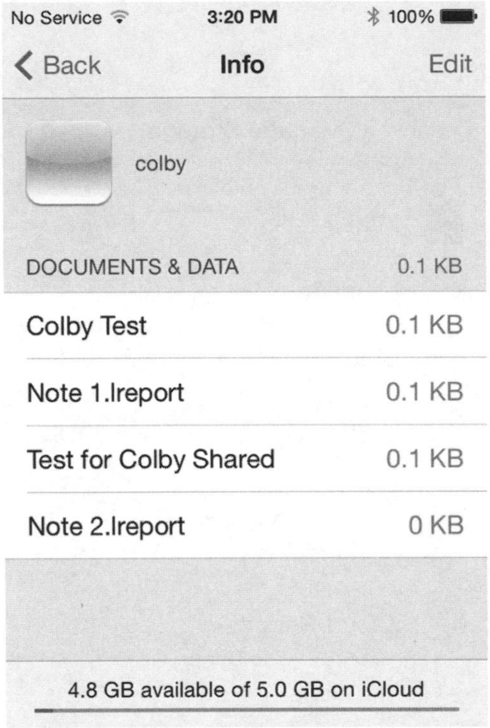

Figure 18.12   Looking inside a ubiquity container

How the Developer Sees the Round Trip

In addition to System Preferences on the Mac and Settings on iOS, there is yet another set of displays that you as a developer can view: developer.icloud.com and the debug gauges in Xcode 5.

Using developer.icloud.com

Log in to developer.icloud.com using the Apple ID for your developer account. This will enable you to see and download the files in your iCloud storage. This feature is not available to users.

> **Note**
>
> Watch out for the address completion in your browser. As soon as you start typing developer, it will probably try to complete it as developer.apple.com when you want developer.icloud.com in this case.

Figure 18.13 shows the interface inside developer.icloud.com. As you can see, you can navigate through the ubiquity containers down to the Documents folder and then, within it, to individual documents. Unlike the user-oriented tools, this tool lets you see folders other than Documents.

Figure 18.13   Viewing files and folders on developer.icloud.com

In addition, when you select a file, you can download it and inspect its modification date, as shown in Figure 18.14.

As you can imagine, this is very valuable for debugging.

Figure 18.14   Downloading files

Using Xcode

Xcode 5 brings debug gauges to the Debug navigator as you run an app from Xcode. The gauges are valuable for analyzing performance, but the focus in this book is on iCloud, so the iCloud gauge is the topic of interest. Like developer.icloud.com, it lets you examine what's going on in the iCloud account. (Remember this is your test account: it's not for user accounts.)

Avoid the iCloud Debugging Trap

The iCloud debugging tools, some of which are new in Xcode 5, answer many of the questions and address many of the problems developers had with the first releases of iCloud. In particular, now you can see what's going on inside the iCloud ubiquity containers.

The tools provide instantaneous access so you can actually watch what's happening and compare it to what you intended to happen.

But be careful.

iCloud is mostly an asynchronous process that generally involves access over the Internet to iCloud resources. The "instantaneous access" just mentioned is instantaneous in the sense that you can see what is happening now. However, the events you are observing are playing out on a different time scale from your desktop as well as being in a different location. All iCloud developers have experienced the frustration of clicking or tapping something that should cause a document to be stored or changed in iCloud, but nothing happens. In the heat of development, it's easy to notice that whatever should have happened didn't happen, and off we go tracking down the bug.

It's hard to break old habits, but it's important to constantly remind yourself of the time frame for iCloud events. The "bug" may disappear if you just walk the dog, have a cup of coffee, or pass some time with email and messaging.

When you are running an app in Xcode either on a Mac or on a device, by default the Debug navigator is shown at the left (you can control this in Preferences). You have a number of debug gauges: click the iCloud gauge, as shown in Figure 18.15.

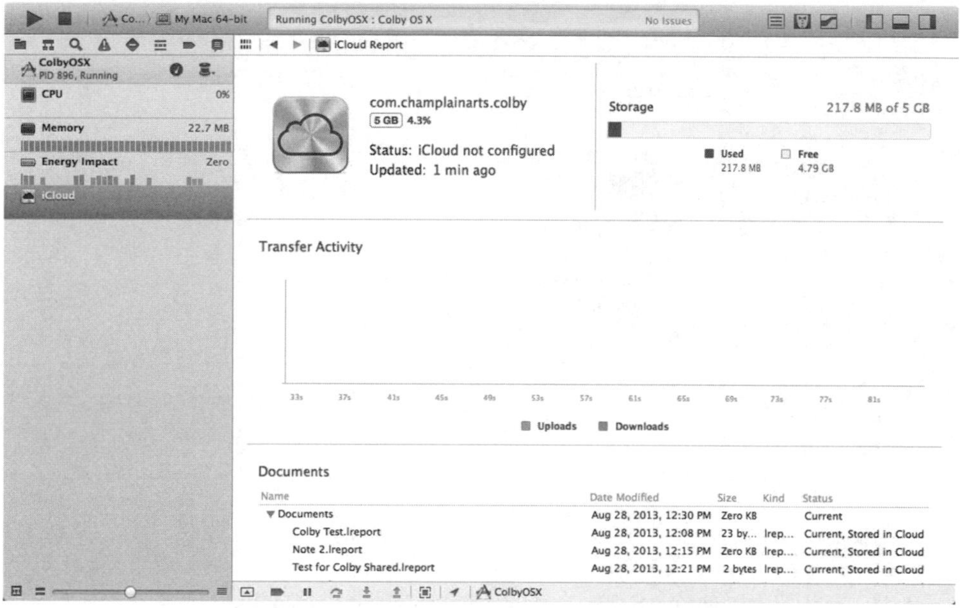

Figure 18.15   Examining iCloud files in the iCloud gauge

At the bottom of Figure 18.15, you can see the same files you saw in the Open dialog for OS X (Figure 18.2), in the master view controller on iPad (Figure 18.3), in the master view controller on iPhone (Figure 18.4), in Settings (Figure 18.12), and in developer.icloud.com (Figures 18.13 and 18.14). (In Figure 18.15, the last line is scrolled out of sight but don't worry: it's there.)

While the app is running, the top of the iCloud gauge shows you the activity that's going on as files move up and down, as you can see in Figure 18.16. In the upper left, you can also watch the progress as the app connects to the ubiquity container.

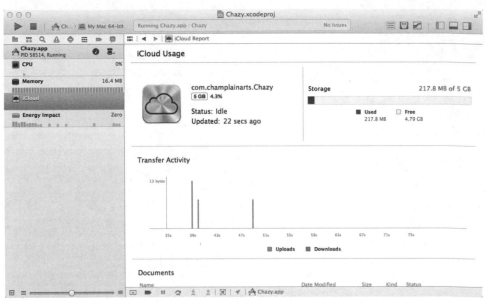

Figure 18.16   Watching uploads and downloads

In particular, pay attention to the Status for each file. Current, Stored in iCloud is generally what you want to see. As the app tries to synchronize files, other status values may appear. During your testing, you can turn Airplane mode on and off on your devices to force iCloud to be available or not available. The statuses should change accordingly—but always allow for the iCloud time lag discussed in the earlier sidebar, "Avoid the iCloud Debugging Trap."

Configuring the Shared Ubiquity Container

In order to implement a Round Trip, you need an iOS app and an OS X app that share a ubiquity container. The easiest way to do this is to create an Xcode workspace for two apps, as described in Chapter 11, "Using Xcode Workspaces for Shared Development." That is the technique used in the downloadable code for this chapter.

The workspace is called Colby (yet another Adirondack lake); one app is called ColbyiOS, and the other is called ColbyOSX. Figure 18.17 shows the General tab for one of the projects.

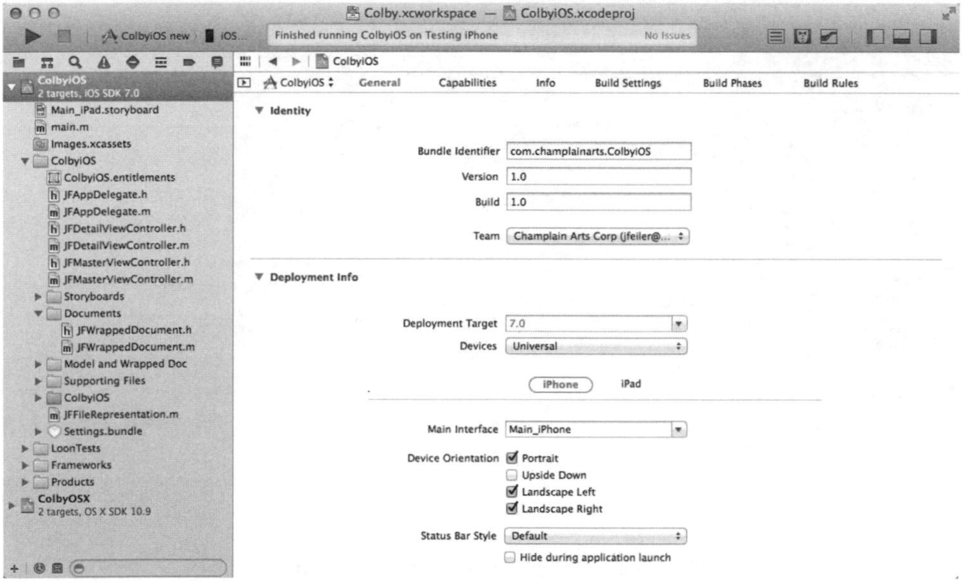

Figure 18.17   Setting up your projects

In the Capabilities tab for both projects, set up a common ubiquity container—colby in this case. (If you follow the naming convention for development mentioned previously, the production version might be Colby.)

Note

Remember that if you change the name of the ubiquity container during development, you should use the Organizer to delete derived data from the Xcode project because that includes the name of the previous ubiquity container.

As you run either app, you should be able to see the ubiquity container in the various debugging tools discussed in this chapter.

Make certain you turn on iCloud in the Capabilities tab for each app, as shown in Figure 18.18.

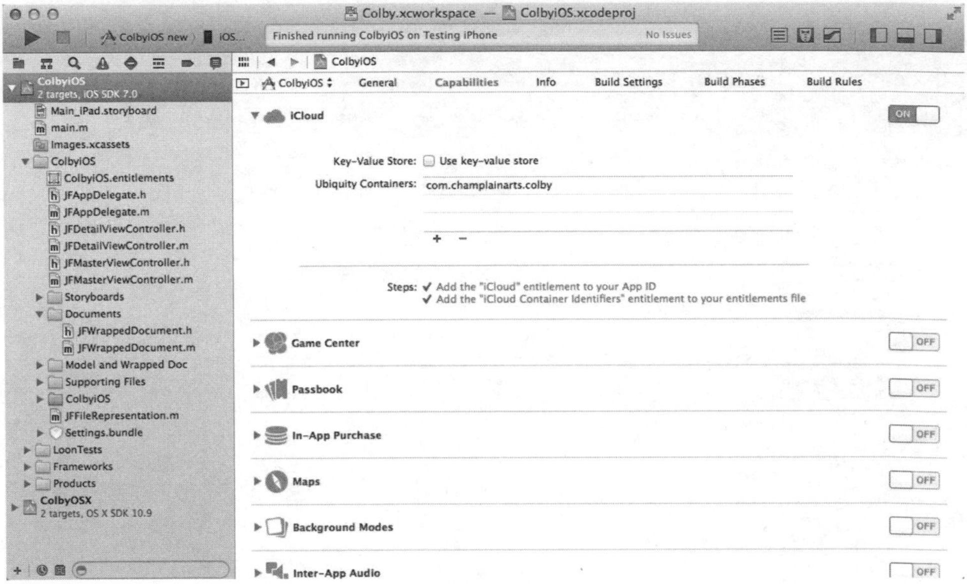

Figure 18.18   Turning on iCloud for each app

The downloadable code puts the two projects in one workspace, but there is no shared code as Chapter 11 implements the concept. One possibility is to place the `WrappedDocument` class into a shared file. Because `loadFromContents:ofType:error:` on iOS and `readFromFileWrapper:ofType:error:` are so similar, you can easily implement both of them side by side in your shared WrappedDocument file: either will be called as needed. (They are very short.)

More significantly, the write methods `contentsForType:error:` (iOS) and `fileWrapperOfType:error:` (OS X) can be rewritten to share a common method that does the processing that is the same for both.

Using a Shared iCloud Controller

In addition to a shared ubiquity container, Round Trip uses a shared iCloud controller. Using the same workspace technique described previously in Chapter 11, "Using Xcode Workspaces for Shared Development," you can create a class that will be built into both the iOS and OS X apps. (Remember, they are separate apps, so it is only the controller source code that is shared: it is not some runtime shared object.)

Implementing the shared iCloud controller is a matter of refactoring the code you've already seen. The new structure is simple: the shared controller contains most of the iCloud code, and the other classes contain the platform-specific code.

Making the App Delegate Link to the Controller

You add a property to the .h file so that the controller is visible. Here is the property for AppDelegate.h:

```
@property (nonatomic, readonly)
  SharediCloudController *iCloudController;
```

It is visible to other classes, such as the master view controller, with this line of code:

```
(JFAppDelegate *)[[UIApplication sharedApplication] delegate]
```

You add an accessor to the app delegate that backs up the property and creates the controller as needed:

```
- (SharediCloudController *)iCloudController {
  if (!_iCloudController) {
    _iCloudController = [[SharediCloudController alloc] init];
  }
  return _iCloudController;
}
```

Declaring the Shared iCloud Controller

Listing 18.1 shows the header file with the properties and methods of the controller that are exposed to clients. All of these have been described in other contexts earlier in this part of the book.

Listing 18.1   **SharediCloudController.h**

```
#import <Foundation/Foundation.h>

@interface SharediCloudController : NSObject

- (NSInteger)numberOfDocuments;                              //1
- (NSString*)stringForDocumentNameAt: (NSInteger)index;      //2
- (id)documentURLAt: (NSInteger)index;                       //3

- (NSString *)newUntitledDocumentName;                       //4
- (void)addDocument: (NSURL *)newDocumentURL;                //5
- (void)deleteDocument: (NSURL *)deleteDocumentURL;          //6
```

```
- (void)checkOnQuery;                                          //7
- (void)setupAndStartQuery;                                    //8

@property NSMutableArray *documents;                           //9

@end
```

1   You save coding time by using the shared code, but you do need to provide a few extra accessors because the documents array is no longer in the master view controller.

2, 3   The UI methods need to be able to quickly get information about the documents.

4, 5, 6   The UI methods in other classes, such as the master view controller, are still called. However, they call these non-UI methods that manage the documents array in iCloud.

7   This is the optional debugging method.

8   This is the method that manages the query that fills the documents array.

9   The documents array is maintained by the shared controller and is exposed to clients such as the master view controller in the UI classes. The methods in lines 1, 2, and 3 may eliminate the need to expose the array, but it is exposed here as a safety valve in case you are converting code that relies on it and doesn't use the accessors at lines 1, 2, and 3.

Implementing the Shared iCloud Controller

The shared controller implementation is shown in Listing 18.2. Key lines are identified in the listing, but the details of the implementations have already been covered in Chapters 15 and 16.

Listing 18.2   **SharediCloudController.m**

```
#import "SharediCloudController.h"
#import "JFFileRepresentation.h"
#import "Constants.h"

@interface SharediCloudController ()                          //1
@property NSMetadataQuery *query;
@end

@implementation SharediCloudController

#pragma mark - initialization
```

```
-(id)init {
  if ( self = [super init] ) {
    [self initializeiCloudAccess];                                //2
    if (!_documents)
      _documents = [[NSMutableArray alloc] init];                 //3
    [self setupAndStartQuery];                                    //4
  }
  return self;
}

- (void)initializeiCloudAccess {                                  //5
      dispatch_async
      (dispatch_get_global_queue
      (DISPATCH_QUEUE_PRIORITY_DEFAULT, 0),
    ^{
        if ([[NSFileManager defaultManager]
          URLForUbiquityContainerIdentifier:nil] != nil)
          NSLog (@"Got iCloud with
            URLForUbiquityContainerIdentifier %@ \n",
          [[NSFileManager defaultManager]
          URLForUbiquityContainerIdentifier:nil]);
        else
          NSLog (@"No iCloud");
      });
}

#pragma mark - managing iCloud data

-(NSMetadataQuery *)textDocumentQuery {
  NSMetadataQuery *aQuery = [[NSMetadataQuery alloc] init];
  if (aQuery) {
    // search
    [aQuery setSearchScopes: [NSArray arrayWithObject:
      NSMetadataQueryUbiquitousDocumentsScope];                   //6

    // add predicate
    NSString * filePattern = [NSString stringWithFormat:@"*.%@",
      SharedReportFileExtension];                                 //7
    [aQuery setPredicate:
      [NSPredicate predicateWithFormat: @"%K LIKE %@",
      NSMetadataItemFSNameKey, filePattern]];                     //8

  //NSLog (@" %@", aQuery);
  return aQuery;
}
```

```objc
- (void)setupAndStartQuery {
  // create if needed
  if (!_query)
    _query = [self textDocumentQuery];                              //9

  // register for query notifications
  [[NSNotificationCenter defaultCenter] addObserver:self
    selector:@selector (processFiles:)
    name:NSMetadataQueryDidFinishGatheringNotification
    object:nil];                                                    //10
  [[NSNotificationCenter defaultCenter] addObserver:self            //11
    selector:@selector (processFiles:)
    name:NSMetadataQueryDidUpdateNotification object:nil];
//start the query
  [_query startQuery];                                              //12

}

-(void)processFiles: (NSNotification*)aNotification {
  NSMutableArray *discoveredFiles = [NSMutableArray array];

  //disable updates
  [_query disableUpdates];                                          //13


  NSArray *queryResults = [_query results];                         //14

  for (NSMetadataItem *result in queryResults) {
    NSURL *fileURL = [result valueForAttribute:
      NSMetadataItemURLKey];
    NSNumber *aBool = nil;

    //don't include hidden files
    [fileURL getResourceValue: &aBool forKey:NSURLIsHiddenKey
      error:nil];                                                   //15
    if (aBool && ![aBool boolValue])
      [discoveredFiles addObject: fileURL];

    JFFileRepresentation *fr = [[JFFileRepresentation alloc]
      initWithFileName: [[fileURL
      lastPathComponent] stringByDeletingPathExtension]
      fileURL:fileURL];
    NSLog (@" %@ %@", fileURL, fr);

  }
```

```
    [_documents removeAllObjects];                              //16
    [_documents addObjectsFromArray: discoveredFiles];

    [_query enableUpdates];                                     //17

    [[NSNotificationCenter defaultCenter]
      postNotificationName:
        SharediCloudControllerDidChangeDataNotification
      object:nil userInfo:nil];                                //18
}

#pragma mark - managing documents array

-(NSString*)stringForDocumentNameAt: (NSInteger)index {        //19
  if ([_documents count] > 0)
    {
    NSURL *theURL = [_documents objectAtIndex: index];
    return [[theURL lastPathComponent]
      stringByDeletingPathExtension];
    }
  return nil;
}

-(NSURL *)documentURLAt: (NSInteger)index {                    //20
  if ([_documents count] > 0)
    {
    NSURL *theURL = [_documents objectAtIndex: index];
    return theURL;
    }
  return nil;
}

- (NSInteger)numberOfDocuments {                              //21
  return [_documents count];
}

- (NSString *)newUntitledDocumentName {                       //22
        NSInteger docCount = 1;
        NSString *newDocName = nil;

  newDocName = @"new doc";
  BOOL done = NO;
  while (!done) {
    newDocName = [NSString stringWithFormat: @"Note %d.%@",
      docCount,
      SharedReportFileExtension];
```

```
      // check for dups
      BOOL nameExists = NO;
      for (NSURL *aURL in _documents) {
        if ([[aURL lastPathComponent] isEqualToString:
          newDocName]) {
          docCount ++;
          nameExists = YES;
          break;
        }
      }

      // if not found, exit WHILE
      if (!nameExists)
        done = YES;
    }
    return newDocName;
}


- (void)addDocument: (NSURL *)newDocumentURL {                          //23
    [_documents addObject: newDocumentURL];
}


- (void)deleteDocument: (NSURL *)deleteDocumentURL   {

    dispatch_async (dispatch_get_global_queue                           //24
                   (DISPATCH_QUEUE_PRIORITY_DEFAULT, 0), ^{
                     NSFileCoordinator *fc = [[NSFileCoordinator
                     alloc] initWithFilePresenter:nil];
                     [fc
                     coordinateWritingItemAtURL:deleteDocumentURL
            options:NSFileCoordinatorWritingForDeleting error:nil
                     byAccessor:^(NSURL *newURL) {
               NSFileManager *fm = [[NSFileManager alloc] init];
    [fm removeItemAtURL: newURL error:nil];
                                            }];
                   });

    [_documents removeObject: deleteDocumentURL];                      //25


}

#pragma mark - debugging
```

```
- (void) checkOnQuery {                                            //26
  if (_query) {
    NSLog (@" %lu", (unsigned long) [_query resultCount]);
    NSLog (@" %lu", (unsigned long) [_query isStarted]);
    NSLog (@" %lu", (unsigned long) [_query isGathering]);
    NSLog (@" %lu", (unsigned long) [_query isStopped]);
    [_query startQuery];
  }
}

@end
```

1	The class extension declares the query to search for iCloud documents.
2	This method forges the link to iCloud that previously was placed either in the app delegate or in the master view controller.
3	This line creates the mutable array.
4	This line runs the query.
5	Get the ubiquity container off the main thread.
6–12	These lines set up the query.
13–17	These lines disable, run, and re-enable the query.
18	This line posts a notification so that the master view controller can reload its data.
19	This line is the accessor to the nth document's name.
20	This line is the accessor to the nth document instance. (Remember, the convention is that the document is represented by its URL; it is up to the detail view controller to actually manage the document object.)
21	This line is the accessor to the count of documents.
22	This line is the same method that you used in Chapters 15 and 16 in the master view controller. It is called in the same way you called it from there.
23, 24, 25	These are the lines to implement the iCloud part of document creation and deletion. The master view controller calls them as needed when it is updating the UI.
26	This line is the optional debugging method that can help you track down issues in the query.

Moving Documents to iCloud

In most cases, the preferred way of writing to iCloud is not to do it. You write to your app's sandbox and then move the written file to iCloud. Because writing directly to iCloud is easier when you are starting out, this book focuses on direct writes to iCloud. (It's easier because there's less code and also because if you create a document directly in iCloud it should show up fairly quickly. If you write to the sandbox and then move the document to iCloud, either the writing or the moving can run into trouble, so it's easier to get basic experience with direct writes.)

The code in Listing 18.3 is based on the common examples on developer.apple.com. The two minor differences are:

- This code uses a JFFileRepresentation object to represent the file with its name and URL. Similar light-weight objects are found in many examples.

- Because this code is envisioned as being part of the shared code, it does not post an error message. You could post a notification or return a value to the calling class.

Listing 18.3 Moving a Document to iCloud

```
- (void)moveFileToiCloud:(JFFileRepresentation
 *)fileToMove {
   NSURL *sourceURL = fileToMove.url;
   NSString *destinationFileName = fileToMove.fileName;
   NSURL *destinationURL = [self.documentsDir
     URLByAppendingPathComponent:destinationFileName];
   dispatch_async(dispatch_get_global_queue
     (DISPATCH_QUEUE_PRIORITY_DEFAULT, 0), ^(void) {
     NSFileManager *fileManager =
       [[[NSFileManager alloc] init] autorelease];
     NSError *error = nil;
     BOOL success = [fileManager setUbiquitous:YES          //1
            itemAtURL:sourceURL
        destinationURL:destinationURL
              error:&error];

     dispatch_async(dispatch_get_main_queue(), ^(void) {
       if (success) {

         JFFileRepresentation *fr =
          [[JFFileRepresentation alloc]
            initWithFileName:fileToMove.fileName
            fileURL:destinationURL];
         [_documents removeObject:fileToMove];
         [_documents addObject:fileRepresentation];
```

```
            NSLog(@"moved to iCloud: %@", fr);
            }
            if (!success) {
              //log error, return value, or set global error
            }
        });
    });
}
```

---

1   This is the line that does the move. Do it on another thread because it can
take time.

Moving Documents from iCloud to Local Storage

The reverse of the process to move a document from iCloud is shown in Listing 18.4.

Listing 18.4   **Moving a Document from iCloud**

```
- (void)moveFileToLocal:(JFFileRepresentation *)fileToMove {

  NSURL *sourceURL = fileToMove.url;
  NSString *destinationFileName = fileToMove.fileName;
  NSURL *destinationURL = [self.documentsDir
    URLByAppendingPathComponent:destinationFileName];

  dispatch_async(dispatch_get_global_queue
    (DISPATCH_QUEUE_PRIORITY_DEFAULT, 0), ^(void) {
      NSFileManager *fileManager = [[[NSFileManager alloc] init]
        autorelease];
      NSError *error = nil;
      BOOL success = [fileManager                              //1
        setUbiquitous:NO
            itemAtURL:sourceURL
       destinationURL:destinationURL
                error:&error];
      dispatch_async(dispatch_get_main_queue(), ^(void) {
        if (success) {
          JFFileRepresentation *fileRepresentation =
            [[JFFileRepresentation alloc]
              initWithFileName:fileToMove.fileName
                           url:destinationURL];
          [_fileList removeObject:fileToMove];
          [_fileList addObject:fileRepresentation];
```

```
           NSLog(@"moved to local storage: %@",
              fileRepresentation);
        }
        if (!success) {
           //log error, return value, or set global error
        }
     });
  });
}
```

1   This is the line that does the move. Do it on another thread because it can
take time.

Chapter Summary

This chapter brought together the components of the Round Trip: an iOS and OS X
app that share the same ubiquity container. It is important to note that many of the
tools that are available in Xcode 5, iOS 7, and OS X Mavericks (10.9) are new. Users
and developers have more control over what is happening and, more important, both
can now observe what is happening.

Exercises

1. Rather than writing directly to the iCloud container, you can (and should) write
    to the sandbox and then move the files to the iCloud ubiquity container. This
    eliminates the delays involved in writing directly to iCloud. Try that with the
    code in the two previous sections. Verify that you have truly moved the files—if
    they wind up in both locations, users will be confused.

2. If you are going to rename a shared ubiquity container as described previously in
    this chapter, do a dry run now to make certain you understand what you have
    to do. (Change the name of the ubiquity container in both apps and discard the
    derived data.)

Index

J

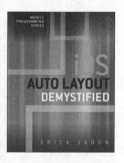

FREE
Online Edition

Safari
Books Online

Your purchase of **Learning iCloud Data Management** includes access to a free online edition for 45 days through the Safari Books Online subscription service. Nearly every Addison-Wesley Professional book is available online through Safari Books Online, along with thousands of books and videos from publishers such as Cisco Press, Exam Cram, IBM Press, O'Reilly Media, Prentice Hall, Que, Sams, and VMware Press.

Safari Books Online is a digital library providing searchable, on-demand access to thousands of technology, digital media, and professional development books and videos from leading publishers. With one monthly or yearly subscription price, you get unlimited access to learning tools and information on topics including mobile app and software development, tips and tricks on using your favorite gadgets, networking, project management, graphic design, and much more.

Activate your FREE Online Edition at
informit.com/safarifree

STEP 1: Enter the coupon code: QLYBNXA.

STEP 2: New Safari users, complete the brief registration form.
Safari subscribers, just log in.

If you have difficulty registering on Safari or accessing the online edition,
please e-mail customer-service@safaribooksonline.com

Addison Wesley   AdobePress   ALPHA   Cisco Press   FT Press FINANCIAL TIMES   IBM Press   Microsoft Press   New Riders   O'REILLY

Peachpit Press   PRENTICE HALL   que   Redbooks   SAMS   SAS Publishing   vmware PRESS   WILEY   wrox